LIBRARY OF HEBREW BIBLE/ OLD TESTAMENT STUDIES

696

Formerly Journal for the Study of the Old Testament Supplement Series

Editors
Claudia V. Camp, Texas Christian University, USA
Andrew Mein, Durham University, UK

Founding Editors
David J. A. Clines, Philip R. Davies and David M. Gunn

Editorial Board
Alan Cooper, Susan Gillingham, John Goldingay,
Norman K. Gottwald, James E. Harding, John Jarick, Carol Meyers,
Daniel L. Smith-Christopher, Francesca Stavrakopoulou,
James W. Watts

PATERNITY, PROGENY, AND PERPETUATION

Creating Lives after Death in the Hebrew Bible

Steffan Mathias

LONDON • NEW YORK • OXFORD • NEW DELHI • SYDNEY

T&T CLARK
Bloomsbury Publishing Plc
50 Bedford Square, London, WC1B 3DP, UK
1385 Broadway, New York, NY 10018, USA
29 Earlsfort Terrace, Dublin 2, Ireland

BLOOMSBURY, T&T CLARK and the T&T Clark logo
are trademarks of Bloomsbury Publishing Plc

First published in Great Britain 2020
This paperback edition published in 2021

Copyright © Steffan Mathias, 2020

Steffan Mathias has asserted his right under the Copyright, Designs and Patents Act, 1988, to be identified as Author of this work.

For legal purposes the Acknowledgements on p. vii constitute an extension of this copyright page.

Cover design: Eleanor Rose

Cover image © Vince Cavataio/Getty Images

All rights reserved. No part of this publication may be reproduced or transmitted in any form or by any means, electronic or mechanical, including photocopying, recording, or any information storage or retrieval system, without prior permission in writing from the publishers.

Bloomsbury Publishing Plc does not have any control over, or responsibility for, any third-party websites referred to or in this book. All internet addresses given in this book were correct at the time of going to press. The author and publisher regret any inconvenience caused if addresses have changed or sites have ceased to exist, but can accept no responsibility for any such changes.

A catalogue record for this book is available from the British Library.
A catalog record for this book is available from the Library of Congress.

ISBN: HB: 978-0-5676-9180-4
PB: 978-0-5677-0332-3
ePDF: 978-0-5676-9181-1

Series: Library of Old Testament Studies, ISSN 2513-8758, volume 696

Typeset by: Forthcoming Publications Ltd

To find out more about our authors and books visit www.bloomsbury.com and sign up for our newsletters.

Contents

Acknowledgments	ix
Abbreviations	xi
Preface	xiii
INTRODUCTION	1
1. Overview	1
2. Outline	5
Chapter 1	
READING POWER AND CULTURE IN FOREIGN LANDS:	
ANTHROPOLOGY, BOURDIEU AND GENDER	9
1. Anthropological Material and Comparison	10
2. Bourdieu	13
3. Gender	23
Chapter 2	
HOW A LAW ABOUT SEX BECAME ABOUT ANYTHING ELSE	27
1. Johannes Pedersen	29
2. Raymond Westbrook	34
3. Eryl Davies	37
4. Herbert Chanan Brichto	40
5. New Avenues	47
6. Widow Inheritance and Ghost Marriage:	
Anthropological Contexts	52
Chapter 3	
DEATH, BURIAL, AND BEYOND	61
1. Status of the Dead	64
2. Burial	71
3. Veneration and Care of the Dead	79
4. Physically Remembering: Monuments	86
5. Conclusion	91

Chapter 4
NAMES 94
1. What's in a Name? 94
2. Anthropological Perspectives on Names and Naming 96
3. The Act of Naming 99
4. Excursus: God's Name 102
5. Human Names 109
6. The Matrix of Names, Descendants, and the Dead 112
7. Social Memory 116
8. Conclusion 122

Chapter 5
KINSHIP: REPRODUCTION AND SEXUALITY 124
1. Anthropological Approaches to Kinship and Sexuality 125
2. Reproduction in Narrative 132
   2.1. Abraham's Promise of Descendants 132
   2.2. Abraham's Covenant 135
   2.3. Rachel and Leah 141
   2.4. The Value of Parenthood 146
3. Regulating Sexuality 150
   3.1. Law and Narrative in Deuteronomy 150
   3.2. Incest Prohibitions: Regulating the Family 154
4. Conclusion 161

Chapter 6
THE HOUSE OF THE FATHER? 164
1. Defining the Family: House of the Father 165
2. Transmitting Property and Family 173
3. Genealogies and Connection 177
4. Regulating the Family: The Fifth Commandment 180
5. Erasing the Family: Cutting Off 183
6. Conclusion 188

Chapter 7
MECHANISMS OF CONTINUITY 190
1. Lot's Daughters: Genesis 19.30-38 190
2. Levirate Law: Context 192
   2.1. Deuteronomy 25.5-10 196
   2.2. Judah and Tamar 205
   2.3. Ruth 214
3. Widow of Tekoa 223
4. Monuments 225
   4.1. Absalom's Monument 225
   4.2. Isaiah 56.3-5 226

| 5. Zelophehad's Daughters | 230 |
| 6. Conclusion | 235 |

CONCLUSION | 237
   1. Overview | 237
   2. Property and Progeny | 241
   3. Gender Reassessed | 246
   4. Conclusion: No Future? | 249

Bibliography | 253
Index of References | 271
Index of Authors | 280

ACKNOWLEDGMENTS

I would like to begin by thanking Theology and Religious Studies at King's College, London for its on-going support over the years, particularly the powers-that-be who allocated me AHRC funding, without which I could not have started – yet alone completed – this project. I offer my thanks to the Arts and Humanities Research Council for the funding, as well as to Jewish Studies at King's, the Office of the Dean at King's, and the Anglo-Israeli Archaeological Society for their generous grants during my doctoral studies. To Paul Joyce and Joan Taylor – thank you for being fantastic supervisors, for your wonderful support and huge freedom you afforded me. To my original supervisor, Diana Lipton, without the encouragement of whom I would probably never have pursued biblical studies, thank you for passing on a sense of wonder and excitement about the text. Several other members of Jewish Studies and Biblical Studies at King's have offered immeasurable support: Laliv Clenman, Sandra Jacobs, and Andrea Schatz. I am grateful to them for reading over my chapters, offering suggestions, and showing an interest in my work with such conviction that it lessened my own doubts.

I also wish to thank Francesca Stavrakopoulou and Ann Jeffers, whose feedback and ideas added huge amounts.

My thanks also go to various PhD friends, and in particular: Mette Bundvad, Jonathan Downing, Ella Fitzsimmons, Michelle Fletcher, Ben Nichols, James Whitfield. Thank you for your support, ideas, and for buying me pints. To my friends, thank you for bearing with me not returning calls, and being constantly broke: Ben, Chris, Estelle, Jez, Nic. Thank you to those who nagged me to do what I needed to do to send my manuscript to a publisher, particularly Jennifer Cooper, and those who have given me the time and space to complete it.

And most of all, thank you to my family - but especially to my parents. I'm so thankful for the complete unconditional love you have shown me, and encouraging me, even when it looked like I was never going to get a real job.

The extract from Theodore J. Lewis's "Family, Household, and Local Religion at Late Bronze Age Ugarit" in Chapter 3 is from *Household and Family Religion in Antiquity*, copyright © 2008 John Bodel and Saul M. Olyan. Used by permission of Wiley Publishing.

Scripture quotations in Chapters 2–6, unless otherwise states, are from New Revised Standard Version Bible: Anglicized Edition, copyright © 1989, 1995 National Council of the Churches of Christ in the United States of America. Used by permission. All rights reserved worldwide. Hebrew words and phrases added to passages are not part of the original translation.

Abbreviations

AB	Anchor Bible
ABD	*The Anchor Bible Dictionary.* Edited by D. N. Freedman. 6 vols., New York, 1992
ABS	Archaeology and Biblical Studies
AIL	Ancient Israel and Its Literature
AOAT	Alter Orient und Altes Testament
AV	Authorised Version
AYBRL	Anchor Yale Bible Reference Library
BA	*Biblical Archaeologist*
BASOR	*Bulletin of the American Schools of Oriental Research*
BDB	F. Brown, S. R. Driver, and C. A. Briggs. *A Hebrew and English Lexicon of the Old Testament.* Oxford, 1907
BHS	Biblia hebraica stuttgartensia
BibInt	*Biblical Interpretation*
BibSem	The Biblical Seminar
BJRL	*Bulletin of the John Rylands University Library of Manchester*
BJS	Brown Judaic Studies
BMW	Bible in the Modern World
BN	*Biblische Notizen*
BZAW	Beihefte zur Zeitschrift für die alttestamentliche Wissenschaft
CBQ	*Catholic Biblical Quarterly*
CC	Continental Commentaries
CHANE	Culture and History of the Ancient Near East
CSHJ	Chicago Studies in the History of Judaism
CSSH	Cambridge Studies in Society and History
DDD	*Dictionary of Deities and Demons in the Bible.* Edited by Karel van der Toorn, Bob Becking, and Pieter W. van der Horst. Leiden, 1995
FCB	Feminist Companion to the Bible
HBM	Hebrew Bible Monographs
HOS	Handbook of Oriental Studies
HSM	Harvard Semitic Monographs
HTR	*Harvard Theological Review*
HUCA	*Hebrew Union College Annual*
IBC	Interpretation: A Bible Commentary for Teaching and Preaching
IEJ	*Israel Exploration Journal*
ITC	International Theological Commentary
JAJ	*Journal of Ancient Judaism*

JBL	*Journal of Biblical Literature*
JBS	Jerusalem Biblical Studies
JHS	*Journal of Historical Studies*
JNES	*Journal of Near Eastern Studies*
JPS	Jewish Publication Society
JPSTC	Jewish Publication Society Torah Commentary
JQR	*Jewish Quarterly Review*
JSJSup	Journal for the Study of Judaism in the Persian, Hellenistic and Roman Period, Supplements
JSOT	*Journal for the Study of the Old Testament*
JSOTSup	Journal for the Study of the Old Testament, Supplement Series
JSS	*Journal of Semitic Studies*
JTS	*Journal of Theological Studies*
LAI	Library of Ancient Israel
LHBOTS	The Library of Hebrew Bible/Old Testament Studies
LTQ	Lexington Theological Quarterly
LXX	Septuagint
NCBC	New Century Bible Commentary
NICOT	New International Commentary on the Old Testament
NIDOTTE	*New International Dictionary of Old Testament Theology and Exegesis.* Edited by William A. VanGemeren. 5 vols. Grand Rapids: Zondervan, 1997
NRSV	New Revised Standard Version
OBT	Overtures to Biblical Theology
OIS	Oriental Institute Seminars
OTL	Old Testament Library
OTR	Old Testament Readings
RIDA	*Revue internationale des droits de l'antiquité*
SBLDS	Society of Biblical Literature Dissertation Series
SBLRBS	Society of Biblical Literature Resources for Biblical Study
SBLStBL	Society of Biblical Literature Studies in Biblical Literature
SBT	Studies in Biblical Theology
SemeiaSt	Semeia Studies
SHCANE	Studies in the history and culture of the ancient Near East
TDOT	*Theological Dictionary of the Old Testament.* Edited by G. J. Botterweck and Helmer Ringgren. Translated by J. T. Willis, G. W. Bromiley, and D. E. Green. 8 vols. Grand Rapids, 1974-
ThTo	*Theology Today*
VT	*Vetus Testamentum*
VTSup	Vetus Testamentum, Supplements
WAW	Writings from the Ancient World
WBC	Word Biblical Commentary
YNER	Yale Near Eastern Researches
ZAW	*Zeitschrift für die alttestamentliche Wissenschaft*

Preface

This project argues for a paradigm shift in understanding texts in the Hebrew Bible that offer responses to men (as opposed to women) dying without sons (as opposed to daughters), principally the practice of 'levirate marriage' (Deut. 25.5-10). It will be argued that this text, and others like it, present the failure to produce sons and protect the transmission of the family line as a failure in masculinity, the male and the social order, leading to the eradication of the name, estate and memory of the man, and so these must be responded to through practices such as levirate marriage and the erection of monuments.

Identity, covenant, name, property and seed are passed down from father to son, and establish both the post-mortem continuity of the deceased and the social reproduction of the בית אב, the house of the father. Using the work of Pierre Bourdieu as well as anthropological and gender-critical insights, the present work will look at eight texts that respond to the threat of men dying without sons: Genesis 19, Genesis 38, Deut. 25.5-10, Ruth, 2 Sam. 14.1-24, 2 Sam. 18.18, Isa. 56.3-5 and Numbers 27 and 36. Instead of reading these texts as reflections of different institutions (such as levirate marriage, inheritance law, or household religion), this work will demonstrate how they are reflective of a single particular social discourse or paradigm, and how ancient family roles were constructed to ensure offspring, or social continuity, for men.

Ancient Judahite and Israelite beliefs about death, burial and memorial will be explored as a context of the fears of social annihilation apparent in these texts. Name, seed, property, inheritance, reproduction and genealogy, all ideas present in these texts in different ways, will then be reassessed to demonstrate how they, rather than being disparate ideas, form part of the same symbolic structures, in which the integrity of the family is protected and passed down through generations of descendants. It will then be shown how these texts construct men as transmitters of identity and women as submissive counterparts, albeit as agents who are not powerless but negotiate the patriarchal system.

Introduction

1. *Overview*

I met a traveller from an antique land
Who said: Two vast and trunkless legs of stone
Stand in the desert. Near them, on the sand,
Half sunk, a shattered visage lies, whose frown,
And wrinkled lip, and sneer of cold command,
Tell that its sculptor well those passions read
Which yet survive, stamped on these lifeless things,
The hand that mocked them and the heart that fed:
And on the pedestal these words appear:
"My name is Ozymandias, King of Kings:
Look on my works, ye Mighty, and despair!"
Nothing beside remains. Round the decay
Of that colossal wreck, boundless and bare
The lone and level sands stretch far away.
Ozymandias, Percy Blythe Shelley[1]

Death and taxes, as the saying goes, are life's only certainties. The human desire for immortality is not only evidenced through ancient fables of the fountain of youth and Achilles' heel; from the commonplace inscription on a park bench, to the 'eternal leader' Kim Il-Sung (still ruling the Democratic People's Republic of North Korea, despite having died in 1992), the human desire to escape and deny the worldly destruction that death brings is so prevalent in our social discourse that it often goes unnoticed. There is nothing shocking to us when we hear of a parent wanting a child to take on their name so that it does not die out, and we understand with relative ease why someone who believes paradise awaits them would so readily give their life in a suicide bombing.[2] Yet the way we perceive mortality, memorialization, continuity, is always contingent.

---

1. Percy Bysshe Shelley, *Miscellaneous and Posthumous Poems of Percy Bysshe Shelley* (London: W. Benbow, 1826), 100.
2. We may be horrified, but we have little difficulty understanding the connection between eternal reward in the afterlife and taking your life in this world.

I will argue that there is a specific paradigm visibly at work in the Hebrew Bible that demonstrates a way (though not the only way) texts viewed existence after death, and sought to ensure and protect it. This paradigm touches on notions of individuality and community; masculinity, femininity, gender and sexual roles; death, afterlife and the underworld; burial, mourning, monuments and associated death rites; names, personhood and social connections; and progeny, descendants and lineage. This project will explore these themes through one specific expression: the death of a male while childless. Male reproduction is presented as necessary for the social perpetuation of the בית אב, or house of the father, and failure to reproduce undermines constructs of power and damages the family unit. We will explore the way that texts respond to this childlessness, particularly the practice of levirate marriage and monuments, and the way female sexuality is utilized and negotiated in service to the responses. There is widespread recognition that 'biblical' conceptions of the 'afterlife' (for example, the shadowy underworld of Sheol) indicate a somewhat inadequate existence, one bleak and unfulfilling. There is also recognition that offspring form a crucial mechanism through which people establish perpetuity for themselves (such as the promise to Abraham that his descendants will be like stars in the sky: Gen. 22.17).

The present project will ask: what is the connection between these two things? I will argue that there is a process at work that attempts to ensure a form of continuity of the person and community to counter what Brian Schmidt terms 'the dreaded death after death',[3] a process which actively attempts to ensure the social presence of the individual through the transmission of identity and memory, and establishment of lineage. I will further argue that this is vital to the continuation of the individual and the community, and that it takes place in and reinforces a patriarchal context in which male reproduction is valorized and women's bodies and sexuality are manipulated and used. The negotiation of women's bodies and sexuality in the service of male reproduction could be resigned to an ancient paradigm divorced from our context, however the way categories of continuity, gender and sexuality are contested and negotiated are always ongoing, particularly when it comes to the Bible. This can be seen perhaps nowhere better than the enduring popularity of Margaret Atwood's *The Handmaid's Tale* or the success of the recent TV adaptation, infused with biblical references such as the Rachel and Leah training centre, and its

---

3. Brian B. Schmidt, 'Memory as Immortality: Countering the Dreaded "Death after Death" in Ancient Israelite Society', in *Judaism in Late Antiquity Part 4: Death, Life-After-Death, Resurrection and the World-To-Come in the Judaisms of Antiquity*, ed. Jacob Neusner and Alan Jeffery Avery-Peck, HOS 49 (Leiden: Brill, 2000), 87.

response to childlessness, both male and female, through the invoking of Rachel's cry that if she does not have children she shall die, and Rachel's offer of Bilhah the 'handmaid'.[4] Biblical texts, replete with categories of gender, sexuality, reproduction and continuity, still hold power to define and negotiate our worldviews; Atwood's dystopia disturbingly and powerfully reads and negotiates contemporary anxieties through ancient texts.

Our focal text will be the law of 'levirate marriage', expressed in Deut. 25.5-10. A dilemma is faced as a man has died sonless, and a task is given to those who survive him: produce a son for him. We are told that this is in order that the son 'shall raise the name of the dead brother (יקום על־שם אחיו המת), that his name may not be blotted (ולא־ימחה שמו) from Israel'.[5] The meaning of *name* is, however, elusive. What does it mean to have one's name 'blotted out' of Israel? This narrative strongly resonates with other texts. In Genesis 19, seemingly believing all others are dead, the daughters of Lot get their father drunk and sleep with him, to create life from him. In Genesis 38 we read the story of Tamar: her husband dies, and her brother-in-law Onan is told to 'Go into your brother's wife and perform the duty of "a brother-in-law"[6] to her; raise up offspring for your brother' (Gen. 38.8). Onan, famously, spills his seed on the ground instead of fulfilling his duty, but Tamar goes to any lengths necessary to produce a son. Ruth, the wife of the deceased Elimelech, returns to Judah from Moab and eventually finds a man, Boaz, to lie with her 'in order that the name of the dead may not be cut off from his kin and from the gate of his place (ולא־יכרת שם־המת מעם אחיו ומשער מקומו)' (Ruth 4.10).

In these texts a widow or daughter or brother or father remain to respond to male childlessness; sometimes, however, these actors are missing and alternative means are sought out to respond to death. A monument is erected, such as Absalom in 2 Sam. 18.18 who laments 'I have no son (בן) to keep remembrance of my name (בעבור הזכיר שמי)'. This theme is taken up in Isa. 56.3-5, where YHWH promises a faithful eunuch a 'memorial and a name, better than sons and daughters'. Sometimes progeny remain, however their role must be renegotiated to protect the legacy of the deceased. In 2 Sam. 14.7 the widow of Tekoa tells that her kinsman is to take revenge on her son, taking his life, lamenting: 'And so, they would extinguish my ember that remains, and leave to my husband neither

---

4. Margaret Atwood, *The Handmaid's Tale* (London: Vintage, 2016), 138.
5. Translations of the core texts, which appear in the Introduction and Chapter 7, are my own. I have attempted, without torturing the text, to maintain Hebrew word order and a literal word-for-word translation, particularly as this highlights gendered language. Other translations, in Chapters 1–6, unless stated, are from the NRSV.
6. The translation of the Hebrew root יבם as 'brother-in-law' will later be critiqued.

name nor remnant (שם ושארית) on the face of the earth'. In Numbers 27, the daughters of Zelophehad, complaining that their father's inheritance will be taken away as he has no sons, argue: 'Why should the name of our father be diminished (יגרע שם־מתוך) from among his clan (משפחתו) because he had no son? Give to us a possession among the brothers of our father (אחזה בתוך אחי אבינו)' (Num. 27.4).

There is a commonality in these texts, which play on the ideas of name, שם, inheritance, נחלה, monuments whether מצבה or יד, on progeny whether firstborn, בכור, son, בן, or seed, זרע; they connect with ideas of memory and death and land. But these texts are rarely considered together, often sectioned off under different disciplinary areas such as inheritance law (in the case of Num. 27) or Israelite household religion (as in the case of 2 Sam. 18.18). In recent scholarship, there have been no comprehensive discussions of this topic. Dvora Weisberg's *Levirate Marriage and the Family in Ancient Judaism* is the only recent full-scale study of the levirate in ancient Judaism, yet even this work devotes just fourteen pages to the biblical period and barely deviates from the standard levirate texts of Deut. 25.5-10, Genesis 38 and Ruth.[7] Some accounts that take into consideration a larger range of texts, such as Jon Levenson's *Resurrection and the Restoration of Israel*, however the relevant discussion only totals four pages.[8]

Rather than divorcing the key texts from their usual sub-disciplines (whether inheritance, household religion, or the status of women in biblical texts), the present project seeks to ask how these different contexts may dialogue with each other. Most interpretations of these texts fail to connect the thematic and symbolic links between them, and instead understand them individually or in relation to a discrete topic. All these texts respond, in some way, to the fear of men (as opposed to women) dying without sons (as opposed to children). They also portray women, especially their sexuality, in service of these men. We will see how biblical texts construct male 'afterlives', which continue to consolidate male power even after their earthly demise, and how these operate in a wider patriarchal discourse of male lineage and descent. It will be demonstrated that when the performance of masculinity fails (i.e. progeny are not produced), mechanisms are enacted which seek to repair this failure.

---

7. Dvora E. Weisberg, *Levirate Marriage and the Family in Ancient Judaism* (Waltham, MA: Brandeis University Press, 2009), 23–37.

8. Jon Douglas Levenson, *Resurrection and the Restoration of Israel: The Ultimate Victory of the God of Life* (New Haven, CT: Yale University Press, 2006), 119–22.

2. Outline

This project is primarily concerned with uncovering a cultural paradigm and exploring how this paradigm establishes relationships of power, particularly around gender. Chapter 1 will outline some of the methodological considerations at hand. To uncover a cultural discourse requires a kind of archaeology which first questions our own cultural understandings and presumptions, and this will be done using comparative anthropology, not to claim it is possible to produce an ethnography of ancient Israel, but to demonstrate the possibility of cultural distance between ourselves and the texts we are exploring. Having cracked open the possibilities in the text, the work of Pierre Bourdieu, particularly his concept of habitus, can be used to see how the different social discourses – death, reproduction, memory – predispose people to act, and how this is embedded in the text. These predispositions are played out particularly in terms of gender, and so Bourdieu's work will be supplemented with contemporary gender and queer theory, using Lee Edelman's idea of reproductive futurism to see how we tend towards constructing 'the future' around the idea of the child.

Chapter 2 will outline four approaches to the law of levirate marriage, three of which characterize a distinct paradigm: that responses to childlessness are about continuing the soul of the deceased (Pedersen), the legal establishment of the man's title (Westbrook), or protection of the widow (Davies). Each of these approaches, however, fails to take account of the fundamental thread through the texts: that they are about sex and reproduction. These will be contrasted Herbert Chanan Brichto's 1973 article, 'Kin, Cult, Land and Afterlife – A Biblical Complex', an important publication that attempted a kind of cultural synthesis of a wider range of material and was successful in offering a new and creative approach, but a work which, however, is now in need of a nuanced revisit and rereading. They will be read alongside recent work by Jacob Wright and Michael Chan, and Francesca Stavrakopoulou, to see how taking the dynamics of procreation and death can seriously begin to open new ways of reading. In response to the more nuanced approaches of Chan and Wright and Stavrakopoulou, this chapter will then argue for the usefulness of using social-scientific material exploring contemporary examples of levirate marriage, widow inheritance, or ghost marriage, not to create an ethnography of ancient Israel, but to question our own interpretative presumptions and cultural biases.

As this study looks primarily at a response to death (contingent on childlessness), Chapter 3 will sketch out the symbolic and social relationship between the living and the dead, both horizontally across communities but also vertically through generations, highlighting areas where the living and the dead interact – in burial, veneration and memorialization, as well as the territorial and political use of the dead. Textual and archaeological evidence will place death in a communal context, which both looks back to ancestors and forward to descendants, for instance in burial where the dead require the living for proper funerary rites, but the living require the dead to establish communal identity. An emphasis on the social interaction between the living and the dead contrasts some of the less nuanced understandings of the dead – such as Schmidt's idea of the beneficent dead – which pervades much scholarship. This will contribute to understanding how practices such as levirate marriage can negotiate the various boundaries between the living and the dead.

The focus of Chapter 4 will be on the name and naming. The שם, name, appears to cross and renegotiate the various boundaries outlined in the previous chapter. Drawing on anthropological understandings of names and naming, this chapter will explore the ontological and symbolic status of the name and how a fresh understanding of this can help us understand the significance of the name in levirate marriage and broader memorializing practices. Outlining scholarship on YHWH's name (with all its anthropomorphic associations) and Name Theology, this will be used to reread texts which discuss the names of humans, and by drawing these into discussion with comparative anthropological material we will be able to assert the social function of names and their ability to cross normal boundaries such as those between the living and the dead. By looking at the ways texts strongly associate names with memory and descendants, we will demonstrate how names do not function in the abstract but instead are parts of extensive social discourses, and function in socially specific ways. I will argue continuation of the name functions as a substantive social existence beyond death in a similar way to proper burial. This substantive social existence will be highlighted through a discussion of the threat of the erasure of names in various texts, offering us a more nuanced understanding of the 'name' when we come to reassess our core texts.

In their responses to death, the texts we will look at find a way of perpetuating the dead; moreover, they centre on the childless man and the reproducing widow. Chapter 5 will explore the way gender and sexuality is constructed and negotiated, and how this produces certain kinds of knowledge about bodies. Drawing on contemporary anthropological understandings of kinship that reject Western models of biological kinship and reproduction as normative, the chapter will explore how reproduction can be understood in radically different ways, and will offer new insights into texts that deal with reproduction. The Abraham narrative will be explored to see the relationship between promise to descendants, name and circumcision, and the relationship between reproduction, progeny and the penis. In the narrative of Abraham's circumcision (Gen. 17) masculinity and the penis are explicitly bound up with perpetuation of the name and seed. Throughout Genesis 30–35, we see how Rachel and Leah compete for status through their ability to reproduce, and how texts may act to articulate women into maternal roles and normalize male procreation. Through exploring these discourses – the focus on male reproduction and the use of women's sexuality – the social dynamics and gendered nature of levirate marriage and the other responses to the failure of a man to leave behind progeny can be demonstrated. Sexuality is also controlled and articulated in legal material, and I will explore two case studies; first, the way sex laws and narrative material in Deuteronomy demarcates and controls the family unit, to ensure its secure transmission into the future; second, the way incest taboo in Leviticus 18 and 20 regulate the internal dynamics of the family.⁹

Building on the previous discussion of gender, Chapter 6 will look at concrete ways that the family is transmitted and maintained. After sketching out the basic social structure of ancient Israel, I will focus in on the smallest social unit, the house of the father, or בית אב. Here the previous discussion on the importance of the dead to the living and the living to the dead, the transmission of name, and the gendered constructions of man and woman will be brought together, and I will explore how they focus around the institution of the בית אב. Individual and communal identity is transmitted in this fundamental social institution, and as we will see in the transmission of property and the establishment of genealogy, the distance between past, present and future generations are collapsed and their autonomy is restrained. The transmission of property and genealogy will be understood in the same context as the regulation of sexuality, as a way of ensuring the security of the male line and the בית אב. We will then look at how these issues relate to the most famous passage of family regulation in the Bible – the commandment to honour father and mother. Having demonstrated how the family unit is to be protected, this will then be contrasted with כרת, the threat of cutting off, which acts as a threat to erase the family unit. This will form the context for the final chapter, by demonstrating how childless death threatens the social fabric of the community and בית אב.

---

9. This will also become significant as Lev. 18 technically prohibits levirate marriage, the sexual relations between a woman and her brother-in-law.

Having outlined the destabilizing reality of childlessness for the individual, the community, and for constructions of gender, Chapter 7 will reassess the primary texts of Lot's daughters (Gen. 19), Judah and Tamar (Gen. 38), the law of levirate marriage (Deut. 25.5-10), the book of Ruth, the narrative of the widow of Tekoa (2 Sam. 13–14), Absalom's monument (2 Sam. 18.18), the promise to the eunuch (Isa. 56.3-5) and Zelophehad's daughters (Num. 27 and 36). Each text will be explored individually and its scholarly discussion will be outlined. Through a thorough analysis of each, the common concerns of the various texts will be highlighted, and the use of the motifs of land, name, progeny, continuity and death will be explored, in order to be compared in the Conclusion. How these various texts, despite substantial differences, exhibit a similar discourse will be demonstrated, revealing a common structure which perceives an interruption to the genealogical flow as a threat to stability. The relationship between property, progeny and gender will be reassessed in the Conclusion and I will demonstrate a paradigm for understanding social continuity and security which pervades disparate biblical texts and how they focus on the בית אב as the centre around which various fields – operations of power which negotiate men's afterlives and women's sexuality – centre. This will offer more comprehensive ways of understanding institutions such as levirate marriage than the abstracted historical institutions much historical criticism has made them, as well as demonstrating how these practices are not isolated from the social context but form part of a wider discourse. This conclusion will also demonstrate how this discourse reinforces constructions of gender, and subsumes masculine and feminine bodies and sexualities into broader institutions of social continuity, of 'reproductive futurism'.

Chapter 1

READING POWER AND CULTURE
IN FOREIGN LANDS:
ANTHROPOLOGY, BOURDIEU AND GENDER

The aim of this project is to explore, define and contextualize a discourse which operates in several texts: the relationship between offspring, death and social reproduction, and specifically offspring as a mechanism to *respond* to male death. Due to the paradigm existing across several texts and genres, the relatively small number of texts that make explicit reference to legal or social responses, and methodological concerns about using texts to reconstruct historical situations, I will not be attempting to reconstruct an Israelite law operating 'behind' the text, but instead will be focusing on the literary products of this paradigm. This does not mean the project is ahistorical; it will utilize archaeological evidence, historical reconstructions, and ancient West Asian literature to explore aspects of the paradigm. Moreover, as most research dealing with these texts operates out of a historical-critical method, it will be necessary to engage with this material, and interrogate its assumptions on its own terms. To examine the cultural fragments of a practice which both operates within its own symbolic discourse, and which requires certain types of behaviour, we will be utilizing anthropological material. This is done for two reasons: first, using cross-cultural examples allows us to challenge our own readings of texts and expose the range of opportunities for how particular concepts and practices have been understood; second, to explore why these concepts influence actions and behaviour, particularly regarding gender.

Opening up new avenues for how people understand the world and act within it raises questions of power: Why does Tamar act not in her own interest but in that of her deceased husband? Why does something such as levirate marriage, which might seem so alien to one culture, make sense to another? What role does masculinity play? We will respond to these questions through the work of Pierre Bourdieu, particularly his understanding of habitus, which articulates the relationship between dynamics of power and culture, and how we as agents respond in ways which make sense only in terms of these dynamics. This articulation of habitus will be supplemented with contemporary gender and queer theory, particularly Lee Edelman's 'reproductive futurism', and how children are used to construct images of the future.

1. *Anthropological Material and Comparison*

Studying ancient texts, the standard biblical studies repertoire of 'linguistics, translation, and literary study' may not always be sufficient; texts leave 'traces' and gaps which elude us. Anthropology and the social sciences can be used to open avenues of thought, as an artist's pencil is used to form an 'outline'.[1] Ken Stone suggests:

> Anthropological concepts can help us to construct and continually reassess our readings frames – that is to say, our ideas about the possible context of symbols and beliefs in terms of which the texts seem to make sense – in a way that at least mitigates our tendency to interpret biblical texts in terms of our own assumptions…to distance ourselves from at least part of what passes as 'common sense' in our own culture.[2]

A now-classic example within biblical studies is Howard Eilberg-Schwartz's work on circumcision, which uses anthropology to tease out implicit meanings that are embedded in a text or practice, which he terms 'symbolic exegesis', recognizing that a symbol might not find explicit articulation in the text.[3] Eilberg-Schwartz recognizes that in biblical studies we are left doing a kind of 'cultural archaeology', unable to 'question natives about the meaning of practices', but using 'symbolic artefacts' such as metaphors to point to 'larger complexes of meaning that never found explicit articulation'. Comparative ethnography of contemporary cultures can suggest new meanings, significantly allowing us to break our own interpretative moulds.[4] Moreover, cross-cultural comparisons are not new to the study of levirate marriage; in the 1940s, Millar

---

1. Johanna Stiebert, *Fathers and Daughters in the Hebrew Bible* (Oxford: Oxford University Press, 2013), 11.
2. Ken Stone, *Sex, Honor, and Power in the Deuteronomistic History*, JSOTSup 234 (Sheffield: Sheffield Academic, 1996), 35–6.
3. Howard Eilberg-Schwartz, *The Savage in Judaism: An Anthropology of Israelite Religion and Ancient Judaism* (Bloomington, IN: Indiana University Press, 1990), 143.
4. Ibid.

Burrows utilized Indian *niyoga* relationships and Persian *čakar* marriages to discuss levirate marriage in the Bible.[5]

The danger of taking an anthropological approach lies in the difficulty of performing contemporary ethnography on the ancient societies. Unlike modern anthropologists who carry out their work in the field, we who work on ancients texts cannot observe what people do, and we only have limited accounts of what they say;[6] we cannot ask the questions we would like to ask.[7] However, ethnographic material can maintain a balance between 'critical distance and cultural empathy', critiquing 'our own Western preconceptions about religion'.[8] This is particularly true when we move away from the social-scientific models employed by Alt, Wellhausen, Pedersen, Albright and Noth, all of which focused on a more positivistic, scientific approach relating to social organization and setting, drawing on early sociology and anthropology,[9] and towards more reflective models, which focus not on 'an experimental science in search of law but an interpretive one in search of meaning'.[10] Doing this allows for a multiplicity of structures 'superimposed upon or knotted into one another', which are 'at one strange irregular and inexplicit'. Clifford Geertz suggests:

> Doing ethnography is like trying to read (in the sense of 'construct a reading of') a manuscript – foreign, faded, full of ellipses, incoherent, suspicious emendations, and tendentious commentaries, but written not in conventionalized graphs of sound but in transient examples of shaped behavior.[11]

---

5. Millar Burrows, 'The Ancient Oriental Background of Hebrew Levirate Marriage', *BASOR* 77 (1940): 5–6. Anthropology and Biblical Studies are both rooted in each other's past and development, although not always in beneficial ways. See: Mary Douglas, *Jacob's Tears: The Priestly Work of Reconciliation* (Oxford: Oxford University Press, 2004), 2, and Robert P. Carroll, 'Poststructuralist Approaches: New Historicism and Postmodernism', in *The Cambridge Companion to Biblical Interpretation*, ed. John Barton, Cambridge Companions to Religion (Cambridge: Cambridge University Press, 1998), 35.

6. Edmund Leach, *Social Anthropology* (New York: Oxford University Press, 1982), 130.

7. For example, if only the biblical text had bothered to articulate what exactly the שם was, this project would be largely redundant.

8. Ronald Hendel, 'Mary Douglas and Anthropological Modernism', *JHS* 8 (2008): 2.

9. Carroll, 'Poststructuralist Approaches', 35.

10. Clifford Geertz, *The Interpretation of Cultures: Selected Essays* (London: Hutchinson, 1975), 5.

11. Ibid., 10.

Does this sound familiar? We cannot create 'first-order' interpretations of a Judahite or Israelite culture, and so we are to be guarded against any attempt to hermetically seal symbolic systems off into neat categories. Instead, we gain access to symbolic systems by 'inspecting events', not 'arranging abstract entities into unified patterns' but by 'tracing the curve of a social discourse' – fixing it into an inspectable form' through 'the microscopic',[12] the 'concrete social events and occasions, the public world of common life'.[13] While we hold to the multivocality and ambiguity of symbols, the way they hold together different ideas, recognizing 'the complexity and uncertainty of meanings of symbols are sources of their strength',[14] we are also required to engage in scholarship that is rigorous. Our control, our guard against excess subjectivity, is close reading, from which we can form, in the words of Geertz, our own *thick descriptions*,[15] allowing us to avoid overly optimistic reconstructions of ancient Israel. When we subject our texts to contemporary anthropological techniques we begin to discover residual traces of structures of meaning. However, we must not fall into the old traps of finding a similarity between a contemporary 'exotic' culture and our texts, and then simply correlating the two. Instead, anthropology is a useful theoretical framework for asking questions about culture, power, kinship and action, one which acts to challenge our cultural perceptions as readers. As such, anthropological material on death, naming, kinship and reproduction will be used to expose our own understanding, so that we can begin to see cultural remains in our texts operating in radically different symbolic systems to our own.

Symbolic systems are never universal, however. The specific texts and laws I will be discussing are not universalist in outlook, but construct identity (man and woman, son and daughter, whole-bodied and non-whole-bodied, reproducing and infertile, powerful and non-powerful) and practice (burial, reproduction, levirate marriage, memorialization, transmission). Accordingly, these texts require us to expose the structures of power at play in the text, to understand how and why people respond the way they do and why the text presents these ways of acting as natural. To approach these texts and ask questions about power, however, requires a robust understanding of the role of power in society, and how power forms understandings of human behaviour, and so we will turn to the work of Pierre Bourdieu, particularly his concept of habitus.

12. Ibid., 20–1.
13. Ibid., 30.
14. David I. Kertzer, *Ritual, Politics, and Power* (New Haven, CT: Yale University Press, 1988), 11.
15. Geertz, *Interpretation*, 30.

2. Bourdieu

Pierre Bourdieu's work explores how power operates within a culture.[16] His anthropological, sociological and theoretical work has been so impactful that it is possible to say he is 'the single most influential sociologist of the later twentieth century', such that his work now pervades not just his own discipline but the full gamut of social sciences and humanities.[17] His work has been taken on by those working on the ancient world, so much so that by 2006 it was possible to say that within Classics Bourdieu's work was already central in trying to understand the dynamics of social power in antiquity.[18] Therefore, Bourdieu's almost complete absence in biblical studies[19] demonstrates a significant gap in theory which can enlighten our understanding of 'the marginalized, the silenced, the un-talked about',[20] as we try to understand how questions of power and performance are present in biblical texts. Bourdieu's work is especially useful for understanding relations of power in terms of social, cultural and symbolic capital, without reducing dynamics of power entirely to economic capital, particularly as his work focuses on pre-capitalist societies, contrasting, for example, the ways levirate marriage has been read solely as a question of inheritance of property or as a form of social security for widows.[21] Bourdieu's work, despite being now several decades old, remains uniquely productive in looking at social and cultural reproduction, while also accounting for how individuals attempt to 'play the game' and negotiate

---

16. I thank Francesca Stavrakopoulou, who wisely suggested Bourdieu, instead of Foucault, as a more productive theorist to work with on for this project.

17. Will Atkinson, *Beyond Bourdieu: From Genetic Structuralism to Relational Phenomenology* (Cambridge: Polity, 2016), 1. Note also Lamont's statement: 'The place of Bourdieu in the small pantheon of individuals who have determined the shape of the social sciences at the beginning of the twenty-first century is beyond question': Michèle Lamont, 'How Has Bourdieu Been Good to Think With? The Case of the United States', *Sociological Forum* 27, no. 1 (2012): 228.

18. Dean Hammer, 'Bourdieu, Ideology, and the Ancient World', *The American Journal of Semiotics* 22, no. 1 (2006): 87.

19. I am aware of a handful of exceptions that use Bourdieu in an extensive way, one being Berlinerblau's article, which will be discussed below. The notable other exceptions I have been able to find are Dermot Nestor's work on Israelite identity and the Merneptah stele, and Donna Laird on power in Ezra-Nehemiah: see Dermot Nestor, *Cognitive Perspectives on Israelite Identity*, LHBOTS 519 (New York: T&T Clark, 2010); idem, 'Merneptah's "Israel" and the Absence of Origins in Biblical Scholarship', *Currents in Biblical Research* 13, no. 3 (2015): 293–329; Donna Laird, *Negotiating Power in Ezra-Nehemiah*, AIL 26 (Atlanta, GA: SBL Press, 2016).

20. Hammer, 'Bourdieu', 87.

21. Ibid., 88.

advantageous positions for themselves. Bourdieu's work also serves as a corrective to 'ideological criticism' as it stands in biblical studies. Jacques Berlinerblau demonstrates how it is tempting for biblical scholars to imply ancient writers '*intentionally constructed* and *promulgated*...ideology', that ancient writers recognized 'what they were up to', all to '*impose* it upon their (seemingly) unsuspecting readership',[22] following the kind of agency-oriented positions of Lenin or Gramsci, where a writer's ideology is a weapon consciously wielded against another class.[23] The texts we are dealing with are multifaceted, and the actions taken by individuals in these texts are nuanced and part of a constant negotiation: What compels Tamar to keep pursuing intercourse with a relative of her deceased husband? What makes the widow of Tekoa's plea to King David so emotionally effective? Why is the thought of memorialization comforting to the childless eunuch of Isaiah 56? Crude understandings of texts as ideology fail to recognize that the workings of power are normally hidden, subtle and internalized.

Bourdieu, in *Outline of a Theory of Practice*, argues that within any system (what he terms 'field') laying below the heterodoxy or orthodoxy of the time (the 'universe of discourse') there resides doxa ('the universe of the undiscussed').[24] Rather than top-down ideology, doxa is something of the shared understandings of power which are common to all within a structure – that which just seems natural or common sense – 'the world of tradition experienced as a "natural world" and taken for granted'.[25] It is this doxa which structures all relations, which provides the commonality in which agents operate, and which begins to make sense of the actions of agents in our texts – why Absalom must erect a monument in place of offspring, or why Tamar would put herself in the situation of prostituting herself to her step-father in service of her deceased husband – without jumping to a crude understanding of texts as propaganda, instead understanding power as cultural and social paradigms which are both *concealed*, and at work through *all* levels of a society. Bourdieu's work situates the subject in the social field, asking how the subject is formed and how society shapes the subject to reproduce constructs of power and capital. A field is a 'place of struggle', a site at which capital is

22. Jacques Berlinerblau, 'Ideology, Pierre Bourdieu's Doxa, and the Hebrew Bible', *Semeia* 87 (1999): 194.
23. Ibid., 198.
24. Pierre Bourdieu, *Outline of a Theory of Practice*, trans. Richard Nice, Cambridge Studies in Social Anthropology 16 (Cambridge: Cambridge University Press, 1977), 168.
25. Ibid., 164.

fought over; here relations between various positions are negotiated and exchanges of capital take place, while relationships of domination are enacted.[26] Moreover, different fields contain what Bourdieu terms 'structural homologies', so what may seem like autonomous fields (church; education; sport) are deeply interrelated (and so, for us, the relationship between death, land, kinship and sexuality).[27] Fields – religious, educational, family, economic – are areas in which one competes, giving us a mediating position between subjectivist and objectivist modes of thought – that we are in complete rational control of our choices, or that we are blindly following the drumbeat of the world – moving away from an approach which makes 'the agent disappear by reducing it to the role of supporter or bearer of the structure', and offering a model which fulfils a 'desire to escape from the philosophy of consciousness without annulling the agent in its true role of practical operator of constructions of the real'.[28] While making significant departures from Marx, Bourdieu's fieldwork and methodology attempted a 'serviceable sociological model for the critique of all forms of social domination',[29] and demonstrated

26. Pierre Bourdieu and Loïc Wacquant, *An Invitation to Reflexive Sociology* (Chicago: University of Chicago Press, 1992), 97.

27. Although Bourdieu does not deal extensively with religion, his work has been used to outline a 'religious' field, a field at work in both the theo-legalistic nature of many of the texts we are looking at, but also alongside the fields of burial, procreation and memorialization. As Rey says: 'The religious habitus is the specifically religious dimension of an individual agent's habitus that manifests itself most apparently, though not exclusively, in the religious field. It is the principle determining subjective (though objectively defined) influence on what particular religious interests, tastes, dispositions and needs that anyone has, on how she or he perceives of, responds to, and uses religious symbols and/or engages in rituals, on her or his reaction to religious leaders, on what forms of religious capital she or he deems worthy of pursuit': Terry Rey, *Bourdieu on Religion: Imposing Faith and Legitimacy* (London: Equinox, 2007), 93. A more religious-informed understanding of Bourdieu can move away from a Durkheimian understanding of religion as society, and away from a naïve understanding of the faith animating the human conscious, instead moving towards a materialist understating, seeing 'that the lived body is an irreducible principle, the existential ground of culture and the sacred' (Thomas J. Csordas, *Body, Meaning, Healing* [Basingstoke: Palgrave Macmillan, 2002], 72).

28. Pierre Bourdieu, *The Rules of Art: Genesis and Structure of the Literary Field*, trans. Susan Emanuel (Cambridge: Polity Press, 1996), 179–80.

29. Rey, *Bourdieu on Religion*, 41. Bourdieu was keen to avoid, on the one hand, theories which made the agent simply a 'supporter or bearer of the structure', and on the other hand 'the philosophy of consciousness', allowing a place for the agent in its role as 'practical operator of constructions of the real': Deborah Reed-Danahay,

that power masks itself, which offers 'a potentially powerful and persuasive tool for the analysis of social action'.[30] This will be essential for understanding the constructs of power and agency at work in our texts, particularly concerning gender roles.

How does the subject operate within this world of doxa? If doxa is that which feels natural, the part of the subject that makes sense of the doxa is the habitus, the genesis of the social person (which Bourdieu terms generative structuralism, or genetic structuralism):

> I am trying to describe and analyse the genesis of one's person. That is, habitus or the notion of habitus. The interest is in understanding how what we call the 'individual' is molded by social structures. That is the problem of the internalization of social structures and the production of habitus as a generative structure. The concept of habitus is generative structure.[31]

Rather than a Durkheimian structuralism, Bourdieu maintained the place of individual agency in contributing to this generative structure; that is, the self in its relation to society is not only *not* a free agent, it also *acts* to perpetuate the socials hierarchies of power. There exist in the world 'objective structures that are independent of the consciousness and desires of agents', and agents gain their social genesis in these worlds.[32] It would be relatively easy to define habitus simplistically as the formation of habits of character with the subject; however, the abiding influence of Bourdieu's work is that the habitus only exists within the broader structures that created it. The most famous definition of the habitus is as follows:

> The conditionings associated with a particular class of conditions of existence produce *habitus*, systems of durable, transposable dispositions, structured structures predisposed to function as structuring structures, that is, as principles which generate and organize practices and representations that can be objectively adapted to their outcomes without presupposing a conscious aiming at ends or an express mastery of the operations necessary in order to attain them.[33]

Locating Bourdieu, New Anthropologies of Europe (Bloomington, IN: Indiana University Press, 2005), 72.
  30. Jeremy Lane, *Pierre Bourdieu: A Critical Introduction* (London: Pluto, 2000), 194.
  31. Bourdieu, quoted in Rey, *Bourdieu on Religion*, 40.
  32. Pierre Bourdieu, *In Other Words: Essays Towards a Reflexive Sociology*, trans. Matthew Adamson (Stanford, CA: Stanford University Press, 1990), 123.
  33. Pierre Bourdieu, *The Logic of Practice*, trans. Richard Nice (Cambridge: Polity, 1990), 53.

So, the *field* and the *habitus* have a 'double and obscure relationship', in which the 'field structures the habitus' while the 'habitus contributes to constituting the field as a meaningful world'.³⁴ Habitus, in its reception, has been interpreted as deterministic. However Loïc Wacquant – who worked and wrote with Bourdieu – responding to this criticism, outlines a genealogy of habitus and argues that there is room for manoeuvre in the habitus, which is not necessarily coherent and unified, and which is capable of 'personal resistance, social innovation, and structural transformation'.³⁵ Moreover, responding to a 'deterministic streak' in Bourdieu, in its recent reception the habitus has been theorized to be more fractured than in Bourdieu's writing.³⁶

What causes us to act per our habitus? Habitus and field are shaped by an addition concept, capital. Symbolic and material capital substantially increases our odds of 'winning at the game'. Forms of capital, the 'possession of which defines class membership' and the 'distribution of which determines positions in power relations', are both 'instruments of power' and stakes in the struggle for power.³⁷ Flowing from the possession of symbolic capital is symbolic violence, crucial for our understanding of domination and power. Symbolic violence is not physical, but is the use of symbolic capital by one in a position of domination on one who is not. Symbolic violence is 'the violence which is exercised upon a social agent with his or her complicity'.³⁸ It is an unknown use of power, and it appears natural. This goes some way to understanding the motivations of an agent not acting out of explicit self-interest (e.g. that the widow requires a child for her own security) but that agents can act for the benefit of the field, because the field has become internalized in the habitus.

To Bourdieu, the quintessential form of symbolic violence is gender oppression, the masked use of symbolic violence against one who does not perceive it.³⁹ In *Masculine Domination* he writes:

---

34. Bourdieu and Wacquant, *Invitation*, 127.

35. Loïc Wacquant, 'A Concise Genealogy and Anatomy of Habitus', in *The Oxford Handbook of Pierre Bourdieu*, ed. Thomas Medvetz and Jeffrey J. Sallaz (New York: Oxford University Press, 2018), 528–33.

36. Reed-Danahay, *Locating Bourdieu*, 156.

37. Pierre Bourdieu, *Distinction: A Social Critique of the Judgement of Taste*, trans. Richard Nice (Cambridge, MA: Harvard University Press, 1984), 315–16.

38. Bourdieu and Wacquant, *Invitation*, 167.

39. Although Bourdieu disavowed feminist theory, his work has reinvigorated a dialogue between feminist theory and social theory; see Lisa Adkins, 'Introduction: Feminism, Bourdieu, and After', in *Feminism after Bourdieu*, ed. Lisa Adkins and Beverley Skeggs (Oxford: Blackwell, 2004), 3–18.

> I have always been astonished by what might be called the *paradox of doxa* – the fact that the order of the world as we find it, with its one-way streets and its no-entry signs, whether literal or figurative, its obligations and its penalties, is broadly respected; that there are not more transgressions and subversions, contraventions and 'follies'…; or, still more surprisingly, that the established order, with its relations of domination, its rights and prerogatives, privileges and injustices, ultimately perpetuates itself so easily…[40]

Symbolic violence can be exercised because it is part of one's habitus; we do not act against it because our habitus has been constituted to internalize it, embody it. Symbolic violence 'can only be exerted on a person predisposed (in his habitus) to feel it', whereas 'others will ignore it'.[41] The internalization of the field, the way negotiating in the field affects how you relate to others, and the accrual of capital and the effect of symbolic violence, defines how people construct their social world, from education to relationships, to questions of taste and beauty; they are tied up, inherently, with relationships of domination.[42] Social exchanges and struggles are not the result of 'the production of a conscious, rational calculation' but manifests as a kind of 'feel for the game', a felt sense of how to navigate the fields of life. This feel for the game is a kind of strategy, where agency negotiates one's place:

> [Strategy is] the product of the practical sense as the feel for the game, for a particular, historically determined game – a feel that is acquired in childhood, by taking part in social activities, especially…in children's games…[43] Because native membership in a field implies a feel for the game in the sense of a capacity for practical anticipation of the 'upcoming' future continued in the present, everything that takes place in it seems sensible: full of sense and objectivity directed in a judicious direction.[44]

How one acts in the field will be seen in the strategies and agency of women in the narratives we look at. For instance, we will look at Rachel and Leah, who attempt to gain symbolic capital despite an inability to produce offspring. However, playing the game does not imply that our possibilities for reconstructing the world are endless: 'we cannot make

---

40. Pierre Bourdieu, *Masculine Domination*, trans. Richard Nice (Cambridge: Polity, 2001).
41. Pierre Bourdieu, *Language and Symbolic Power*, ed. John Thompson, trans. Gino Raymond and Matthew Adamson (Cambridge: Polity, 1991), 51.
42. Bourdieu, *Outline*, 115.
43. Bourdieu, *Logic*, 62.
44. Ibid., 66.

history just as we please'.[45] Agency, counterintuitively, is not always autonomous. The acquisition of habitus is:

> A practical *mimesis* (or memeticism)...and the process of reproduction – a practical reactivation that is opposed to both memory and knowledge – tend to take place below the level of consciousness, expression and the reflexive distance which these presuppose... [The body] does not represent what it performs, it does not memorize the past, it *enacts* the past, bringing it back to life. What is 'learned by the body' is not something one has, like knowledge that can be brandished, but something that one is.[46]

Bodies, whether reproductive or entombed, enact power. Power is not just internalized, but embodied, and so the most 'insignificant techniques of the body – ways of walking or blowing one's nose, ways of eating or talking – engage the most fundamental principles of construction and evaluation of the social world'.[47] What is more, one can never wholly *know* what one is doing, and personal style is generally seen as Bourdieu as 'never more than a deviation in relation to the style of a period of class':[48] our 'arms and legs are full of numb imperatives'.[49] Social meaning, situated in bodies, living and dead, is therefore in itself reproducing, especially as social meaning and the structures of power become entwined with the habitus of personal sexual reproduction.

Our inability to know the structures that constitute us and how they form habitus, our inability to actively – cognitively – choose to alter our habitus in relation to the fields we find ourselves in, allows Bourdieu, as suggested above, to be charged with a rigid structuralism that takes away agency. Crucially, however, Bourdieu's theory leaves room for resistance: 'we are like a conductorless orchestra, which offers small opportunities for change'.[50] Hoy, responding to criticism of Bourdieu's work as overly deterministic, suggests:

---

45. Richard Harker, Cheleen Mahar and Chris Wilkes, 'The Basic Theoretical Position', in *An Introduction to the Work of Pierre Bourdieu: The Practice of Theory*, ed. Richard Harker, Cheleen Mahar and Chris Wilkes (London: Macmillan, 1990), 11–12.
46. Bourdieu, *Logic*, 73.
47. Bourdieu, *Distinction*, 466.
48. Bourdieu, *Logic*, 60.
49. Ibid., 69.
50. Bourdieu states: 'in other words, by being produced by a *modus operandi* which is not consciously mastered, the discourse contains an 'objective intention'... which outruns the conscious intentions of its apparent author and constantly offers new pertinent stimuli to the *modus operandi* of which it is the product'. Ibid., 57.

> The habitus does not work via a rigid mechanical causation... [I]nstead, it has a certain plasticity due to the fuzziness, irregularity, and even incoherencies of a few principles that must be easy to master and use. This plasticity allows for the generation of improvisations.[51]

Criticism that habitus is overly deterministic has affected its reception in feminist studies. However, in understanding its usefulness for resistance Steph Lawler helpfully suggests: 'Bourdieu is often (rightly, in my view) characterized as pessimistic; and this pessimism is often (wrongly, in my view) characterized as determinism'.[52] This does not mean resistance will be easy: because of the flow of symbolic capital in the fields of practice, because of our habitus formed within these structures which constantly strive to renew themselves, resistance, while not futile, will be difficult. According to Bourdieu, 'resistance may be alienating and submission may be liberating. Such is the paradox of the dominated, and there is no way out of it'.[53] Put plainly by Lawler:

> How liberating is it to have your clothes, your speech, your appearance vilified? On the other hand, how liberating is it to cast off these marks of difference and to adopt a normalized (middle-class) habitus?[54]

The exercise of power, of symbolic violence, of the reproduction of power in the habitus, in dispositions and tastes and bodies, explains the *endurance* of structures of power:

---

51. David Couzens Hoy, 'Critical Resistance: Foucault and Bourdieu', in *Perspectives on Embodiment: The Intersections of Nature and Culture*, ed. Gail Weiss and Honi Fern Haber (New York: Routledge, 1999), 86. Atkinson's recent work outlines responses over the past twenty years to Bourdieu's work, and in his view, the misreading which suggest it is too deterministic or unable to account for social change: Atkinson, *Beyond Bourdieu*, 1–10.

52. Steph Lawler, 'Rules of Engagement: Habitus, Power and Resistance', in Adkins and Skeggs, eds., *Feminism after Bourdieu*, 124. Others have suggested avenues to break out of an overly deterministic mind-set: Crossley has suggested a soft restoring of Bourdieu's phenomenological roots to cater for a greater degree of messiness and agency in encountering fields (Nick Crossley, 'The Phenomenological Habitus and Its Construction', *Theory and Society* 30, no. 1 [2001]: 95–7); Mahmood, in comparing Butler and Bourdieu, suggests not every modality through which the body acts can be 'captured within the dualistic logic of resistance and constraint' (Saba Mahmood, *Politics of Piety: The Islamic Revival and the Feminist Subject* [Princeton, NJ: Princeton University Press, 2005], 26 n. 46).

53. Bourdieu, *In Other Words*, 155.

54. Lawler, 'Rules of Engagement', 122.

> The *habitus*, a product of history, produces individuals and collective practices – more history – in accordance with the schemes generated by history. It ensures the active presence of past experience, which, deposited in each organism in the form of schemes of perception, though and action, tend to guarantee the 'correctness' of practices and their constancy over time, more reliably than all formal rules and explicit norms. This system of dispositions – *a present past that tends to perpetuate itself into the future by reactivation in similar structured practices.*[55]

This perpetuation takes place partially through the exercise of *doxa*, in which 'relations of order' structure both 'the real world and the thought world', and are therefore 'accepted as self-evident',[56] where doxa is the naturalness which conceals domination. The site for this durability, for Bourdieu, is not in intellectual argument but contained in the body:

> Bodily hexis is political mythology realized, *em-bodied*, turned into a permanent disposition, a durable way of standing, speaking, walking, and thereby of feeling and thinking.[57]

Bourdieu's work has helped develop a move towards a more materialist understanding of religious practice. Take, for instance, Catherine Bell's now classic work on ritual, using Bourdieu to move away from ritual as an object which reveals a social process to one of an understanding of ritual as 'a way to distinguish and privilege what is being done in comparison to other, usually more quotidian, activities', in which the body takes precedence: 'no longer mere physical instrument of the mind, it now denotes a more complex and irreducible phenomenon, namely the social body'.[58] Through this Bourdieu has helped to bring the body to centre stage as a place for sociological analysis, and his work has been significant for theorists of the body.[59] Catherine Connell and Ashley Mears assess Bourdieu as *the* contributor who brought the body into

---

55. Bourdieu, *Logic*, 54. Italics mine.
56. Bourdieu, *Distinction*, 471.
57. Bourdieu, *Logic*, 69–70.
58. Catherine M. Bell, *Ritual Theory, Ritual Practice* (New York: Oxford University Press, 1992), 74, 96.
59. Shilling provides a precis of Bourdieu's theorizing of the body, but also draws some of the limitations in his analysis, particularly highlighting those places in which the lived experience of the body cannot be reduced to physical capital, but 'transcend the profane parameters of economic interest' (Chris Shilling, *The Body and Social Theory*, 3rd ed. [London: SAGE, 2012], 135–61). Shilling points to the work by

study of class reproduction, though they highlight that in the reception of his work many offering understandings of bodily capital in contexts such as body building and fashion modelling ignore Bourdieu's critique of class domination, taking for granted that the holder of bodily capital is the 'beneficiary of its value'.[60] They cite, as a contrast, the work of Kimberly Hoang, whose ethnography of sex work in Ho Chi Min City showed how hostesses in bars allow Vietnamese business men to secure deals with foreign investors;[61] studies such as these demonstrate 'bodily capital is not *only* the property of individuals; it is often situated in a structure of relations in which individual bodies *function* as property for those with the structural power to harness it'. Connell and Mears highlight the need to attend to the mechanisms of appropriation, which 'seem to often have an affective dimension', suggesting we must attend to 'the pleasures of exploitation and consider how affect is being manipulated to appropriate individuals' bodily capital with one hand and to sell it back to them with the other'.[62] Through Bourdieu's focus on the body as the site of social reproduction, the body will be central to how the bodies we will look at – dead and living, male and female, reproducing non-reproducing – perpetuate social reproductions of power. Despite opportunity for change and resistance, structures of power are durable, and this durability resides forcefully in the body. This durability goes some way permitting understanding of commonality of practice over the long period of the texts we are looking at, but its durability in the body also goes some way to explaining the diversity of responses to crisis in our texts: crisis is not responded to by a single rationalised practice (e.g. levirate marriage) but through the bodily hexis: the inability of the body to not respond.

Mahmood on Islamic piety which highlights the fact that, despite Bourdieu's focus, embodied practice 'is not exhausted by its ability to function as an index of social and class status or a group's ideological habitus': Mahmood, *Politics of Piety*, 26.

60. Catherine Connell and Ashley Mears, 'Bourdieu and the Body', in Medvetz and Sallaz, eds., *The Oxford Handbook of Pierre Bourdieu*, 562–3. They cite, as an example, Catherine Hakim's study of erotic capital, though they critique her focus on a sexual marketplace and her failure to take into account unequally distributed capital: Catherine Hakim, *Erotic Capital: The Power of Attraction in the Boardroom and the Bedroom* (New York: Basic Books, 2011).

61. Kimberly Kay Hoang, *Dealing in Desire: Asian Ascendancy, Western Decline, and the Hidden Currencies of Global Sex Work* (Oakland, CA: University of California Press, 2015).

62. Connell and Mears, 'Bourdieu and the Body', 567.

3. Gender

Bourdieu argued that gender is fundamental to the exercise of capital, symbolic violence and the reproduction of structures of power. This drive of reproduction – central to our discussion of the importance of the reproduction of the male, the בית אב, and social structures and norms – has been picked up by gender and queer theorists. Lee Edelman's groundbreaking *No Future: Queer Theory and the Death Drive* rejects the symbolic figure of the 'Child', and forms a useful dialogue partner with Bourdieu's emphasis on social reproduction. The Child, argues Edelman, is the figure around which the symbolic system is build. Pope Benedict XIV, for example, speaking against gay marriage, said of children that they 'are the greatest treasure and the future of every society'.[63] However, constructing the future around the child, Edelman argues, is not limited to conservative pronouncements. It pervades all rhetoric. Edelman cites the use by proponents of abortion rights, who frame the political struggle as a 'fight for our children – for our daughters and our sons'.[64] The image of the child pervades not just political rhetoric but art, film and music. Our political and social rhetoric, whether from the political left or the right, congeals around the figure of the Future, embodied in the Child, in what Edelman terms 'reproductive futurism'. This reproductive futurism rejects the 'queer', that which ruptures or disfigures normal gender, sexual or reproductive norms, in favour of social reproduction. This reproductive futurism is used by both liberal and conservative, in an unending rhetoric of the 'future', and Edelman, speaking specifically to a queer audience, calls on them to reject the Child and its hold on our discourse and rhetoric, and with that the position that for the marginalized or those outside of the domains of power 'the future is mere repetition and just as lethal as the past'.[65] This involves not just a rejection of that which we would

---

63. On the 8 March 2012, http://w2.vatican.va/content/benedict-xvi/en/speeches/2012/march/documents/hf_ben-xvi_spe_20120309_us-bishops.html [last accessed: 14 May 2019]

64. Lee Edelman, *No Future: Queer Theory and the Death Drive* (Durham, NC: Duke University Press, 2004), 2, quoting a speech by Donna Shalala at the 150th Anniversary of the First Women's Rights Convention, Seneca Falls, New York, 17 July 1998.

65. Ibid. Edelman's work has been particularly influential within queer theory, and his appropriation of the Lacanian notion of the death-drive has significantly influenced my thinking around personhood and reproduction. See also Carolyn Dinshaw et al., 'Theorizing Queer Temporalities: A Roundtable Discussion', *GLQ: A Journal of Lesbian and Gay Studies* 13, no. 2 (2007): 177–95; Lee Edelman, 'The

cast as negative (sexism, homophobia, patriarchy), but a rejection of the system as a whole, a rejection of assimilation, of the fallacy of 'equality' (same-sex marriage, gay nuclear families).

Edelman's work has been drawn upon by others working in queer theory as an embrace of *failure*.[66] Edelman's thesis is bold and provocative, and draws on post-Victorian texts to explore the way that society projects the idea of the Child. Its starkness holds up a mirror to the texts we are looking at, highlighting how subtle and pervasive its own paradigm of reproductive futurism is. The symbolic *Child* is arguably absent from the text of the Hebrew Bible; there are few sentimental appeals to 'the child' being of importance in and of itself.[67] However, a kind of reproductive futurism pervades the text, from YHWH's promise of descendants to Abraham (Gen. 22.17), to the raising of the name of the dead (Deut. 25.5-10), to the tears of Rachel over her descendants going into exile (Jer. 31.15). Edelman's work is crucial in terms of allowing us to step back and see how 'reproduction' is deeply ingrained both in social structures and how we internalize this (similar to the habitus). This project is informed by this idea of 'reproductive futurism' and queer, feminist and gender-critical theory more widely, understanding gender and sexuality as a kind of discourse, not a given reality or 'essential state'.[68] If, then, gender is not an essentialist state, Judith Butler proposes it is a kind of fantasy, 'instituted and inscribed on the surface of bodies', a product of discourse.[69] To Butler, gender is the *performance* of repeated acts, which 'congeal over time to produce the appearance of a substance, of a natural sort of being', and are:

Future Is Kid Stuff: Queer Theory, Disidentification, and the Death Drive', *Narrative* 6, no. 1 (1998): 18–30; Robert L. Caserio et al., 'The Antisocial Thesis in Queer Theory', *PMLA* 121, no. 3 (2006): 816–28; Judith Halberstam, *The Queer Art of Failure* (Durham, NC: Duke University Press, 2011); José Esteban Muñoz, *Cruising Utopia: The Then and There of Queer Futurity* (New York: New York University Press, 2009); Elizabeth Freeman, *Time Binds: Queer Temporalities, Queer Histories* (Durham, NC: Duke University Press, 2010).

66. See, for example, Halberstam, *The Queer Art of Failure*. An example of this kind of 'queer' thinking would be the rejection of gay, or equal, marriage, as something understood as a form of assimilation.

67. Though there are exceptions, as will be discussed below.

68. Nikki Sullivan, *A Critical Introduction to Queer Theory* (New York: New York University Press, 2003), 81.

69. Judith Butler, *Gender Trouble: Feminism and the Subversion of Identity* (New York: Routledge, 1990), 136.

> *Performative* in the sense that the essence or identity that they otherwise purport to express are *fabrications*... That the gendered body is performative suggests that it has no ontological status apart from the various acts which constitutes its reality.[70]

These constructions preserve particular purposes and institutions.[71] Gender, then, is seen as a 'regulatory fiction',[72] which treats anything outside of this as an anomaly. Social stigma conceals gender's genesis:

> The tacit collective agreement to perform, produce, and sustain discrete and polar genders as cultural fictions is obscured by the credibility of those productions – and the punishment that attend not agreeing to believe in them.[73]

The failure to repeat a performance 'exposes the phantasmatic effect of abiding identity as a politically tenuous construction',[74] and would be liable to the kind of symbolic (or actual) violence Bourdieu theorised. Butler states the importance of destabilising these constructs, as 'identity categories tend to be instruments of regulatory regimes...as the normalizing categories of oppressive structures'.[75] By doing this we can create a 'hermeneutical stance borrowed from contemporary gender theory that deconstructs the phenomenon "women" as the constructed "other"'.[76]

This work, although having a historical and anthropological bent, cannot shy away from political questions of how texts construct gender and personhood, and how these texts dialogue with contemporary culture and religion. By demonstrating that the text creates a category of 'woman', and places her in a position of submission and marginalization, we can recognize, and therefore deconstruct, the dominant discourses at work in the Bible. By cutting the text free from any 'monolithic' discourse it is possible to find 'varieties of constructions of gender that

---

70. Ibid. See Lovell for an engagement of Butler and Bourdieu: Terry Lovell, 'Thinking Feminism With and Against Bourdieu', *Sociological Review* 1, no. 1 (2000): 11–19.
71. Sullivan, *A Critical Introduction*, 82.
72. Annamarie Jagose, *Queer Theory: An Introduction* (New York: New York University Press, 1996), 83–4.
73. Butler, *Gender Trouble*, 140–1.
74. Ibid., 141.
75. Judith Butler, 'Imitation and Gender Insubordination', in *Inside/Out: Lesbian Theories, Gay Theories*, ed. Diana Fuss (New York: Routledge, 1991), 343.
76. Deborah Sawyer, *God, Gender and the Bible*, Biblical Limits (London: Routledge, 2002), 4.

compete and contradict across the breadth of the canon'.[77] We can also see how constructions of masculinity are normalized and how failures in masculinity, failures to repeat a performance such as reproduction, are masked or dealt with. The academic study of masculinity has grown over the past two decades, and a few studies have started to emerge in relation to the Bible.[78] As noted by Ovidiu Creangă, most works take a critical approach to masculinity as a complement to feminist-critical approaches. Masculinity, as the expression of an unequal balance of power, is one that perpetuates itself, and becomes 'embedded in power structures'.[79] Despite attempt of masculinity, particularly a reproductive masculinity, to portray itself as natural, it is fundamentally a construct, one that is 'very shaky indeed', and which must constantly adapt and shape itself.[80] The texts we are looking at deal, in part, to when the reproductive masculinity fails. Therefore, in assessing the texts we will look at, the 'shaky' notion of gender will be explored; through this, following Bourdieu, we will be able to see how texts such as Deut. 25.5-10 do not simply display certain ideas of gender, but negotiate them, reinforce them, and mask their instability. This will run counter to dominant readings of levirate marriage, which understand it as a form of inheritance law, widow protection, of ancestor veneration, paradigms which have become deeply embedded in scholarship. We will now turn to four dominant examples of these paradigms.

77. Ibid., 13.
78. Ovidiu Creangă, ed., *Men and Masculinity in the Hebrew Bible and Beyond*, BMW 33 (Sheffield: Sheffield Phoenix, 2010); Roland Boer, *The Earthy Nature of the Bible: Fleshly Readings of Sex, Masculinity, and Carnality* (Basingstoke: Palgrave Macmillan, 2012); Janice C. Anderson and Stephen D. Moore, eds., *New Testament Masculinities*, SemeiaSt 45 (Atlanta, GA: Society of Biblical Literature, 2004); David J. A. Clines, *Interested Parties: The Ideology of Writers and Readers of the Hebrew Bible*, JSOTSup 205 (Sheffield: Sheffield Academic, 1995); Howard Eilberg-Schwartz, *God's Phallus and Other Problems for Men and Monotheism* (Boston: Beacon, 1994).
79. Susan Haddox, "Favoured Sons and Subordinate Masculinities', in Creangă, ed., *Men and Masculinity*, 2–19.
80. Roland Boer, "Of Fine Wine, Incense and Spices: The Unstable Masculine Hegemony of the Book of Chronicles', in Creangă, ed., *Men and Masculinity*, 21–2.

Chapter 2

How a Law about Sex Became about
Anything Else

Of all the core texts, most scholarly work has been written about 'levirate marriage', focusing on Deut. 25.5-10, Genesis 38 and Ruth. In 1976, in a scathing review of Donald Leggett's *The Levirate and Goel Institutions in the Old Testament*, Etan Levine wrote:

> The *G^eUllah* [redemption of land], *Yibbum* [levirate marriage] and related institutions of the Bible have been subject to such intensive and extensive research that the author of any new study is perforce obliged to justify his enterprise. Such legitimation should include the usual constituents: definition of the problem(s), critical evaluation of previous investigations, disclosure of the implicit assumptions in the author's methodology, and presentation of new conclusions. These conclusions, in substance or in emphasis, should provide new information, or, at the very least, reveal a new perspective to guide further research.[1]

Levine was right; by the early 1980s, a mass of literature had developed around the three texts looking at the institution of levirate marriage and seeking out its historical development, its meaning and its purpose.[2]

---

1. Etan Levine, 'On Intra-Familial Institutions of the Bible', *Biblica* 57, no. 4 (1976): 544.
2. The following is a list of journal articles and books dedicated *solely* to the subject of Levirate marriage: Millar Burrows, 'Levirate Marriage in Israel', *JBL* 59, no. 1 (1940): 23–33; Burrows, 'Background'; Eryl W. Davies, 'Inheritance Rights and the Hebrew Levirate Marriage: Part 1', *VT* 31, no. 2 (1981): 138–44; idem, 'Inheritance Rights and the Hebrew Levirate Marriage: Part 2', *VT* 31, no. 3 (1981): 257–68; Dorothy Thompson and Thomas Thompson, 'Some Legal Problems in the Book of Ruth', *VT* 18, no. 1 (1968): 79–99; Derek R. G. Beattie, 'The Book of Ruth as Evidence for Israelite Legal Practice', *VT* 24, no. 3 (1974): 251–67; Samuel Belkin,

Levine's critique of Leggett's book hints at the wider problems of the scholarship in the field:

> The book under review has not adequately respected these criteria. It consists largely of fragmentary, and frequently irrelevant or unsubstantiated, quotations punctuated by remarks of the author that oscillate between the self-evident and the unverifiable. Assertions are 'proved' by assertions of previous authors, without scholarly investigation of primary sources. The uncritical use of secondary sources, combined with the citation of positions that are mutually exclusive, conspire to form a confused and confusing whole, requiring several readings to determine whether the author has a position, and, if so, what the precise nature of the position is, and how it is related to the quoted material.[3]

The literature on the subject became trapped in a self-referential cycle, large enough that it was possible to find enough supporting statements to assert something about the texts under question without engaging with the actual texts themselves, or to assert statements about words or phrases without proper contextual study. Attempts to trace historical developments of legal institutions, to substantiate legal practice from narrative texts, and to offer interpretations without a proper contextual study of agnate texts had stifled discussion, and by the 1990s there appears to have been a vacuum of journal articles or monographs dealing with the subject matter.

In the attempts to explain the purpose of the levirate, three paradigms emerged in the scholarship. Broadly speaking, the first paradigm suggested levirate marriage is enacted to keep the name alive, which somehow means the dead live on; the second viewed the name as a legal term which applies to property and inheritance; the third, while drawing on the first two, suggested a purpose of the law is to protect the widow left behind by the death of the man. However, all three fail to note some of its fundamental

---

'Levirate and Agnate Marriage in Rabbinic and Cognate Literature', *JQR* 60, no. 4 (1970): 275–329; Ernst Kutsch, 'יבם', *TDOT*; Harold H. Rowley, 'The Marriage of Ruth', *HTR* 40, no. 2 (1947): 77–99; Donald A. Leggett, *The Levirate and Goel Institutions in the Old Testament: With Special Attention to the Book of Ruth* (Cherry Hill, NJ: Mack, 1974); Baruch Levine, 'In Praise of the Israelite *Mišpāḥâ*: Legal Themes in the Book of Ruth', in *The Quest for the Kingdom of God: Studies in Honor of George E. Mendenhall*, ed. Herbert Huffmon, Frank Spina, and Alberto R. Green (Winona Lake, IN: Eisenbrauns, 1983), 95–106; Raymond Westbrook, 'The Law of the Biblical Levirate', *RIDA* 24 (1977): 65–87.

3. Levine, 'On Intra-Familial Institutions of the Bible', 544.

dynamics, and arguably shy away from the sexual, reproductive, thrust of the texts. I will now outline each of these explanations by reference to three scholars who epitomized the various approaches: Johannes Pedersen, Raymond Westbrook and Eryl Davies, before contrasting them with the work of Herbert Chanan Brichto, who attempts a broader cultural synthesis of kin, cult, land and afterlife.

1. *Johannes Pedersen*

Pedersen's epic *Israel: Its Life and Culture* (1926) is regularly footnoted in discussions of levirate marriage. Pedersen attempts a kind of anthropology of ancient Israel, and makes connections regarding levirate marriage that many contemporary scholars have failed to account for. He notes that interpretations had taken into consideration the welfare of the widow and the property of the family.[4] However, following the text of Deuteronomy, he states that the 'object of the law is to get progeny for a man without sons, that his name may be preserved and his house not be blotted out'. In his exegesis, Pedersen presumes that 'dwell together' in Deut. 25.5 means in the 'same town' and that it is meant to release obligations when the husband has left his kindred. He states:

> If a man, after having contracted a marriage, dies without sons, then he dies entirely. It is this blotting out of life which is to be avoided. His nearest of kin, the brother, must perform this office of love in order to protect him from extermination. The wife, whose object in life it is to bear him a son in whom his life is resurrected, must be enabled to do her duty towards him… The name once more comes to life in him.[5]

Pedersen suggests the wife's primary role in the passage is to 'supply the man with progeny, in which his life may be maintained', and the brother's duty is meant to come out of love for the deceased, and his refusal 'is also a violation of her rights, in that he prevents her from fulfilling her most exalted duty'.[6] Pedersen discusses the three texts, Deut. 25.5-10, Genesis 38 and Ruth, as examples of the same process under different contingencies: Deuteronomy lays the responsibility on the brother of the deceased man, whereas Genesis leaves open the possibility of the

---

4. Johannes Pedersen, *Israel: Its Life and Culture* (London: Oxford University Press, 1926), 78.
5. Ibid.
6. Ibid.

father-in-law acting, and in Ruth the responsibility goes to the nearest agnate relative.[7] The key to Pedersen's interpretation lies in his phrase 'in whom his life is resurrected', and this resurrection, Pedersen later suggests, takes place in through the שם, or name:

> The soul in its entirety, with all its blessing and honour, finds expression in the name, *shēm*... The name is the appellation characterizing each individual soul. In so far it may be said that the name is part of the soul, seeing that it is possessed by it like the body, and everything wherein it manifests itself... It is to be understood quite literally that the name is the soul.[8]

Pedersen surveys texts that refer to the name of YHWH, with Israel trusting in the name or longing for it (Ps. 33.21; Isa. 26.8), or the name supporting the king (Ps. 20.2). He relates this to depictions of the human name such as Qoh. 6.4, where the name of the child is covered in darkness 'for no one knows its soul'; and to the name of the wicked perishing (Prov. 10.7) as 'the name is so identical with the soul in the whole of its weight and extent'.[9] He further suggests there is an 'intimate relation between soul and property', expressed by the name being called after that of the owner (Ps. 49.12; 2 Sam. 13.28). He understands the erection of monuments as related to names, such as David's pillar in 2 Sam. 8.13, and relates this explicitly to Absalom's monument in 2 Sam. 18.18, stating:

> It contains the name of the man, and so protects his soul against extermination, when it cannot be preserved in a natural manner by being maintained in the son. The pillar is equal to the name, and the name is equal to the soul.[10]

He then relates this to the promise to the eunuch in Isa. 56.3-5, and specifically links the text to the inclusion of ancestors' names:

> The man bears the name of his fathers, and the meaning of that now appears quite clearly. The name is the soul; the heritage consisting in the name is not an empty appellation, a sound, but the substance of a soul. In the heritage of the name the psychic community is expressed. The house bears the name of the father of the house, and this implies that his soul imbues the whole of the family with everything that belongs to it.[11]

---

7. Ibid., 79–80.
8. Ibid., 245.
9. Ibid., 246.
10. Ibid., 251.
11. Ibid., 254.

Despite the problematic use of the term 'soul' by Pedersen, he does attempt to contextualize it:

> We are unable to understand this manner of thinking, unless we look upon it from the psychological standpoint of the Israelite. We must realize what is implied by the soul not be limited to the ego, the conscious, finished personality. The soul is in everything that fills it, in the renown, in the property, in everything wherein it works.

He suggests that the soul 'may live, even though the ego disappears'.[12] He understands the desire to continue the soul as a 'desire to live'; 'he desires that life is never to run out, but is to be constantly renewed. Therefore, he desires sons more than anything else on this earth. It is his desire to live which demands them; for the son bears his name, in him his life and soul live continually'. He understands this in relation to the 'seed':

> The progeny, the 'seed', is identical with the name. 'For as the new heavens and the new earth, which I will make, shall remain before me, saith Yahweh, so shall your seed and your name remain' (Is. 66,22)… It is really a promise to Abraham himself and the other patriarchs that the earth is to be blessed by their seed, because it is identical with their own soul.[13]

Pedersen argues extermination of the name is akin to 'complete annihilation',[14] connecting the widow of Tekoa to the narratives of both Zelophehad's daughters and Ruth. To prevent the annihilation, 'the brother of the deceased must come to the fore and offer disinterested help' in the form of the levirate: 'By providing progeny for his brother he maintains his name…he guards his soul against obliteration'.[15] This is further connected to memory (Jer. 11.19) and he states: 'the word memory or remembrance, *zēkher*, is used in exactly the same manner as *shēm*, in order to designate the name, and so also the soul'.[16] He continues:

---

12. The English translation was undertaken with the help of Aslaug Møller at the University of Copenhagen; Pedersen notes 'the character of the subject has sometimes necessitated the finding of expressions which, like their Danish equivalents, may strike the reader as peculiar and perhaps not in strict accordance with the common *usus loquendi*'. Pedersen, *Israel*, Preface. For a recent discussion of the nuances of Pedersen's understanding of the נפש, see Matthew J. Suriano, *A History of Death in the Hebrew Bible* (New York: Oxford University Press, 2018), 136–8.

13. Pedersen, *Israel*, 254.

14. He references Josh. 7.9; 2 Kgs 14.27; Deut. 7.24; 9.14; 12.3; Isa. 14.22; 1 Sam. 24.22.

15. Pedersen, *Israel*, 256.

16. Ibid.

> The man wants to be remembered; thus his name is made to live. The substance of his soul must be so strong that it does not perish, but works through the generations. If he has no sons, then he may seek compensation in setting up a memorial, into which his name has been laid so as to be preserved. It may have its value, perhaps even if he has sons. But it can never be full compensation for the life which the name continues in the new souls through the descendants. It sounds very strange when Yahweh says to the most rejected people, the eunuchs, that to them will be given a memorial and a name better than that of sons and daughters (Is. 56,5).[17]

Pedersen makes many of the connections made in this project. His 15-page analysis of the 'name' is a tour de force, so relentless in its wide range of texts, of its creative connections, and its unapologetic certainty in its argument that it cannot be ignored. However, texts are often referenced (or sometimes quoted) and briefly commented on without any form of rigorous examination; his use of categories like 'soul' and 'resurrection', while partially qualified, are problematic, and Pedersen is generally overconfident in the claims he can make. That said, the opportunities he presents to rethink the topic at hand are enormous. He begins to make connections that this project will make, in terms of understanding how the seeming metaphysical nature of the שם relates to its more concrete connections such as that of property or progeny. As we shall see in the next section, someone like Westbrook limits his understanding of 'the name' to a legal term meaning 'title' to property, and excludes examination of further meanings of שם. What Pedersen has done is build a solid context for why it is not possible to delineate between legal and non-legal meanings of a concept like the שם. Further, he has made concrete attempts to demonstrate how, despite the shortcomings of the term soul, the name takes on a real social role beyond something metaphysical in its connection to memory, to progeny, to the household and its property.

Pedersen idea of the name is explicitly referenced by scholars discussing levirate marriage.[18] While his work is no longer referenced in more recent literature, his influence can be traced through later scholarship. For example, Millar Burrows, whose article on levirate marriage is widely cited, suggests:

---

17. Ibid., 257.
18. See Leggett, *Levirate and Goel*, 51–4; Leonard Mars, 'What Was Onan's Crime?', *CSSH* 26, no. 3 (1984): 435, 436; Thompson and Thompson, 'Legal Problems', 87 n. 3.

> An important factor, doubtless, was man's natural dread of annihilation and his craving for some kind of immortality. In part what was desired was simply to be remembered. But the continuance of the name meant more than that. To the Israelite the 'name' included practically what we call the 'self'. The extinction of the self, his own life, was what a man avoided by having a son.[19]

When we reach footnote 18 on that page, however, we find this is referenced entirely through both Pedersen's arguments around levirate marriage and his whole discussion of the 'name'. This connection between immortality and memory emerges recently in other places, without reference to Pedersen, for example in Brian Schmidt's essay 'Memory as Immortality: Countering the Dreaded "Death after Death" in Ancient Israelite Society', where he argues for a relatively powerless afterlife, with the dead 'weak and frail'. He sets up the context of commemoration cults at Ugarit, which he argues focus on the prevention of *eternal anonymity*.[20] For Schmidt, the Babylonian exile resulted in 'significant transformations' of Judahite beliefs about death and afterlife, arguing 'while notions of immortality were possibly afloat in various periods of Israelite religious history, only with the passage of time were certain forms singled out for fuller elaboration and development'.[21] He suggests:

> The evidence suggests that what occupied a more central place in the thought and action of ancient Israelites as they contemplated their prospects beyond the grave was the concern to perpetuate the memory of the deceased in the minds of the living. Prior to the exile, the ancient Israelites…placed primary, if not sole, emphasis on the perpetuation of the memory of the family dead and on making the best of life on this side of the grave. Both commoner and elite went to some length to ensure that the family name epitomized by the multigenerational graves containing the bones of family dead and located on family land would never be neglected, let alone forgotten. By regularly performing various communal and public rituals, the names and memories of deceased kin were preserved from oblivion, thereby avoiding the dreaded 'death after death'.[22]

---

19. Burrows, 'Levirate Marriage', 31. He references pp. 71–81, 94–5, 245–59 in Pedersen, which relate exactly to his discussions.
20. Brian B. Schmidt, 'Memory as Immortality: Countering the Dreaded "Death after Death" in Ancient Israelite Society', in *Judaism in Late Antiquity, Part 4: Death, Life-After-Death, Resurrection and the World-To-Come in the Judaisms of Antiquity*, ed. Jacob Neusner and Alan Jeffery Avery-Peck, HOS 49 (Leiden: Brill, 2000), 92–6.
21. Ibid., 97.
22. Ibid., 99.

Schmidt's analysis resists some of the pitfalls of Pedersen, notably his uncritical use of terms like 'soul', while maintaining the importance of social continuity in some form as a kind of afterlife. However, while Schmidt appears to have reduced his emphasis on a powerless, weak dead as articulated in his earlier work,[23] he still relies heavily on a negative sense of memorialization where certain acts preserve the fragile life of the dead, which will be discussed in more depth in the next chapter. However, where this strain of thinking around death and afterlife as the context of levirate marriage has been influential and productive, it is in need of reassessment.

2. Raymond Westbrook

Westbrook attempted a radically different understanding of the purpose of levirate marriage, one which has had considerable influence.[24] Westbrook writes partly against attempts to understand the differences between Deut. 25.5-10, Genesis 38 and Ruth as indicating historical development, stating instead that the differences between the texts are omissions, not contradictions; he argues that the assumption that Deuteronomy 25 is a 'comprehensive account' of the law of the levirate is in conflict with ancient West Asian law forms which are not 'a comprehensive statement of general principles'. He suggests therefore that Ruth and Genesis 38 are written with the assumption the reader would know the legal material, and that the writer 'assumes knowledge of the law on the part of the reader and only concerns himself with some unusual, and for that reason interesting, application thereof'.[25] For Westbrook, the concept of the man's memory

---

23. Brian B. Schmidt, *Israel's Beneficent Dead: Ancestor Cult and Necromancy in Ancient Israelite Religion and Tradition* (Winona Lake, IN: Eisenbrauns, 1994).

24. Dvora E. Weisberg, 'The Widow of Our Discontent: Levirate Marriage in the Bible and Ancient Israel', *JSOT* 28, no. 4 (2004): 403–29; Adele Berlin, 'Legal Fiction: Levirate Cum Land Redemption in Ruth', *JAJ* 1, no. 1 (2010): 5; Pnina Galpaz-Feller, 'The Widow in the Bible and in Ancient Egypt', *ZAW* 120, no. 2 (2008): 236; Ziony Zevit, 'Dating Ruth: Legal, Linguistic and Historical Observations', *ZAW* 117, no. 4 (2006): 489; Carolyn Pressler, 'Sexual Violence and Deuteronomic Law', in *A Feminist Companion to Exodus to Deuteronomy*, ed. Athalya Brenner, FCB 6 (Sheffield: Sheffield Academic, 1994), 53–8; Rachel Adelman, 'Seduction and Recognition in the Story of Judah and Tamar and the Book of Ruth', *Nashim: A Journal of Jewish Women's Studies & Gender Issues* 23 (2012): 92 n. 23; Deborah L. Ellens, *Women in the Sex Texts of Leviticus and Deuteronomy: A Comparative Conceptual Analysis*, LHBOTS 458 (New York: T&T Clark, 2008), 252–60.

25. Raymond Westbrook, *Property and the Family in Biblical Law*, JSOTSup 113 (Sheffield: Sheffield Academic, 1991), 71.

being preserved by the levirate is not justified, as in both the narratives, Genesis 38 and Ruth, 'the offspring of the levirate union is subsequently referred to as the issue of the levir, Judah and Boaz respectively, and not of the deceased, Er and Mahlon'.[26]

For Westbrook, the book of Ruth demonstrates a further condition for the performance of the levirate: that there must be land available. Since the kinsman in Ruth is only liable to perform the levirate if he redeems the property of the deceased man, Westbrook concludes 'that there must be land for the issue of the levirate to inherit'. He follows:

> If then we take the two conditions precedent thus posited as essential: that the deceased be childless and that there be land of his available...for the issue of the levirate, we may by a simple process of inversion deduce that the main purpose of the levirate was to provide the deceased with a successor to his estate.[27]

He relates Ruth 4.10, להקים שם־המת על־נחלתו ('raise up the name of the dead *upon his inheritance*'), to Deut. 25.6, יקום על־שם (which he translates 'stand up upon the name'), as similar, and suggests that, as the names of the deceased in Genesis and Ruth are not included in the genealogies, 'we are therefore justified in seeking for this context a meaning of the word "name" other than its literal one'. Westbrook suggests taking into account the wide range of meanings in the word 'name' is unnecessary, stating 'a legal term may have several meanings, but usually has only one in any single context'.[28] He suggests, referencing Numbers 27 and Zelophehad's daughters, that the term 'name' may mean something akin to the English legal term 'title', 'which refers not to the property itself but to a man's right to a particular piece of landed property'.[29] So, therefore, 'the issue of the levirate would succeed to the dead brother's title and the deceased's title would thus avoid extinction'.[30] While Westbrook notes that Genesis 38 makes no reference to inheritance, he claims that if Onan does not perform the obligation, he would take the inheritance of Er, and therefore 'in this context the reluctance of the levir contemplated in Deuteronomy and the reluctance of Onan in Genesis are understandable', and that Onan thinks of a trick to avoid *anyone* creating an heir for the

---

26. Ibid., 73.
27. Ibid., 74.
28. Ibid., 75 n. 1.
29. Ibid., 75. He suggests a similar usage in Ezek. 48, where the 'names of the tribes' go on to delineate the 'portions of land allotted to each' (see especially n. 3).
30. Ibid., 75–6.

deceased. Westbrook concludes 'property was thus the background to this narrative as well'.[31]

For Westbrook, the three sources depict different operations of the law: when the father is alive and the brothers are still living together in the same house (Gen. 38);[32] immediately after his death when the brothers have not divided his estate (Deut. 25.5-10); and where the land has been alienated where the nearest relative would repurchase it (Ruth).[33] There is, according to Westbrook, a fourth impossible scenario, where the brothers have divided the land and the surviving brother inherits as an heir of the deceased. He suggests there is no levirate because the title to the land would already have been established; once the legal title has been established the property can be inherited under the normal chain of succession.[34] However, he goes on to state:

> The reasons why the fictional maintenance of a separate title was considered so important are beyond the scope of a legal discussion, but just how important it was considered is shown by the plea of the daughters of Zelophehad.[35]

It is at this point that Westbrook, in a footnote, suggests 'the theological importance of keeping ancestral property in the correct descendant line has been fully discussed by H. C. Brichto, in his article 'Kin, Cult, Land and Afterlife – A Biblical Complex'.[36] Westbrook's understanding appears clean and succinct; however, his failure to consider the other contexts of the term שם are limiting to his discussion. This failure is highlighted in his pointing to Brichto (discussed below), as his argument cannot account for the *why* of levirate marriage, suggesting instead a purpose without a meaning. However, it is in the *meaning*, in the symbolic context, that the law cannot be reduced to something as limited as 'title', and so this will require us to look more deeply at the name and its symbolic import. This will be further explored in relation to texts such as Isa. 56.3-5 which are not about land, but appear to function in a similar symbolic system.

---

31. Ibid., 76.
32. Ibid., 82. He suggests that in this situation the father would enforce the law as it is in his 'interest', suggesting the intergenerational dynamic of the law.
33. Ibid., 78. For Westbrook, the term 'when brothers dwell together' should be understood spatially rather than temporally, suggesting the phrase refers to the time after the death of the father when the sons have not yet divided the estate; cf. Gen. 13.6; 36.7.
34. Ibid., 80.
35. Ibid.
36. Ibid., 80 n. 2.

3. *Eryl Davies*

Ephraim Neufeld, influentially, claimed the purpose of the law of Deut. 25.5-10 was to provide protection for the widow, and went as far as to suggest that the working of the law (implying that the raising of a son was for the name of the deceased) is simply a matter of the author making their intention more palatable to the audience.[37] A more nuanced proposal of this view can be seen in Davies' two-part article 'Inheritance Rights and the Hebrew Levirate Marriage'. Davies's perspective is arguably made clear by his title, which draws attention to the issue of inheritance rights in the text. The opening line of *Part I* begins: 'The right of a widow to inherit the property of her deceased husband was…generally recognized in the cultures of the ancient Near East',[38] before briefly recounting Babylonian, Hittite, Nuzi, Ugaritic and Assyrian material which all suggests widows could inherit from men. However, notes Davies, it is not so in the biblical texts. There is, for Davies, one law that suggests a provision for the widow in levirate marriage: 'the brothers of the deceased had the responsibility of providing the widow with male heirs', further noting that 'the three references…suggest that the primary purpose…was to provide a son for the childless widow'.[39] In connecting inheritance and levirate marriage, Davies makes a significant assumption: the text is about obligating the *brothers* to provide a male heir for the *widow*.

For Davies, this is implied by Deut. 25.5 as there is no male issue, as well as in Judah's command to Onan to go into his brother's wife in Gen. 38.8, and Boaz and Ruth in Ruth 4.13. However, Davies suggests this raising an heir for the widow takes place through the continuation of the male line.[40] Acknowledging the end of the line would mean the end of family and self (cf. 2 Sam. 18.18 and Amos 8.10), and so, recognizing a range of coping strategies (polygamous marriage, female slaves, possibly adoption),[41] he notes that scholars, especially in 'early times', argued

---

37. Ephraim Neufeld, *Ancient Hebrew Marriage Laws: With Special References to General Semitic Laws and Customs* (London: Longmans, Green & Co, 1944), 29–40.
38. Davies, 'Inheritance I', 138–9.
39. Ibid., 139.
40. Ibid., 140. However, he goes on to say 'the duty involved raising offspring for the deceased', which seems to suggest an ambiguity about whether the offspring are for the deceased or the widow. Again, in relation to Ruth and Boaz he observes 'continuation of the line of her deceased husband by providing her with male offspring'.
41. Ibid.

'perpetuation of male descent' as the sole purpose of the levirate, and that if this had been accomplished the obligation was fulfilled. Notably, he suggests it is probable that there was more involved.[42]

Suggesting the emphasis on the name 'was not to be taken literally', as neither Tamar nor Ruth named their children after the deceased (Gen. 38.29-30; Ruth 4.17), Davies connects the name to land, citing three passages in support:[43] (1) Num. 27.1-11 and Zelophehad's daughters, where the father's name is 'preserved as long as his descendants remain associated with his property';[44] (2) 2 Samuel 14 and the widow of Tekoa, where 'her plea contains a subtle suggestion that by destroying the heir the kinsmen would also be securing for themselves the inheritance, since in the absence of any children the inheritance would pass automatically to them'; (3) Ruth, where 'to raise up the name of the dead in his inheritance' operates in the context of Levirate marriage. While acknowledging that the property connection is not explicit, he suggests that 'this is surely the implication behind the statement that the first-born son of the levirate union would succeed to the name of the dead',[45] and associates the name with the inheritance of property, and, by extension suggests the practice also served to prevent the alienation of the ancestral estate.

Davies then suggests a further purpose, which is the protection of the widow; stating the easiest way for this to have been accomplished was through marriage. Acknowledging that Genesis 38 fails to mention marriage, he asserts:

> Despite these arguments, however, it is probable that the levirate duty, even in the early period, normally involved marriage between the widow and the brother of the deceased.[46]

Supporting this, he suggests the text does not preclude marriage, and that Tamar being accused of playing the harlot is because she was not given

42. Ibid., 141. He explicitly notes Rowley, 'Marriage', 177 n. 3.
43. He also cites Leggett, *The Levirate and Goel Institutions in the Old Testament*, 48–54.
44. Davies, 'Inheritance I', 142. See also Martin Noth, *Numbers: A Commentary*, trans. James Martin, OTL (London: SCM, 1968), 221. Noth suggests the text 'presupposes that the "name" of the man...could be preserved only in association with the inheritance of the land by his descendants'.
45. Davies, 'Inheritance I', 142 n. 15–16. He cites Josephus (*Ant.* 4.8.23) who appears to link Levirate marriage with continuation of estate and the alleviation of widow's misfortune. However, Davies notes that Assyrian and Hittite laws are 'conspicuously' absent of references to keeping the estate.
46. Ibid., 143.

to Shelah 'in marriage'.⁴⁷ Furthermore, he suggests Naomi, by sending Ruth to Boaz, 'was probably seeking to arrange a marriage based on Boaz's relationship as kinsman', and suggests Ruth's request 'to spread your skirt over your maidservant' (Ruth 3.9) is a request for marriage (cf. Ezek. 6.8). Davies concludes that 'the view that the levirate duty was limited to the one purpose of raising an heir for the dead is too narrowly defined to do justice to the nature of the obligation as presented in the Old Testament'. However, Davies's analysis never actually explores the concept of providing an heir to the dead in any detail, while his argument that name equates to property is underdeveloped and the notion that the levirate equates to marriage – which equates to protection – fails to take into account the use of women's bodies and sexuality in various texts.

In *Part II*, Davies suggests Onan's refusal to perform the levirate duty in Genesis 38 is the result of a fear of the son inheriting, which he derives from interpolating Onan's thoughts and Num. 27.8-11.⁴⁸ Davies proceeds to look at the book of Ruth, arguing that the kinsman reacts against impairing his inheritance, as it 'would suggest that his personal estate would somehow be affected in a deleterious way if he were to agree to undertake the levirate obligation'.⁴⁹ He suggests this may be understood by suggesting the child born inherits both the property of the dead man and a share of the levir's own, premised on the presumption that the kinsman already had a wife and family of his own and would not want to divide his inheritance.⁵⁰ Davies proposes that as Boaz does not have an heir, 'any son born of this levirate marriage would be fully Boaz's heir as well as the heir of Elimelech',⁵¹ suggesting that the levir would become administrator and would have time to use his brother's land. It is in this context, where the raising of a son can have a detrimental effect on one's wealth, that Davies goes on to discuss whether the levirate is binding or not. He suggests there was no penalty and that the removal of the shoe was a 'ceremony' for refusal, apparently diminishing the shaming aspects of the removal of the sandal in Deut. 25.5-10. He takes Genesis 38 as evidence that in an early phase it was 'an unavoidable obligation',⁵² as Onan had to 'resort to a secret act of defiance' to avoid it.⁵³ Davies states

47. He suggests Gen. 29.28; 30.4, 9; 34.8, 12 as examples where לאשה + לו + נתן are used 'to express marriage': ibid., 143 n. 18.
48. Ibid., 257.
49. Ibid., 258.
50. Ibid., 259.
51. Ibid.
52. Ibid., 260.
53. Ibid., 261.

that the ceremony benefitted the widow and brother-in-law, as while the brother-in-law was released from the obligation, the widow was free to marry.[54]

Davies's articles have impacted on Carolyn Pressler's extensive exploration of the law of levirate marriage in *The View of Women Found in the Deuteronomic Family Laws*, which is an explicitly feminist analysis of Deuteronomic law.[55] Pressler suggests that although a secondary aim of the law,

> It seems clear that the institution of levirate marriage would have provided the wife of the deceased man an important means of economic security and social status.[56]

This interpretation – that the law is for the widow's benefit – appears in scholarship either as *the purpose* of the law, or, as in the case of Pressler, as a secondary benefit. We will explore this interpretation throughout this project, looking in more nuanced detail at how the women and men in the various texts are constructed, and whether economic protection of the widow is internal to the discourse of any of the texts.

4. *Herbert Chanan Brichto*

Brichto's 'Kin, Cult, Land and Afterlife – A Biblical Complex' is probably the most significant piece of secondary literature in relation to this project. Published in 1973, Brichto's 54-page article reassesses some of the questions tackled by the above scholarship, by drawing on social theory outside of biblical studies, notably Coulanges's *The Ancient City*, as well as reassessing the core texts in light of other biblical texts in order to establish not just the workings of a legal mechanism but a

---

54. Ibid., 262.
55. See also Cheryl Anderson, *Women, Ideology and Violence: Critical Theory and the Construction of Gender in the Book of the Covenant and the Deuteronomic Law*, JSOTSup 394 (London: T&T Clark, 2004), 47, 55. Anderson adopts Davies's argument when discussing the status of the widow as marginalized. However, she recognizes more generally that the primary purpose is the perpetuation of the male line, and so thus restricts the woman, bringing her under control of the father/husband.
56. Carolyn Pressler, *The View of Women Found in the Deuteronomic Family Laws*, BZAW 216 (Berlin: de Gruyter, 1993), 72. Others have come to this conclusion independently of Davies: George W. Coats, 'Widow's Rights: A Crux in the Structure of Genesis 38', *CBQ* 34, no. 4 (1972): 461–6; Susan Niditch, 'The Wronged Woman Righted: An Analysis of Genesis 38', *HTR* 72, nos. 1–2 (1979): 143–9.

whole symbolic paradigm, as highlighted by his title 'a biblical complex'. Brichto's essay smashes through the established conclusions of preceding research and attempts to understand the various dynamics of texts as symbolically coherent in a particular cultural context. Whereas Levine had been so critical of others in his above-quoted review of Leggett, he said of Brichto's essay:

> ['Kin, Cult, Land and Afterlife'] is a study which deals with these ideas and institutions in a brilliant, meticulous and original manner. This example of biblical scholarship at its best proves that there remains pay-dirt to be mined from the study of the *yabam*, the *go'el*, and the Book of Ruth. The author is invariably provocative, and generally convincing.[57]

Brichto's work has been influential, but it has never been revisited in any systematic way. Theodore Lewis has stated that 'the interconnected relationship between kin, land, and death has nowhere been more articulately described than in Brichto's treatment',[58] while Francesca Stavrakopoulou has observed that Brichto's study is 'the most detailed and clearly articulated' of the 'interrelation of ancestral tombs and territoriality in the Hebrew Bible'.[59] Westbrook's analysis, as noted above, points to Brichto's essay to assess the 'theological' implications of the transmission of land that Westbrook himself shies away from approaching.[60] The creativity of the article comes primarily from a similar starting point to this project: an engagement with ancient perspectives on the afterlife and how these might dialogue with issues of kinship or land – or, as emphasized here, reproduction.

Brichto's opening is the rupture Mitchell Dahood's *Psalms I & II* caused in the prevailing consensus that any notion of immortality was late if not entirely absent in the Hebrew corpus.[61] He states that given the scholarly battle lines, he will take a different approach, to explore 'the iceberg's surface with a view to what lies beneath', to see whether in the 'biblical thought-world' death was an end or a transition, and if the latter,

---

57. Levine, 'On Intra-Familial Institutions of the Bible', 554 n. 1.
58. Theodore J. Lewis, 'The Ancestral Estate (נחלת אלהים) in 2 Samuel 14:16', *JBL* 110, no. 4 (1991): 608.
59. Francesca Stavrakopoulou, *Land of Our Fathers: The Roles of Ancestor Veneration in Biblical Land Claims*, LHBOTS 473 (New York: T&T Clark, 2010), 8.
60. Westbrook, *Property*, 80 n. 2.
61. Mitchell J. Dahood, *Psalms I: 1–50. Introduction, Translation, and Notes*, AB 16 (New York: Doubleday, 1966).

how far this way of thinking 'permeated the consciousness of ancient Israel' and how this affected ethics, law and institution.[62]

For Brichto, some of the biblical texts were already fossilized remains at their time of writing; however, he still suggests they contain aspects which were meaningful throughout the whole 'biblical period'.[63]

Taking Sheol as a starting point, particularly Saul's communication with Samuel in 1 Samuel 28, he suggests an animated afterlife, in possession of memory, consciousness and speech.[64] He then surveys burial culture and states that, despite a belief in the continued existence of the dead, there is not an accompanying 'lessening of the importance of burial'.[65] He goes on to link the importance of burial with ownership of land,[66] citing Abraham's payment for the plot at Machpelah in Genesis 23, emphasizing the requirement for 'clear and absolute' possession.[67] He notes further that any understanding of ancestor worship and ancestral ownership of land must be understood in the context of the belief that the land ultimately belongs to YHWH.[68] Brichto now makes a jump and moves to an extensive discussion of levirate marriage as it relates to kinship, land and immortality, taking the book of Ruth as his primary text.[69] He states that levirate marriage is the instrument which achieves continuation of the

---

62. Herbert Chanan Brichto, 'Kin, Cult, Land and Afterlife – A Biblical Complex', *HUCA* 44 (1973): 3.

63. Ibid., 6.

64. He is here particularly arguing against those such as Bruce Vawter who tried to make a division between ancient West Asian necromancy as superstition and a kind of superior Israelite humanism which set them apart (Bruce Vawter, 'Intimations of Immortality and the Old Testament', *JBL* 91, no. 2 [1972]: 170).

65. Brichto, 'Kin', 8.

66. Brichto imagines a kind of vertical and horizontal ownership: vertically, he looks at the way property belongs to unborn descendants in the future and dead ancestors in the past – 'it is a *sine qua non* of their stake in immortality'. Horizontally, property relates to the family in that each individual possesses a share of the land 'subject to the overriding ownership of the family as a whole'. It is worth nuancing the relationship between 'vertical' ownership of land and burial; for example, he suggestively states 'whether the ancestors had to be consulted if a parcel of their property was to be alienated we do not know', despite a seeming absence in biblical texts (except for 1 Sam. 28) of how this would take place.

67. Brichto, 'Kin', 10.

68. Ibid., 11.

69. Ibid. This is as he emphasizes that through the connection with the land and YHWH, it is possible to state that to enter the עם of YHWH 'was to enter the worship of YHWH and vice versa'.

line, a union between the widow and 'next-of-kin' to produce a son, who, in order to preserve the ancestral line, is 'the son of the deceased'.[70]

He suggests the opening prayer of Ruth 1.9, which asks YHWH to grant rest, מנוחה, stands for the eternal rest, which, through the death of their sons, is denied to Naomi, her dead husband, and their deceased sons.[71] Their dialogue invokes themes of death, land and kinship: the promise to go wherever Naomi goes and be buried wherever she is buried. Brichto continues with a close reading of the text, emphasizing the recurrence of his themes, such as Naomi's response, blessing YHWH who has not forgotten the living or the dead, and immediately following this with a reference to Boaz as kinsman redeemer.[72] This theme of loyalty to the dead is drawn out by Brichto, with Ruth refusing to run after young men and personal happiness, instead seeking, 'single-mindedly', a union with the kinsman who may act as levir and produce a son, 'for him'.[73] Brichto appears to understand the institution of redemption and levirate as being merged in the book of Ruth.

Brichto explores the final chapter of Ruth, where most dialogue referring to redemption or levirate takes place. He understands the nearest kinsman-redeemer's readiness to redeem the land as evidence that redemption is a privilege; however, he suggests the right also carries the obligation of levirate marriage: the readiness of the kinsman to redeem the plot of Elimelech attests to the fact it is a privilege; the other fact, the obligation, causes the kinsman to reverse his decision: 'Acceptance of the privilege to redeem is obligation to raise the name of the dead up on his legacy. The two go hand in hand.'[74] Brichto reads the *go'el*'s fear to be that he will damage his own נחלה to be evidence of concern for it after his death. Presuming he would have usufruct of the redeemed plot in his lifetime, Brichto suggests that the fear lies in that the *go'el* bears the cost of redeeming the dead man's plot, has to support the man's widow and has 'to raise another man's son to guarantee the afterlife of that other'. Brichto states that the 'welfare of the dead is somehow connected with the continuation of his line upon his inherited property and the more sons the greater the deceased's security (מנוחה)'.[75] He also understands this as the root of Onan's failure to raise seed for his brother in Genesis 38, with

---

70. Ibid., 12.
71. Ibid.
72. Ibid., 13.
73. Ibid., 14.
74. Ibid., 15.
75. Ibid., 15–16.

Onan potentially losing the double-share of the firstborn by raising an heir for the dead;[76] and we see from Genesis 38 that the widow is 'tied to her husband', even though he is dead.[77] The levir, despite it denying him property, is a duty: 'the *go'el* is he who redeems the dead from the danger to his afterlife by continuing his line'.[78] He relates this to the final verses of Ruth:

> Our suggestion is that the word שם has the metonymic force of 'family-line' comparable to that same force for בית 'house'. The expression לקרא שם in this context then is equivalent to להקים שם המת in Ruth 4:5 and והקם זרע in Gen. 38:8. The expression קרא שם in this context would simply stand for 'continue/perpetuate (the) family line'.[79]

Brichto proceeds to make a connection between the transition to Sheol, the huge importance in the Hebrew Bible of male progeny, and the 'the failure to recognize שם and its synonym זכר stand for '(line of) descendant(s)' and not merely for 'name' or 'memory'.[80] For Brichto, the key is to move away from an understanding of the concern for descendants as a 'peculiar, sentimental desire' to be held in remembrance by giving your child your name, arguing instead that Israelites did not give children the name of ancestors or take surnames, as evidenced by the lack of repetition in genealogies; he states that apart from eponymous ancestors whose name is taken by a tribe, a patronymic normally only goes back one generation; even in the case of a son being characterized as 'the one through whom a father's "name is to be called"', neither bear the name of the father and they are both known as sons of that father, such as Ishmael and Isaac; moreover, with the increase of genealogical material in literary form, 'the average Israelite could hardly fail to note how many names were lost and forgotten'.[81] Brichto, therefore, conceives of 'the name' as having an expansive social function, over the more limited definitions of Westbrook, and taking on various symbolic associations.

---

76. Ibid., 16.
77. Ibid., 19.
78. Ibid., 21. For example, Brichto offers an analogy between the biblical practice and the Kaddish, the Jewish hymn recited by the son for a deceased parent, 'in keeping with a tradition that such recitation is effective in redeeming the dead from sufferings in Gehenna. By metonymic extension a father (to this very day) will refer to his firstborn or only son as his "kaddish". But for anachronism, Ruth's firstborn was the kaddish of Naomi.' Ibid., 21 n. 30.
79. Ibid., 22.
80. Ibid., 23.
81. Ibid., 24.

Brichto catalogues the vocabulary of continuation (or extermination) of the line, and for progeny/posterity. The nouns include בית, זרע, זכר, שם, פרי, אחרית; and the verbs זכר, קרא, אבר, שמד, מחה, כרת.[82]

Brichto then moves on to examine several narratives under the 'complex' he has suggested. For example, he re-examines patriarchal narratives such as Lot's daughters' incest with their father, or Abraham's sacrifice of Isaac in terms of the importance of assured progeny.[83] He then focuses on texts which demonstrate a dependence on the living from the dead, arguing that on the Coulanges model, the dead require specific acts or rites by the living, and includes a discussion of biblical prohibition of offerings to the dead.[84] Brichto suggests that the obligation to honour one's father and mother contains, at least in part, a requirement to respect *post-mortem* through rites or offerings. He suggests the right to kill the son in Deut. 21.18-21 stems from a realization that the son is selfish and cannot be depended on to perform mortuary rites which is the duty the son 'the line of which he is the next living link'.[85] Brichto considers the character of Rachel in the book of Jeremiah, noting Jeremiah has a certain penchant for invoking exposure of corpses, disturbance of the afterlife, ancestral land, exile by YHWH, and the theme of the family-line in danger. He focuses in on Jer. 31.15, which recounts Rachel weeping from her tomb for her children in exile, to which YHWH responds that she shall be rewarded by her descendants returning to their own borders. He states that the association here of land, descendants, return and exile, in the context of the complex he has established, shows that the dead Rachel lives and that her reward for her work in life is the preservation of her descendants on the ancestral land, 'from whose fate her own cannot be sundered'.[86] This, argues Brichto, is not simply a sentimental attachment to land. Jeremiah's decision to purchase his kinsman's land on the eve of Babylon's conquest of Jerusalem (Jer. 32.8) draws these themes together, and the narrative impact of the text cannot be understood except in the

---

82. Ibid., 24–5, 26 n. 41. Brichto then gives examples, which will be discussed below and so are not explored here, that cover core texts such as Isa. 56.3-5 and 2 Sam. 18.18. He suggests the discussion of memory in the latter should not be seen as 'an indication of immortality as mere remembrance', though he does not say why.

83. He argues that their lament there is no man to have typical sexual relations with them highlights concern primarily for their own afterlife and secondarily for their father: Ibid., 27 n. 42.

84. Ibid., 28.

85. Ibid., 32–3. See also Prov. 20.20 and Prov. 30 which links this with a privation of burial.

86. Ibid., 39.

terms of this 'complex of land-kinship-immortality-religion'.[87] The tearing from the land is a death sentence to the living and the dead, the end of the line for the past, present and future of the people, 'the end of its religion'.[88] In this context of Rachel, Brichto can discuss texts such as Exod. 1.15-21, Gen. 16.2 and Ps. 113.9, where the building up of the house is discussed in relation to women. Brichto is not simply attempting to demonstrate a particular *function* of a social institution, but instead to attempt a kind of anthropology, to understand the limits and expanses of a symbolic system of thought and how what may seem disparate actually operates in union, even to the extent of how this symbolic system constructs sex and gender. This exegesis is repeated with other texts, and through this Brichto attempts to tease out specific contextual understandings of words or rites, and to demonstrate the existence of a discourse that operates in a particular cultural context.[89]

While stimulating, the essay also suffers from certain methodological flaws. As noted, Brichto's study makes heavy use of Coulanges's *The Ancient City*, originally published 1864 as *La Cité Antique*.[90] Coulanges sketches a kind of rough anthropology of ancient civilizations where kinship is formed around ever-perpetuating families: religion is a form of ancestor veneration, and property is subsumed into these two aspects and a means of perpetuation. The impact on Brichto is considerable, especially his use of Coulanges's construction of the ancient Indo-European 'mind' and its idea of the 'life-dead-life continuum', and allows him to use comparative material from other ancient cultures uncritically. Coulanges's research influenced anthropological thinking about how religion *functions* in a society and how this is connected to other areas of culture, and foregrounds kinship in his study of the ancient city-state. However, by the time of Brichto's writing, *The Ancient City* was already over a century old, with evolutionary models of anthropology long rejected;[91] as such, later scholars have criticized its impact on biblical studies.[92] While

87. Ibid.
88. Ibid., 40.
89. Discourse here is used in a Foucauldian sense. Brichto constantly attempts to break the terms of the debate as they stood; for example, he seeks to reject the distinction between a Greek dualistic and Semitic monistic view.
90. Moses I. Finley, 'The Ancient City: From Fustel de Coulanges to Max Weber and Beyond', *Comparative Studies in Society and History* 19, no. 3 (1977): 305–27.
91. Ibid., 110–14.
92. For example, Mary Douglas states 'according to Fustel de Coulanges a people organized by patrilineal inheritance and succession would be expected to pay respect to the points of articulation by which they themselves enter the lineage system. Their ancestor cults would reinforce hereditary principles and disperse centres of power

Brichto does acknowledge that any comparison is to be only logical or analogical, noting 'we are all too keenly aware of the mischief wrought in Biblical scholarship by loose and irresponsible use of comparative anthropology', at times, such as his understanding of ancestor cults, he seems overly tied to Coulanges's work. There are also further methodological problems. Stavrakopoulou notes that Brichto is overconfident in how he reads 'the biblical texts as a direct reflection of the historical realities of mortuary culture'.[93] Furthermore, his treatment of mortuary culture *per se* is overly fixated on a specific form of ancestor veneration, as will be discussed below. Stavrakopoulou also notes: 'given the more socially-nuanced perspectives of contemporary biblical scholarship, some of the concepts and labels Brichto employs are now best considered somewhat unwieldy, out-dated or uncritical – particularly his imaging of "property"'.[94] Therefore, while this project will build on Brichto's work, notably his creative comparative material, it will seek to reassess some of its approaches and conclusions.

5. *New Avenues*

Although Brichto's seminal essay has been cited widely (along with Pedersen, Schmidt, and Westbrook), there has not been, to my knowledge, any attempt to reassess the wide range of texts he takes in or paradigms he constructs. Despite this, in the past decade there has been a renewal of interest in the texts of Deut. 25.5-10, Genesis 38, Ruth, and their relation to levirate marriage. This has been inspired, in part, by developments in both intertextuality, narrative criticism and gender-critical approaches, as well as studies approaching the texts from new perspectives.[95]

---

over the territory... It is not at all certain[, however,] that the society of Israel was ever organized into strong lineages in the way that Fustel de Coulanges described': Douglas, *Jacob's Tears*, 183–4.

93. Stavrakopoulou, *Land*, 10.

94. Ibid., 9. Or, for example, Brichto's insistence on an Israelite belief in 'blood-kinship' as opposed to its neighbours is drawing on anthropological models which no longer carry weight in anthropological discourse. This will be discussed further in a later chapter. See Brichto, 'Kin', 29.

95. See Adelman, 'Seduction and Recognition'; Berlin, 'Legal Fiction'; W. Gafney, 'Mother Knows Best: Messianic Surrogacy and Sexploitation in Ruth', in *Mother Goose, Mother Jones, Mommie Dearest: Biblical Mothers and Their Children*, ed. C. A. Kirk-Duggan and T. Pippin, Society of Biblical Literature Semeia Studies (Atlanta: Society of Biblical Literature, 2009); T. Sutskover, 'The Themes of Land and Fertility in the Book of Ruth', *JSOT* 34, no. 3 (2010): 283–94; F. van Dijk-Hemmes, 'Tamar and the Limits of Patriarchy: Between Rape and Seduction (2 Samuel 13

Two recent articles by Jacob Wright, one co-written with Michael Chan (which will be discussed in detail when looking at Isa. 56.3-5), have offered fresh insight into a stale topic. Wright's 'Making a Name for Oneself: Martial Valor, Heroic Death, and Procreation in Ancient Israel' will be discussed here in detail as, first, it offers a perspective on our subject from a different angle, and, second, it demonstrates how looking at the perpetuation of the self through the lens of gender can offer further insights. Wright examines the notion of 'making a name for oneself' in the context of warfare.[96] He states:

> The biblical authors assign priority and primacy to procreation as a means of making and perpetuating one's name. While they countenance and even condone name-making through martial valor, they cast aspersions on heroic death. By attending to the attitudes of biblical authors to these three strategies of name-making, we can better appreciate what prompted and sustained the formation of biblical literature. The driving force was, I will argue, a concern to build a robust and sustainable nation after the defeat of the state and the loss of territorial sovereignty.[97]

Wright outlines what he perceives as a difference between pre-modern and modern notions of identity, and reverses the contemporary response that death at war is especially devastating when the father has a child and wife:

> In the ancient world, the reverse is supposed to have been the case: dying without having first 'made a name' in the form of progeny (a genealogical namesake) was considered completely devastating, while the news that the man left behind a (male) child would have brought some relief. Such a generalization is of course risky, yet it points to what many see as a late development in the *histoire des mentalités*: In modern times, the self (one's name) is conceived individualistically, while in pre-modernity, identity (one's name) is constructed according to collective—most fundamentally, familial—parameters.[98]

and Genesis 38)', in *The Double Voice of Her Desire: Texts*, ed. J. Bekkenkamp and F. Dröes, trans. D. E. Orton (Leiderdorp: DEO, 2004); A. I. Abasili, 'Genesis 38: The Search for Progeny and Heir', *Scandinavian Journal of the Old Testament* 25, no. 2 (2011): 276–88; M. George, 'Masculinity and Its Regimentation in Deuteronomy', in Creangă, ed., *Men and Masculinity*, 64–82.

96. Jacob L. Wright, 'Making a Name for Oneself: Martial Valor, Heroic Death, and Procreation in the Hebrew Bible', *JSOT* 36, no. 2 (2011): 6. Wright also draws on Brichto's work.

97. Ibid., 131–2.

98. Ibid., 133.

Wright surveys a range of ancient West Asian and Second Temple sources which look at 'name making', particularly highlighting the importance of death on the battlefield, for example 1 Macc. 6.4, where Eleazer stabs an elephant in battle while under it, as he thinks it carries the enemy king. His suicidal mission is undertaken, according to the author, in order to 'save his people and win for himself an everlasting name'. However, examining war battle narratives, Wright notes:

> While biblical authors sanction name-making through martial valor (after re-contextualizing it), they leave no room for name-making through *heroic death*. This fact is remarkable given that commemoration of the war dead occupies such a central place in public ritual and space in cultures from antiquity to the present. We would expect, for example, that the book of Joshua would contain a scene in which the nation's leader exhorts his soldiers not to shirk their duties but to be willing to die a noble death, as Judas enjoins his men in 1 Maccabees. Likewise, the biblical authors had many occasions to tell how Israel mourned those who fell in the wars of conquest, commemorating their names and sacrifice for the nation.[99]

Astonishingly, we find nothing of the sort; warriors 'venerated in biblical literature die in peace, with many children to mourn them'.[100] For example, in the book of Judges the deaths of the most illustrious figures are either not told or depicted as occurring peacefully (Gideon, Judg. 8.32), contrasted to villains such as Abimelech, who begs to be finished off so that he is not remembered dying at the hands of a woman (9.53-54). Even Samson's unique example of noble death is presented as being 'of real pragmatic value', as opposed to, say, the suicide during the siege of Masada.[101] In contrast to other ancient laments, Wright notes that texts such as the lament for Saul (2 Sam. 1) are notably different, since 'the lament does not praise these warriors for bravely sacrificing their lives... instead, it presents their deaths as completely tragic, without any redeeming esthetic value' – the text states: 'Tell it not in Gath, proclaim it not in the streets of Ashkelon...' (2 Sam. 1.20).

Wright connects this to texts such as Deut. 24.5, which applies to a man who takes a new wife:

> When a man is newly married, he shall not go out with the army or be charged with any related duty. He shall be free at home [לביתו] for one year, to be happy [ושמח] with the wife whom he has married.

---

99. Ibid., 147. He notes that 1 Kgs 11.15 is an exception 'that proves the rule'.
100. Ibid., 148.
101. Ibid., 148–9.

Wright renders לביתו 'for the sake of his household' and argues 'house' and 'name' are interchangeable,[102] while suggesting ושמח may be a euphemism for pregnancy, and claims the law creates 'conditions for Israelite soldiers to produce progeny before performing military service'. He also relates this to Deut. 20.7, in which deferral is demanded for anyone betrothed 'or he might die in battle and another marry her'; thus, he establishes legal claims over house, vineyard and wife. Wright connects the concern for land to the perpetuation of the family name, drawing on Ruth 4 and connecting it to the law of levirate marriage.[103] Wright also takes the lack of commemoration for fallen soldiers and interprets it in dialogue with the emphasis on procreation, ultimately arguing it was 'the *loss* of statehood and conditions of *defeat* that explain the paradigm he has outlined'.[104] For example, in the first chapter of Exodus, the fear of the Egyptian king that the Israelites may 'increase and join our enemies and fight against us', is followed by his command to destroy male infants. Wright notes, interestingly, that the action of the midwives is divinely rewarded with 'houses' being built for them.[105] In Genesis 32–33, the wives and children of Jacob stand against Esau and his warriors. Particularly interesting in this context is Ruth:

> The book of Ruth imagines an alternative society to that depicted in Judges: war is completely absent, Israel is sustained by name-making through offspring, and a גבור חיל is not a 'warrior' but rather a man of noble virtue and social status, who plays a key role in the decisive act of procreation.[106]

To Wright, the Pentateuchal emphasis on procreation is the 'primary means of Israel's existence', not just in its production but its survival.[107] The focus on gender and reproduction is seen in an earlier monograph, Pressler's *The View of Women found in the Deuteronomic Family Laws*, which discusses aspects of this project in terms of gender. Pressler, rather than focusing on laws in isolation, demonstrates how Deuteronomy controls sexuality in the service of patriarchal perpetuation of male lines between generations. This kind of approach will become critical in our final analysis of the texts approached.

---

102. Cf. 2 Sam. 7.
103. Wright, 'Name', 150–1.
104. Ibid., 152.
105. Ibid., 152 n. 46.
106. Ibid., 153.
107. Ibid.

Stavrakopoulou's 2010 book, *Land of Our Fathers: The Roles of Ancestor Veneration in Biblical Land Claims*, explores similar issues but from the perspective of use of the dead in establishing claims to land, with land in the Hebrew Bible 'a narrated topography of cultural memory'.[108] Stavrakopoulou notes, significantly, that little attention 'has been paid to the ways in which the dead mark or mar many of the territorial agendas' in biblical literature, connecting explicitly with Brichto's essay, in exploring the relation between tombs and territoriality.[109] We see this connection, for example, in Prov. 22.27-28 in which 'the reader is warned not to remove the ancient landmarks set up by his ancestors in order to pay off his debts by selling his ancestral estate and its family tomb (here reading משכב as "grave", rather than "bed")'.[110] Standing stones also perform territorial functions, and construct what Stavrakopoulou termed a 'mortuary landscape', 'the boundaries of which are marked by the graves of the dead'.[111] For example, Joshua is buried upon the boundary of his ancestral estate (Josh. 24.30; Judg. 2.9); the boundary of Benjamin is marked 'by the tomb of the "local" ancestress, Rachel' (1 Sam. 10.2); the grave of the Canaanite king Ai is placed at the city gate (Josh. 8.29); and Achan's corpse is buried in the Valley of Achor (Josh. 7.26), which Stavrakopoulou connects to the boundary between Benjamin and Judah (Josh. 15.7). Stavrakopoulou suggests 'the boundaries within the landscape are materialized and memorialized by the graves of the dead in a way significantly similar to the *monumental* materialization and memorialization of boundaries in other texts'.[112] Stavrakopoulou focuses on the materiality of death and burial and the way it 'imbues burial with a cultural and social agency', which is not 'only "remembered" or assumed, but experienced visually'. The 'material memorialization of the mortuary landscape goes some way to giving places socio-cultural "genealogies", rooting them to the past and structuring intergenerational social responses to the landscape'.[113] In reassessing the real and present social import of memorialization of ancestors, Stavrakopoulou offers a new perspective on Schmidt's narrow understanding of a beneficent dead – that memorialization and social integration of the dead into the social landscape does not necessarily imply the dead are weak, but instead

108. Stavrakopoulou, *Land*, 7.
109. Ibid., 8.
110. Ibid., 11.
111. Ibid., 12.
112. Ibid., 13. See 1 Sam. 7.12; 2 Sam. 8.3; Josh. 15.6; 18.7; 1 Sam. 20.19; 1 Kgs 1.9; Isa. 19.19.
113. Stavrakopoulou, *Land*, 14.

that they are important for a community's own narrative of the past and present. While this is only a part of this project (though it is significant, and will be drawn upon throughout), Stavrakopoulou's work is instrumental in terms of approach. Rather than simply offering a historical approach, Stavrakopoulou interacts with historical material (both written and material), doing so with a keen eye to the use of anthropology and wider cultural studies to understand the significance of burial, ancestors and land claims in terms of their social role. It is this specific focus on the social context of ancient practices, rather than an attempt to narrowly define texts in terms of, say, their legal application, which will be drawn on. Moreover, her nuanced understanding of social relations between the living and the dead, mortuary culture in Israel, and understanding of the political importance of ancestors will inform the present project throughout.

6. *Widow Inheritance and Ghost Marriage: Anthropological Contexts*

Rather than the narrow, isolated understandings of levirate marriage that have pervaded scholarship, Brichto's article suggests seeing levirate marriage as embedded in a cultural system. Several current or historical social practices share similarities with biblical levirate marriage and open ways in which practices dialogue with the fields in which they occur. Commonly termed levirate, widow inheritance, wife inheritance, or ghost marriage, there are anthropological examples from sub-Saharan Africa, South and East Asia and South America.[114] As will be seen, their social and symbolic function varies and should not be considered mirror images of practices attested in the Hebrew Bible.[115] Several studies from Africa

---

114. While there is a seeming similarity between the biblical practice and widow inheritance, it is significant, as Lemos notes, that despite the availability of proprietary language, it is only in Ruth 4.10 that the root קנה is used; neither Deut. 25.5-10 nor Gen. 38 characterize Levirate marriage as the inheritance of widows: see Tracy M. Lemos, *Violence and Personhood in Ancient Israel and Comparative Contexts* (Oxford: Oxford University Press, 2017), 76.

115. Margaret Owen, *A World of Widows* (London: Zed, 1996), 102–24. Owens summarizes a huge number of widow marriage customs; both custom and purpose vary massively from society to society. See also the survey of the practice in South Africa in M. E. Baloyi, 'The Christian View of Levirate Marriage in a Changing South Africa', *Journal of Sociology and Social Anthropology* 6, no. 4 (2015): 483–91. In a different context, Smita Sahgal's study of the historic institution of Niyoga in early India describes it as a 'strategy of heirship', 'a response to the *āppati* (emergency)

look at how widows negotiate the practice of widow inheritance, and the practice of brothers of family members 'inheriting' the widow from the deceased brother. However, very little research has been done in the past twenty years. Betty Potash explores widow inheritance in rural Luo communities in South Sudan:

> The levir is usually a married man who lives in his own home. His responsibilities and interests are directed primarily to his wives and legal sons, who are part of his descent line. These sons will inherit from him and carry on his name. By contrast, the widow's children, including natural offspring sired by the levir, belong to the deceased husband's line and will inherit there.[116]

Despite the children being legally the children of the deceased, the genitor 'is always accorded some degree of recognition…some children take the genitor's name'. The level of this recognition is based largely on the quality of the relationship between him and the children.[117] Potash found the focus of the widow, however, is on 'safeguarding her children's property' and providing 'for the economic support', allowing the widow to maintain control of property. The practice among the Luo is not dependent on a lack of progeny: some widows choose to enter the unions to keep custody of the children of the deceased who would otherwise come under the guardianship of the deceased's family. Moreover, she questions the term 'widow inheritance': the widows are not inherited but chose the union and partner.[118] Rather than a cohabiting union, they are characterized by separate residences, with the widow living in the husband's home; the widow is not obliged to provide domestic assistant to the levir and the levir does not have to provide economic assistance to the widow.[119] Leviratic relationships were impermanent, 'some relationships lasted a few days; others endured for as long as fifteen years'.[120] Potash's study is significant for highlighting the material nature of the unions, as well as the importance of negotiation for understanding the motivations of the people

---

occasioned by childlessness [which] belonged to the category of practices excused by *āpaddharma* or laws of exigency'. See Smita Sahgal, *Niyoga: Alternative Mechanisms to Lineage Perpetuation in Early India: A Socio-Historical Enquiry* (Delhi: Indian Council of Historical Research, 2017).

116. Betty Potash, 'Wives of the Grave: Widows in a Rural Luo Community', in *Widows in African Societies: Choices and Constraints*, ed. Betty Potash (Stanford: Stanford University Press, 1986), 44.

117. Ibid., 59.

118. Ibid., 63.

119. Ibid., 44.

120. Ibid., 63.

involved. Regina Oboler's study of the Nandi of Kenya has the children of a union belonging 'to her "house" and thus will be considered descendants of her first (and only) husband, whoever their genitor may be'. And yet, inheritance is not the issue: the wife inherits the dead husband's property for the continuation of her life, and she more or less has freedom in choosing a sexual partner. If there are a number of children from the deceased husband the widow is unlikely to take a levir; however, there is pressure to build up the household if there are no or few children.[121] Jane Guyer, writing in the same volume as Oboler, highlights the difficulty of tracing the institution – her context being the Beti in southern Cameroon – over long periods; the various functions of widow inheritance 'have been attached to and detached from the institution of widow inheritance over the course of this history'.[122] Rather than understanding the practice in terms of anthropological models of kinship where it had been understood 'as a means of reproducing structural relationships across the vicissitudes of the human life cycle', she argues that the historical importance of the practice was based in a period where the 'nature and value of assets at stake were changing rapidly; it must therefore be understood in relation to accumulation and resource control by men'.[123]

The role of the widow in negotiating her place and union is explored in several studies. Edwin Gwako charts the various reasons given for women choosing widow inheritance among the Maragoli of western Kenya. The reasons given and the rate at which they were given are:

Our tradition	16.3%
To access productive resources	15.4%
To benefit from deceased husband's estate	15.0%
For children to benefit from education fund	14.2%
To get financial support	12.9%
To have a son	10.7%
Childless – to have children	6.9%
Not to be implicated in husband's death	3.9%
Needed a companion	3.0%
To benefit from deceased husband's estate	15.0%

---

121. Regina Smith Oboler, 'Nandi Widows', in Potash, eds., *Widows in African Societies*, 76–9.

122. Jane I. Guyer, 'Widow Inheritance and Marriage Law: A Social History', in Potash, ed., *Widows in African Societies*, 194.

123. Ibid., 192–4.

Women articulated that it was a social tradition they had no option but to engage in.[124] At the same time, Gwako also found that there was a much higher rate of consenting widows among those who were poor, younger, less educated or had no sons, whereas richer widows resisted social pressure.[125] One woman, Emily, stated:

> Without a child I am a nobody in this clan. I need a child in order to confirm my status, among other things. In this clan, a woman's post-widowhood child is more socially accepted when fathered by a levir proposed by the clansmen. These are some of the factors which influenced my consent to the practice of widow inheritance.[126]

Social pressure is not just restricted to widows. Stella Nyanzi found pressure on men to have intercourse with widows whose husbands were known to be HIV positive; rather than understanding the men as 'perpetrators of this supposed social evil', Nyanzi questions how the practice is 'socially scripted and negotiated'. In her study of the Masaka district of Uganda, Nyazi found that:

> Widow inheritance also transcends notions of gender asymmetry – that is, of male dominance and women's lowly status. In part, it is about social interpretations and cultural enactments of responsibility towards the dead. Kinsmen, clan and society owe a deceased man the care and support of his offspring, widows and other dependants. Male members of the line are obliged to settle the deceased's property matters, cover his outstanding debts, and propagate the family line so that he 'can rest tranquilly'. Likewise, a widow does not just owe it to her deceased husband to obey his wishes for her future. She must also act to safeguard the interests of her dependent children, who are deemed to belong to the patrilineal clan. The widow must leave them with her dead husband's heirs if she decides to return to parents or marry into another clan. Maternal attachment, anxiety over children's future welfare, and the social meaning that children bestow on women – increased status, marital security, recognition of maturity, old-age insurance – all inhibit widows from leaving.[127]

Rather than a static practice, widow inheritance, as attested across Africa, is continually negotiated and changing.

124. Edwins Laban Moogi Gwako, 'Widow Inheritance among the Maragoli of Western Kenya', *Journal of Anthropological Research* 54, no. 2 (1998): 182.
125. Ibid., 181.
126. Ibid., 183.
127. Stella Nyanzi, 'Widow Inheritance', in *Men of the Global South: A Reader*, ed. Adam Jones (London: Zed, 2006), 63.

A similar social practice is ghost marriage: the marriage of a deceased person's ghost to a living person, a deceased person or a doll. Ghost marriage is particularly pertinent as it is concerned with post-mortem continuity but is not predicated on inheritance or sexual relationships. Ghost marriage is particularly useful for probing levirate marriage in that it 'tends to contradict almost every definition of the term 'marriage' that anthropologists have proposed', such as marriage defined through sexual and economic union, permanence, reciprocal rights between spouses, or social standing of children born.[128] Among the Nuer in South Sudan, if a man dies 'his widow may choose to live with one of his brothers... the former husband is still the legal pater, and the "pro-husband" is a member of his lineage'. However, if she lives with a lover not of her husband's family, 'the children are still considered part of her legal husband's lineage'. The practice goes further however: 'If a man dies without male heirs, a kinsman frequently marries a wife to the dead man's name. The genitor then behaves socially like the husband, but the ghost is considered the pater.' The 'ghost-pater' may also be a kinswoman who is infertile; she may be married to another woman and 'the role of genitor is delegated to a lover, while the children belong to the lineage of the female household'.[129] Here an entire range of strategies coexist side by side to continue lineage and name, including ghost marriage. However, unlike widow inheritance, such strategies do not necessarily include the transfer of a widow. A similar form of ghost marriage exists among the Atuot in the same region of South Sudan, and the designation for a ghost marriage, *cuong*, connotes 'to hold straight, upright', expressing the name of the man being held up straight, so 'he will "stand" or be remembered'. It is used to appease the spirit of the deceased and prevent vengeance, and only used when the 'next in line' to be marries dies.[130]

This practice contrasts with the kind of ghost marriage in East Asia, which does not necessarily involve the creation of offspring. Ellen Schattschneider has explored bride-doll marriage in northern Japan. A

---

128. Lucas Schwartze, 'Grave Vows: A Cross-Cultural Examination of the Varying Forms of Ghost Marriage among Five Societies', *Nebraska Anthropologist* 25 (2010): 82–4. Schwartze notes through the article that there is disappointingly little theoretical work done on Ghost marriage.

129. Alice Singer, 'Marriage Payments and the Exchange of People', *Man* 8, no. 1 (1973): 83.

130. John W. Burton, 'Ghost Marriage and the Cattle Trade among the Atuot of the Southern Sudan', *Africa: Journal of the International African Institute* 48, no. 4 (1978): 402–3. Burton acknowledges a disappointing lack of information about ghost marriages, partially through unwillingness of the offspring of the unions to admit to it.

hanayome ningyô, 'bride doll', is a box containing a photograph of a person who died before marriage, along with an opposite-sex figurine, 'believed to be animated with the miraculous power of Jizô, a prominent Buddhist Bodhisattva'. The couple are enshrined in a temple for around 30 years, and Jizô is believed to guide the dead person 'stranded between worlds, towards successful rebirth and eventual salvation'.[131] Sometimes dolls are used for both the spirit spouse and the deceased. A written text memorialized the name, death date, home village, person who offers the doll, and the name of the spirit spouse. The doll can also be referred to as *musume* (daughter) or *musuko* (son).[132] Additionally, 'many bereaved families place small dolls depicting children of the spirit couple in the memorial box'.[133] The practice has grown in popularity in the Tsugaru region of northern Japan over the past six decades, initially among those who lost children in military campaigns, particularly those who did not have the remains of the deceased. The practice 'serves to reinstitute proper, limited-exchange relationships between the living and the dead'.[134] Through the materiality of the doll box, the living can fulfil their obligations to the deceased, who have died 'without knowing the comforts of marriage and without leaving behind a tangible posterity in the form of children', simulating features of 'conventional marriage among the living'. Schattschneider contrasts doll marriages with Chinese ghost marriages, as north Japanese descent lines tend to encompass only a few generations, whereas Chinese descent lines are extended and the dead can be included in a family altar:

> Many commentators assert that throughout China, spirit marriage is more commonly performed for dead female children, because a dead male child's soul can be memorialized through an ancestral tablet in his father's family ancestral altar. In contrast…a dead female cannot be memorialized in her natal family's altar – in principle, she should not even die within the central room of her father's house.[135]

Without Chinese-style family altars, 'the dead soul in Japan seems to require a more permanent image, lasting for the initial years of memorialization'.[136] The dolls perform several functions:

---

131. Ellen Schattschneider, '"Buy Me a Bride": Death and Exchange in Northern Japanese Bride-Doll Marriage', *American Ethnologist* 28, no. 4 (2001): 854.
132. Ibid., 860.
133. Ibid., 862.
134. Ibid., 854.
135. Ibid., 856.
136. Ibid.

Over the years, in my many conversations with spirit mediums and bereaved families, survivors have articulated a range of motivations for dedicating a doll and for periodically paying rededication fees. Nearly all emphasize the tremendous pity they feel for the deceased and express the hope that the doll spouse will bring comfort in the other world. Many assert that the doll marriage will 'send the child to heaven', or allow it to attain rebirth and the status of Jôbutsu. Others have told me that the doll, like a dedicated Jizô, helps them 'to remember' the deceased and is a more suitable place to memorialize the prematurely deceased soul than the family domestic altar *(butsudan)*, which is principally oriented toward ancestral figures.[137]

After a period, normally 30 years, once the soul has attained Buddhahood, the dolls are ritually disposed of, and they are 'subsumed into the collective identity of its natal family's ancestors'.[138] The marriages allow both the continuation of kinship with the deceased, and the post-mortem continuity and safeguarding of the spirit. Jizô is a particularly significant Bodhisattva in this context, widely regarded to have 'the capacity to forge a tangible substitute for kin links, to re-create the elemental bonds of familial unity after all such bonds appear to have been shattered'.[139] The spirit marriage therefore reinstitutes 'proper exchange relations with the dead'; in addition, it safeguards the social stability of the living kin group:

> Bridedoll spirit marriage...produces form and lineal continuity out of formlessness and non-continuity, but with some striking twists: It foregrounds a deceased relative, who by virtue of dying too early has become a potential danger to the family, and through marriage reconverts this person into an ally.[140]

This social stability, however, is not contingent on permanent bounds to a descent group: the spirit must surrender ties to the living by becoming socially situated among the 'collective, generic status of benevolent ancestors'. Children and grandchildren are not integral parts of both proper kinship bonds or post-mortem rest.[141]

Diana Martin's essay on ghost marriage demonstrates a similar practice, but within a different social paradigm. She situates ghost marriage not in short-term attainment of Buddhahood, but in *Xiao*, the duty of a son to keep alive the patriline and provide descendants to venerate ancestors.

137. Ibid., 858.
138. Ibid., 860.
139. Ibid., 863–4.
140. Ibid., 865.
141. Ibid., 866.

The ideal death of parents is in the central room of the house alongside the ancestral altar, containing tablets of names, titles, dates of birth and dates of death, which are to be venerated with incense and food offerings on the anniversary of a death. However, 'reality frequently fails to fit the model, and so there exist various well-established remedies for correcting the defects'. If, for example, there are no children, a son may be adopted into the family, or if there is only a daughter a husband may be sought who will contract to take on the matrilineal grandfather's name. An heir may be adopted posthumously for a dead son.[142] Ghost weddings are understood within this context: for example, the deceased may be married to the husband or wife of a sibling, and a child produced by their union will be considered the child of the deceased. In one case, several years after a ghost wedding, Martin records, 'the girl-ghost's mother adopted her son-in-law's brother's child on behalf of the couple. The child is being brought up by his own parents. When he is older, he will have the duty of worshipping his deceased adoptive parents'.[143] The practice also provides a post-mortem continuity for deceased daughters who cannot be placed on her biological family altar – her ghost may be married to a man and then her ancestral tablets placed on his family altar.[144] This is highlighted in Taiwanese anecdotes that a male ghost does not require a marriage, as through appropriate mediums he can request the family adopt an heir: 'they are from birth potential contributors to the lineage and hence entitled to a place on the altar'; the adopted son is needed not to guarantee a place but instead to guarantee veneration.[145] Throughout Martin's collected examples, there occurs again not a defined static practice but a wide range of mechanisms to respond to non-ideal situations. Ghost marriage, while rare, 'encompasses a broad spectrum of cultural practices', ranging from the material preservation of property and kin group, to the Japanese context which though material in form has a more transcendent context.[146] It, along with examples of widow inheritance, demonstrates how marriage can be used to negotiate several less than ideal outcomes for an individual and community; moreover, these marriage negotiations can cross social boundaries, including those between the living and the dead. The broad range of ways these negotiations are articulated also guards against being

---

142. Diana Martin, 'Chinese Ghost Marriage', in *An Old State in New Settings: Studies in the Social Anthropology of China in Memory of Maurice Freedman*, ed. Hugh D. R. Baker and Stephan Feuchtwang (Oxford: JASO, 1991), 25–6.
143. Ibid., 31.
144. Ibid., 32–3.
145. Ibid., 41.
146. Schwartze, 'Grave Vows', 93.

too determined by purpose: there are a range of competing motivations at play in the examples given. They also guard against narrow interpretations of the biblical texts: the presence of widows does not necessarily suggest a question of widow welfare, just as inheritance is not the dominant factor in some of the cases cited.

As discussed above, some of the more traditional historical-critical approaches to levirate marriage became overly self-referential, in terms of both the primary and secondary sources that were consulted, becoming concerned with the precise operation of an ancient law and less so with the symbolic context in which it existed. In what follows I will examine these primary texts and their secondary literature in detail, but will widen the project by considering texts that exhibit similar concerns, language and responses, and by bringing all these texts into an extensive dialogue with their cultural context, looking at death, burial, name, remembrance, family, land, sexuality and gender. Taking into account the limits of Brichto's research, this project will be asking similar questions, drawing on his outstanding creativity, and will apply insights gleaned from narrative approaches, anthropology and gender-critical approaches, along with more traditional historical-criticism. Each of our key texts respond to the death of a male, and so the next chapter will begin looking at the context of death, burial and veneration of the dead.

Chapter 3

DEATH, BURIAL, AND BEYOND

Tombs, ancestors and genealogy create ties of loyalty and obligation and also ones of identity and narrative. Our key texts respond to the failure of men to reproduce before their death, and so this chapter will sketch Israelite discourses around 'afterlife', burial, ancestor veneration and memorial, allowing us to delineate in what ways the responses in our texts (levirate marriage, erecting a monument) allow for social interaction between the living and the dead. Through this we will begin to uncover how the fields of death and burial are symbolically linked to wider social discourses.

Qohelet imagines the bleak scenario of one being forgotten:

> The living know that they will die, but the dead know nothing; they have no more reward, and even the memory of them is lost. (Qoh. 9.5)

However other texts, such as 1 Samuel 28, which recount Saul bringing up the ghost of Samuel, may suggest a more vibrant existence. The discussion about the afterlife in the Hebrew Bible has undergone distinct waves in the past century, often coloured by theological presuppositions and competing methodologies. Elizabeth Bloch-Smith outlines the broad fluctuation over the last century between a 'maximalist' and 'minimalist' position: scholarship originally perceived a vibrant and ubiquitous cult of the dead, which tamed and controlled the wild forces of one's predecessors through elaborate mortuary rites; there was then a shift towards recognizing a post-mortem existence that was all but denied and where ancestor veneration was negligible; and scholars then again adopted a maximalist approach, which now appears to be diminishing.[1]

---

1. Elizabeth Bloch-Smith, 'Death in the Life of Israel', in *Sacred Time, Sacred Place: Archaeology and the Religion of Israel*, ed. Barry M. Gittlen (Winona Lake, IN: Eisenbrauns, 2002), 139–43.

Due to the strong bearing of material remains on the textual evidence, there is a tension in scholarship, with two camps that position themselves along the spectrum between archaeological and textual approaches. When ancient West Asian materials are used, it is often done over-confidently, as a means of interpreting biblical texts and archaeological remains. Many approaches have not considered diachronic changes and thus have ignored the 'distinguishing developments during the critical period of national and religious formation'.[2] There is one significant challenge in any approach: a lack of evidence. As Wayne Pitard notes,

> One of the most striking aspects about the Hebrew Bible is how little it actually talks about death and afterlife. The subject does not form a primary theme in any book of the Hebrew Bible. What we find instead are (at best) scant, rather off-hand, ambiguous and nonspecific references and allusions to the subject in a variety of contexts. These passages are not particularly harmonious in their views.[3]

Pitard concludes that the absence of texts may have been a deliberate choice by the religious leadership of Judah,[4] further complicated by economic and political factors such as the burial of royals.[5] There is a broad consensus that 'our inability to arrive at a full and accurate synthesis needs to be underscored'.[6] Pitard highlights the difficulties of interpreting even contemporary culture's responses to death, where

---

2. Elizabeth Bloch-Smith, *Judahite Burial Practices and Beliefs about the Dead*, JSOTSup 123 (Sheffield: JSOT, 1992), 17. See also Suriano, who suggests while providing us with non-Western perspectives, they 'risk obscuring the cultural distinctiveness of the Levant': Suriano, *History*, 2.

3. Wayne T. Pitard, 'Tombs and Offerings: Archaeological Data and Comparative Methodology in the Study of Death in Israel', in Gittlen, ed., *Sacred Time, Sacred Place*, 146.

4. Ibid.

5. Jason S. Bray, 'Genesis 23 – A Priestly Paradigm for Burial', *JSOT* 60 (1993): 69–73; Joseph Blenkinsopp, 'Deuteronomy and the Politics of Post-Mortem Existence', *VT* 45, no. 1 (1995): 1–16; Bloch-Smith, *Burial*, 130–2; Bloch-Smith, *Burial*, 18.

6. The acknowledgment that the extant evidence can only form a partial reconstruction is acknowledged by a wide range of scholars: Theodore J. Lewis, 'How Far Can Texts Take Us? Evaluating Textual Sources for Reconstructing Ancient Israelite Beliefs about the Dead', in Gittlen, ed., *Sacred Time, Sacred Place*, 161; Bloch-Smith, 'Death in the Life of Israel'; Ron Tappy, 'Did the Dead Ever Die in Biblical Judah?', *BASOR* 298 (1995): 66; Pitard, 'Tombs and Offerings', 147; Saul M. Olyan, 'Some Neglected Aspects of Israelite Interment Ideology', *JBL* 124, no. 4 (2005): 609–10 n. 25; Schmidt, *Israel's Beneficent Dead*, Chapter 1; Stavrakopoulou, *Land*, 23.

'extensive documentation and living informants are available'.[7] Every aspect of burial is significant and may be interpreted from an economic, political, social, psychological or religious perspective.[8]

We can, however, attempt to critique some of the approaches to understanding ancient mortuary cultures, which have been heavily influenced by out-dated anthropological models such as the one usd by Coulanges.[9] Stavrakopoulou argues that there is a modernist Western bias, which states that death 'irrevocably breaks the active social relationship between the newly deceased and the living community'.[10] For example, Schmidt's *Israel's Beneficent Dead* is based on anthropological models which,[11] according to Stavrakopoulou, over-emphasize a distinction between the social and anti-social aims of responding to death and dying: mortuary rituals consist of separative acts, as opposed to 'death cult' rituals which enable actively accessing the dead, an approach which ignores the 'socially transformative, inclusive and constructive function of mortuary practices'.[12] In 'a majority of known societies, the biological death of the body 'articulates a boundary' that is not an 'end' but an 'event-horizon'. Therefore, 'whether or not the dead are worshipped or merely commemorated, post-funerary practices articulate the ongoing social presence of the dead among the living, rather than their social absence'.[13]

Seeing death as the rearticulating of the relationship between living and dead, as a process rather than a static event, mitigates against a Western cultural bias and can bring about a re-imagining of our data in a way that avoids constructing artificial dichotomies of official vs. popular religion, or minimalist vs. maximalist positions. We will explore the status of the dead in the Bible, the burial of the dead in textual and material remains, the veneration or care of the dead, and the physical remembering of the dead through monuments.

7. Pitard, 'Tombs and Offerings', 145.
8. See the literature listed in Bloch-Smith, *Burial*, 18 n. 1.
9. Finley, 'The Ancient City.'
10. Stavrakopoulou, *Land*, 20–1.
11. Schmidt works with: Ian Morris, 'Attitudes toward Death in Archaic Greece', *Classical Antiquity* 8, no. 2 (1989): 296–320; Max Gluckman, 'Mortuary Customs and the Belief in Survival after Death among the South-Eastern Bantu', *Bantu Studies* 11, no. 1 (1937): 117–36; Meyer Fortes, 'Some Reflections on Ancestor Worship in West Africa', in *African Systems of Thought: Studies Presented and Discussed at the Third International African Seminar in Salisbury, December 1960*, ed. Meyer Fortes and Germaine Dieterlen (London: Oxford University Press, 1965).
12. Stavrakopoulou, *Land*, 22.
13. Ibid., 23. Suriano approaches the 'process' of death from a ritual perspective: Suriano, *History*, 19–27.

1. *Status of the Dead*

We use various terms to describe the state of the dead: from the contemporary 'life after death', to the Hebrew idiom 'gathered to one's kin'. The terms we use flit from describing the poetic or metaphorical, to the concrete and real: 'gathered to one's kin' could suggest one is buried in a family tomb, or it could refer to the spirit being reunited with one's ancestors. We will use, herein, the term 'afterlife', which in no way describes what state the individual continues after death, but does suggest that the individual exists in a substantive and real way, beyond the physical remains of a corpse or the cognitive working of memory. While some have suggested evidence of an Israelite belief in some form of beatific afterlife,[14] or even resurrection,[15] some texts show a general agnosticism towards the idea of an afterlife: 'Who knows whether the human spirit goes upwards and the spirit of animals goes downwards to the earth?' (Qoh. 3.21). The referents for the dead suggest broad and conflicting states: 'those who pass over', העברים (Ezek. 39.11); *elohim*, אלהים (1 Sam. 28.13); 'mutterers', האטים (Isa. 19.3); *nephesh*, נפש (Lev. 19.28); 'ghosts', אוב (Isa. 29.4); 'knowing ones', הידענים (Isa. 8.19); 'holy ones', קדושים (Ps. 16.3); rephaim, רפאים (Isa. 14.9).[16] The language of dying implies something other than simply burial: the contrasting 'and he slept/lay down' and 'was gathered to his kin/ancestors' in Gen. 25.8, if understood as parallel phrases, suggest communal burial was tantamount to being gathered to one's ancestors in the afterlife.[17] Matthew Suriano contrasts the terms used in 1 Kgs 2.10, וישכב דוד עם־אבתיו, and Gen. 15.15, תבוא אל־אבתיך, with the Akkadian 'go to one's fate', arguing that based on the use of the former in dynastic succession in Kings, the Hebrew terms refer not to a reified fate, but consist in proper burial with progeny. In Gen. 15.16 this fate is tied up with references to the 'fourth generation', and within the epilogues of Kings there is a logical structure: 'ancestors, burial, progeny'. Death is 'idealized through themes of succession and inheritance'; it is relational, tied to descendants. Moreover, the 'generational depth' relates to the kinship unit of the בית אב, centred on four generations: this can be compared to

---

14. Klaas Spronk, *Beatific Afterlife in Ancient Israel and in the Ancient Near East*, AOAT 219 (Neukirchen-Vluyn: Butzon & Bercker Kevelaer, 1986).

15. Dahood, *Psalms I*, e.g. 4–5, 99, 183, 222, and passim in all three volumes.

16. Bloch-Smith, *Burial*, 109. Suriano suggests that while in Ugaritic literature the *repi'u* are royal ancestors, the rephaim in the Hebrew Bible, appearing as characters vanquished in the past by Moses and David (Deut. 3.11; 2 Sam. 21.15-22; 1 Chron. 20.6-8) are potentially the 'ancestors of Israeli's enemies': Suriano, *History*, 31.

17. Bloch-Smith, *Burial*, 110.

the punishment to the third and fourth generation (Exod. 20.5; Deut. 5.9; Num. 14.18) – the idealized family unit in life and death.[18] However, these idioms also occur in narratives without family burial as such, which indicates physical proximity is not requisite.[19] For instance, Deut. 32.50 says that Moses is to die on the mountain he ascends and be gathered to his kin, despite the text affirming that Aaron died on a different mountain and was gathered to his kin.

If being gathered to one's ancestors implies a communal aspect to burial, then other texts suggest additional social dynamics, such as descriptions in Isa. 14.9-10 of dead leaders becoming weak in death. The dead are sometimes said to abide in שאול, Sheol; the word 'earth', ארץ, can designate this underworld, as can שחת and בור, both meaning 'pit'; אבדי, Abydon, is often translated as 'perdition' or 'place of destruction'.[20] There is no consensus on the etymology of שאול, and, compared to other ancient West Asian realms of the afterlife, the Bible is fairly non-descriptive,[21] while the existence of the term in cognate languages remains unproven.[22] The realm of the afterlife is variously described as somewhere one 'goes down' to (Num. 16.30; Job 7.9; Isa. 57.9), the lowest place imaginable (Deut. 32.22; Isa. 7.11), with its depth emphasized by it is modifier תחתי (Deut. 32.22; Ps. 86.13; Ezek. 31.14-18). It is connected to water imagery (Jonah 2.3-6; Ps. 88.6-7); it is sometimes gated (Isa. 38.10); sometimes barred (Jonah 2.7; Job 38.10); it is sometimes a land of no return (2 Sam. 22.6; Job 7.9); it is often dark (Job 17.13; cf. Lam. 3.6; Job 18.18);[23] is it characterized by dust (Job 17.16; 21.26; Ps. 7.6) and

18. Suriano, *History*, 9–10.

19. Olyan, 'Neglected Aspects', 608 n. 23; Lewis, 'How Far Can Texts Take Us?', 173; Stavrakopoulou, *Land*, 9.

20. Theodore J. Lewis, 'Dead, Abode of the', *ABD*, 101.

21. Ibid., 102, notes the Egyptian *duat*, and the Mesopotamian story of the descent of Isthar. John Healey notes how the Ugaritic deity Mot dwells explicitly in the underworld, with Baal dispatching messengers to him (KTU 1.4 viii), where he rules over a city reached through the base of a mountain (KTU 1.6 vi.27-29). However in texts such as Hab. 2.5 where death appears personified as Mot, the relationship to Sheol is ambiguous (see also Ps. 49.15; Hos. 13.14; Isa. 5.14): John F. Healey, 'Mot', *DDD*.

22. Dominic Rudman, 'Mitteilungen: The Use of Water Imagery in Descriptions of Sheol', *ZAW* 113, no. 2 (2001): 241.

23. Note that necromancy is depicted as taking place at night: 1 Sam. 28.8; Isa. 45.18-19; 65.4; possibly to consult those that dwell in darkness. See Theodore J. Lewis, *Cults of the Dead in Ancient Israel and Ugarit*, HSM 39 (Atlanta, GA: Scholars Press, 1989), 12.

silence (Ps. 31.17-18). Sometimes God has dominion over it (Deut. 32.22; 1 Sam. 2.6; Isa. 7.11; Prov. 15.11; Hos. 13.14; Amos 9.2). Rainer Albertz and Rüdiger Schmitt attempt a topography, 'four areas in which the realm of the dead could be located, none of which was necessarily distinct from another'. According to them, Sheol is:

1. Part of the visible world located in the far west or north
2. Within the empirical realm of the dead: the grave as the necropolis;
3. A liminal realm with ambiguous borders: for instance, caves, graves, the necropolis, the desert; but also the sea
4. A mythical realm of the underworld, underneath the waters.[24]

It is often characterized in an extremely negative fashion:[25]

> For in death there is no remembrance of you;
> in Sheol who can give you praise? (Ps. 6.5)

> What profit is there in my death,
> if I go down to the Pit [שחת]?
> Will the dust praise you?
> Will it tell of your faithfulness? (Ps. 30.9; see also Ps. 88.5-6)

Sheol is sometimes characterized as outside YHWH's jurisdiction, where the dead will forget and cease to praise YHWH. Dominic Rudman argues that the dichotomy between the heavens, as the sky, and Sheol cannot fail to define Sheol as a geographical location, and some texts rely on the reader's awareness of Sheol as somewhere so deep it is beyond comparison:[26]

> Though they dig into Sheol,
> from there shall my hand take them;
> though they climb up to heaven,
> from there I will bring them down. (Amos 9.2)

---

24. Rainer Albertz and Rüdiger Schmitt, *Family and Household Religion in Ancient Israel and the Levant* (Winona Lake, IN: Eisenbrauns, 2012), 431.
25. See further: 'For Sheol cannot thank you, death cannot praise you; those who go down to the Pit cannot hope for your faithfulness' (Isa. 38.18); and '…for there is no work or thought or knowledge or wisdom in Sheol, to which you are going' (Qoh. 9.10).
26. Rudman, 'Mitteilungen', 241.

Despite some suggestions otherwise,[27] the good and the bad alike go down to Sheol:

> Who can live and never see death?
> Who can escape the power of Sheol? (Ps. 89.48)[28]

Rudman states: 'the fact that references to Sheol occurs relatively infrequently in relation to the deaths of "good" people and is emphasised in the cases of the wicked', 'is probably due to literary considerations, rather than witness to a belief in any distinction between the ultimate fates of those groups'.[29] A good life is emphasized in terms of long life and progeny (Gen. 25.8; 46.30).[30]

Of the 66 occurrences of שאול,[31] only a handful refer to a concrete example of an individual residing there: Gen. 37.35 recounts Jacob's belief the Joseph is in Sheol, and that he will descend there still mourning; Num. 16.33 recounts how, due to the rebellion of Korah, Dathan and Abiram caused an unspecified number to be swallowed into Sheol alive; Ezek. 37.17 refers to those killed in a battle residing there, as does Ezek. 31.22, 25. All other references to Sheol either refer to someone in the future being killed, the personification of Sheol as death, a physical location that the living would escape to, or other non-specific descriptions. Confident reconstructions of Sheol, such as those in the *ABD*,[32] miss the point that in a mere 66 descriptions, Sheol is used in such a variety of ways that reconstructions can only work by excluding the majority of references. Sheol is envisaged as a place, a threat, a force; it is somehow representative of death, sometimes representative of torment, sometimes representative of the tomb. Suriano suggests, partially through his survey

---

27. See R. Laird Harris, 'Why Hebrew *Shĕ'ōl* Was Translated "Grave"', in *The Making of a Contemporary Translation: New International Version*, ed. Kenneth Barker (London: Hodder & Stoughton, 1987), 76.
28. See also Qoh. 9.1-10.
29. Rudman, 'Mitteilungen', 241.
30. Ibid., 242.
31. Gen. 37.35; 42.38; 44.29, 31; Num. 16.30, 33; Deut. 32.22; 1 Sam. 2.6; 22.6; 1 Kgs 2.6, 9; Job 7.9; 11.8; 14.13; 17.13, 16; 21.13; 24.19; 26.6; Pss. 6.5; 9.17; 18.5; 30.3; 31.17; 49.14-15; 55.15; 86.13; 88.3; 89.48; 116.3; 139.8; 141.7; Prov. 1.12; 5.5; 7.27; 9.18; 15.11, 24; 23.14; 27.20; 30.16; Qoh. 9.10; Song 8.6; Isa. 5.14; 7.11; 14.9, 11, 15; 28.15, 18; 38.10, 18; 57.9; Ezek. 31.15-17; 32.21, 27; Hos. 13.14; Amos 9.2; Jonah 2.2; Hab. 2.5.
32. Lewis, 'Dead, Abode of the'.

of Sheol in the Psalms, that Sheol can be seen as a liminal place, relating to the 'period of time within which the defunct individual is no longer part of a living community but not yet joined to the ancestors', a liminal place in space and time 'negotiated through ritual practices'.[33]

Bloch-Smith, drawing largely on the material remains of ancient burial sites, states 'narrative and prophetic passages relate the dead's benevolent and malevolent powers to foretell the future, create life, revive life and exact vengeance'.[34] While it is true that in 1 Sam. 28.19 Samuel does correctly foretell of the defeat and demise of Saul and his line, and the text does not doubt the efficacy of the consultation,[35] certain other texts suggest a more complicated relationship. There are commands not to consult the dead through certain forms, normally intermediaries (Lev. 19.31; Deut. 18.11), and Isa. 8.19-20 warns against inquiring of the dead via divination.[36] Evidence of the ability of the dead to provide blessings and protection is also somewhat weak. The possibility that Elkanah's annual sacrifice at Shiloh in 1 Samuel 1 is in order to encourage ancestral blessing for fertility is essentially without evidence.[37] In the narrative of 2 Kgs 13.21 it is evident that Elisha's bones were used to revive a dead man. However, it is possible that this has more to do with the importance of Elisha and his unique position, as well as the continuation of the power he had in life (2 Kgs 4.17-37), rather than providing evidence that the corpses of prophets had any innate power simply because they were dead. In the priestly text the bones carry ritual impurity,[38] implying a liminal state between life and death; therefore, it could be the remnants of life that cause the bones to heal, not the power of death.[39] Moreover, there is no suggestion in

33. Suriano, *History*, 242–8.
34. Bloch-Smith, *Burial*, 121.
35. Though compare with some texts that see the dead as having no knowledge, such as Job 14.21 and 21.21. Kaufmann, however, sees these as unrepresentative of the wider Bible: Yeḥezkel Kaufmann, *The Religion of Israel: From Its Beginnings to the Babylonian Exile*, trans. Moshe Greenberg (London: Allen & Unwin, 1961), 312.
36. Karel van der Toorn, *Family Religion in Babylonia, Syria and Israel: Continuity and Change in the Forms of Religious Life*, SHCANE 7 (Leiden: Brill, 1996), 218–25. It is also possible the *teraphim* (2 Kgs 23.24) were ancestor figurines used for divination.
37. Bloch-Smith, *Burial*, 122.
38. Num. 19.16-18.
39. This is partially based on Milgrom's assertion that the rationale behind the Priestly purity system is a symbolism of death (e.g. skin disease, dead bodies, menstruation) in Jacob Milgrom, 'The Dynamics of Purity in the Priestly System', in *Purity and Holiness: The Heritage of Leviticus*, ed. Marcel Poorthuis and Joshua

the text of any sort of pilgrimage cult or specific veneration attached to Elisha's body or tomb. Adolphe Lod's argument that David's removal of the hands and feet of Ishbaal's murderers (2 Sam. 4.12)[40] is intended to prevent their vengeance in the afterlife is an argument that overlooks the wider context of the passage; David's actions are presumably better seen as an appropriate form as corpse-abuse and shaming of the men who beheaded Ishbaal. It has been argued that Samuel's complaint about being disturbed in 1 Sam. 28.15 serves as a warning against disturbing the dead lest they become vengeful. However, this does not consider the other possibilities – namely, that Samuel is simply objecting to being unsettled. Notably, the term used in the Samuel narrative, רגז, is also used in the Tabnit inscription in relation to the violation of tombs.[41]

During the encounter between Saul and the dead Samuel, the necromancer states:

> The king said to her, 'Have no fear; what do you see?' The woman said to Saul, 'I see a divine being [אלהים] coming up out of the ground'. (1 Sam. 28.13)

When Saul is asked why he summoned Samuel, he responds:

> ...'I am in great distress, for the Philistines are warring against me, and God [אלהים] has turned away from me and answers me no more, either by prophets or by dreams...' (1 Sam. 28.15)

While many have suggested the term אלהים refers to the deification of the dead,[42] Theodore Lewis has suggested that as Saul previously refers to the deity as YHWH,[43] the narrative is using the possibility of referring to the dead as אלהים as a literary device – Samuel is called an אלהים as Saul has lost access to his אלהים – rather than making any point about the deified nature of Samuel. Lewis argues that the confusion in the text arises

---

Schwartz, Jewish and Christian Perspectives 2 (Leiden: Brill, 2000), 31–2. However I would argue that certain sources of impurity such as ejaculation (Lev. 15.18) and childbirth (Lev. 12.18) are in fact symbolic of life, and the source of impurity therefore is not purely death but instead the liminal state between life and death.

40. Adolphe Lods, *Israel: From Its Beginnings to the Middle of the Eighth Century*, trans. Samuel H. Hooke, The History of Civilization (London: Routledge & Kegan Paul, 1932), 220.

41. Peter Kyle McCarter Jr., *I Samuel: A New Translation with Introduction, Notes and Commentary*, AB 8 (New York: Doubleday, 1980), 421.

42. Bloch-Smith, *Burial*, 123.

43. Lewis, *Cults of the Dead*, 116.

because of the poverty of ancient West Asian vocabulary – we have here a reference to 'preternatural nature' rather than deification.[44] Moreover, as Suriano notes, necromancy 'is distinct from mortuary practices': it does not take place at the tomb or require a body, and Samuel is not Saul's ancestor.[45] Kaufmann suggests the dead's description as אלהים refers to it as 'a disembodied spirit whose existence is unlike that of the living', suggesting 'no other divine quality is referred to, either as a recognized belief or as a condemned popular error'. Yeḥezkel Kaufmann denies the dead any demonic power, contrasting with the idea of them at peace asleep in their graves or Sheol (Job 3.12; 14.12; Dan. 12.2).[46] For example, the heifer rite (Deut. 21.1-9) is aimed not at appeasing the murdered man's ghost, but is instead directed to YHWH; the famine in David's time is not the revenge of the murdered Gibeonites, but God's wrath; and David hangs and exposes Saul's sons to propitiate YHWH, not the ghosts of the murdered (2 Sam. 21.5-9). Similarly, the blood of Abel (Gen. 4.10) cries out, not to seek its own vengeance, but instead to plead to YHWH.[47] In 2 Sam. 12.22-23, the victimized royal dead cannot return to console survivors or avenge themselves.[48]

The sheer diversity of texts and their redaction by parties which may wish to deny practices which compete with the centralized cult suggest a diversity of custom and understanding. However, we can broadly reject a thesis of the dead as omnipotent beings, though the tombs of ancestors formed important sites of local veneration in different periods.[49] Contextual evidence from Mesopotamia suggests a more nuanced reciprocal relationship:

---

44. Lewis, 'How Far Can Texts Take Us?', 198. See also Tappy, 'Review', 62; J. Day, 'The Development of Belief in Life after Death in Ancient Israel', in *After the Exile: Essays in Honour of Rex Mason*, ed. J. Barton and D. J. Reimer (Macon, GA: Mercer University Press, 1996), 233.

45. As Suriano notes the *hapax legomenon* אטים in Isa. 19.3, referring to the dead used in necromancy, is a loan word from the Akkadian *etemmu*, 'a problematic type of dead spirit that required exorcism to be removed', hardly a deified spirit: Suriano, *History*, 31–2.

46. Kaufmann, *Religion*, 313.

47. Ibid., 313–14.

48. Tappy, 'Review', 298.

49. Herbert Niehr, 'The Changed Status of the Dead in Yehud', in *Yahwism After the Exile: Perspectives on Israelite Religion in the Persian Era*, ed. Rainer Albertz and Bob Becking, Studies in Theology and Religion 5 (Assen: Royal Van Gorcum, 2003), 158.

Come, (O dead ancestors), eat this, drink this and bless Ammisaduwa son of Ammiditana, the king of Babylon.[50]

Here, a more mutual relationship takes place – a kind of communal meal and blessing. The evidence for a substantial afterlife is weak and conflicting. Crucially, however, this does not contradict the *importance* of the dead. By turning to ancient Judahite burial practices, we will be able to see in more depth how the dead exist alongside the living.

2. *Burial*

Texts of burial are often descriptive and carry no theological or cultic interpretation, which may lead to a sense that burial is a mechanical rite. Tombs, on the other hand, carry an array of objects, which has led to various hypotheses as to their purpose. Bloch-Smith acknowledges the archaeological data is sketchy, drawn from an arbitrary selection of sites, and potentially skewed by the fact that burial sites associated with the wealthy tend to be better constructed and are thus better preserved.[51] There are additional difficulties in dating, due to prolonged usage of tombs, issues of selective presentation of material and the vast gap between population size and burials found.[52] However, there appears to be a surprising degree of homogeneity in burials in the highlands of Judah, as opposed to the lowland practices designated 'Canaanite' within the Bible. Out of around 850 burial reports Bloch-Smith examines, she distinguishes eight different burial forms.[53] From the late eighth century to the fall of the southern kingdom, 'the bench tomb was the characteristic Judahite form of burial, as demonstrated by its virtually exclusive use at twenty-four sites throughout Judah'; the only variant forms existed at the cosmopolitan centres of Jerusalem and Lachish.[54] Moreover, 'there are sufficient examples of pit graves cut into bedrock (Lachish, Megiddo) and bench tombs hewn in coastal Kurkar with pillars added to support the ceiling (Ashdod-Yam, Nahshonim) to demonstrate that culture and not geology was the determining factor in choice of

---

50. Lewis, *Cults of the Dead*, 2. Lewis's translation.
51. Bloch-Smith, *Burial*, 21.
52. Ibid.
53. Receptacle containing the body: jar, anthropoid coffin and bathtub coffin; lacking a vessel: simple grave, cist grave, cave tomb arcostolia/bench tomb; and cremation. See ibid., 26. Moreover, there are examples of cross-usage, for example vessels in tomb burials; see ibid., 57.
54. Elizabeth Bloch-Smith, 'The Cult of the Dead in Judah: Interpreting the Material Remains', *JBL* 111, no. 2 (1992): 216.

burial type'.[55] We can broadly maintain that from the eleventh and twelfth centuries, the number of bench tomb burials began to increase from the main concentration in the Shephelah and with the fall of the northern kingdom the bench tomb burying population swelled in numbers and settled throughout the southern highlands of Judah.[56] Moreover, very few burials have been located in the northern kingdom, perhaps due to survey techniques, but perhaps due to the use of a form of burials that left behind little or no material remains.[57] The correlation of the distribution patterns of burial types and the settlement of different cultural groups is very high:[58] the bench tomb is the only burial type to change its distribution pattern, from coastal-lowland regions to the highlands.[59] This rise in bench tombs and decrease in pit tombs may be motivated by economics, but may also reflect a cultural expression of Judahite identity or YHWH worship.

The common form was multiple burials within the same plot, with the movement of skeletal remains to the cave periphery in order to create a cleared space in the centre. The tomb involved a doorway in a rock-cut facade, a five-square-meter chamber with waist-high benches arranged around the perimeter of the room. Additional chambers and benches were sometimes added. Individuals were 'reposed, extended on their backs, with their heads on stone pillows or headrests when provided'.[60] When space was limited, previous interments were moved to a repository pit carved inside the tomb. The archaeological remains show that both sexes and all ages were buried together. Bloch-Smith suggests: 'A nuclear family most likely maintained the tomb, since most undisturbed burials housed only fifteen to thirty individuals of varying ages, which would represent three to five generations'. Moreover, Suriano emphasizes the relatedness of the four-room house and the bench tomb, suggesting 'the similarities do reveal a conservativeness that was rooted in the idea of the family', creating a 'house' for dead bodies.[61]

55. Ibid.
56. Bloch-Smith, *Burial*, 52.
57. Ibid.
58. Ibid., 55.
59. Ibid., 57.
60. Bloch-Smith, 'Cult', 217.
61. Suriano, *History*, 94–6. Suriano is building on particularly: Shlomo Bunimovitz and Avraham Faust, 'The Judahite Rock-Cut Tomb: Family Response at a Time of Change', *IEJ* 58, no. 2 (2008): 150–70; and Alexander Fantalkin, 'The Appearance of Rock-Cut Bench Tombs in Iron Age Judah as a Reflection of State Formation', in *Bene Israel: Studies in the Archaeology of Israel and the Levant during the Bronze and Iron Ages in Honour of Israel Finkelstein*, ed. Alexander Fantalkin and Assaf Yasur-Landau, CHANE 31 (Leiden: Brill, 2008), 17–36.

Many of the descriptors of Sheol, as somewhere one 'goes down into', somewhere dark, dusty and silent, allude to the tomb. Entry into the tomb may have mirrored entry into the underworld, although we have no textual descriptions of entry into the underworld (save being swallowed up whole).[62] Suriano persuasively outlines a relationship between the corpse and the tomb, using ritual theory; while he maintains that postmortem existence is predicated on the fate of the body, he suggests a more nuanced way of understanding the relationship.[63] He moves away from an idea of transition from earth to an ethereal place, instead suggesting the body exists first as an individual and then as a collective: 'conversion of status where collection of bones inside each bench tomb represented the transcendent state of the collective dead: the ancestors'. The status of the person changed in line with the corpse's decomposition, and 'this transition should be understood as a process'.[64] He maintains the architecture of the bench cut tomb with the individual bench and collective repository for bones suggest a 'dialectic relationship inside the tomb between the different conditions of the dead, first as an intact corpse and then as a collection of disarticulated bones', and through this dialectic the tomb is understood as a ritual space'.[65] The transportation of the body to an extramural (outside of the town) burial creates ritual boundaries,[66] and the ritual transformation inside the tomb consists of a first (individual) and second (collective) burial, with a liminal phase that spanned the two burials.[67] Expanding on the liminal phase, Suriano explores the placement of lamps next to the body: several examples exist of a smoothed surface

---

62. There is an argument that Sheol does not refer to a realm, the most vocal proponent of this view being R. Laird Harris, who states explicitly that his problem with Sheol is a theological one: the notion that the righteous (Gen. 38.25) and wicked (Num. 16.3) going to the same place. He fails to take into account any references which imply a meaning of Sheol beyond a grave, such as the gates of Isa. 38.10; moreover, his insistence on using New Testament texts imply a certain theological bias: see Harris, 'Shĕ'ōl', 76.

63. Suriano is particularly informed by Catherine Bell's work on ritualization, the 'interrelationship of action and meaning within a specific setting' and ritual as created through systems of binary opposition: Suriano, *History*, 19–28.

64. Ibid., 40–1.

65. Ibid., 43.

66. Extramural burials are found at Gibeon, Beth-Shemesh (Tell er-Rumeileh), Tell Beit Mirsim, Khirbet el-Qôm (Makkedah), Lachish, Tel 'Ira and Tel Ḥalif. Jerusalem appears to be the exception, with Iron Age cemeteries in Silwan, the Hinnom Valley, and north of Damascus Gate. Ibid.

67. Ibid., 46.

carved adjacent to the headrest, and there are examples in undisturbed tombs of lamps still in situ, as well as evidence of soot marks, all indicating deliberate placement next to the head of the corpse.[68] The ritual action spanned 'both time (from primary to secondary burial) and space (bench and repository)',[69] with the meaning of the body shifted through each location. Suriano suggests:

> By allowing the natural course of action — namely, the decomposition of the flesh — to take place, the survivors of the dead were able to control the uncontrollable, giving power to ritual through periodic routine... In this sense, liminality represented the marginality of the dead person as they transformed from corpse to ancestor. The repository symbolized the collective preservation of past generations, but the dead existed inside this space in an undifferentiated mass.[70]

Stavrakopoulou has explored how burial *ensures substantive continuity after death and the ways privation of burial is used as punishment*, enabling the living community to negotiate and reframe their relationship with that individual.[71] She argues that there is a paradigm of ideal/anti-ideal burial, demonstrating a division in thought between what is acceptable, what facilitates the transformation of the individual and what inhibits or prevents this transformation. Interment 'in the family tomb on ancestral land facilitated the transition of the dead into the underworld and manifested the integration of the individual into the realm of the ancestors'. This has social implications: it 'transformed the corpse from its liminal state into a once-living-now-dead member of the social group, thereby reincorporating the individual into the community, and it embodied and reinforced the territorial claims of the deceased's living descendants and their socioeconomic well-being'.[72]

This positive burial is further emphasized through accounts of non-ideal burial, where retribution is carried out through the treatment of the corpse. Saul Olyan creates a schema of interment types which function along this ideal/anti-ideal paradigm.[73] At the pinnacle of the hierarchy is

---

68. Ibid., 48.
69. Ibid., 50.
70. Ibid., 52.
71. Francesca Stavrakopoulou, 'Gog's Grave and the Use and Abuse of Corpses in Ezekiel 39:11-20', *JBL* 129, no. 1 (2010): 67.
72. Ibid., 68.
73. Olyan, 'Neglected Aspects'.

honourable burial in the family tomb,[74] evidenced by the duty which lay on kin or those bound by formal relationships to transport the corpse.[75] Jacob expresses his wish to be buried at the site of Abraham and Sarah, Isaac and Rebekah, and where he buried Leah (Gen. 49.29-32), which his forefather purchased from the Hittites. Jacob reiterates the associations between his people and their proper ownership of the land, and his kin fulfils this in Gen. 50.13. Burial away from the family tomb is 'cast as punishment by various texts';[76] see, for example, 1 Kgs 13.21-22, where the man of God who came from Judah is told his body shall not come to his ancestral tomb in punishment for rebellion.[77] Moving down Olyan's schema, we find evidence that interment in a substitute for the family tomb seems to have been considered honourable:[78] the burial of Eshbaal's head in Abner's tomb (2 Sam. 4.12) demonstrates the desirability that kin should be buried together even if denied the family tomb and patrimony (2 Sam. 3.31-32).[79] 2 Samuel 21.12-14 shows David transporting Saul and Jonathan to the family tomb in Benjamin, which demonstrates salutary transfer of remains, and that despite the substitution burial, the family tomb is still the ideal.[80] Archaeological evidence for secondary interment seems to suggest that movement of bones was a legitimate act, possibly beneficial and possibly related to the textual terms referring to an afterlife with ancestors.[81] Moreover, in light of purity rules, the preoccupation with secondary interment may reflect 'a distinct theology of afterlife which made care of the bones take precedence over the reluctance for

---

74. Ibid., 603. Suriano, based on arguments by Hays, suggests the polemic against Shebna's tomb in Isa. 22, possibly associated with the royal steward of Silwan's Tomb 35, may be the decision to 'build his own tomb rather than choosing interment in a family tomb': Suriano, *History*, 108–10; Christopher B. Hays, 'Re-Excavating Shebna's Tomb: A New Reading of Isa 22,15–19 in Its Ancient Near Eastern Context', *ZAW* 122, no. 4 (2010): 558–75.

75. Olyan, 'Neglected Aspects', 603; see, e.g., 2 Sam. 2.32; 2 Kgs 23.30. On the obligation of the son and other male kin to ensure burial, see Gen. 49.29-31; 50.5-6 and Judg. 16.31; on obligation of non-kin bound by formal relationship, see 2 Kgs 9.28.

76. Olyan, 'Neglected Aspects', 604.

77. See also the burial of sinful Kings in 2 Chron. 12.20; 24.25; 28.27.

78. Olyan, 'Neglected Aspects', 604–5.

79. See also 1 Sam. 21.13, and the Royal Tomb in 1 Kgs 2.10.

80. Olyan, 'Neglected Aspects', 612.

81. Ibid.; Matthew J. Suriano, 'Death, Disinheritance, and Job's Kinsman-Redeemer', *JBL* 129, no. 1 (2010): 58.

touching them',[82] particularly as secondary interment appears well after the assumed rise of the Priestly School.[83] The last form of honourable interment is attested in 1 Kgs 13.30, describing the interment of the disobedient man of God, where the prophets honour him with burial, albeit within someone else's family tomb.

'Dishonourable' burial is inferior to honourable burials, but preferable to non-burial.[84] For example, Jehoiakim will not be lamented but cast into the grave of an ass, thrown out (והשלך) beyond the gates of Jerusalem (Jer. 22.18-19). Numerous texts recount bodies being cast, שלך (a verb associated with animal burial),[85] piled over with stones, placed in common tombs, not being lamented, and even being buried in an animal's grave.[86] However, these are still better than non-burial or consumption of the cadaver by animals, which is used as a threat (Deut. 28.26; Jer. 16.4). The dishonour of mutilation by animals is threatened by enemies (Ps. 79.2) and prevented by kin, friends and allies (2 Sam. 21.10), or mitigated and reversed through interment and mourning, such as 1 Sam. 31.8-13, where, upon hearing of the mutilation of Saul and his sons, the inhabitants of Jabesh-Gilead travel through the night, collect the bodies, burn and bury them, before fasting seven days. Here corrective measures are taken to ensure Saul's post-mortem security. This contrasts with the treatment of Jezebel's body in 2 Kgs 9.34-37, a text which makes clear that, as the king's daughter, Jezebel is to be buried. Notably, those tasked with burial find only her skull, feet and hands, and the lack of remains is interpreted as divine retribution, brought about by Jezebel's flesh being eaten by dogs, like 'dung', דמן, a term associated with corpses,[87] and so being disfigured no one can say 'This is Jezebel'. It is 'as though there is not enough left of her corpse to warrant transferral into the grave and transformation into post-mortem existence':[88] Without a grave to mark, mortuary and remembrance rituals cannot be performed, rendering Jezebel unremembered and

---

82. Eric M. Meyers, 'Secondary Burials in Palestine', *BA* 33, no. 1 (1970): 15.

83. Ackerman and Cox argue that Rachel's burial away from the family tomb is due to the social stigma attached to dying in childbirth, either due to pollution or 'ghost' worries: Susan Ackerman and Benjamin D. Cox, 'Rachel's Tomb', *JBL* 128 (2009): 135–48.

84. Olyan, 'Neglected Aspects', 606.

85. As contrasted to נוח in the hiphil, 'to set at rest' (ibid., 607).

86. 2 Sam. 18.17; Josh. 7.25-26; 8.29; 10.26-27; Jer. 26.23; 41.9.

87. It is used in Ps. 83.11 and throughout Jeremiah; in Jer. 25.33 it is used in contrast to mourning, gathering, burying. See Suriano, *History*, 195.

88. Stavrakopoulou, 'Gog's Grave', 74.

so non-existent. It is 'uncontrolled, unregulated loss and disposal'; rather than being fed, the dead will become food, signifying their total abandonment.[89] Stavrakopoulou highlights the social importance of the materiality of the cadaver, which is 'both person and object, so that the placing and presence of a corpse or its remains (whether real or presumed) are critical to its symbolic efficacy and social significance'.[90] Stavrakopoulou discusses this in the context of Josiah at Bethel (2 Kgs 23.15-20), which is understood not just as a case of desecrating the sacred place through the presence of bones:[91] Josiah is 'eliminating Bethel's ancestral potency by destroying the corpse and thereby annihilating the dead'.[92] This form of corpse punishment can involve the removal of bones after burial, such as Isa. 14.19-20, which expresses the King of Babylon being cast out of his tomb:

> but you are cast out, away from your grave,
> like loathsome carrion,
> clothed with the dead, those pierced by the sword,
> who go down to the stones of the Pit,
> like a corpse trampled underfoot.
> You will not be joined with them in burial,
> because you have destroyed your land,
> you have killed your people.
> May the descendants of evildoers
> nevermore be named!

The destruction of the cadaver, public dishonouring and absence of mortuary rituals mark the 'deliberate social dislocation of the dead': the 'unwelcome damage or destruction of the corpse or its parts might be understood to render the deceased somehow socially unidentifiable, disabled, displaced, or distressed in the post-mortem state', limiting their post-mortem transition.[93]

Mutilation serves a decisively political motivation, both demonstrating socio-political control over the community by exerting symbolic power over the rulers, but also showing that political dominion can extend to the

---

89. Ibid., 75.
90. Ibid., 76.
91. Even if we were to make the presumption that bones would desecrate all sanctuaries to all deities.
92. Stavrakopoulou, 'Gog's Grave', 76.
93. Ibid., 73.

post-mortem world.⁹⁴ This model is supported by archaeological remains which show threats to those who disturb the dead. The fragmentary Royal Steward inscription (KAI 191) from Silwan, which, according to Olyan, 'is not atypical of this genre'. Olyan translates:

> This is [the tomb of] Yahu who was over the house. There is no silver or gold here. Only [his bones] and the bones of his female slave with him. Cursed be the person who will open this.⁹⁵

This kind of inscription stresses the importance of safeguarding the dead inside the tomb, with a particular emphasis on memory, and the name of the dead preserved. Suriano argues the use of the curses suggests 'the dead were not disconnected from their deity'.⁹⁶ We find in other ancient West Asian contexts that the same actions carry direct consequences: the description by Ashurbanipal of the Elamite royal tombs links the carrying off of exhumed bones to Assyria 'in order to impose restlessness on their "spirits" and to deprive them of food offerings and libations'.⁹⁷ Texts such as *Gilgamesh* XII:151 state that the unburied 'is not at rest in the underworld',⁹⁸ though Olyan does note that no direct evidence of this remains in the Bible.⁹⁹ In Jer. 8.1-2, the bones of the kings, officials, priests, prophets and inhabitants shall be brought out of their tombs, as punishment for incorrect worship; they are not to be 'gathered or buried' but shall be like 'dung'. The removal of bones 'is presented as a post-mortem punishment of previous generations of rulers…perhaps assuming that such removal would disrupt the afterlife of those affected'.¹⁰⁰ This could be simply an act of shaming, somehow using the bones of the dead to warn others, or to enact some form of vague revenge on the perpetrators of the act. However, considering that the removal of the bones of previous generations is seen as such a grotesque act, alongside the terms

---

94. Seth Richardson, 'Death and Dismemberment in Mesopotamia: Discorporation Between the Body and Body Politic', in *Performing Death*, ed. Nicola Laneri, OIS 3 (Chicago: Oriental Institute of the University of Chicago, 2007), 191.

95. Saul M. Olyan, 'Unnoticed Resonances of Tomb Opening and Transportation of the Remains of the Dead in Ezekiel 37:12-14', *JBL* 128, no. 3 (2009): 614. Olyan's restoration.

96. Suriano, *History*, 126–7.

97. Olyan, 'Unnoticed Resonances', 496, referencing Rykle Borger, *Beiträge zum inschriftenwerk Assurbanipals* (Wiesbaden: Harrassowitz, 1996), 55, prism VI 70-76.

98. A. R George, ed., *The Babylonian Gilgamesh Epic: Introduction, Critical Edition*, 2 vols. (Oxford: Oxford University Press, 2003), 1:734.

99. Olyan, 'Unnoticed Resonances', 498.

100. Stavrakopoulou, 'Gog's Grave', 72.

used to describe post-mortem existence and burial and their association with Sheol, the inference of the social dynamic of the tomb, and the evidence of disturbance from other ancient West Asian cultures, it is highly probable that the negative act caused a disturbance or cessation of the individual or group's post-mortem existence. Correct burial facilitated safe transition for the dead.

Drawing on the work of Bloch-Smith, Stavrakopoulou and Olyan, we have seen how the communal existence of the dead appears to have concrete social consequences, to the extent that incorrect burial can act as a form of punishment: a sharp depreciation of social and symbolic capital even after death. Burial culture suggests a way in which the living community is responsible for the social wellbeing of the dead, and is obligated to correct failures in proper burial. When we come later to look at the importance for the living of the presence of the dead, we will be able to demonstrate the inherent instability caused by death without offspring, as it disrupts the normal patterns of descent. However, burial did not take place in isolation; instead, it was set alongside additional commemorative rites, which can be understood as veneration and care for the dead.

3. *Veneration and Care of the Dead*

The debates around veneration, care or worship of the dead have remained 'stubbornly sluggish' in adopting newer perspectives, with mortuary rites persistently categorized as an aspect of 'popular religion'. As Stavrakopoulou notes,

> ...the persistent 'popularizing' of rituals associated with the dead is particularly curious given the near certainty that mortuary practices of some sort or another were performed at all levels of society by all social groups, however configured. After all, everybody dies. It might thus be expected that death cults would be treated as a more normative and mainstream aspect of religious practice, so that the only justification for their being termed 'popular' would be their widespread, common occurrence.[101]

Ezekiel 43.7-9 indicates a royal cult of the dead operating near the temple, which YHWH declares to be his throne, objecting that there is only a wall between him and the corpses, and calls on the people to no more

---

101. Francesca Stavrakopoulou, '"Popular" Religion and "Official" Religion: Practice, Perception, Portrayal', in *Religious Diversity in Ancient Israel and Judah*, ed. Francesca Stavrakopoulou and John Barton (New York: T&T Clark, 2010), 45. See also Bloch-Smith, 'Death in the Life of Israel', 142.

defile his holy name: '...neither they nor their kings, by their whoring, and by the corpses of their kings at their death... Now let them put away their idolatry and the corpses of their kings far from me, and I will reside among them for ever.' While the text casts the cult as negative, to be operating in such proximity must have indicated partial or temporary approval or instigation from political or religious authorities, possibly functioning in complement to the central cult of YHWH. Interestingly, Isa. 56.6 sees YHWH himself setting up a memorial monument and invoking the name of the dead in his temple. Moreover, 2 Sam. 21.9-14 implies the public performance of mortuary rites secures blessing, while Jer. 8.1-3 suggests ritual reversal of these public practices cause curses. As such, any assumption that mortuary rituals 'were socially, spatially and conceptually peripheral to mainstream or normative Yhwh worship – and thus in essence "popular" – is difficult to defend'.[102] Certain biblical texts, however, modify mortuary rituals and demarcate certain practices as 'foreign' to mainstream YHWH worship. Deuteronomy 18.9-12 instructs the people when they enter the land not to 'imitate the abhorrent practices of those nations', including making a son or daughter pass through fire, practicing divination, being a soothsayer, augur, sorcerer or spell caster, consulting ghosts or spirits or seeking oracles from the dead (see also Ps. 106.28). Difficulty comes, however, in attempting to interpret these acts, especially when their meaning would have changed over time and they operate in a symbolic mortuary system so different to a contemporary Western system; interpretation can become an 'intellectualist' endeavour, attempting to tease out belief from descriptions of ritual acts.[103]

There is textual evidence for a range of practices associated with mourning. While some funerary rites were prohibited, such as shaving the head or gashing the body (Lev. 21.5; Deut. 14.1),[104] others were deemed appropriate: rending of garments, donning of mourner's garb, perhaps fasting (2 Sam. 1.11-12; 3.31); a week of intense mourning (Gen. 50.10); rolling in ashes (Jer. 6.26); laments (Jer. 9.17-20).[105] We find burial rites beginning at the home of the deceased (Num. 19.14; Amos 6.10) and culminating at a tomb following a procession (2 Sam. 3.31-37). When we look to material remains, we find an array of items placed in tombs that

---

102. Stavrakopoulou, '"Popular" Religion and "Official" Religion', 46.
103. Schmidt, *Israel's Beneficent Dead*, 4.
104. cf. Isa. 15.2-3; Mic. 1.16.
105. Carol Meyers, 'Household Religion', in Stavrakopoulou and Barton, eds., *Religious Diversity in Ancient Israel and Judah*, 127–8.

are never listed in the biblical texts:[106] bowls, jugs, lamps, jars, juglets for scented oils, perfumes, spices, oil for lamps, jewellery, tools, household implements, and items of dress, grooming, amusement and identification.[107] There is 'no explicit and unambiguous discussion of the meaning of food placed in tombs in the Hebrew Bible (or, for that matter, in Canaanite/ Ugaritic texts)',[108] though 'to conclude that the Israelites did not perform such offers [would] be a very dangerous argument from silence'.[109] There has been a tendency to over-interpret, over-generalize and over-rely on meagre and weak evidence.[110] While mortuary provisions could be evidence of an extensive 'cult of the dead', the data themselves are ambiguous; food, for example, could suggest a funerary meal rather than the feeding of the dead.[111]

Bloch-Smith argues: 'the belief in the empowered dead, with the attendant practices stemming from that belief, is here interpreted as a cult of the dead'.[112] Here Bloch-Smith presumes a great deal about beliefs in the powers of the dead, and suggests a cult which acts to negotiate the power of the dead. However, 'one must remain careful not to equate signs of caring for the dead with an organized cult of the dead, where the spirits of deceased persons can help and sometimes harm the living'.[113] This is a specific concern when using comparative ancient West Asian data, where two similar sets of material remains can only in 'exceptional cases suggest

106. Lewis, 'How Far Can Texts Take Us?', 274.
107. Bloch-Smith, 'Cult', 218–19.
108. Pitard, 'Tombs and Offerings', 150.
109. Ibid., 155. Pitard offers the example of Ribar's hypothesis, in John Whalen Ribar, 'Death Cult Practices in Ancient Palestine' (PhD diss., University of Michigan, 1973), 55–63, of holes over tombs to provide food and drink offerings to the dead, which Pitard discredits. The hypothesis is based on two tombs from Bet-Shemesh, dating to the eighth to sixth centuries, along with other examples from the wider area. However, many of the examples are not widely accepted as tombs, some of the tombs had been covered up, and the two examples from Iron Age Israel and Judah, Tombs 1 and 2, had shafts of c. 1 meter in diameter and c. 1 meter in length, which arguably is too wide to be considered a useful opening for offerings, Moreover, Ribar is using comparative evidence from Ugaritic which has been discredited (see Pitard, 'Tombs and Offerings', 153–4). Even if the most likely (Tomb 2) is accepted, 'how can the installations found in such a tiny number of tombs be used to delineate the funerary practices of a culture?'.
110. Pitard, 'Tombs and Offerings', 147.
111. Tappy, 'Review', 61.
112. Bloch-Smith, 'Cult', 213.
113. Tappy, 'Review', 66.

a one-to-one correlation' in terms of culture.[114] Lewis argues based on Ugaritic evidence for a cult of the dead in Israel,[115] arguing that we are to stop thinking of 'the Bible *and* the ancient Near East, as if the former were not a part of the latter'.[116] While this is true, it is equally important to understand the Bible as an *expression* of ancient West Asia, operating within a broad cultural framework but still distinct, as are all ancient West Asian cultures (not to mention differences within societies). The process in which Israel/Judah self-identified as distinct from its surrounding cultures (whether real or imagined, organically occurring or dictated by the Deuteronomist/Priestly schools) occurred over time, geography, culture, language, socioeconomic development and 'religion'. There has been a tendency to presume ancient West Asian evidence corresponds directly to Israelite or Judahite beliefs and practices;[117] however, better criteria need to be developed for using ancient West Asian texts. While this is not the place to establish such criteria, it is worth noting that it may be constructive to only allow ancient West Asian material to determine our interpretation of a biblical text when there is a *high degree of correlation* between the non-biblical and biblical material. That is, in those places where the Bible leaves gaps in our knowledge, and a seemingly corresponding system is found operating in another cultural landscape, it might be reasonable to use the similar material to enlighten our view of the Bible (or vice versa). However, considering the great gaps (for example, in time) between the Bible and some of the ancient West Asian material used, it seems methodologically foolish to over-interpret the correspondence between these two systems. Grave goods, for example, rather than identifying a cult of the dead, can suggest any number of social and religious understandings. Ethnography from the Lugbara of Uganda shows that burial and tomb goods have 'no purpose connected with the afterworld; they are simply the visible expression of part of a person's social personality' – that is, the funerary rites are primarily directed at the social relationship of the living and the dead. This notion of 'social personality' is humorously applied by Peter Ucko to the large amounts of goods left during burials at Woodlands Private Animal Cemetery in Burwash, Sussex: the goods reflect emotional connotations and not any beliefs about a journey to the underworld. Conversely, among the Lober

---

114. Peter J. Ucko, 'Ethnography and Archaeological Interpretation of Funerary Remains', *World Archaeology* 1, no. 2 (1969): 263.
115. Lewis, *Cults of the Dead*.
116. Lewis, 'How Far Can Texts Take Us?', 206.
117. Pitard, 'Tombs and Offerings', 147.

of Ghana, no goods are placed in the tomb as they are symbolically placed with the deceased before burial; however, there is a prevalent belief the dead takes the goods with them.[118] Ucko warns against some of the pitfalls of ethnography through archaeology:

> It must be realised that where one particular cultural trait has remained the same over time, it does not necessary follow that other cultural traits have not changed either – where the same pottery types of funerary practices continue over a space of time, religious beliefs may just as well change as remain static.[119]

In common West African practice, the body lies on its left or right side depending on its sex; however, ethnographically there is no religious significance associated with this variable, though presumably there once could have been, as there still is in a few Nigerian and Ghanaian groups.[120] Conversely, 13 years after the 1902 Regular Cremation Act in the UK there were only 1,400 cremations; by 1960 35 per cent of the population was cremated, and evidence from Roman Catholics cremation statistics suggest this change was not associated with a change in religious beliefs.[121] While there is Judahite evidence of food the provision of food for the dead,[122] there is no guarantee of what significance these acts carried. The difficulty of interpretation is compounded when we consider the diversity of practice recorded in the Bible and the period over which the texts were produced. Moreover, we have to consider the diachronic changes that may have come with the introduction of certain funerary restrictions;[123] any elements suggesting a cult of the dead could 'only reach us after they have undergone a thorough editing'.[124] Despite this, Karel van der Toorn argues that many elements of the framework of a cult of the dead inherited from old Semitic traditions, such as patrilineal inheritance, are present in the text, reflected, for example, in genealogy, land being named after individuals (e.g. Josh. 19.12) and the transference of blessing (Gen. 25.11).[125] Necromancy is referenced multiple times, albeit negatively,

---

118. Ucko, 'Ethnography and Archaeology', 265.
119. Ibid., 263.
120. Ibid., 272.
121. Ibid., 274.
122. Ibid.; Bloch-Smith, 'Cult', 218–19.
123. Bloch-Smith, *Burial*, 222–4; Bray, 'Genesis 23'; Blenkinsopp, 'Post-Mortem Existence'.
124. Lewis, *Cults of the Dead*, 99.
125. Van der Toorn, *Family Religion*, 206.

which implies it was perceived as being practiced.[126] As discussed above, certain acts are prohibited and certain acts allowed,[127] and although the rationale behind these acts is not easily understood,[128] some see them as bringing about intimacy between the living and the dead by infusing the dead with the substance that symbolized the living.[129]

The debate around a possible cult for the dead is also influenced by constructions of sacrifices intended for the dead. Deuteronomy 26.14 prohibits offering tithed (sacred) food 'to' the dead, למת. At the same time, this same text appears to allow for the offering of 'secular' food.[130] Lewis emphasizes the problem of the ל: we cannot rule out that the offering is 'to' the dead, as opposed to 'for' the dead, indicating a cultic act directed to the dead as opposed to mere provisioning.[131] Alan Cooper and Bernard Goldstein argue that אלהים sacrifices in the Pentateuchal narratives refer to divine ancestors.[132] They note, for example, Gen. 31.53-55, which reads:

> '…May the God of Abraham [אלהי אברהם] and the God of Nahor' – the God of their father [אלהי אביהם] – 'judge between us'. So Jacob swore by the Fear of his father Isaac, and Jacob offered a sacrifice on the height and called his kinsfolk to eat bread…

However, their understanding of אלהים as referring to the deified dead is not convincing.[133] Moreover, we do not understand the origin of sacrifice; our main understanding is derived from the way the text imagines the central cult as functioning.[134] Accordingly, any indication of sacrifice to ancestors does not take us further in understanding the purpose. In addition, William Albright's inference that the standing stones (Gen. 35.20)

---

126. Lev. 19.31; Deut. 18.11; Isa. 8.19-20a; 19.3; 29.4; 1 Sam. 28.19; 2 Kgs 21.6; 23.24.

127. See also Lev. 19.28; 21.5; Isa. 15.2; 22.12; Jer. 16.6; 41.5; 47.5; 48.37; Ezek. 7.18; Amos 8.10; Mic. 1.16.

128. Lewis, *Cults of the Dead*, 101.

129. Van der Toorn, *Family Religion*, 210.

130. Compare to the secularization of sacrifice (Deut. 12.1-18). A 'secularization' of death cults – a concept that seems alien to us – could have served to prevent the conflation of the worship of YHWH and the veneration of ancestors.

131. Lewis, *Cults of the Dead*, 103.

132. Alan Cooper and Bernard Goldstein, 'The Cult of the Dead and the Theme of Entry into the Land', *BibInt* 1, no. 3 (1993): 285–303; Bloch-Smith, *Burial*, 123.

133. Tappy, 'Review', 62.

134. Jonathan Klawans, 'Pure Violence: Sacrifice and Defilement in Ancient Israel', *HTR* 94, no. 2 (2001): 136–7.

were places of sacrifice[135] has not been accepted.[136] There are references to clan sacrifices, זבח משפחה, such as the yearly sacrifice for the whole clan in 1 Sam. 20.6 (see also 1 Sam. 20.29). However, the term לכל־המשפחה is ambiguous and obscures the purpose of the sacrifice. Psalm 16.4 may refer to libations and invocation of the name of the dead.[137] In addition, rites associated with food offerings at graves appear in late texts, such as Tob. 4.17 (see also Sir. 30.18). These texts may reference earlier rites or be later developments. It should be noted that while there are references to highly ritualized funerary banquets (Jer. 16.5), along with archaeological remains of grave goods, it is unclear how often these invocations or offerings may have occurred.[138] Other texts suggest something closer to 'care' for the dead. 2 Kings 9.34 states:

> Then he went in and ate and drank; he said, 'See to [פקדו] that cursed woman and bury her; for she is a king's daughter'.

Lewis argues that פקדו means to 'care for', a reference to the specific mortuary rites deemed appropriate in a royal death cult[139] evidenced by the role of the 'caretaker', *pāqidu*, in the Mesopotamian cult of the dead.

These possible references to death/mortuary cults offer us an image of some practices; however, they are often presented in negative and polemical contexts. By not overemphasizing the separation between living and dead, and taking into account the range of practices which appear to have taken place, we can affirm transformative, inclusive and constructive functions of mortuary rites.[140] Given the seeming likelihood that the dead were 'recipients of cultic activities reaching beyond mere commemoration', the use of the term 'worship' 'is in many ways a question of the perspective of the interpreter, as much as a question of evidence'.[141] What we can state instead is that there was continued social interaction between living and dead, so much so that certain rites were deemed to

---

135. William Albright, 'The High Places in Ancient Palestine', in *Volume du Congrès, Strasbourg 1956*, ed. G. W. Anderson, VTSup 4 (Leiden: Brill, 1957), 243.

136. Charles A. Kennedy, 'Dead, Cult of the', *ABD*, 106.

137. Lewis, *Cults of the Dead*, 166.

138. Saul M. Olyan, 'Family Religion in Israel and the Wider Levant of the First Millennium BCE', in *Household and Family Religion in Antiquity*, ed. John Bodel and Saul M. Olyan, The Ancient World: Comparative Histories (Malden, MA: Blackwell, 2008), 119.

139. Lewis, *Cults of the Dead*, 121.

140. Stavrakopoulou, *Land*, 23.

141. Ibid.

be antipathetic to YHWH worship; the fact certain homogenizing texts took to renegotiating mortuary practices rather than complete rejection should, rather than suggesting a negation of ancestor veneration, in fact affirm the existence of widespread practices which facilitate social continuity between generations. One parallel practice which seems to indicate care for the dead, and an ongoing social relationship, was the erection of monuments for the dead, and notably those dying without progeny.

4. *Physically Remembering: Monuments*

Monuments form a type of on-going social interaction between the living and the dead; moreover, monuments act generally as a response to death, but more specifically as a response to *childless* death.[142] Among other uses, monuments are used as memorials of people, and this can include the living or the dead.[143] While we find some clear references to the erection of memorial monuments, most notably that of Absalom in 2 Sam. 18.18,[144] many texts may indicate memorial monuments, such as the פגרי מלכיהם in Ezek. 43.7-9, which may be memorial steles or the bodies of the kings.[145] We are given a few brief details regarding the size, shape or stone-type of the biblical מצבה (or the lesser-used term יד)[146] (memorial pillars/standing stones/stele), and Bloch-Smith suggests they are neither 'structural [n]or functional' but primarily 'prominent or conspicuous', focusing the

---

142. There is a strong ancient West Asian context for understanding mortuary monuments: their 'frequent place in (perhaps higher status) mortuary and ancestor cults is now broadly accepted', particularly because of Egyptian, Mesopotamian and Phoenicio-Punic inscribed monuments, and the Ugaritic Tale of Aqhat. See Stavrakopoulou, *Land*, 15. Zevit surveys a wide range of מצבות, and suggests the information available from classical authors, inscriptions, excavated cult sites and other artefacts indicate cultic and funerary roles; see Ziony Zevit, *The Religions of Ancient Israel: A Synthesis of Parallactic Approaches* (London: Continuum, 2001), 256–9.

143. LaRocca-Pitts cites Gen. 35.20, Exod. 20.4 (representing the twelve tribes); 2 Sam. 18.18 and Isa. 6.13. Curiously she does not include in her discussions texts such as Isa. 56.5-10 which use the term יד: Elizabeth C. LaRocca-Pitts, *Of Wood and Stone: The Significance of Israelite Cultic Items in the Bible and Its Early Interpreters*, HSM 61 (Winona Lake, IN: Eisenbrauns, 2001), 212.

144. See also Gen. 35.20; Isa. 56.5; 57.8-15.

145. Lewis, *Cults of the Dead*, 142.

146. Zevit outlines the diversity of terms: they are made of stone (Gen. 22.18; 31.13, 45); they were constructed (Exod. 24.4; 1 Kgs 14.23); placed (Gen. 28.18); raised high (Gen. 31.45); stood up (Lev. 26.1; Deut. 16.22); set erect (Gen. 35.14, 20; 2 Kgs 17.10). They can also be dressed up artificially (Hos. 10.2), and are usually single but in Exod. 24.4-12 and Jer. 43.13 there are many: Zevit, *Religions*, 259.

viewer's attention, with a shape that makes it notably a standing stone 'rather than a random rock'.[147] Defined by their presence, the monument is to be a standing stone which carries with it a set of meanings. However, Elizabeth La-Rocca Pitts notes Isa. 6.13, in which a tree stump represents the remnant of Israel: 'the use of the term *maṣṣēbôt* for a tree stump is curious here unless one understands that the wordplay that evokes the image of the commemorative *maṣṣēbāh*, in this case, a stump which witnesses to both the fallen glory of Israel as well as the survival of the remnant'.[148] We have little information about their usage, and we should be aware that their functions may well be overlapping (commemorative, legal, cultic, etc.).[149] They appear to be a part of family piety (Gen. 35.20; Isa. 56.6), 'the duty of a son to commemorate his parents after their death'.[150] Standing stones are used as a form of commemorative markers across cultures throughout ancient West Asia. However, it is unclear to what extent these stones 'manifest, deify, or merely symbolize or represent the dead'. Such likely 'depends on the (changing) context-specific particularities of the stones themselves, including, perhaps, the perspective of the viewer before whom the stone is exhibited'.[151] It also highlights the 'mortuary landscape' outlined by Stavrakopoulou, above.

Mortuary monuments are not simply markers of death or individual memory, but take on a social function that links communities through generations and mediates cultural memory. Some texts situate the stones at the grave (e.g. Gen. 35.20), while Absalom's monument in 2 Sam. 18.18 is set up before his death.[152] We cannot be certain to what extent these stones mark a specific burial site, or function 'as a memorial indexing more broadly the presence of the dead (whether there or elsewhere)'.[153] While

---

147. Elizabeth Bloch-Smith, 'Will the Real Massebot Please Stand Up: Cases of Real and Mistakenly Identified Standing Stones in Ancient Israel', in *Text, Artifact, and Image: Revealing Ancient Israelite Religion*, ed. Gary M. Beckman and Theodore J. Lewis, BJS 346 (Providence, RI: Brown Judaic Studies, 2006), 65.

148. LaRocca-Pitts, *Wood and Stone*, 212.

149. Bloch-Smith, 'Will the Real Massebot', 78.

150. Albertz and Schmitt, *Family and Household*, 460.

151. Stavrakopoulou, *Land*, 15.

152. Rüdiger Schmitt, '"And Jacob Set up a Pillar at Her Grave...": Material Memorials and Landmarks in the Old Testament', in *The Land of Israel in Bible, History, and Theology: Studies in Honour of Ed Noort*, ed. Jacques Ruiten and J. Cornelis de Vos, VTSup 124 (Leiden: Brill, 2009), 394. Stavrakopoulou notes 1 Kgs 7.15-22, Isa. 56.5 and possibly Gen. 28.18, 35.14, where the site appears to be cultic: Stavrakopoulou, *Land*, 16.

153. Stavrakopoulou, *Land*, 16.

some texts portray standing stones negatively, others take more positive approaches, including YHWH establishing them himself,[154] as well as them taking on more territorial associations, such as Gen. 31.44-54 where they are set up to mark boundaries in the names of ancestral deities.[155]

While certain scholars would like to attribute these מצבות to a flourishing cult of the dead,[156] there is a lack of evidence.[157] Comparative approaches can be extremely tempting; for example, KTU 1.17.2.12-23 reads:

> Let there be a son in his house
> A descendant in his palace;
> One who sets up the stela of his divine ancestor,
> In the sanctuary, the marker of his clansman;
> One who delivers his life from the Underworld,
> One who guards his footsteps from the Dust;
> One who squelches his detractor's slander,
> One who drives away those who act against him.[158]

The reference to the divine ancestor may imply either the deceased's ancestor as a god, or worship of the same god in solidarity with one's ancestors.[159] Here a son is longed for to set up a stela of his 'divine ancestor', as well as perform the necessary functions, which will take care of the deceased. However, as B. G. Ockinga notes, there is a dissonance

---

154. For negative connotations, see Exod. 23.24; 34.13; Lev. 26.1; Deut. 7.5; 12.3; 16.22; 1 Kgs 14.23; 2 Kgs 3.2; 10.26-27; 17.10; 18.4; 23.14; 2 Chron. 14.3; 31.1; Jer. 43.13; Mic. 5.13. However, YHWH establishes monuments in Isa. 56.3-5, and Stavrakopoulou also notes more positive representations: Gen. 28.18, 22; 31.13; 35.14, 20; Exod. 24.4; Hos. 3.4. References appear in E, the Covenant Code, Exod. 34, H, D, Dtr, the Chronicler, Hosea, Micah, First Isaiah, Jeremiah and Ezekiel, and they are understood positively or negatively, generally dependent on whether they are dedicated to other gods. D, Dtr and the Chronicler express disapproval without reference to their being dedicated (Deut. 16.22; 1 Kgs 14.23; 2 Kgs 17.10; 18.4; 2 Chron. 14.2; 31.1), although some explicitly reference others gods (2 Kgs 3.2; 10.26, 27; 23.14); the only reference in this material which is with approval is in 2 Sam. 18.18, which LaRocca-Pitts suggests may be, like Gen. 35.20, explicitly dedicated to a person: LaRocca-Pitts, *Wood and Stone*, 209–11.

155. Stavrakopoulou, *Land*, 16–17.

156. Cooper and Goldstein, 'Cult of the Dead'.

157. Stavrakopoulou, *Land*, 17; Lewis, 'How Far Can Texts Take Us?', 187.

158. Reproduced from Lewis's 'Family, Household, and Local Religion at Late Bronze Age Ugarit', *Household and Family Religion in Antiquity*, copyright © 2008 John Bodel and Saul M. Olyan. Used by permission of Wiley Publishing.

159. Ibid., 68–9. Compare, e.g., the biblical 'God of Abraham, Isaac and Jacob'.

with biblical descriptions such as 2 Sam. 18.18 and Isa. 56.3-5 (which will be discussed in detail in a later chapter) as these refer to the setting up of a monument in *place* of offspring.[160] Ziony Zevit argues that there are hints, in the wider geographical and cultural context, of 'immanent presence' being represented at the standing stones, at least relating to deities.[161] This is hinted at in polemical texts, for example Exod. 23.24, 34.13, and Deut. 7.5, 12.3, where the intensity of the verb used for the destruction of the monuments, שבר, is 'proportional to the perceived inherent sacred power that they were thought to possess',[162] although Zevit acknowledges this does not necessarily imply cultic rites at the sites. For example, he looks at the site at Bethel:

> The angel of God said to me in the dream '...I am the God of Bethel [אנכי האל בית־אל], where you anointed a pillar [מצבה] and made a vow to me. Now leave this land at once and return to the land of your birth'. (Gen. 31.13; cf. Gen. 28.10-22)

While suggesting that the name Bethel implies the monument is in some ways 'animated', he states:

> In both of these Bethel traditions no mention occurs that sacrifices were made at the spot, no incense burnt, no prostrations made to the stone, and no provision made for the standing stone to be protected from natural elements. The *massebot* were set up and then left. Their role seems to have been simply to be present, to be dedicated to a particular deity, and somehow to assure the god's presence. Both physically and metaphysically, they represented, expressed, and guaranteed a continuous, immanent presence.[163]

This is particularly interesting if we look at two texts – Gen. 31.13, where the stone commemorates a vow to the God of Bethel, and the story of Absalom's monument in 2 Sam. 18.18, where it functions as a personal marker – in terms of both the broad use of the term, מצבה, and because in both texts they seem to act as more than a static memorial marker, suggesting something of an immanent presence. However, there is no 'textual evidence at all that stelae were inhabited by dead spirits or that acts of veneration were performed in front of them'; 'the presence of the dead as marked by stelae was not intended to denote any sort of actual presence; it was intended to represent symbolically an ongoing

---

160. B. G. Ockinga, 'A Note on 2 Samuel 18.18', *BN* 31 (1986): 32.
161. Zevit, *Religions*, 261.
162. Ibid.
163. Ibid.

relationship between the dead and the bereaved'.[164] Suriano explores some north Semitic inscriptions bearing references to *npš*, a cognate to נפש, where *npš* refers to the monument itself, providing 'excellent examples of how the term *npš* could represent the reification of the self in a material object'.[165] For example, a Persian-period inscription from Anatolia, KAI 258, reads:

> This is the relief Nanshati established
> Before Adonis, his provider-of-care.
> My defunct soul (*npš*) belongs to it. But if anyone evil
> acts destructively with this relief
> may Sahar and Shamash seek him out![166]

According to Suriano, the inscription assigns the *npš* a physical presence in the relief 'because the relief, which probably was accompanied by an image...encompassed elements of Nanshati's selfhood, chiefly his name'. Suriano suggests a commonality with the נפש as corpse, in that the 'dead are personified in an object that is attended to by the living'.[167] Textual evidence is quite clear in linking memorial monuments with names. The monument and the name are linked in Isa. 56.5 where the eunuch is promised a יד ושם, a hand/memorial/phallus and a name, which may suggest more than simply being complementary – the two are conceptually linked. In 2 Sam. 18.18 the monument acts both in replacement of a name (brought by offspring) and in order to keep his name in remembrance (the monument acting in the place of offspring). Suriano suggests the use of the root זכר in 2 Sam. 18.18 could indicate a performative aspect of possible writing on the pillar, as the מצבה is meant to accomplish the remembrance.[168] The pillar may indicate the on-going social tie between living and dead, the importance being the connection to the presence of the dead person, not the 'spirit' of the dead.[169] Memorials for individuals are further recorded for Saul:

> ...Saul went to Carmel, where he set up a monument [יד] for himself, and on returning he passed on down to Gilgal. (1 Sam. 15.12)

---

164. Albertz and Schmitt, *Family and Household*, 461.
165. Suriano, *History*, 151.
166. Ibid., 152. This is a reproduction of Suriano's translation.
167. Ibid., 150-4.
168. Suriano, 'Death, Disinheritance, and Job's Kinsman-Redeemer', 52.
169. Schmitt, 'Pillar', 394.

We read of Rachel that she dies and is buried outside the communal family tomb on the way to Ephrath:

> ...and Jacob set up a pillar at her grave [מצבה על־קברתה]; it is the pillar of Rachel's tomb, which is there to this day. (Gen. 35.20)

As with Absalom, the pillar of Rachel's tomb is distinct from the tomb itself, and its function is separate. These references suggest something beyond simply graves or tombs:[170]

> By the erection of imaginary memorials the landscape has been semiotisized and thereby becomes a 'mnemotope' for the collective cultural memory and identity of Israel... [They are] markers in the landscapes of imagination with a variety of meanings, which transform the landscape of reality into a mnemotope for the cultural remembrance, and both the religious and national identity of Israel.[171]

As with more general mortuary culture, memorial markers form an ongoing social relationship between the living and the dead, tying once-living members of the community who view them with the monuments, and ensuring a commonality of identity between generations. Monuments will be discussed in the final chapter, which will explore Isa. 56.3-5 and 2 Sam. 18.18 in more detail.

5. Conclusion

The evidence we have shows the dead were thought to continue in a real, substantive and social way after death, although the biblical texts offer various, competing and partial suggestions of what the afterlife was like. It is tempting to suggest elaborate mortuary cults or a belief in the powerful dead, but a lack of textual evidence restricts this. Moreover, anthropological research that suggests meaning cannot be derived from practice limits our ability to interpret material remains. This does not mean that there was not some form of ongoing social relationship between the living and the dead, and we should be cautious about suggesting an artificial social division caused by death. There is a well-evidenced ideology relating to burial, with archaeological and textual sources agreeing that burial involves a communal continuation, and that care is taken to look after the remains of the dead. In addition, partially due to a correlation

---

170. Ibid., 389. See also 2 Kgs 23.17.
171. Ibid., 402, 403.

between the tomb and Sheol, we can substantiate that burial was seen to safeguard the post-mortem existence of the dead, and that burial with kin was considered the ideal. Material relating to both burial and mortuary practices makes clear the strong familial dimension of the dead, which emphasizes the transformation of the deceased from a living member of the community to a dead member; moreover, a range of practices are known to have carried out after the death of an individual, including the erection of physical reminders which act to create, along with tombs, a kind of mortuary landscape. We appear to have a field in which actors still struggle to negotiate their place and that of their kin, and that this takes place in an embodied way.

The language used, such as 'gathered to his fathers', is gendered, though texts also emphasize the burial of women. Indeed, with Rachel we have not only burial and the erection of monuments, but she is also the most prominent description of an ancestral intercessor available to us, and her tomb appears to act as a claim to land.[172] Jezebel, conversely, is denied burial and her body is mutilated in post-mortem punishment. What has been demonstrated through this discussion is that despite uncertainty about the significance of certain practices and rites, there is a strong emphasis on burial, veneration and memorialization, suggesting the social importance of the dead, with the living responsible for their proper care. This is epitomized in the existence of standing stones, which materially function to represent the dead among the living and may offer something of a continued existence to the dead. The chief social concern for and about the dead is that they continue to exist in social dynamic with their kin, in their family tombs on their family inheritance. Moreover, as highlighted in the work of Brichto and Stavrakopoulou outlined in the Introduction, the dead are vital for the community and offer both physical and symbolic claims to land and identity. Through an exploration of the importance of proper burial and memorialization, we are also able to reassess Schmidt's notion of the 'dreaded death after death'.[173] I would argue that his emphasis is overly negative regarding the status of the dead and their reliance on the living, and denies the vibrant connections which are constantly negotiating the boundaries between the living and the dead. However, we have been able to see the importance of proper practice towards the deceased and that a form of post-mortem corpse abuse and neglect is clearly detrimental to the wellbeing of the deceased, acting as a kind of 'death after death'. It is clear that social and symbolic capital do

172. Ibid., 87.
173. Schmitt, 'Pillar', 394.

not cease to matter post-mortem, and symbolic and actual violence can be done to a still-embodied person. This capital is also clearly important to the living, and can be manipulated through connections of burial and land claims. Having established the importance of social continuity and relationship between the living and the dead, and the co-dependency of each, we can now look at the importance of names, and their capacity to cross boundaries of death and reinforce social connection.

Chapter 4

NAMES

1. *What's in a Name?*

Almost all our key texts are concerned with the perpetuation of the שם, the name. There are around a thousand occurrences of שם in the Hebrew Bible, the vast majority not descriptions of a person's name,[1] but rather where the name itself appears to take on an *ontological* presence distinct from the embodied person. We see Saul make David promise:

'…Swear to me therefore by the LORD that you will not cut [תכרית] off my descendants after me [את־זרעי אחרי], and that you will not wipe out [ואם־תשמיד] my name from my father's house [שמי מבית אבי]'. (1 Sam. 24.21)

There is an association between descendants, or זרע, seed, name and ancestral land, with the name taking on substance after Saul's death. Many interpretations of the place of names suggest that when the text speaks of an individual's name not being wiped out, it is a metaphor for their memory, for their offspring, for their inheritance, or their land. However, this chapter will demonstrate that ensuring one's name was perpetuated after death – that it is not wiped out – was of primary importance to men in and of itself,[2] because, as is widely recognized, the name is in some way of the same substance as the human being in the Bible and ancient West Asia.[3] Moreover, the continuation of the name is treated in such a way that

---

1. E.g. 'his name was Samuel'.
2. The texts do not seem concerned with the perpetuation of the woman's name, which will be explored in later chapters.
3. On the names of people, see Victor A. Hurowitz, 'Name Midrashim and the Word Plays on Names in Akkadian Historical Writings', in *A Woman of Valor: Jerusalem Ancient Near Eastern Studies in Honor of Joan Goodnick Westenholz*, ed. Wayne Horowitz, Uri Gabbay and Filip Vukosavovic, Biblioteca Del Próximo

a great deal of symbolic capital is associated with it. By excavating down and uncovering the discourse that surrounds names and naming, we can see how names function in the core texts of this study as connected with the perpetuation of the individual and community.

The cornerstone for understanding anthropological research on names is that names are not labels but speech-acts. Names are not classifiers, but are always performative speech; they bring the fleeting and indefinable ideas of the self and the social into concrete existence.[4] This sense of personhood and recognition of the individual bridges the previous discussion of death and burial with the discussion here of names – naming, burial and memorialization contribute to the personhood of an individual. Lemos draws upon and synthesizes recent work on what defines personhood, finding the most common definition 'is the criterion of social recognition': our personhood is defined by other people's recognition of our personhood. Lemos suggests 'the most salient foci of anthropological treatments' of personhood defines personhood as '*social recognition of*

Oriente Antiguo 8 (Madrid: Consejo Superior de Investigaciones Científicas, 2010), 101; Michael Hundley, 'To Be or Not to Be: A Reexamination of Name Language in Deuteronomy and the Deuteronomistic History', *VT* 59, no. 4 (2009): 549; William Morrow, '"To Set the Name" in the Deuteronomic Centralization Formula: A Case of Cultural Hybridity', *JSS* 55, no. 2 (2010): 379; F. V. Reiterer, H. Ringgren and H. J. Fabry, 'שם', *TDOT*; Johann Jakob Stamm, 'Names: In the Bible', *Encyclopedia Judaica* 14:766; Walther Eichrodt, *Theology of the Old Testament*, trans. J. A. Baker, OTL, 2 vols. (London: SCM, 1961), 1:206; Yael Avrahami, 'Name Giving to the Newborn in the Hebrew Bible', in *These Are the Names: Studies in Jewish Onomastics* (Hebrew), ed. Aaron Demsky, Studies in Jewish Onomastics 5 (Ramat-Gan: Bar-Ilan University Press, 2011), 19. On the names used for God, see Victor A. Hurowitz, 'Review of Sandra L. Richter, The Deuteronomistic History and the Name Theology: *Lešakkēn šemô šām* in the Bible and the Ancient Near East', *JHS* 5, Review (2004) (Hurowitz recognizes name theology as being perceived by scholars as being *the* hallmark of Deuteronomic name theology); Horst Dietrich Preuss, *Old Testament Theology*, trans. Leo G. Perdue, OTL, 2 vols. (Louisville, KY: Westminster John Knox, 1995), 2:45; Rainer Albertz, *Israel in Exile: The History and Literature of the Sixth Century B.C.E.*, trans. David Green, SBLStBL 3 (Atlanta, GA: Society of Biblical Literature, 2003), 295; William M. Schniedewind, 'The Evolution of Name Theology', in *The Chronicler as Theologian: Essays in Honor of Ralph W. Klein*, ed. Steven L. McKenzie, Matt Patrick Graham and Gary N. Knoppers, JSOTSup 371 (London: T&T Clark, 2003), 232–5.

4. Maurice Bloch, 'Teknonymy and the Evocation of the "Social" Among the Zafimaniry of Madagascar', in *An Anthropology of Names and Naming*, ed. Barbara Bodenhorn and Gabriele vom Bruck (Cambridge: Cambridge University Press, 2006), 113.

value, based upon criteria that are often variable both between and within societies and marked by the *attribution of jural rights* and *agency* in legal or in less formal social contexts; and/or by *rituals conveying status*'.[5] That is, a person is recognized as having personhood by 'having value, not as a commodity but as a participant in social relations'. Personhood 'is a way of thinking about the relationship between the physical body and social status, about the limits of what we can do to bodies'.[6] Personhood can be 'full' or 'partial', and can be taken away.[7] Personhood, even if not explicitly stated, affects how individuals are differentiated.[8] Names – or a lack of them – form one of the primary methods of personhood. I will first discuss the anthropological framework through which to understand names and naming in their social context, before looking at the substance of a name in the Bible through this framework. Within this context, I will explore the relation between names, descendants and death. Finally, I will reverse this and look at what occurs when a name is forgotten, which I will show is a form of symbolic violence, removing personhood from an individual.

2. *Anthropological Perspectives on Names and Naming*

Name discourse, the way we use, think of and symbolize names, is deeply connected to the structures of power and capital, of both those named and those who name them. Names and naming are fundamental aspects of social processes, which have a profound impact on anthropological understanding of personhood, kinship and gender.[9] It is perhaps easy to assume concepts of names and naming function in a broadly similar system to one's own because names at once seem so important (we would never expect to meet someone without a name) and at the same time so ordinary (universality suggesting a level of banality). The differences in name ideology between cultures, however, are as ubiquitous as any other social difference. There is no such thing as a 'naming system', but names and naming form part of the whole complex of society: 'the total system of village life that exists through a multitude of individual

---

5. Lemos, *Violence*, 11.
6. Ibid.
7. Ibid., 12.
8. Ibid., 14.
9. Barbara Bodenhorn and Gabriele vom Bruck, 'Entangled in Histories: An Introduction to the Anthropology of Names and Naming', in Bodenhorn and vom Bruck, eds., *An Anthropology of Names and Naming*, 4.

acts, of which linguistic acts are a significant element'.[10] Understanding its symbolic importance allows us to see 'patterns in what might at first glance seem to be simply cultural variations'.[11] Names constitute part of social interactions and are never used as isolated acts; they form part of a series of designating devices (eye contact, pronouns, titles, gestures etc.) and 'the choice involved in using names must be understood in terms of these always available alternatives'.[12] They are in these ways inherently social choices, bridging and crossing social boundaries and invoking and reproducing history.

What is a name? According to Maurice Bloch, names should not be understood along the 'old and dangerous semiotic model of the signifiers signifying signifieds'; words are not classifiers, and if we mistake them as such we forget that names *do* things. Names 'are one of the ways in which phantasmagorical images of the "social" are given fleeting phenomenological existence',[13] giving subsistence to individuals and constituting social relations.[14] They are both performative as symbolic expression of something, but at the same time, crucially, they are effective action in terms of constructing kinship, gender, bodies and personhood.[15] Names do not 'evoke' a social system, but rather the individuals in themselves are 'an equally immaterial entity whose phenomenological existence is created by acts such as using personal names'.[16]

Through names we can express relation between others and ourselves. But what is the relationship between the name and the named? Naming is state monitored in our societies today, and the eradication of the name is an act of symbolic violence – so much so that the right to a name is enshrined in the UN Convention on the Rights of the Child,[17] 'recognizing the implications of carrying a name that begin at the earliest moments of social being'.[18] Barbara Bodenhorn and Gabriele vom Bruck suggest:

10. Bloch, 'Teknonymy', 113.
11. Bodenhorn and Bruck, 'Entangled', 2.
12. Bloch, 'Teknonymy', 98.
13. Ibid., 99.
14. Bodenhorn and Bruck, 'Entangled', 5.
15. Ibid.
16. Bloch, 'Teknonymy', 101.
17. UN General Assembly, *UN Convention on the Rights of the Child*, Treaty Series 1577, 1989.
18. Bodenhorn and Bruck, 'Entangled', 3.

> The potential for the name to become identical with the person creates the simultaneous potential to fix them as individuals and as members of recognized social groups. It is their detachability that renders names a powerful political tool for establishing or erasing formal identity, and gives them commodity-like value. And it is precisely their detachability that allows them to cross boundaries.[19]

This tension between the ability to attach and detach creates a space, an opportunity for human agency to manipulate the relationship between name and named. This space is the place where political, religious and social powers attempt to define personhood, identity and relationships:

> That identities can be stolen, traded, suspended, and even erased through the name reveals the profound political power located in the capacity to name; it illustrates the property-like potential in names to transact social value; and it brings into view the powerful connections between name and self-identity.[20]

Names are property and commodity-like entities that carry value, revealing crucial information about gender, kinship, geographical origin or religion. Names carry with them the capacity not only to delineate the boundaries of social status, but also to bridge them.[21] At the same time, they may also provide the vehicle for crossing boundaries between those very same categories, as well as between life and death, past and future, humans and non-humans.[22] The potential to fix and detach identities to persons and communities exposes the 'moral and cultural instability' involved in naming, and helps us to understand how they socially interconnect histories.[23] In individual and unique ways, naming systems bear the weight of the past, and entangle our histories with those past, present and future in our social systems.[24] They function vertically through time, horizontally through different social boundaries, and 'diagonally', between the realm of gods and the realm of the dead. This theoretical context will allow us to explore naming and names – both of humans and gods – in the Hebrew Bible.

19. Ibid., 4.
20. Ibid., 2.
21. Ibid., 3.
22. Ibid., 4.
23. Ibid., 2.
24. Susan Benson, 'Injurious Names: Naming, Disavowal, and Recuperation in Contexts of Slavery and Emancipation', in Bodenhorn and vom Bruck, eds., *An Anthropology of Names and Naming*, 179.

3. *The Act of Naming*

The very act of giving a name is performative, and an exercise of power. That words have agency as performative utterances or speech-acts is well attested in ancient West Asia. However, it is critical to recognize that the mechanism through which they act is both hard to define and deeply specific to each culture.[25] The idea that words have universal agency has been critiqued,[26] and it is possible to express more nuanced understandings where words do not have automatic potency, but where their potency depends on 'the power and authority of the person who utters them'.[27] So, for example, in Isa. 55.11 YHWH states that the word that goes out 'from my mouth...shall accomplish that which I purpose'. The word, personified as an actor with agency, is depicted as leaving God's mouth and returning, succeeding in its task. The act of naming is integral to the act of creation:[28]

> ...Who created [ברא] these?
> He who brings out their host and numbers them,
> calling them all by name [יקרא בשם];
> because he is great in strength,
> mighty in power,
> not one is missing. (Isa. 40.26)

Here the speech-act is included in the matrix of things that assist the creative act; it is via name-giving that the act of creation is completed.

Linda Layne notes that the act of naming transforms new-borns into 'somebodies', and an absence of naming provokes a heightened anxiety, suggesting loss of pregnancy is a particular site of struggle over the

---

25. Seth L. Sanders, 'Performative Utterances and Divine Language in Ugaritic', *JNES* 63, no. 3 (2004): 161–6. See also Delbert Hillers, 'Some Performative Utterances in the Bible', in *Pomegranates and Golden Bells: Studies in Biblical, Jewish, and Near Eastern Ritual, Law, and Literature in Honor of Jacob Milgrom*, ed. David P. Wright, David N. Freedman, and Avi Hurvitz (Winona Lake, IN: Eisenbrauns, 1995), 757–66.

26. James Barr, 'The Symbolism of Names in the Old Testament', *BJRL* 52, no. 1 (1969): 19; George W. Ramsey, 'Is Name-Giving an Act of Domination in Genesis 2:23 and Elsewhere?', *CBQ* 50, no. 1 (1988): 31; Anthony C. Thiselton, 'The Supposed Power of Words in the Biblical Writings', *JTS* 25, no. 2 (1974): 283–99.

27. Ramsey, 'Name-Giving', 31.

28. Avrahami, 'Name Giving', 23.

construction of identity.[29] In this context, she points out the increasing tendency, encouraged by US pregnancy loss support groups, to name miscarried or stillborn infants, often using their 'womb-names'. Naming here is demonstrative of discourse regarding personhood:

> The social construction of personhood is particularly well illustrated in cases where the social dimensions are decoupled from the biological – either where a name is given to an entity that lacks the biological potential to develop into an infant; or where a name is withheld from an entity that does.[30]

Whereas biological birth is a 'one-time' irreversible event, personhood is continuous and mutable, and can even be annulled. By inscribing a name, the baby is 'being constructed as part of the collective identity of the family'.[31] Within the contexts of the support groups, space was constructed for the opportunity to speak the name of the baby verbally,[32] inscription on monuments was encouraged,[33] and others were encouraged to speak the name, which normalized the personhood for the parents.[34] In one example the names were written on paper and planted under a tree, therefore nourishing and living in the tree.[35] Here we see the physical inscription of the name losing importance to a symbolic life it had taken on, but also embodying it in another object. Names, here, allow the remembrance of an entity as a person, and construct personhood in response to tragedy; in receiving a name, the infants become people, and are distinguished from the biological process of pregnancy to become social agents.

The formation of identity which naming brings means that on each appearance of the object or person, we can acknowledge some self-sameness.[36] Although names can be used as a mean of control, 'the name is [primarily] an affirmation, by others, of our existence, hence a vehicle for realizing it for ourselves'. Through 'endowing its referent with

---

29. Linda Layne, '"Your Child Deserves a Name": Possessive Individualism and the Politics of Memory in Pregnancy Loss', in Bodenhorn and vom Bruck, eds., *An Anthropology of Names and Naming*, 34.
30. Ibid., 36–7.
31. Ibid., 44.
32. Ibid., 43.
33. Ibid.
34. Ibid., 42.
35. Ibid., 46.
36. Michael Lambek, 'What's in a Name? Name Bestowal and the Identity of Spirits in Mayotte and Northwest Madagascar', in Bodenhorn and vom Bruck, eds., *An Anthropology of Names and Naming*, 118.

identity', the name 'fulfils a necessary, if not sufficient, condition for realizing that object as an entity'.[37] We can see acts of naming less in the context of giving a name to a person, than of 'conjoining of person with name'.[38] Due to its significance in the Genesis creation narrative concerning the relationship between man and woman, naming is of interest to feminist critics. Trible suggests: 'the act of naming, which can mean either power over an object or recognition of the object, requires the noun *name* joined to the verb *call*. Alone, the verb *call* does not signify naming.'[39] For example, Gen. 2.20 states ויקרא האדם שמות לכל־הבהמה (which, if we translate literally, reads 'and called *ha'adam* names to all the beast/cattle'). James Barr describes the naming of the woman in Gen. 2.23 as 'a cry of discovery, of recognition'.[40] The biblical text reads:

> This at last is bone of my bones
> and flesh of my flesh;
> this one shall be called Woman [לזאת יקרא אשה],
> for out of Man this one was taken [כי מאיש לקחה־זאת].

The name is joined to the *physical* substance of the person, in response to the internal recognition of the name-giver. Trible notes the formula used for the woman, for whom it is stated לזאת יקרא אשה, is different from the formula ויקרא האדם שמות, used for the animals. The act of recognition and the giving of the name calls into social relationship, while acknowledging difference: 'Because others name us, the act of naming has the potential to implicate infants in relations through which they become inserted into and, ultimately will act upon, a social matrix'.[41]

For Butler, the subject exists precisely by being distinguishable through the name, which draws it into bonds.[42] This corresponds to the change of name the woman of the creation narrative undergoes; it is not until calling her Eve that the Adam takes ownership of her.[43] Her name draws her into a social matrix that is now differently configured to express a new reality – that she is (according to some readings) under the dominion of the man, a kind of primordial symbolic violence of male domination.

---

37. Ibid., 119.
38. Ibid., 142.
39. Phyllis Trible, *God and the Rhetoric of Sexuality*, OBT 2 (Philadelphia: Fortress, 1978), 100.
40. Barr, 'Symbolism', 35.
41. Bodenhorn and Bruck, 'Entangled', 3.
42. Judith Butler, *Excitable Speech: A Politics of the Performative* (New York: Routledge, 1997), 29–30.
43. Trible, *God and the Rhetoric of Sexuality*, 134.

Joseph receives a new Egyptian name (Gen. 41.45), signifying a new identity within the Egyptian role. Warriors named conquered sites after themselves (Num. 32.41-42), and David notably calls his conquered Zion 'City of David' (2 Sam. 5.6-9). At times the deity takes over the naming of the child from the parents (Gen. 16.11; 17.19; Isa. 7.14; Jer. 23.6), or to signify a change in status, such as the giving of the name Abraham to Abram because he is to be 'the ancestor of a multitude of nations' (Gen. 17.5). Here, although agency is removed from Abraham, the name is imbued with social capital. Jacob is given the name Israel in recognition that he has struggled with God and human and prevailed (Gen. 32.28). In both these narratives it is after foundational and definitive events that the identity of the patriarchs is shifted through a change in the name, with de-naming and re-renaming akin to a re-personalization. The name 'comes to stand for the person, operating synecdochally to epitomize the essence of his or her being as well as his or her time'.[44] Name changes are expressive of changes in social status and social situation, and reflect the ability of names to embody the personalization of individual.[45] They are both fundamental to how we relate to one another, as well as our own identity – they allow us to operate in the social field and to negotiate our own and others place in it. Having established a context of the social importance of names, we will now move on to look at the *substance* of names, both human and divine.

4. *Excursus: God's Name*

Due to theological importance and relevance to understanding Deuteronomic theology, a great deal of scholarship has been applied to the meaning and function of YHWH's name, יהוה. YHWH's name is generally discussed separately from human names (though with some exceptions, such as Pedersen). However, as will be shown, there is arguably an overlap between the way the name of YHWH and the name of people are conceptualized. If, as will be shown, YHWH's name takes on a substantive reality, this may inform our discussion of human names. The ability of words and names to have potency in and of themselves can be seen in the text of the Sotah, in which details of the 'trial' of a woman suspected of adultery are given. Subjected to inquisition by her husband and the priest, the accused is dragged before the presence of YHWH, whereupon the priest says to the woman:

---

44. Lambek, 'What's in a Name?', 132.
45. Bloch, 'Teknonymy'.

> ...let the priest make the woman take the oath of the curse and say to the woman – 'the LORD make you an execration and an oath among your people, when the LORD makes your uterus drop, your womb discharge; now may this water that brings the curse enter your bowels and make your womb discharge, your uterus drop!' And the woman shall say, 'Amen. Amen'. (Num. 5.21-22)

After stating the curse, the priest writes it down on paper, and washes the words, which includes יהוה, off into 'the water of bitterness', transferring its potency into the liquid, which the woman is made to drink (vv. 23-34).[46] One may expect that the act, which could potentially end in discharge from the uterus or womb, would take place outside of the sacred space. However, the woman is both dragged before YHWH, and is made to digest his name. YHWH is both judge and punisher, with the divine name mediating the trial, showing agency in and of itself.

Most scholarship on the name of YHWH has grown from Gerhard von Rad's hypothesis that Deuteronomy is replacing the 'old crude' idea that YHWH resides physically at the temple with a 'theologically sublimated idea' that only his name resides in the temple, while his real self resides in heaven.[47] For example, in Deut. 12.11, the people are to bring sacrifices and tithes to 'the place that the LORD your God will choose as a dwelling for his name [לשכן שמו שם שמה]'. Von Rad suggests that the Deuteronomist is exercising YHWH's כבד (glory) from the temple as a polemical correction of the former 'crude' idea of God's actual presence. He suggests the name instead may be 'established in a particular place', the conception of which 'verges closely upon a hypostasis'.[48] This thesis has been reworked and nuanced, but the central tenets continue to reappear in scholarship.[49] In recent years, however, the thesis of name theology has, from a place of almost complete dominance, come under attack. Sandra Richter launches two critiques of name theology; her thesis is that לשכן שמו שם is a calque of the Akkadian expression *šuma šakānu*,[50]

---

46. Jack Sasson, 'Numbers 5 and the "Waters of Judgement"', in *Women in the Hebrew Bible: A Reader*, ed. Alice Bach (New York: Routledge, 1999), 484.

47. Gerhard von Rad, *Studies in Deuteronomy*, trans. David Stalker, SBT 9 (London: SCM, 1953), 39.

48. Ibid., 30.

49. Hurowitz recognizes that name theology is perceived by scholars as being *the* hallmark of Deuteronomy and the Deuteronomistic History: Hurowitz, 'Review of Sandra L. Richter'; Preuss, *Old Testament Theology*, 45; Albertz, *Israel in Exile*, 295; Schniedewind, 'The Evolution of Name Theology', 232–5.

50. A calque is a semantic borrowing without phonetic copying, such as the French *eau de vie* from the Latin *aqua vitae*.

which expresses not the presence of the thing named, but rather connotes symbolic ownership, particularly in the context of victories.[51] First, Richter rejects the paradigm of 'evolution', the move from primitive to developed religion,[52] including 'nominal realism' – the idea that the word is the same as the thing.[53] And yet, she does not fully articulate how terms *should* be understood that appear in biblical texts.[54] Her second attack on name theology is the idea of 'illegitimate totality transfer', the premise that a word in all its occurrences will not carry the same meaning,[55] interpreting the particular expression לשכן שמו שם as an idiom by transferring other meanings onto it.

It is odd that Richter at once critiqued 'illegitimate totality transfer' in the context of the Bible, yet in a sense applies it to her own analysis of the relation between the Deuteronomic Hebrew expression and the Akkadian *šuma šakānu*. William Morrow accepts the central tenet of a transmission from the Akkadian term to the Hebrew; however, he critiques the idea that the meaning of the term was passed down with its incorporation into Hebrew.[56] Moreover, there is no Akkadian instance of the gods attaching a name, and the Akkadian expressions carry a larger range of nuances than Richter is willing to express in her own work.[57] Morrow supposes instead that the term is best explained based on the native expression לשום שם, and suggests the range of meanings it carries are broad, and can include ideas of presence, ownership and fame.[58] Ian Wilson compares suggestions of divine presence in the Tetrateuch and Deuteronomy,[59] and finds

---

51. Sandra L. Richter, *The Deuteronomistic History and the Name Theology: Lešakkēn šemô šām in the Bible*, BZAW 318 (Berlin: de Gruyter, 2002).

52. Ibid., 8.

53. Ibid., 15–22.

54. Hundley further supports this contention, describing Richter's approach as 'unfinished': Hundley, 'To Be', 543.

55. Moisés Silva, *Biblical Words and Their Meaning: An Introduction to Lexical Semantics* (Grand Rapids, MI: Zondervan, 1983), 25.

56. Morrow, '"To Set the Name"', 374–8. This is based on potential routes of transmission, levels of Akkadian literacy (biblical scholars often state literacy levels in tension with Assyriologist's scepticism), the potential time periods the term would have been incorporated, and use of Aramaic as a diplomatic language, suggesting it would take a limited not robust knowledge of Akkadian to be familiar with the term.

57. Hundley, 'To Be', 545–6.

58. Morrow, '"To Set the Name"', 379–81.

59. Ian Wilson, *Out of the Midst of the Fire: Divine Presence in Deuteronomy*, SBLDS 151 (Atlanta, GA: Scholars Press, 1995), 211. He compares D with the Tetrateuch and finds several instances of divine presence in D which is absent in parallels elsewhere (Deut. 5.4-5, 23-27; 9.10, 12, 15-16).

an *affirmation* of divine presence in Deuteronomistic texts, where the allusions to divine presence are 'parallel in five instances, heightened in six, and absent only in two'.[60] Wilson's critique of traditional articulations of name theology suggests not that the dwelling of the name in the temple implies an 'evolution' from primitive religion, but that it allows to a far greater extent YHWH's presence of earth. Moreover, Michael Hundley suggests that the construction of a rigid cosmological distinction between heaven and earth is questionable – as he notes, clouds and birds are clearly associated with heaven.[61]

Morrow further responds to Richter with the phenomena of 'colonial mimicry', which involves 'cleaving' a colonial term's definition away, and simultaneously attaching the term to a different meaning. The use of the loan term could at once acknowledge Neo-Assyrian hegemony while also subverting it by attributing it to the local deity YHWH.[62] In its different occurrences, 'placing one's name shares a common basis; it ensures that the individual named gets whatever benefits are to be had, with the result that the individual named accrues certain obligations and consequences'.[63] Hundley suggests the that the Deuteronomistic History is too at ease the idea that language suggests presence to want to eradicate it entirely, arguing that such a transformation from earlier theologies would be an extreme departure, especially as nothing is articulated explicitly to suggest removal of presence.[64] Moreover, texts such as 1 Kgs 8.27 imply that the temple cannot contain YHWH, not that he does not dwell there.[65] Richter acknowledges that in other texts the name does appear to stand in for the deity, such as the name of God being protection (Ps. 20.1), or something to trust in (Ps. 33.21), where the divine name is the subject of devotion and agency. Within Deuteronomy itself we find the instruction to fear 'this glorious and awesome name, the LORD your God' (Deut. 28.58). Additionally, in Exod. 20.24 remembrance of the name and presence are connected, where in every place 'I cause my name to be remembered I will come to you and bless you'.

---

60. Wilson, *Out of the Midst*, 210. See also Hundley, 'To Be', 537–41.

61. Hundley, 'To Be', 539 n. 27. For example in some texts heaven is not depicted as a distinct reality: while riding, Absalom's head gets caught and we are told 'he was left hanging between heaven and earth [בין השמים ובין הארץ], while the mule that was under him went on' (2 Sam. 18.9). Hundley is referencing an argument made by Ziony Zevit at IOSOT 2007.

62. Morrow, '"To Set the Name"', 382.

63. Hundley, 'To Be', 534.

64. Ibid., 551. See 1 Kgs 8.

65. Ibid., 551 n. 27.

The שם serves to 'simultaneously guarantee YHWH's practical presence and to abstract the nature of that presence'.[66] According to Hundley,

> Like YHWH and his glory, the name and YHWH are so intimately allied that the two could be equated yet distinguishable enough that the one does not encapsulate the other... The name communicates that God attaches himself...to the temple, yet he does so without revealing the nature of his presence.[67]

Anthropological comparisons have the potential to suggest new ways of understanding the relationship between the individual and the name in the Hebrew Bible. Bodenhorn highlights the case of Iñupiaq communities living on Alaska's north slope:

> It seems to me that the problem of meaning must...recognize the possibility that names in a non-trivial way must *be* the things named (that is, they are the same, not the same as). They form a real identity...that goes beyond both connotation and denotation. Inupiaq names are meaningful because of who they are and what they do.[68]

Bodenhorn teases this out in his descriptions of the Iñupiaq question 'Who is your name?',[69] being deeply connected to the life force of the person.[70] Names can be so associated with the physical person that in Mongolian naming culture, the naming of sick children is avoided, and they are instead given names such as 'no-name', 'who knows', 'bad dog', 'smelly', 'not human'; once the link between the name and the name-bearer is broken, the one speaking the name can deflect the attention of the spirits who may want to attack the vulnerable.[71] Within this system 'there is presumed to be an identity between the person and their name, a connection so intimate that some people say that the name *is* the person'.[72]

---

66. Ibid., 552.
67. Ibid., 551, 553.
68. Barbara Bodenhorn, 'Calling into Being: Naming and Speaking Names on Alaska's North Slope', in Bodenhorn and vom Bruck, eds., *An Anthropology of Names and Naming*, 141.
69. Ibid., 140.
70. Caroline Humphrey, 'On Being Named and Not Named: Authority, Persons, and Their Names in Mongolia', in Bodenhorn and vom Bruck, eds., *An Anthropology of Names and Naming*, 159.
71. Ibid., 169.
72. Ibid., 160.

The name of an adult cannot be given to a child, as it would express the child is somehow 'the same' as him or her,[73] and the use of an older, powerful person's name is side-stepped due to the recognition that 'the name is a part of a person and that power is at issue'.[74] The tie between the name and the person is expressed through the respect it is due, and a series of taboos which surround it, especially when we consider the agency of names, as well as the fact that that the name 'often plays a critical role in the social life'.[75] Whereas titles can 'modulate and conceal', names can 'expose', and according to Michael Lambek this is why addressing by direct name, in many cultural contexts, can be considered rude or invasive.[76] For example, when we consider the intimacy between YHWH and the name in Exod. 3.13-15, where the name is revealed and its 'root' makes clear some sense of 'I Am' or being:

> But Moses said to God, 'If I come to the Israelites and say to them, "The God of your ancestors has sent me to you", and they ask me, "What is his name?" what shall I say to them?' God said to Moses, 'I AM WHO I AM' [אהיה אשר אהיה]. He said further, 'Thus you shall say to the Israelites, "I AM has sent me to you".' God also said to Moses, 'Thus you shall say to the Israelites, "The LORD, the God of your ancestors, the God of Abraham, the God of Isaac, and the God of Jacob, has sent me to you":
> This is my name for ever,
> and this my title for all generations.'

Slightly further through the narrative we read:

> God also spoke to Moses and said to him: 'I am the LORD. I appeared to Abraham, Isaac, and Jacob as God Almighty, but by my name "The LORD" [יהוה] I did not make myself known to them'. (Exod. 6.2-3)

The permanence of the deity expressed through his appearance to different patriarchs is now concretized in his name YHWH: it is forever and for all generations, and so attaches an identity to the deity. The text constructs a situation where a level of knowledge of God is hidden from the people, and it is not that YHWH is recognized through his name, but that somehow through the name he – himself – is known. Similarly, we read of the מלאך יהוה:

---

73. Ibid., 159.
74. Ibid.
75. Bodenhorn and Bruck, 'Entangled', 3.
76. Lambek, 'What's in a Name?', 122.

> Then Manoah said to the angel of the LORD, 'What is your name, so that we may honour you when your words come true?' But the angel of the LORD said to him, 'Why do you ask my name? It is too wonderful.' (Judg. 13.17-18)

The messenger repeatedly refuses to give his name, which is described as פלאי (wonderful, secret, incomprehensible), implying it is the fact of his status as other than human which leads to the exceptionality of his name. The name does something more than present itself, it expresses the 'existential "I"', and to invoke it unnecessarily is both rude and threatening but also violating and profaning.[77] If the name carries potency, rich in symbolic capital, and operates within a hierarchy of relationships – giving it a distinct advantage in playing the game of the field – the potency (mental, physical, ritual) dictates the appropriateness of its use.[78] We see this demonstrated in the taboo around blasphemy:

> The Israelite woman's son blasphemed the Name and cursed... The LORD spoke to Moses' saying... "Take him who cursed to outside the camp and then let lay all who heard him their hands on his head and let all the congregation stone him. And to the sons of Israel you shall speak, saying, whoever curses his God shall take their sin. And whoever blasphemes the name of YHWH surely shall be put to death, and all the congregation shall surely stone him – the stranger, as well as he who is born in the land, when he blasphemes the name shall be put to death. And whoever kills any life of a human surely shall be put to death. And he who kills the life of an animal shall make good, life for life. And if a man causes the disfigurement of his neighbour, as he has done so shall be done to him. Fracture for fracture, eye for eye, tooth for tooth; as he has caused disfigurement of a man so shall it be done to him. Whoever kills an animal shall make good, but whoever kills a man shall be put to death..." And Moses spoke to the sons of Israel and they took him who had cursed to outside the camp and stoned him with stones. (Lev. 24.11-23, author's translation)

The principle of *lex talionis* is invoked, and the narrative of the punishment for blasphemy is encased around this principle: the blaspheming of the name of YHWH is akin to the murder of the man, reinforcing the gravity of the act. The name only exists in its verbal or written form: to misuse its form takes the entirety of the name and distorts it; the punishment, equal to the crime, is death. Having outlined the relationship between YHWH's

---

77. Ibid., 129.
78. Humphrey, 'Being Named', 167.

name and being, and the arguments that YHWH's name is representative of YHWH's self, which can dwell and be feared and is an object of trust, this can now be compared to the importance of human names.

5. *Human Names*

The relative individuality of names in the Hebrew Bible is striking, and we do not find people named after major figures like Abraham, David, Ruth or Rachel.[79] We do have evidence that the ancient West Asian context was one that saw names as profoundly linked to the individual, often with what is classed as a 'magical' or at least performative role that can affect change.[80] As for the importance of the meanings of names, James Barr comments that a high proportion of names make assertions not about the one who bears the name but about God, such as Nathaniel, נתנאל, 'God has given a child'.[81] Barr also calls into question the literal etymologies given, such as whether Huldah of Josiah's reign was really thought to be like a 'mole-rat', or that Habakkuk symbolized the household plant 'ocimum basilicum'.[82] Barr notes that while 1 Sam. 25.25 suggests Nabal means 'churlish fool', this should not be indicative that his parents chose to name him 'churlish fool' and instead functions as a nickname.[83] We also find in material remains, as we move later into the Iron Age and closer to Jerusalem, a near-total absence of personal names compounded with theophoric elements other than YHWH or El.[84] In addition to this, Karel van der Toorn notes the occurrences of kinship terms (father, brother) in lieu of divine terms, such as Abinadab, Ahinadab or Jonadab, a phenomenon which he suggests is the kinship term functioning in place of the designation of a deity.[85] While van der Toorn suggests this is indicative of an ancestor cult,[86] it is also arguable that kinship elements in names could have served as a way to establish social connections

---

79. Barr, 'Symbolism', 12.
80. Hurowitz, 'Name Midrashim'.
81. Barr, 'Symbolism', 20.
82. Ibid., 21.
83. Ibid., 22–7.
84. See Richard Hess, 'Aspects of Israelite Personal Names and Pre-Exilic Israelite Religion', in *New Seals and Inscriptions, Hebrew, Idumean, and Cuneiform*, ed. Meir Lubetski, HBM 8 (Sheffield: Sheffield Phoenix, 2007), 301–13.
85. Karel van der Toorn, 'Ancestors and Anthroponyms: Kinship Terms as Theophoric Elements in Hebrew Names', *De-DE* 108, no. 1 (1996): 1.
86. For example, *Abiasaph*, 'The Father Has Added [a child to the family]'.

through generations and lineage systems, especially when we consider the frequency of patronymic descriptions in biblical texts. Moreover, while non-YHWHistic names declined, kinship elements in names did not, which suggests the continuing religious and social significance of kinship and family structures.[87]

The Hebrew word שם has semantic overtones of fame, honour and influence, suggesting nuances of power and capital. Rural villages of Hong Kong can offer us insight into how names connect with status and importance, and how a name is reflective of personhood. Individual men gain names throughout their lives, and, as they become people of higher social standing – at marriage, entry to a profession, or childbirth – their number of names increases. Women, however, remain mostly nameless,[88] losing their name when they reach marriage. If they fail to produce an heir, they even lose kinship terms,[89] becoming known merely as 'old woman'. Their lack of social importance, inheritance rights, and exclusion from genealogies, mean they are excluded from name-bearing and thus excluded from full personhood.[90] Full personhood is not acquired at birth, but is a process: 'In Ha Tsuen the ultimate goal of all males is to produce an heir, to have a grandson at one's funeral, to leave property that guarantees the performance of one's ancestral rites. The possession of many names testifies to the fact that a man has completed the cycle of life.' Personhood extends even beyond death as the named ancestor interacts with the living, increasing one's bind to society, becoming at once more integrated to social structures yet also more distinct.[91] However, neither process happens to peasant women, who in life as in death remain 'suspended between the anonymous world of anybodies and the more sharply defined world of somebodies'.[92]

Taking into account the concrete link between personhood and names, we can see how this applies in the act of remembrance, where remembrance of names is not described as casual or passive:

> So Aaron shall bear the names of the sons of Israel in the breastpiece of judgement on his heart when he goes into the holy place, for a continual remembrance before the Lord. (Exod. 28.29)

---

87. Van der Toorn, 'Ancestors and Anthroponyms', 11.
88. Rubie S. Watson, 'The Named and the Nameless: Gender and Person in Chinese Society', *American Ethnologist* 13, no. 4 (1986): 619.
89. Ibid., 627.
90. Ibid., 626.
91. Ibid., 627.
92. Ibid., 629.

The bearing of the names is – presumably – not to prevent God forgetting; instead, the names are necessary for the active representation and embodiment of the tribes of Israel, giving agency to the tribes and patriarchs. As with the men of rural Hong Kong, it is precisely by having names that their identity is materialized. This materialization becomes clearer if we borrow Lambek's theory on the naming of spirit, where he recognizes the realization of the spirit as dialectic between embodiment on the one hand, and objectification on the other:

> The embodied qualities of spirits are manifest in the experience of possession for the host and onlookers, their appearance in dreams, and their impact on wellbeing in daily life. Yet because their embodiment is contingent and unstable, the objectification by means of names is even more critical in realizing their identity as persons than is the case for human persons.[93]

Considering the material existence of spirits is contingent, it is through the objectification brought about by the naming that the embodiment can become stable, and through identification and differentiation of the spirit from the 'other' that continuity between events is achieved. Lambek continues:

> The constitutive function of names is surely strongest in delineating noumenal beings, creatures who are primarily unembodied or not 'in focus'…until they have been named. Names help to *realize* spirits: noumenal beings are brought to sustained human attention and become relatively fixed in their names, such that we may speak of an identity relation, in part through the process of naming.[94]

Naming allows us to distinguish individuals who are not bodily present from others, and to attribute identity to them. By inscribing the tribes of Israel, Aaron is not simply reminding YHWH of their existence but is carving out and fixing them. Thanks to the detachability of the name from the body, names create connections with the individual but also allow for social communication across boundaries. We need the names of the dead, spirits and deities because as entities we can only envisage them partially or as ambiguously embodied: names allow us a level of permanence, of identity, we would find hard to formulate otherwise. Considering the social importance of naming, the naming of spirits suggests that there is capacity for social relations with, and the exercise of power upon, those

---

93. Lambek, 'What's in a Name?', 127.
94. Ibid., 118.

not physically present. By establishing permanence through a name, the speaker is establishing continuity and the capacity for commitment and reciprocity.[95] Names of the dead are in many communities not to be mentioned, since doing so brings their unsettling presence too close to the living.[96] For some Mongolian groups: 'the calling out of one's name inevitably attracts one's attention and it is somehow injurious to seniors to compel them in this way… [If they call on the ancestors it will cause] their bones to ring out.'[97] The uncontrolled use is thought to 'hit' the ancestors' names and is to be done with caution.[98] The remembrance of the name maintains personhood, identity and continuity; it is deeply connected to the person. It appears to allow a form of even partial materiality to a disembodied being. However, its detachability can cross boundaries, particularly the boundaries between the living and the dead. Having established this, we can now see how names are used to perpetuate the existence of the dead and the legitimacy of the community.

6. *The Matrix of Names, Descendants, and the Dead*

The Genesis narratives establish genealogical relationships between the patriarchs based around their names:

> I will make of you a great nation [לגוי גדול], and I will bless you, and make your name great [ואגדלה שמך], so that you will be a blessing. (Gen. 12.2)

This promise is continued through the narrative, with Jacob stating of his children:

> …and in them let my name be perpetuated, and the name of my ancestors Abraham [ויקרא בהם שמי ושם אבתי אברהם] and Isaac; and let them grow into a multitude on the earth'. (Gen. 48.16)

In this second text, the primary link between the 'multitude' and the name remains; however, an additional dynamic is brought in, one between Jacob's name and the original promise to Abraham's name. The text constructs a genealogy which links the names of the patriarchs as symbolic of their lineage and descendants; through the multitude, the name of Jacob is perpetuated, but this has the effect of also influencing Abraham and

---

95. Ibid., 127.
96. Bloch, 'Teknonymy', 109.
97. Humphrey, 'Being Named', 167.
98. Ibid.

Isaac's name: the text presupposes the importance of descendants as the vital mechanism in perpetuating ancestral names. This occurs at times in other texts, for example:

> Thus David son of Jesse reigned over all Israel. (1 Chron. 29.26)[99]

The label 'son of Jesse' clearly does not act as an identifying mark – David having already been well established within the narrative – but implies that for at least one generation the father's name is still invoked.

This capacity of names to transmit identities, crossing the boundaries of death, is prominent in many cultures. In the Orokaiva name system, of Papua New Guinea, the transmission of names is indispensable for staying catastrophes. This is achieved by keeping the gap between the primordial time and the present wide.[100] If there are no children, the individual 'invests' their name somewhere in the group, to prevent disappearance.[101] They do not expect to be individually recalled, but expect that once their memory has faded, their name will remain by being circulated within the community. By passing on a name, therefore, their name is prolonged in time beyond the capacity of personal memory.[102] The name retains a social life of its own above and beyond that of the person it represents, concurrently subsuming the person into the life it maintains. This success relies heavily on the successful establishment of a prosperous village and a lineage of offspring, creating a 'big name' that will be transmitted to his sons. However, if those he leaves fail to prosper as he did, the names are more likely to be forgotten.[103] If they fail, the genealogy of 'big names' shortens and the present community slips further back towards the apical time and ancestors – a time of cannibalism, incest, strife between animals and people and an absence of cultivation and prosperity.[104] This establishment of a chain that crosses time is interrupted if the individual fails to produce children. Accordingly, the village has a series of strategies, manipulating horizontal and vertical relations – manipulation of kinship ties, child and village initiation – to ensure durability and social

---

99. See also 1 Chron. 10.14; Ps. 72.20.
100. André Iteanu, 'Why the Dead Do Not Bear Names: The Orokaiva Name System', in Bodenhorn and vom Bruck, eds., *An Anthropology of Names and Naming*, 69.
101. Ibid., 64.
102. Ibid., 59.
103. Ibid.
104. Ibid., 60.

continuity.¹⁰⁵ Here the importance of ensuring a proper genealogical succession is highlighted through its role in securing social structures. If we turn again to Saul's request of David in 1 Sam. 24.21, we see that to cut off Saul's line would not only wipe out his name, but would compromise his father's house, which was already established and transmitted through genealogical descent. While the symbolic capital of names has notably become integrated with Saul's habitus, this habitus has also incorporated the structures of power and reproduction of his father's house and status. Saul's lineage transcends his future (his descendants), his present self (his name) and his past (his father's house). For Saul, as for the Orokavia, the continuation of the name is not solely a self-interested strategy, but one that is necessary for the protection of a lineage system, and so individual and collective interests touch.

As with ideal and non-ideal forms of burial, there is an idealized form of naming, as well as the non-ideal removal of names. Jeremiah 11 begins with a prophetic warning, which invokes, repeatedly, the ancestors of the community addressed. We are told the community of Anathoth seeks the life of Jeremiah, saying:

> ...Let us destroy the tree with its fruit,
> let us cut him off from the land of the living [לנכרתני מארץ חיים],
> so that his name will no longer be remembered [ושמו לא־יזכר עוד]! (Jer. 11.19)

YHWH responds that he will punish them, their sons and daughters, so that 'not even a remnant shall be left of them...' (Jer. 11.22-33). The tree and fruit symbolize the descendants and the seed of Jeremiah,¹⁰⁶ and the remembrance of the name can be seen explicitly linked with existence in the land of the living. If the name is extinguished the mechanism of contact between the two realms of the living and the dead is broken; without the ability of the name to cross the social boundary, Jeremiah would be lost. In Isaiah 14, Isaiah seeks to administer justice and prophesies nothing less than the complete destruction of the Babylonian kings *after* their death:

---

105. Ibid., 61.
106. Jer. 16.2 subsequently sees God instructing Jeremiah not to marry or have children, due to the calamities which will befall that place: the children and parents will die, they will not be lamented, nor be buried, and will be as 'dung' on the ground, their bodies to be eaten by wild animals.

> Sheol…rouses the shades to greet you,
>> all who were leaders of the earth…
>> 'You too have become as weak as we are!…
> Your pomp is brought down to Sheol,…
>> maggots are the bed beneath you,
>> and worms are your covering…
> You said in your heart,
>> 'I will ascend to heaven…
> But you are brought down to Sheol,
>> to the depths of the Pit…
> Those who see you will stare at you,
>> and ponder over you:
> 'Is this the man who made the earth tremble,
>> who shook kingdoms,
> who made the world like a desert
>> and overthrew its cities,
>> who would not let his prisoners go home?'
> All the kings of the nations lie in glory,
>> each in his own tomb;
> but you are cast out, away from your grave…
>> like a corpse trampled underfoot.
> You will not be joined with them in burial,
>> because you have destroyed your land,
>> you have killed your people.
> May the descendants of evildoers
>> nevermore be named!
> Prepare slaughter for his sons
>> because of the guilt of their father.
> Let them never rise to possess the earth
>> or cover the face of the world with cities.
> I will rise up against them, says the Lord of hosts, and will cut off from Babylon name and remnant, offspring and posterity [והכרת לבבל שם ושאר ונין ונכד], says the LORD. (Isa. 14.9-22)

Sheol will hold for them a reversal of their worldly power and here they shall join the other dead to be powerless. The disruption of burial is symbolically connected with the destruction of name and descendants. Their descendants are not to be named, destroyed for the guilt of their fathers; their personhood is erased, and the king's post-mortem existence is to be distinguished. Their claim to land and cities is denied, and YHWH will cut off from Babylon 'name and remnant, offspring and posterity'. This is nothing less than complete annihilation of the person, from their corpse to their integration with the community of the dead, to their social existence through the sons who take their place, transmit their name and keep them in remembrance. Descendants, the name and the afterlife are interconnected; the name can be used as a tool to perpetuate the dead, and its eradication can be used to destroy them and their community. As an aspect of a person which can transcend the boundaries between the living and the dead, the name forms part of the substantive existence of the deceased in the social world of the living, one that relies critically on procreation and lineage. This is highlighted by narratives that suggest that it is possible to manipulate either the endurance of continuity (such as Saul begging David, 1 Sam. 20.20-21) or the eradication of continuity (Isa. 14.9-22). Therefore, the importance of responding to childless death through mechanisms such as levirate marriage, which renegotiate the social reality left by mortality, can be further contextualized as part of a wider discourse.

7. *Social Memory*

The past is used in the present to understand identity and heritage. According to Paul Connerton,

> We experience our present world in a context which is causally connected with past events and objects, and hence with reference to events and objects which we are not experiencing when we are experiencing the present. And we will experience our present differently in accordance with the different past to which we are able to connect that present.[107]

It is at this site of interaction that our personal and social memories are brought into expression – the past and present constantly redefine each other. In the social context where memory is 'shared and articulated it becomes a "social fact"'.[108] Social memory, however, is not stable as information, but, 'rather, at the level of shared meanings and remembered images'.[109] Here, on the one hand, social memory defines the simplest of social interactions and gestures: how we greet one another or dine together. On the other, it underpins our social cohesion and its malleability allows it to become a social tool.[110] This political nature of memory may

---

107. Paul Connerton, *How Societies Remember*, Themes in the Social Sciences (Cambridge: Cambridge University Press, 1989), 2.

108. John Tosh, 'Reviewed Work: Social Memory by James Fentress, Chris Wickham', *Social History* 19, no. 1 (1994): 130–1.

109. Ibid.

110. Athalya Brenner and B. O. Long, 'Introduction', in *Performing Memory in Biblical Narrative and Beyond*, ed. Athalya Brenner and Frank H. Polak, BMW 25 (Sheffield: Sheffield Phoenix, 2010), 4.

not rely on living memory, but leaders may (literally) dig up evidence from the past that was not of significance at the time, in order to shape the present.[111] Social memory is not egalitarian, with different (and often privileged) groups attempting to shape the way we collectively view the world, both codifying official histories that record one group's social memory, while also attempting to eliminate alternatives.[112] This can be enacted at the level of state or nation, but can also function on a household or lineage level.[113] It legitimates 'a present social order', and in order to participate in this social order, one must 'presuppose a shared memory'.[114] According to Connerton, what binds together memories is not the fact that they are contiguous in time, but that they form part of 'a whole ensemble of thoughts common to a group',[115] and the memories of the individual and group are negotiated.[116]

Connerton suggests we find social memory in action in the existence of commemorative ceremonies, but he defines these ceremonies as commemorative only in so far as they are performative, involving habit, which he argues cannot 'be thought without a notion of bodily automatisms'.[117] Commemoration inhabits not just one's mental faculties but the body and materiality, through which the community is 'reminded of its identity as represented' by a 'master narrative', a collective autobiography.[118] Collective memories are something in addition to personal and cognitive memory – to be persuasive involves habituation and bodily performance.[119] This background on memory is useful for our purposes, as the recitation of names is not just an act of memory but is also 'an active not-forgetting, that validates the present order'.[120] Names do not just tell stories but construct a master narrative. Memory and names are deeply intertwined tools, and these take place not just at the cognitive level, but at the symbolic and physical level. Names, spoken or remembered, inhabit the same symbolic landscape as funerary monuments or tombs as markers of land and identity. This notion of active not-forgetting will now be contrasted with the active blotting out of a name: Amalek.

111. Charles Golden, 'Where Does Memory Reside, and Why Isn't It History?', *American Anthropologist* 107, no. 2 (2005): 272.
    112. Ibid., 271.
    113. Ibid., 272.
    114. Connerton, *Societies*, 3.
    115. Ibid., 36.
    116. Golden, 'Where Does Memory Reside?', 271.
    117. Connerton, *Societies*, 4.
    118. Ibid., 70.
    119. Ibid., 71.
    120. Bodenhorn and Bruck, 'Entangled', 2.

Two particularly enigmatic passages deal with the issue of forced extermination of a memory:

> Then the LORD said to Moses, 'Write this as a reminder in a book and recite it in the hearing of Joshua: I will utterly blot out the remembrance of Amalek from under heaven'. (Exod. 17.14)

> Therefore when the LORD your God has given you rest from all your enemies...you shall blot out the remembrance of Amalek from under heaven; do not forget. (Deut. 25.19)

Diana Lipton suggests the context of these two texts as further demonstrative of their point: Exod. 17.8-16 uses the term יד (hand, memorial, phallus) in the context of a memorial banner, and the Deuteronomy passage comes immediately after reference to a יד and אבן, reminiscent of memorial stones.[121] Moreover, Deut. 25:19 occurs after the passage on levirate marriage and the commandment to raise the name of the dead, that his name may not be blotted out of Israel. It is in the strangeness of the text – forgetting by remembering – that the relationship between erasure and presence is explored.[122] These texts take on a performative role, invoking 'the efficacious power of language'.[123] Elsewhere the physical name is associated with existence and erasure with non-existence:

> 'But now, if you will only forgive their sin—but if not, blot me out of the book that you have written'. But the LORD said to Moses, 'Whoever has sinned against me I will blot out of my book...' (Exod. 32.32-33)

> ...Let me alone that I may destroy them and blot out their name from under heaven; and I will make of you a nation mightier and more numerous than they. (Deut. 9.14)[124]

---

121. Diana Lipton, 'Remembering Amalek: A Positive Biblical Model for Dealing with Negative Scriptural Types', in *Reading Texts, Seeking Wisdom: Scripture and Theology*, ed. Graham Stanton and David F. Ford (London: SCM, 2003), 151.

122. Brian M. Britt, 'Erasing Amalek: Remembering to Forget with Derrida and the Biblical Tradition', in *Derrida's Bible: Reading a Page of Scripture with a Little Help from Derrida*, ed. Yvonne Sherwood, Religion/culture/critique (New York: Palgrave Macmillan, 2004), 63.

123. Ibid., 63.

124. See also 2 Kgs 14.27; Deut. 7.24; 12.3; 29.20; Judg. 21.17; 1 Sam. 24.21; Pss. 9.5; 69.28; 109.13.

Each text uses מחה (to blot, destroy, wipe away), a term which also occurs in Neh. 4.5 with reference to the blotting away of sins, Gen. 7.23, in relation to the blotting away of living things during the flood, and Judg. 21.17, which speaks of the blotting away of an entire tribe of Israel. Here we see two loci for the existence of the names: Exodus supposes a book, a text that records the names of people, and Deuteronomy suggests a presence of the names in the human world 'under heaven', suggesting a relationship between the textual recording of a name and the social existence of a name. Brian Britt suggests that negation and affirmation are always connected, and it is through the establishment of a name that the threat of the eradication is understood.[125] In order to actively blot out the name, the blotting-out must be remembered. The Phoenician inscription of Azatiwada, dating from the end of the eighth or beginning of the seventh century reads:

> Now if a king among kings or a prince among princes, if a man, who is a man of renown, who shall erase the name of Azatiwada from this gate, and shall place (his) name (on it);
> if indeed he shall covet this city, and shall tear away this gate, which Azatiwada has made, or shall make for himself a different gate, and place (his) name on it; if from covetousness he shall tear (it) away; if from hate or from evil he shall tear away this gate;
> then shall Ba'al Shamem and El, creator of the earth, and Shemesh, the eternal, and the whole group of the children of the gods erase that kingdom, and that king, and that man who is a man of renown.
> Only may the name of Azatiwada be forever like the name of the sun and the moon![126]

The text, which follows an account of Azatiwada's life and his great achievements, places a curse on any who would remove the name of Azatiwada from the gate which he had built. This in itself is significant, yet the text ends with the expressed wish that only the name of Azatiwada would 'be forever like the name of the sun and the moon!' We see the name take on an abstracted form and seek immortality, symbolized by the sun and moon expressing eternity.[127] This text is complemented by a significant number of other West-Semitic curses which deal with

---

125. Britt, 'Erasing Amalek', 63.
126. III.12–IV.3, translation in K. L. Younger, 'The Phoenician Inscription of Azatiwada: An Integrated Reading', *JSS* 43, no. 1 (1998): 11–47.
127. Younger, 'The Phoenician Inscription of Azatiwada', 28.

preventing the removal of the name of the one inscribed, and destruction of the stele which memorialize them.[128]

While not offering a solution to the puzzle of Amalek, Britt raises the question:

> Biblical curses of erasure, in other words, take familiar customs to a new level by incorporating them in a growing biblical tradition constituted largely by recitation, ritual, and commentary. The question is how such speech and writing are understood: is the curse on Amalek an efficacious speech act that somehow *performs* the erasure of this people, and if so, what are its ontological implications?

Schmidt discusses Ugaritic ritual, which comprised commemoration which both sustained the memory of the dead in the minds of the living (individual and community), and legitimatized living claims to birthright and land ownership.[129] Central to this is the public recitation of names of the dead, which lie at the heart of the mortuary rites of the elites of Ugarit. These seek to perpetuate the dead's memory and the maintenance of the dead's genealogical ties.[130] RS 24.257[131] lists kings, each associated with their dynastic god, and RS 34.126,[132] a funerary text, calls on dead kings below to await the arrival of the deceased weak and frail king.[133] The liturgy served not necessarily as worship of the dead but as a balance to any social loss the dead may have suffered.[134] Importantly, however, through the recitation of the names and the restoration of the dead the community could also legitimate their interests. The consequence of the destruction of the name articulated by the anthropologist Roy Rappaport:

---

128. Stanley Gevirtz, 'West-Semitic Curses and the Problem of the Origins of Hebrew Law', *VT* 11, no. 2 (1961): 137–58. See also the infamous account of Thutmose III erasing the name of Hatshepsut from inscriptions, which was also understood to correspond to a destruction in the afterlife; see David B. O'Connor, 'Thutmose III: An Enigmatic Pharaoh', in *Thutmose III: A New Biography*, ed. Eric H. Cline and David B. O'Connor (Ann Arbor, MI: University of Michigan Press, 2006), 33.

129. Schmidt, 'Memory as Immortality', 94.

130. Ibid.

131. Nick Wyatt, *Religious Texts from Ugarit: The Words of Ilimilku and His Colleagues*, 2nd ed., BibSem 53 (London: Sheffield Academic, 2002), 399–403.

132. Dennis Pardee, *Ritual and Cult at Ugarit*, WAW 10 (Atlanta, GA: Society of Biblical Literature, 2002), 85–8.

133. Schmidt, 'Memory as Immortality', 85.

134. Ibid., 95.

> That is, a performative expression which in its liturgical utterance establishes some cosmic entity, quality or power as a social or cultural fact makes it subsequently possible to construe that self-same expression as a statement. To establish God's existence as a social fact through the ritual recitation of, say, the *Shema*, makes it immediately possible to interpret the sentence 'The Lord Our God, the Lord Is One' as a report or description of a state of affairs existing independently of the sentence or, at least, any instance of its utterance. Such a construction is, of course, validated by the enduring public nature of the Ultimate Sacred Postulates. None of those who have recited the *Shema* in the last 3,000 years or so has enunciated it *de novo*. They have been reiterating a formula which had established the One God long before they were born. Ultimate Sacred Postulates thus appear as statements to those who give voice to them.

That is, due to over familiarity, we interpret acts as fundamentally descriptive not performative. However:

> Their ultimately performative grounding nevertheless becomes clear when the effects of the cessation of their liturgical expression is considered. If no one any longer recited the *Shema*, 'The Lord our God the Lord is One' would cease to be a social fact, whatever the supernatural case might be. As far as present day society is concerned, Jupiter, Woden, En-Lil, and Marduk are no longer anything more than figments of ancient imaginings, for no one continues to establish or re-establish their being by calling their names in ritual.[135]

Thus, when we recognize the performative nature of perpetuating the name of the dead we see its importance in keeping the activity of the person (individual, social, religious) vibrant. The evidence then begins to suggest that what occupied thought and action was the perpetuation of the name. Great effort went into ensuring 'the family name epitomized by the multigenerational graves containing the bones of family dead and located on family land would never be neglected, let alone forgotten'.[136] By rituals, legal channels and social norms, names become preserved 'from oblivion' and avoid the death after death.[137]

---

135. Roy A. Rappaport, *Ritual and Religion in the Making of Humanity* (Cambridge: Cambridge University Press, 1999), 297.
136. Schmidt, 'Memory as Immortality', 99.
137. Ibid.

8. Conclusion

Having established a theoretical context for discussing names and naming – one which emphasizes the performative function of names and their ability to draw separate entities into relationship – we surveyed biblical texts which explored the importance of names and naming to form personhood and create dynamics of power, imbuing individuals and social relationships with symbolic capital. Having established the performative aspect of names, this allowed us to review scholarship on name theology and reassess the influential work of Richter, whose work attempted to downplay an aspect of 'presence' from Deuteronomistic language of YHWH's name dwelling in the temple; it was argued, however, that YHWH's name reflects a concrete attachment to the deity, emphasized by taboos around the use of his name. Rather than disconnecting this from discussion of human names, I have suggested that both could form part of a wider name discourse in which rather than descriptors, names play a concretizing social role, making the named present; it allows them to operate over various fields, to negotiate and renegotiate their place on the field. The particularity of the detachability of names allows for the representation of beings that are not present corporally. Likewise, the importance of transmitting names through descendants is highlighted, as demonstrated by looking at texts that posit the transmission of names as essential in ensuring the post-mortem vitality of the deceased. Moreover, those in positions of power can exert symbolic violence, manipulating lines of descent to eradicate the transmission of the name.

Having established this, it is possible to understand the importance of responding to childless death. According to the work of Rappaport, the remembering and the recitation of names in a tangible way ensure the social continuity of the individual: and so the threat to eradicate the name of the deceased can be understood in all its terror. Here the importance of names can be seen as being internalized in a habitus, as with those who protest the destruction of their name. Moreover, the capital attached to names in the field relates not just to the individual, but to their ancestors and progeny, and so the place of names is constantly negotiated and fought over.

The importance attached to a name and to offspring becomes politicized, rendering it a tool for erasing identity and personhood, which at once destroys the memory and therefore the social life of the individual, and at the same time de-legitimizes the social order. However, the reverse is true: the establishment of the name, such as the name of the patriarchs in Gen. 48.16, in which the name is perpetuated through descendants, means that the establishment of a name and the proliferation of progeny bolsters power and reinforces patriarchal structures and norms. The patriarchal nature is especially seen in the repeated gendered emphasis: the texts are concerned with the name of the male and father, most commonly safeguarded by the production of sons. This will be demonstrated in the next chapter through texts which emphasize male reproduction through the use of women's bodies and sexualities; through this, we will see how the text valorizes gender roles and creates secure modes of transmission for male lines. We will also witness how the female habitus reproduces these structures of power.

Chapter 5

KINSHIP: REPRODUCTION AND SEXUALITY

Our texts deal with what I am arguing is seen as a failure in male reproduction: a man dying before producing a child or son. To trace why responses to childlessness are gendered, it is necessary to see how biblical texts articulate kinship, reproduction, and male and female difference. Texts construct gendered bodies into doxic sexual roles, and these sexual roles play into larger patriarchal structures of power – structures which, I will argue, insist on male reproduction and the continuation of the family line to perpetuate the social order, a kind of 'reproductive futurism'. Discourses of sex – from reproductive technology, questions of adultery, or the phenomenon of celibacy – are always discourses that bring an actor or a body into relations. For example, a comparative study of infertility treatments in the Middle East and Mexico demonstrates how male infertility, more than a failure of masculine roles, compromises the man's ability to form expected bonds within his kinship group, whether in his ability to procreate or to satisfy sexual partners.[1] It is by understanding the sexual field at work across the biblical texts we are looking at, that we can understand the failings of male childlessness, the dramatic loss of capital, and the failure to maintain ideas of kinship. Furthermore, we can understand texts dealing with childlessness not as responding to a sentimental desire for children, but as responding to a failure to play the game, and fulfil one's role in the patriarchal system. We are also able to see how the text presents as natural a female habitus which has at its core a desire to produce children for men. This requires us to ask questions about kinship in the Bible, and to explore how this gender dynamic is played out in narrative and legal material which construct and regulate sexuality.

1. Marcia C. Inhorn and Emily Wentzell, 'The Male Reproductive Body: Reproducing Masculinities through Sexual/Reproductive Medicine in the Middle East and Mexico', in *A Companion to the Anthropology of Bodies and Embodiment*, ed. Frances E. Mascia-Lees (New York: Wiley-Blackwell, 2011), 307–19.

1. *Anthropological Approaches to Kinship and Sexuality*

Kinship, as suggested, underlies understandings of sex and reproduction, that sex and reproduction do not exist in isolation but bring people into social relationship. Kinship studies, once a staple of anthropology, underwent a crisis in the 1980s in large part due to David Schneider's *A Critique of the Study of Kinship*,[2] a work which undermined the notion of the universality of kinship and the projection of Western (Anglo-American) notions of biological kinship, primarily consanguinity, onto profoundly different societies. For example, early anthropologists discuss an 'ignorance of paternity' among certain social groups who 'failed' to recognize biological understandings of paternity.[3] Edmund Leach, for instance, in 'Virgin Birth', describes paternity as a kind of observable fact.[4] Carol Delaney suggests paternity or kinship was understood purely in terms of Western 'knowledge' that did not recognize that kinship can be configured in different ways.[5] An example of a radically different structure of kinship can be found in Raymond Kelly's ethnography on the Etoro of Papua New Guinea, demonstrating how sexual relations can be understood in terms of its relation to an entire system of thought. For the Etoro, social life is organized around communities living in longhouses together, and men and women sharing separate areas. The life-force, or *hame*, of the man is concentrated in the semen, and the *hame* the man expends in intercourse augments the nascent *hame* implanted by the ancestral spirits in the womb of the woman. Consequently, the *hame* of the man is expended each time sexual intercourse takes place – the loss of *hame* contributing to the demise and eventual death of the man. Because of this, male–female sexual relations are severely restricted, taking place for only around 100 days of the year, and only in the wooded area far away from the communal centre. However, to gain life force, young men must gain *hame* through pederastic relationships and the oral ingestion of semen from the older men, without which they cannot grow to maturity. However, here sex and reproduction are not isolated facets of social life: in this system sexual relations and witchcraft are integrated into a highly

---

2. David Murray Schneider, *A Critique of the Study of Kinship* (Ann Arbor, MI: University of Michigan Press, 1984).

3. Patrick Heady and Peter Loizos, 'Introduction', in *Conceiving Persons: Ethnographies of Procreation, Fertility and Growth*, ed. Patrick Heady and Peter Loizos (London: Continuum, 2003), 2.

4. Edmund Leach, 'Virgin Birth', *Proceedings of the Royal Anthropological Institute of Great Britain and Ireland* (1966): 39–49.

5. Carol Delaney, 'The Meaning of Paternity and the Virgin Birth Debate', *Man* 21, no. 3 (1986): 494–513.

complex matrix of sexual and food taboos. Pederastic relations in the Etoro community take place *despite* the risk of *hame hah hah* (the loss of life) because of the supreme importance of passing something on. The example of the Etoro demonstrates how a rare way of conceiving sex actually functions within a broader discourse which takes into account other areas of social life, and emphasizes the bodily and material constitution of kinship.[6]

Although Schneider's critique had become synonymous with the 'death of kinship', there has been a revival of kinship studies in the past decade, both rejecting the traditional model as well as the complete denial of kinship by Schneider.[7] This approach, influenced by feminist criticism,[8] acknowledges the fluidity and diversity of kinship relations within and between contexts, and has drawn on changing dynamics of family life in Europe and North America, such as reproductive technology, the instability of the nuclear family, and the LGBT movement.[9] Newer kinship work should cause us to question our understandings of relations within the Bible, how those relations are formed, and the obligations those relations bring. The predominant approach among anthropologists now is that kinship does not

---

6. Raymond Kelly, *Constructing Inequality: The Fabrication of a Hierarchy of Virtue among the Etoro* (Ann Arbor, MI: University of Michigan Press, 1993), 149–57, 521–3. This more recent work is based on his original ethnography: Raymond Kelly, 'Witchcraft and Sexual Relations: An Exploration in the Social and Semantic Implications of the Structure of Belief', in *Man and Woman in the New Guinea Highlands*, ed. Paula Brown, Georgeda Buchbinder, and David Maybury-Lewis (Washington, DC: American Anthropological Association, 1976), 36–53. While Kelly's work is with the Etoro community, similar practices have been recorded throughout Papua New Guinea and Vanuatu; for a survey of studies see: Michael Allen, 'Male Cults Revisited: The Politics of Blood Versus Semen', *Oceania* 68, no. 3 (1998): 189–99.

7. Heady and Loizos, 'Introduction', 7.

8. See, for example, the work of Gayle Rubin, 'The Traffic in Women: Notes on the "Political Economy" of Sex', in *Toward an Anthropology of Women*, ed. Rayna R. Reiter (Routledge: Monthly Review Press, 1975), 157–210.

9. For new approaches which incorporate Schneider, see: Sarah Franklin and Susan McKinnon, eds., *Relative Values: Reconfiguring Kinship Studies* (Durham, NC: Duke University Press, 2001); Marilyn Strathern, *Reproducing the Future: Essays on Anthropology, Kinship and the New Reproductive Technologies* (Manchester: Manchester University Press, 1992); Mary Jo Maynes et al., eds., *Gender, Kinship, Power: A Comparative and Interdisciplinary History* (New York: Routledge, 1996); Elisa J. Sobo and Sandra Bell, eds., *Celibacy, Culture, And Society: Anthropology of Sexual Abstinence* (Madison, WI: University of Wisconsin Press, 2001); Patrick Heady and Peter Loizos, eds., *Conceiving Persons: Ethnographies of Procreation, Fertility and Growth* (London: Continuum, 2003).

have its 'base in nature',[10] and moreover, that 'cultural ideas of reproductive biology must necessarily vary in a way that corresponds to differing systems of kinship'.[11] However, this nuanced biological understanding itself has come under attack: non-biological means of relations can at times override biological, as in most cases a series of competing and coexisting metaphors are manifest at one time.[12] Within a given system, a form of 'performative kinship' can be more dominant than a substantial (e.g. blood) kinship: here concepts of 'doing' over 'being' dominate.[13] Crucially, there will be 'unresolved tension' within each and every structure, so attempts to comprehensively explain a particular kinship system will always fail.[14] Even within highly patrilineal controlled societies, there are legal recourses to deal with the tensions that are inherent in these structures, such as lack of an heir.[15] Kinship systems are seen as a 'classificatory technology', which signify both connection but also 'disconnection and exclusion', as well as the inevitable boundary-crossing which 'confound such classifications'; and, since as a technology it is imbued with relations of power, 'kinship is also utilized to articulate the possibilities for social relations of equality, hierarchy, amity, ambivalence and violence'.[16] Between anthropological theory and practice is the space in which lives are lived out, and this site, this 'paradox', is one of the places where feminist criticism can best manifest,[17] pointing out 'the ruptures, gaps, elisions' in any discourse of bodies, kinship or reproduction.[18]

While practices such as marriage brokering may be presented with a certain amount of uniformity, ethnographies demonstrate a diversity of practices in all societies.[19] Understanding the negotiated nature of

10. Sarah Franklin and Susan McKinnon, 'Introduction', in Franklin and McKinnon, eds., *Relative Values*, 2.

11. Heady and Loizos, 'Introduction', 5.

12. Ibid., 6–9.

13. Philip Thomas, 'No Substance, No Kinship? Procreation, Performativity and Temanambondro Parent-Child Relations', in Heady and Loizos, eds., *Conceiving Persons*, 39–41.

14. Heady and Loizos, 'Introduction', 15.

15. Ann Waltner, 'Kinship between the Lines: The Patriline, the Concubine, and the Adopted Son in Late Imperial China', in Maynes et al., eds., *Gender, Kinship, Power*, 71.

16. Franklin and McKinnon, 'Introduction', 15.

17. Strathern, *Reproducing the Future*, 94.

18. Ibid., 65.

19. Cynthia R. Chapman, 'The Biblical "House of the Mother" and the Brokering of Marriage: Economic Reciprocity Among Natal Siblings', in *In the Wake of Tikva Frymer-Kensky*, ed. Steven Holloway, JoAnn Scurlock, and Richard Beal, Gorgias Précis Portfolios 4 (Piscataway, NJ: Gorgias, 2009), 162.

kinship is highly informative for an analysis of levirate marriage, in which 'everyday' forms of kinship have failed, and alternative forms of reproduction are utilized; this is compounded when we consider that even within sanctioned or articulated forms of kinship there will nevertheless be methods with which to 'play the game'. Contemporary anthropology has highlighted alternative or negotiated kinship, such as reproductive technologies, as a site at which our desire to separate nature and culture, as fixed categories, is brought into question. Ethnographies of reproductive technologies demonstrate that as soon as tension in our understanding becomes apparent, 'the choreography between the natural and cultural is managed flexibly by ordinary people'.[20] However, negotiated kinship is not 'artificial': Signe Howell has demonstrated in contexts typically dominated by biological notions of kinship, international adoption creates new ways of understanding kinship; she finds these notions of kinship are not 'artificial', instead preferring the term 'self-conscious kinship' as one which is determined and chosen.[21] Moreover, self-conscious kinship can be a deliberate act of *resistive* to dominant notions of biology and culture.[22] As an example, we can note that the Shakers, although at first rejecting sexual practice due to religious rationales, came to develop a particularly materialist understanding:

> Private property is based on the family and on inheritance along one line of descent or another, according to custom. In order to abolish the cause of greed and violence one needs to abolish private property, and in order to abolish private property one needs to abolish the traditional family... The keystone of the family is the procreating couple, and only after the legitimacy of this relationship has been denied can the basis of private property be suspended.[23]

Even suspending sexual relations draws us into forms of kinship; for the Shakers, a radical rejection of society and sexual intercourse is at the same time an embrace of community. Biblical texts which respond to failures in

---

20. Charis Thompson, 'Strategic Naturalizing: Reproduction in an Infertility Clinic', in Franklin and McKinnon, eds., *Relative Values*, 198.
21. Signe Howell, 'Self-Conscious Kinship: Some Contested Values in Norwegian Transnational Adoption', in Franklin and McKinnon, eds., *Relative Values*, 220.
22. Mary Weismantel, 'Making Kin: Kinship Theory and Zumbagua Adoptions', *American Ethnologist* 22, no. 4 (1995): 686.
23. Peter Collins, 'Virgins in Spirit: The Celibacy of the Shakers', in *Celibacy, Culture, and Society: Anthropology of Sexual Abstinence*, ed. Elisa J. Sobo and Sandra Bell (Madison, WI: University of Wisconsin Press, 2001), 114.

kinship are not necessarily doing so to create a 'legal fiction', but instead negotiating the boundaries of kinship.

Delaney's work in central Anatolia explores paternity in a wider cultural context.[24] For Delaney, procreation is a cultural construction, and 'paternity and maternity are concepts embedded in such a system from which they cannot be abstracted'. Rather than arguing paternity is physiological, Delaney instead suggests the bio-physical elements of procreation 'are utilized for expressing social meaning, for example, gender, authority and kinship'. Here Delaney draws on the example of the Virgin Birth story, where the father is divine and has the primary, creative and essential role in reproduction – a notion she terms 'monogenetic', which she views as consistent with the theological doctrine of monotheism.[25] Delaney recounts the notion of procreation among this particular Turkish village:

> The male is said to plant the seed and the woman is said to be like a field. Occasionally villagers refer to the Koran to support their view: 'Women are given to you as fields, go therein and sow your seed'. (Sura 2:223)[26]

Critiquing previous ethnographies in which figurative language has been viewed as the decorative veil that conceals the naked 'true' reality, Delaney re-evaluates the language used:

> *Tohum'dan çoçuk gelir* – the child comes from the seed; *erkek'ten çoçuk gelir* – the child comes from the man. When I suggest to villagers that one could not have a child without a woman, it was clear to them I had missed the point. Men give the seed which encapsulates the potential child. A woman's body, like soil, provides the nurturing context for the foetus.

The woman's body, while nourishing, 'does not affect its essential identity; that comes from the father'.[27] The term *Döllenmenk*, to inseminate, incorporates 'the word *döl*, meaning seed/foetus/child, which is implanted in

---

24. Delaney, 'Virgin Birth', 495.
25. Ibid., 496.
26. Ibid.
27. Ibid., 497. Emily Martin, 'The Egg and the Sperm: How Science Has Constructed a Romance Based on Stereotypical Male–Female Roles', *Signs* 16, no. 3 (1991): 485–501, critiques scientific explanations for failing to describe the relationship between the sperm and egg outside of highly gendered notions, such as the sperm 'penetrating' the egg. See also Waltner, 'Kinship between the Lines: The Patriline, the Concubine, and the Adopted Son in Late Imperial China', 71, and historical texts in China describing a 'seed and field' construct, where the substance of the child was seen as derived from the father.

the *dölyolu* (seedpath or vagina) into the *dölyatağı* (seedbed or womb), and people wish pregnant women "may it come out as easily as it went in".' The seed carries the spark of life, which is eternal but must be passed down through the generations, as reflected in sayings such as: 'a boy is the flame of the line, a girl the embers of a house'. If a man has no sons, it is said: *ocağı sonmus*, 'his hearth has been extinguished'.[28] Women's bodies, in this conception, are 'relatively undifferentiated, like soil', and are distinguished primarily by whether they are fertile or 'barren', and since female bodies provide something ambiguous, it is crucial to 'guarantee that a man's child is from his own seed'.[29] Delaney demonstrates how particular understandings of procreation and kinship can be reflective of extensive social practices. Notions of seed and the focus on the procreative importance of the father, with the woman as the nurturing receptacle, resonate with biblical texts, especially when the dominance of male names in genealogies is considered. Moreover, Delaney's research suggests how the passing down of seed may be a form of transmission of kinship; the lament for the childless man, 'his hearth has been extinguished', reverberates with the fear of erasing the name of the dead.

Cynthia Chapman argues that דם, blood, is rarely if ever used in the Hebrew Bible as a substance that establishes kinship relationships. Instead, the preferred biblical terminology is 'seed', which denotes semen and a lineal relationship, and 'bone and flesh', which she describes as more ambiguous, and also a more malleable, kinship term.[30] However, responding to, among others, Delaney, particularly her application the 'monogenetic' theory to biblical material in her later work,[31] Chapman argues that other forms of kinship are neglected by these approaches.[32] These approaches accept the patrilineal ideal described in some texts as reflective of reality, and so ignore other biblical materials that 'point to a mother's contribution to the substantive forming of her child'. Chapman argues that the father transmits name, house, land and monument, and she understands the covenant as mediating 'a great name', blessing, land and protection, 'all of which are values within an idealized patrilineality'. However, while seed relates to the 'ideal of patrilineality', she argues it does not describe the passing on of physical or character traits between

---

28. Delaney, 'Virgin Birth', 498.
29. Ibid.
30. Cynthia R. Chapman, *The House of the Mother: The Social Roles of Maternal Kin in Biblical Hebrew Narrative and Poetry*, AYBRL (New Haven: Yale University Press, 2016), 126.
31. Carol Delaney, 'Cutting the Ties that Bind: Sacrifice of Abraham and Patriarchal Kinship', in Franklin and McKinnon, eds., *Relative Values*, 93–4.
32. Chapman, *House*, 126.

father and child.³³ One of the areas for women's kinship formation Chapman examines is breastfeeding. For example, Chapman suggests the term 'brother who nursed at my mother's breast' (Song 8.1) means biblical scholars need to take account of the possibility breast feeding and breast milk, rather than only seed or blood, 'establish kinship bonds'.³⁴ Chapman explores studies of Islamic, Irish and Abkhazian approaches to breastfeeding and kinship. In discussion of hadith literature around how much milk (from a drop to two years of feeding) establishes kinship bonds, social access is negotiated: 'for example, a Muslim woman could meet her milk brother unveiled, and a wet nurse would have free, familial access to a male child she nursed for his entire life'.³⁵ Building on this, Chapman explores the role of breastfeeding in metaphors around Jerusalem: in Isaiah 60, breastfeeding is a literary trope that shows the transformation of Jerusalem from an abandoned woman to being majestic forever; in Isaiah 49, exiles are made royal through breastfeeding with both kings and princesses 'serving as their wet nurse'.³⁶ Isaiah 66.12-13 imagines Jerusalem and God in feminine terms: 'only through a rebirth by their capital city and through ingesting the milk of Jerusalem's breast can they regain their ethnic status as the new Israelites marked by "glory", a repeated epithet of Yahweh's royal power'.³⁷ In Song 8.1-2 the relationship the female speaker imagines with the brother who nursed at her mother's breast is one where 'she could kiss him in public and no one would censure the activity'.³⁸ Chapman further suggests this is significant in the breastfeeding of Isaac: Isaac is weaned, ending with a great feast (Gen. 21.8), by Sarah. Yet 'because Sarah had a younger, fertile, Egyptian slave woman in her household at the time of Isaac's birth, one might assume that Hagar would become Isaac's wet nurse';³⁹ however, it is

33. Ibid., 122.
34. Ibid., 126.
35. Ibid., 131. Chapman cites Avner Giladi, *Infants, Parents and Wet Nurses: Medieval Islamic Views on Breastfeeding and Their Social Implications* (Leiden: Brill, 1999), 13–40. Giladi references both Quranic and Hadith literature on breastfeeding as establishing kinship. Among others, Chapman looks at Peter Parkes, 'Fosterage, Kinship, and Legend: When Milk Was Thicker than Blood?', *CSSH* 46, no. 3 (2004): 587–615. Parkes explores, in the context of fosterage, milk-kinship practices in Abkhazia into the twentieth century, as well as legend and literature in ancient Greece, Eurasia and Ireland. Parkes does highlight the ambiguity of perspectives in his fieldwork in South Asia.
36. Chapman, *House*, 132.
37. Ibid., 133.
38. Ibid., 133–4.
39. Ibid., 139.

Sarah's breastfeeding that establishes his ethnic status. Similarly, Moses is nursed at the breast of a Levite woman, even though he was in Egyptian custody.[40] Kingship is neither a biological fact nor a male preserve: instead it is constantly negotiated and dependent on material contact.

2. *Reproduction in Narrative*

As outlined, within any system there are competing and complementing forms of understanding kinship. Narrative material in the Bible presents, on the one hand, a highly idealized form of reproductive kinship; however, as will be seen, the text has gaps which reveal alternative places of kinship. The promise to Abraham connects reproduction to covenant, remembrance of name and the male body. The narrative of Rachel and Leah complement this as a case study of how the text presents female reproduction, in the service of men, as normalized and natural. However, in both texts competing images arise.

2.1. *Abraham's Promise of Descendants*

In the first chapters of Genesis, the God of the first creation narrative encourages and endorses the flourishing of plant life (Gen. 1.12), animal life (1.20-22) and human life (1.26-28). The האדם of v. 27 is blessed, and God says to them (להם), with undifferentiated gender, to be fruitful (פרו) and multiply (רבו), and to fill the earth and control or subdue it. The secondary narrative of creation develops this account with a relational aspect introduced, with God saying it is not good for האדם to be alone. Needless to say, things deteriorate, and within a short time the woman is told she shall have trouble in childbirth, and that she shall desire her husband and he shall rule over her (3.16). In addition, we are told האדם calls woman by the name חוה, because כי הוא היתה אם כל־חי, she would be the mother of all living (3.20). Generations pass, punctuated with lineages and genealogies (4.17–5.32), fertility blessings (9.1, 7) and lists of men 'begetting' (יולד) men, without the mention of women (11.10-24).[41]

40. Ibid., 142.
41. Boer, 'Fine Wine', 26, discusses such genealogies in Chronicles. He states: 'The problem with all of this is that at a basic level the holidh formula leaves the mother entirely out of the process... With holidh we have a different form of the verb (hiphil), which means strictly, "A caused to bear B." So the question then becomes: whom did he cause to bear?' The text, however, does not include the obvious answer, the mother, effacing (with a few exceptions) women from genealogy. Boer's reading points to an inherent instability in the androcentrism of the text: its masculine presentation reveals its bias.

This form of tracing descent, focusing exclusively on men, is particularly reflective of patrilineal descent, and allows a kind of 'eternal' genealogical continuity to be established.[42] These genealogies, according to Boer,

> tell a story of embodied sexual practices, recited in a cadence of names almost without any action at all, or at least no action except for intercourse and childbirth. The narrative exists with no characterization and no plot, yet it progresses over centuries with nothing but sexuality and procreation to tie the tale together... Through the kinship related in the genealogies and the shorter genealogical notes, the narrative forms a connection to the intended reader who was also part of (a later) Israel. The narrative shapes identity in the readers by co-opting them into kinship ties claimed within the story itself. At the core of this narrative structure, therefore, is sexuality, for the genetic ties hold the kinship together.[43]

These genealogies create identity through this fast-paced recitation of 'begettings', and are performative in and of themselves as a form of kinship, functioning without the woman's role highlighted. This absence of women's role articulates ideas of sexuality and reproduction:

> If they chose to mention multiplication without reference to its vehicle, this can only mean that social ideology – monogamous liaisons, regulated procreation – rather than biology is on their agendas. And in their religious ideopicture, sexuality is secondary to the higher status of procreation – for both males and females, in that order.[44]

Following a kind of doxic interpretation outlined in the Introduction, however, suggests the text is not so much ideological or agenda-driven, but unconsciously reflecting a kind of symbolic violence to women: by divorcing procreation from the women involved, generational descent becomes a gendered, masculine form of kinship. Generations later, we read that Terah was father of Abram, Nahor and Haran:

> Abram and Nahor took wives; the name of Abram's wife was Sarai... Now Sarai was barren (עקרה); she had no child. (Gen. 11.29-30)[45]

42. Nancy Jay, 'Sacrifice, Descent and the Patriarchs', *VT* 38, no. 1 (1988): 56.
43. Jon L. Berquist, *Controlling Corporeality: The Body and the Household in Ancient Israel* (New Brunswick, NJ: Rutgers University Press, 2002), 51–2.
44. Athalya Brenner, *The Intercourse of Knowledge: On Gendering Desire and 'Sexuality' in the Hebrew Bible*, BibInt 26 (Leiden: Brill, 1997), 54.
45. For a discussion of infertility in the Bible, see Joel S. Baden and Candida R. Moss, *Reconceiving Infertility Biblical Perspectives on Procreation and Childlessness* (Princeton, NJ: Princeton University Press, 2015).

The first eleven chapters of Genesis whizz from the very specific (Eden, Noah, Babel, etc.) to the very long-term (genealogies), on a roller-coaster narrative. The racing text and genealogy is brought to focus on a pairing, and we are told twice that Abram's wife was Sarai, and that she is unable to conceive and without child. The composite text of Genesis 1–11 is composed of many themes; however, reproduction, childbirth, lineage and fertility have been amply introduced. It is at a moment of discontinuity, of infertility, that the text introduced its first epic, that of Abram and Sarai. YHWH tells Abram to leave his country, kin, and father's house, and go to the land he will show him, and that he will '…make you a great nation (ואעשך לגוי גדול), and I will bless you, and make your name great (ואגדלה שמך), so that you will be a blessing' (Gen. 12.1-3). Abram is approached after his father's death, creating a radical separation from his kinship roots.[46] It is significant, as Athalya Brenner identifies, that despite repeated references to progeny the texts are not 'paedocentric';[47] the concern with offspring does not seem interested in the offspring themselves but with lineage and posterity, and progeny 'is depicted as basic and intrinsic, but nothing is mentioned about an instinct for fatherhood'.[48]

Abram makes it to the land of Canaan and is, if we translate זרע as seed,[49] told that he will give the land to his seed.[50] As noted above, seed dominates as the image of male reproduction; however, the angel declares to Hagar that he will multiply her זרע, seed or offspring, so that they cannot be counted (16.10). The ambiguity of the term זרע is highlighted here; referring to the זרע of a woman either suggests the term can function without the semantic reference to seed/semen, or that it may be borrowed from references to the seed of a man. After a brief excursion in Egypt, Abram settles the land and is told: 'for all the land that you see I will give to you and to your offspring (זרע) for ever. I will make your offspring like the dust of the earth; so that if one can count the dust of the earth, your offspring also can be counted' (Gen. 13.15-16). After another excursion to save Lot, YHWH promises Abram he will be rewarded, and Abram replies that he is still childless, and that his heir is to be a slave born in his house (15.2). However, the word of YHWH comes to him:

46. Gerhard von Rad, *Genesis: A Commentary*, trans. John Marks, rev. ed., OTL (London: SCM, 1972), 159.
47. Brenner, *Intercourse*, 55 n. 12.
48. Ibid., 55.
49. At times זרע carries the specific meaning of semen; see Num. 5.28; Lev. 22.4; 15.16-18; 19.20; Num. 5.13; Jer. 31.27. It also carries agricultural associations, for example in sowing; see Gen. 47.24; Lev. 27.16; Num. 20.5; Ezek. 17.5.
50. The NRSV, among other translations, translate זרע as 'offspring', but translations here will maintain 'seed'.

...'This one shall not be your heir; but rather one who comes out from your own inner parts/internal organs (אשר יצא ממעיך),[51] he shall be your heir'. And he brought him outside and said, 'Look now toward heaven and count the stars... So shall be your seed.' (15.4-5, own translation)

While many translations, such as the NRSV, euphemize אשר יצא ממעיך with something like 'your very own issue', a literal translation has the effect of blurring the distinction between the seed of Abram and his descendants. Rather than 'offspring', his *seed* will become great, and his heir is promised to be one who comes out from his inner parts/organs; the text emphasizes the materiality of the semen, descendants, and Abram's body: the material passing on of patrilineality. YHWH takes the point of Terah's death and moves Abram to associate him with a new land (of Canaan), forging a new kinship relation, and repeatedly makes the promise of a multitude of descendants in stark contrast to 'barrenness'. Our new narrative has begun, and it is one that is tied up with reproduction and descendants. However, almost as soon as it is begun, it is retold, and it is in this retelling that we can begin to see competing constructs.

2.2. *Abraham's Covenant*

In Genesis 17, El Shaddai appears to Abram,[52] introducing himself and again promising to make him exceedingly numerous, though this time with a differently articulated blessing:

> When Abram was ninety-nine years old, the LORD appeared to Abram, and said to him, 'I am God Almighty (אל שדי); walk before me, and be blameless.[53] And I will make my covenant between me and you, and will make you exceedingly numerous'. Then Abram fell on his face; and God said to him, 'As for me, this is my covenant with you: You shall be the ancestor of a multitude of nations. No longer shall your name be Abram, but your name

---

51. BDB, 'מעי'.
52. Trible, *God and the Rhetoric of Sexuality*, 61. Trible notes possible representations of the God figure in a fertility role: Gen. 49.25 makes a play between El Shaddai (שדי), breasts (שדים) and womb (רחם). David Biale, *Blood and Belief: The Circulation of a Symbol between Jews and Christians* (Berkeley: University of California Press, 2007), 26, is among those who argue El Shaddai is derived from 'God of the Breasts'.
53. Lawrence A. Hoffman, *Covenant of Blood: Circumcision and Gender in Rabbinic Judaism*, CSHJ (Chicago: University of Chicago Press, 1996), 35, translates התהלך לפני והיה תמים as 'walk before me in a state of completion'. Hoffman relates תמים to the Levitical sacrifice as wholeness/without blemish, and so makes sense of the wholeness of Abraham in terms of circumcision. There is a particular irony in the Levitical insistence in undamaged genitalia for participation in the cult.

shall be Abraham (אברהם); for I have made you the ancestor of a multitude (המון) of nations. I will make you exceedingly fruitful; and I will make nations of you, and kings shall come from you. I will establish my covenant (בריתי) between me and you, and your offspring (זרעך) after you throughout their generations, for an everlasting covenant, to be God to you and to your offspring (ולזרעך) after you. And I will give to you, and to your offspring after you, the land where you are now an alien, all the land of Canaan, for a perpetual holding; and I will be their God.' (Gen. 17.1-8)

This repeated promise of descendants is hyperbolic, especially when contrasted with the previous covenant in Genesis 13. El Shaddai continues:

God said to Abraham, 'As for you, you shall keep my covenant (בריתי), you and your offspring (זרעך) after you throughout their generations. This is my covenant, which you shall keep, between me and you and your offspring after you: every male among you shall be circumcised (המול). You shall circumcise the flesh of your foreskins (בשר ערלתכם), and it shall be a sign (לאות) of the covenant (ברית) between me and you (וביניכם). Throughout your generations every male among you shall be circumcised when he is eight days old, including the slave born in your house and the one bought with your money from any foreigner who is not of your offspring. Both the slave born in your house and the one bought with your money must be circumcised. So shall my covenant be in your flesh (בבשרכם) an everlasting covenant (לברית עולם). Any uncircumcised male (וערל) who is not circumcised in the flesh of his foreskin shall be cut off (ונכרתה) from his people; he has broken my covenant.' (Gen. 17.9-14)

Eilberg-Schwartz has interrogated the role of masculinity in the text and critiqued received wisdom on the function of circumcision. Circumcision is to function as a sign of the covenant, and Eilberg-Schwartz argues it has a symbolic function in Priestly literature:

Since circumcision is described as a symbol of the covenant between Abraham and God, one is led to the conclusion that the practice has an intimate connection with the content of that covenant. The centerpiece of this covenant is God's promise that Abraham will have vast numbers of descendants... This writer is pre-eminently concerned with human reproduction and its implications. In narrating world and Israelite history, this writer emphasizes in seven separate contexts the importance of human fertility.[54]

The Priestly writer has an intense focus on genealogy.[55] Eilberg-Schwartz's argument relates the covenant to the penis, which is the primary vehicle

---

54. Eilberg-Schwartz, *Savage*, 147. Gen. 1.22; 9.1, 7; 28.3; 35.11; 48.3; Exod. 1.7.
55. E.g., Gen. 5.1-28, 30-32; 10.1-7; 11.10-26; 25.12-18; 36.1-14; 46.6-27.

'by which reproduction and intergenerational continuity are ensured'.⁵⁶ This is evidenced by the function of 'uncircumcised' in other contexts: uncircumcised organs are equated with improperly functioning organs,⁵⁷ and uncircumcised (עָרֵל) fruit trees are not harvested (Lev. 19.23-25).⁵⁸

This interpretation is especially poignant in relation to anthropological research on circumcision, which suggests circumcision solidifies male lines of descent; the ritual allows men to assert their genealogical tie to the child, which is always more precarious than the relationship between a child and his or her mother.⁵⁹ Following Eilberg-Schwartz's interpretation of anthropological data, it is possible to see circumcision as a mechanism which mediates and relieves some of the contradictions inherent in a heavily patrilineal system. Moreover, as well as navigating the uncertainties of paternity, it can work to form kinship bonds between father and son, making 'tangible the links among generations of men'. Max Gluckman, in his study of circumcision in Barotseland, Southern Africa, argues that men assert their ownership over the sons against the women, who wish to 'grab' the children during the rite of circumcision.⁶⁰ The instigator and recipient in circumcision are men, and this forms a connection that denies the mother's role, and during rites of circumcision

---

56. Eilberg-Schwartz, *Savage*, 148. The specificity of the sexual organ is often sidelined. In Gen. 24 Abraham tasks his servant to find a wife for Isaac not from the Canaanites, but from the land of his birth; his servant is to place his hand 'under my thigh' (ידך תחת ירכי). Von Rad argues ירכי is euphemistic of the testicles, though attributes no particular significance to the genitals as the site of the oath, instead supposing that its 'special sanctity' is no longer present in this period (von Rad, *Genesis*, 254). The other occurrence, Gen. 47.29, takes place again at the end of life (Claus Westermann, *Genesis 12–36: A Commentary*, trans. John J. Scullion [London: SPCK, 1985], 384) though this time in the context of being gathered to one's kin. Boer suggests the sacredness of the organ would enhance the solemnity of the oath, while also suggesting the narrative of Jacob fighting with the divine figure in Gen. 32.26 and subsequent explanation of why the Israelites do not eat a certain part of the body actually refers to the testicles: Boer, *Earthy Nature*, 54–5.

57. Eilberg-Schwartz, *Savage*, 149. E.g. the heart (Jer. 9.25; Deut. 10.16), the ears (Jer. 6.10), the heart in priestly material (Ezek. 26.41; 44.7), lips (Exod.6.12, 30, cf. 'heavy of lips' in the J text Exod. 3.10).

58. Eilberg-Schwartz, *Savage*, 150. Eilberg-Schwartz develops the relationship between fruit, horticulture and offspring throughout pages 156–60.

59. See Jay, 'Sacrifice, Descent and the Patriarchs'; Nancy Jay, *Throughout Your Generations Forever: Sacrifice, Religion, and Paternity* (Chicago: University of Chicago Press, 1993).

60. Max Gluckman, 'The Role of the Sexes in Wiko Circumcision Ceremonies', in *Social Structure*, ed. Meyers Fortes (Oxford: Clarendon, 1949), 158.

references are frequently made to patrilineal ancestors. Among the 'Wiko' people, it is believed that circumcision blood is threatening to female reproduction, as circumcision is perceived as a fundamentally male way of establishing kinship.[61] According to Eilberg-Schwartz, this is useful as a parallel for understanding the Priestly system, which is based primarily on descent and not election, particularly as he perceives the writer operating during a period of discontinuity,[62] interested in the pre-Abraham history and 'communal self-definition'.[63] Eilberg-Schwartz suggests that Lev. 21.2-4, which allows a priest to bury his nearest kin *except for* a non-virgin sister, combined with Lev. 22.12-14, which prohibits the daughter of a priest who has married a non-priest from eating of the priestly rations,[64] suggest exclusion of women from the patriline due to their sex status.[65]

The term בשר, flesh, in P and cognate literature is both used in terms of kinship (Gen. 2.23; 29.14; 37.27; Lev. 18.6) and of the penis (Lev. 17.13; 15.2-3; Ezek. 16.26; 23.30; 44.7), which 'reflects the conceptual association between the penis and the relations of kinship',[66] whereas J never uses the term for the penis.[67] The notion of fertility, kinship and lineage is inscribed explicitly on the male body:

> The association between the male organ and the idea of kinship made the penis doubly appropriate as the spot for the symbol of God's covenant. God had promised to make Abraham fertile and provide him with a successful progeny. As we have seen, the removal of the foreskin symbolizes the fertility of the organ. But the cut also suggests that this lineage, represented by the penis, is set apart from all others. In this way, circumcision symbolizes and helps create intergenerational continuity between men. It graphically represents patrilineal descent by giving men of this line a distinctive mark that binds them together.[68]

---

61. Ibid., 155.
62. He compares Ezra 2.61-63 and Neh. 7.64 (Eilberg-Schwartz, *Savage*, 165–6).
63. Eilberg-Schwartz, *Savage*, 166.
64. Unless she is widowed/divorced and has no descendants.
65. Eilberg-Schwartz, *Savage*, 170.
66. Ibid.
67. For a discussion of the development of circumcision in non-P and prophetic material, see Hoffman, *Covenant*, 27–32, and Leonie Archer, 'Bound by Blood: Circumcision and Menstrual Taboo in Post-Exilic Judaism', in *After Eve: Women, Theology and the Christian Tradition*, ed. Janet Martin Soskice (London: Collins Marshall Pickering, 1990), 36.
68. Eilberg-Schwartz, *Savage*, 171.

The male body and the male organ become the locus of patrilineal identity and descent, and something substantive and material is passed down through the men in their ability to serve in the priesthood, notably the position of high priest. Leviticus 12.2 makes clear that after childbirth the woman is unclean seven days, and on the eighth day the new-born is to be circumcised. The rite transfers the infant from the realm of women to the realm of men, with the female infant remaining impure for longer (Lev. 12.3). The spilling of the infant's blood may symbolically relate to the blood of the woman.[69] Ilona Rashkow argues that within a patriarchal system not simply women's but all sexual expression must be heavily controlled. Additionally, she notes that the male organ forms a point of control in other ancient West Asian systems:[70]

> The Hebrew Bible posits the human penis as the explicit, emblematic, and exclusive symbol of religious identity and membership of the communal order. Thus, the penis symbolizes the special link between this society's God and the (male) members of the community. It serves as a physical reminder both of inclusion *in* the community and exclusion *from* it.[71]

This male way of presenting lineage and descendants, as the multiplication of men, is particularly successful: by the time Jacob goes to Egypt he has acquired 66 bloodline descendants, 64 of them men. The vitality of this process is seen through the way a particular social role, the priesthood, is transmitted through this line of succession – a real and substantive form of social perpetuation. While Eilberg-Schwartz's thesis is not without

---

69. Ibid., 174–5. Archer, 'Bound by Blood', 53, states: 'the blood of circumcision served as a symbolic surrogate for the blood of childbirth, and because it was shed voluntarily and in a controlled manner, it transcended the bounds of nature [the blood flow of the mother at birth]'.

70. Ilona N. Rashkow, *Taboo or Not Taboo: Sexuality and Family in the Hebrew Bible* (Minneapolis, MN: Fortress, 2000), 30. For example, article 20 of the Middle Assyrian Code mandates castration as punishment for male–male intercourse – the choice of castration is presumably a symbolic form of punishment relating to the use (or 'abuse') of the male organ. On the role of the penis in sexual relation in rabbinic texts (specifically in their interpretation of biblical texts) where sexual relations are constituted through the penis, see Daniel Boyarin, 'Are There Any Jews in "The History of Sexuality"?', *Journal of the History of Sexuality* 5, no. 3 (1995): 333–55.

71. Rashkow, *Taboo*, 75. Rashkow presents a psychoanalytic approach to circumcision, which further emphasizes the dynamic between God and men, placing the ultimate power over both the penis and procreation in the hands of the divine: 'in Lacanian terms, Abraham and his offspring may possess the penis but never the Phallus, the ultimate symbol of paternal authority and the privilege it signifies'.

critics,[72] Sandra Jacob's points out that the very notion of an everlasting covenant is always tied up with questions of succession and heredity.[73]

The Priestly source takes an established discourse of procreation, already focused around the man, and ties it up with the penis, creating a robust notion of male performance as sexually active. Social and symbolic reproduction come to be materially united with bodily reproduction. Here the field – and habitus – become concentrated in the embodied penis. In its interest in male lines, it also partially erases women from the process. However, this is not to say women are absent, or that they cannot form substantive kinship bonds and even create dynasties. Hagar is promised the multiplication of seed. The text is at pains to point to Sarah as the one who weans Isaac, and the narrative takes seriously the promise to her.[74] In Gen. 16.2 Sarai tells Abram that by the slave-girl she may be אבנה, built up, בנה to build also a pun on sons, בנים.[75] Genesis 17.16 states לגוים מלכי עמים ממנה יהיו,[76] as will be discussed in the next chapter. However, the construction in 17.21, יצחק אשר תלד לך שרה, still appears to view Isaac's birth through Abraham. Reproduction in the narrative is directed towards the covenantal relationship with Abraham, one which coalesces around name, progeny and land.

---

72. Most recently, see David A. Bernat, *Sign of the Covenant: Circumcision in the Priestly Tradition*, AIL 3 (Atlanta, GA: Society of Biblical Literature, 2009). For a thorough and useful critique of Bernat's critique, see Sandra Jacobs, 'Divine Virility in Priestly Representation: Its Memory and Consummation in Rabbinic Midrash', in Creangă, ed., *Men and Masculinity*, 146–70.

73. Jacobs, 'Divine Virility'.

74. This is not to say that women are absent from the narrative, but that they are actors primarily in relation to the men, as will be shown in the Rachel and Leah narrative. For a fuller discussion of the role of Sarah and Hagar, see Jay, 'Sacrifice, Descent and the Patriarchs'; Esther Fuchs, *Sexual Politics in the Biblical Narrative: Reading the Hebrew Bible as a Woman*, JSOTSup 310 (Sheffield: Sheffield Academic, 2000), 46–52, 150–4; Danna N. Fewell and David M. Gunn, *Gender, Power, and Promise: The Subject of the Bible's First Story* (Nashville: Abingdon, 1993), 89; Athalya Brenner, 'Female Social Behaviour: Two Descriptive Patterns within the "Birth of the Hero" Paradigm', in *Feminist Companion to Genesis*, ed. Athalya Brenner, FCB 2 (Sheffield: Sheffield Academic, 1993), 212.

75. The JPS translation renders the Hebrew 'perhaps I shall have a son through her', adding the note that the literal 'be built up' is a play on both son and build up, while the NRSV gender-inclusive further obscures the Hebrew by rendering the text 'obtain children by her'.

76. This is often rendered 'mother of kings of nations', however 'mother' is not explicit in the Hebrew.

2.3. *Rachel and Leah*

Within narrative material that looks at reproduction, a women's need or desire for a son is distinct form a husband's need for an heir. Chapman notes the difference in titles for a first son: to the father it is 'the first fruits of his vigour' and to the mother 'the one who opens the womb'. The child establishes the mother's house within the larger household of the father (as will be discussed in the next chapter). A son builds up the mother by raising her status, he secures her economic life, and within a polygynous household creates aspiring heirs.[77] However, this kind of fight for symbolic capital, as will be seen in the narrative of Rachel and Leah, while 'building up' the women can be unsettling to read. In Genesis 29, Jacob agrees to serve Laban seven years in order to take his daughter Rachel as a wife. However, Laban tricks Jacob into marrying Leah (29.23), and Jacob works another seven years to take Rachel (29.27). Leah is given Zilpah as a maidservant and Rachel is given Bilhah, and we are told that Jacob loves Rachel more than Leah (29.30). The text has set a scene for a drama of reproduction: Jacob, having been given the blessing, is assured to have his descendants multiplied; he has been given two wives and two maidservants, and he has a clear preference between them. The proceeding passage (29.31–30.24) is, in one reading, reading a fast-paced account of a family drama. However, it creates a context in which ability to reproduce sons (one daughter, out of a total of thirteen offspring, is produced throughout the entire scene) is inscribed as a battle for affection and approval from the patriarch, and reproduction becomes the want, desire and need of every woman: 'there is nothing worse for a woman than to be infertile (that is, sonless), especially when her husband is not'.[78] Moreover, it presumes the sexual use of maidservants, suggesting normalized sexual slavery. Here the desire to produce children is further complicated by rivalry between sisters. YHWH initially notices Leah is unloved and 'opened her womb', but Rachel has not given birth (עקרה). Leah conceives and bears a son she names Reuben, ראובן, which she declares means 'Because the LORD has looked on (ראה) my affliction'. Yet the text also tells us 'surely now my husband will love me (יאהבני)' (29.32), reflecting a bitter sadness. She conceives again and names this son שמעון, Simeon, declaring: 'Because the LORD has heard (שמע) that I am hated, he has given me this son also' (29.33). She bears another son and names him לוי, Levi, declaring: 'Now this time my husband will be joined (ילוה) to me, because I have borne him three sons' (29.34). Again,

---

77. Chapman, *House*, 151.
78. Brenner, *Intercourse*, 56.

she bears a son she names יהודה, Judah, saying, 'This time I will praise (אודה) the LORD', and then we are told her reproduction stops (29.35). The various names have undergone layers of redaction, being crafted into a narrative focusing on YHWH's actions in the birth of the children.[79] Leah's fertility serves in the production of four offspring for Jacob, yet does not change her status, which is perceived primarily in relation to her husband: she is the unloved sister.

Rachel sees that Leah has born 'to Jacob' (ליעקב), and becomes envious:

> And she said to Jacob, 'Give me children – if not I will die!' And the anger of Jacob was kindled against Rachel, and he said, 'Am I in the place of God, who has withheld from you the fruit of the womb?' And she said, 'Here is my maidservant Bilhah; go in to her, that she may bear on my knee, that built up also I am by her'. (Gen. 30.1, own translation)

Rachel's distress at not providing children (בנים) is said to be so severe she believes she will die, the passage purveying both the agony she is in, but also the desperation she will go to compete. There is an obvious difficulty in the translation of בנים, which literally may mean sons but can also be used in a gender-inclusive way to mean children; I will use the term sons throughout to reflect the androcentric context. Jacob is incensed at her questioning and reaffirms that it is God who is in control of her womb. Furthermore, he reaffirms his lack of involvement in Rachel's infertility. Fuchs notes that the denial of male impotence and sterility serves a patriarchal strategy of denial of the father's interest in a male heir, which is displaced onto the woman:

> Significantly, although the father's name, patrilineage and inheritance are at stake, the biblical narrative projects onto the mother-figure the concern for patrilineal continuity; the mother-figure rather than the father-figure is most interested in giving birth to a male heir, though her name will inevitably be omitted from the patrilineal genealogy she tries so hard to sustain.[80]

In reaction (or desperation) Rachel tells Jacob to use her maidservant Bilhah, and that she will bear on Rachel's knees and Rachel will be built up from her (ואבנה גם־אנכי ממנה). Rachel's jealousy stems from her reaction to Leah bearing children for Jacob; however, she is hoping she specifically would be built up through her maid producing offspring. It

---

79. Westermann, *Genesis 12–36*, 472. Oratorically the etymologies are playful and should not be considered etymologies *per se* (von Rad, *Genesis*, 294).
80. Fuchs, *Sexual Politics*, 48.

is in the physicality of the act that tensions and ambiguities inherent in a notion of succession are brought out. Even if a dominant motif sees the production of children as primarily for the male, we have noted texts where the multiplication of seed is promised to women. Moreover, the tension between competing women does not just reflect a desire for the affections of the male. The use of the verb בנה portrays the building up of the woman through her progeny. While some refer to the bearing on the knees as a ritual of adoption,[81] there is considerable ambiguity in the act; the physicality of the maid bearing on Rachel's knees suggests a sharing by Rachel of the birthing process, a kind of embodied adoption, she must mimic the act of childbirth itself.[82]

Tikva Frymer-Kensky notes that adoption was very common throughout ancient West Asia, and that it was not used only in cases of childlessness, but in cases where it is very clear the adopter already has children.[83] It is particularly interesting in this context that matriarchs appear to prefer a process of giving their slaves, and many scholars have noted the complications inherent in the maid/slave narratives, which have been described as exploitative. Moreover, the text is ambiguous regarding whether it presents the abuse of power as problematic.[84]

Jon Berquist states that as any social system is always fragmented, there will always be competing ideas about the body, and that power relations between groups influence the way that ideas about the body interrelate, which provokes forms of resistance.[85] In the bearing of the child taking place on her knees, the boundaries between Rachel's body and Bilhah's body become fluid, and Rachel stakes a claim to the primary maternal role. From a Bourdieuian approach, the habitus of the women, to compete in the field, internalizes the male reproductive structure as doxic; to accrue symbolic capital she must reproduce – it she is unable, the use of female slaves offers a kind of playing of the field offering the woman a distinct advantage in play. Rachel names the child Dan, דן, stating 'God has judged me (דנני), and has also heard my voice and given me a son' (30.6). Bilhah again bears ליעקב, to which Rachel names the child נפתלי,

---

81. Westermann, *Genesis 12–36*, 474.

82. Cf. Joseph in 50.23, who has previously been left without heir through Jacob's adoption of his sons. See also Ephraim Speiser, *Genesis: Introduction, Translation and Notes*, AB 1 (New York: Doubleday, 1964), 230, who states it is usually performed by the father.

83. Tikva Frymer-Kensky, *Studies in Bible and Feminist Criticism* (Philadelphia: Jewish Publication Society, 2006), 230.

84. Fewell and Gunn, *Gender, Power, and Promise*, 45.

85. Berquist, *Controlling Corporeality*, 9.

Naphtali, stating 'With mighty wrestlings (נפתלתי) I have wrestled with my sister, and have prevailed', emphasizing conflict (30.8). Leah gives Zilpah to Jacob, who bears two sons – גד, Gad, as she states 'Good fortune (גד)!' and אשר, Asher, as she states 'Happy am I! For the women will call me happy (באשרי)!' (30.13). That God has rewarded her for giving Jacob her maid, further reveals a dynamic of patriarchal power in the text: Leah offering a woman she is in control of, for the sexual service of her husband and his lineage. The sexual domination of Zilpah by Jacob is both rewarded and not interrogated – she is Leah's to give, and she (Leah) is to give freely (despite Jacob already having a substantial progeny), in service of the patriarch. Reuben is said to come upon some mandrakes in the field, and Rachel asks for some from Leah (30.14), to which Leah responds: 'Is it a small matter that you have taken away my husband? Would you take away my son's mandrakes also?' (30.15), mandrake being possibly an aphrodisiac or fertility drug in the ancient world.[86] Rachel uses access to Jacob as a bargaining tool for the mandrake, and Leah says to Jacob that he must 'come in to' her as she has hired him with the mandrake, the text suggesting Jacob acts as a passive bystander who must be persuaded to enter the narrative, while at the same time reasserting his sexual hegemony. Leah bears a fifth son to Jacob, named יששכר, Issachar, for she states 'God has given me my hire [שכרי] because I gave my maid to my husband', then bears to Jacob זבלון, Zebulun, stating 'God has endowed me with a good dowry [זבדני]; now my husband will honour me [יזבלני], because I have borne him six sons' (30.18-20). Finally, she bears him a daughter, named Dinah, for whom no etymology is given, possibly as she will not come to head a tribe. The birth of the final child is expressed still with a longing that Jacob will respond to her.

With Leah's childbearing having now run its course, we are told:

> Then God remembered Rachel, and God heeded her and opened her womb. She conceived and bore a son, and said, 'God has taken away (אסף) my reproach'; and she named him Joseph (יוסף), saying, 'May the LORD add (יסף) to me another son!'

Rachel bears the son who is to become Jacob's favourite and occupy most of the rest of Genesis. Jacob is renamed Israel (twice: 32.29; 35.10); God, now appearing as El Shaddai, blesses him, stating 'be fertile and multiply', that nations will come from him, kings will come from his loins, and that his offspring will dominate the land (35.10-12). Finally, at Ephrath, while Rachel is in labour, we read:

---

86. Fewell and Gunn, *Gender*, 78.

> When she was in her difficult labour, the midwife said to her, 'Do not be afraid; for now you will have another son'. As her soul was departing (for she died), she named him Ben-oni [בן־אוני]; but his father called him Benjamin [בנימין]. So Rachel died, and she was buried on the way to Ephrath (that is, Bethlehem). (35.17-20)

The midwife suggests the bearing of a son should negate Rachel's fears, and in the moments of dying, she names him Ben-Oni, 'son of my suffering'.[87] Jacob's change of name, whether intentionally or not, erases Rachel's ability to name Ben-Oni.

The particularity of the 'barren' motif occurs here and throughout the Hebrew Bible. Brenner suggests: 'if women concur with this assessment of their nature, the repetition and emphasis might be redundant. The repetition, then, sounds like too much of a protest. It sounds problematic. Perhaps it points to a need to socialize women into internalizing the requirements of community survival in terms of personal desire.'[88] There is a kind of interplay between Brenner's more ideological criticism and an understanding of doxa; that female infertility is presumed as part of the structuring of bodies and reproduction, but that within a literary narrative it becomes a prominent motif in a text negotiating gender and reproduction, and strays into the literary territory of role models.[89] That Rachel's death is the only occurrence of mortality in childbirth throughout Genesis is particularly noteworthy, and Brenner argues that the pressure to procreate must have carried known risks for women, and to ensure compliance the social status of childbirth has to be enhanced in a way that adds to their families and their own 'security, prosperity and labour power'.[90]

Childbirth leads to high risk of death, yet without it women face social death; indeed 'the risks and sorrows, the ambiguities and the ironies, are all but passed over in the rush to tell a man's story'.[91] This is particularly poignant when we consider that the battle to reproduce is valorized through the Bible: Rachel and Leah are said to have 'together built up the house of Israel' (Ruth 4.11). However, the two women also build up themselves:

---

87. Derived from אנה, to be in sorrow (Westermann, *Genesis 12–36*, 555). Another 'possibility is to associate *'ônî* with *'ôn*, "vigor, strength"' (Victor P. Hamilton, *The Book of Genesis: 18–50*, NICOT [Grand Rapids, MI: Eerdmans, 1995], 383 n. 8).

88. Brenner, *Intercourse*, 58.

89. Even if the Genesis account is ambiguous about whether the women are presented as role models, when we come to look at Ruth they are clearly extolled as a model to Ruth.

90. Brenner, *Intercourse*, 68.

91. Fewell and Gunn, *Gender*, 79.

the sons of Rachel and Leah are differentiated from the 'sons of Bilhah and Zilpah' in Gen. 37.2, accentuating 'the distance, the non-relationship between Joseph and the sons of Jacob my maidservants'.[92] Moreover, the subdivision between the houses of Rachel and Leah becomes the southern kingdom of Judah and the northern kingdom of Israel, with the biblical narrative presenting the two kingdoms as 'nested sub-houses' within the paternal house of Jacob.[93] Chapman argues that throughout the early kinship dynasties, Rachel emerges as the 'preeminent royal house', with Gideon of Manasseh, Saul of Benjamin, and Jeroboam of Ephraim, and with Saul's kinship receiving confirmation at the tomb of Rachel, 'the physical site of her enduring house'. Even David the Judean must 'insinuate himself into the house of Rachel', which he does through marrying into, absorbing, and eradicating Saul's Benjamite house, and 'locating his own ancestry at the site of Rachel's tomb'.[94]

The text draws the story of Rachel and Leah through various strands which dialogue with the reader; in reading, Brenner argues, women 'are encouraged to become willing madonnas and they internalize the message, to their own and their society's detriment'. She further states that even feminist critics have 'acquiesced' and appropriated this 'idealized picture of biblical desire for motherhood as their own'.[95] The text presents as natural the will to procreate for the husband, and even valorizes competition between women; in the book of Ruth, they become known for their loyalty to Israel, both man and nation. There is an obviousness to the way Rachel and Leah's habitus negotiates their place; there is a subtle distinction in what is valuable to them, however: the product of reproduction, and the value placed on parenthood.

2.4. *The Value of Parenthood*

Progeny are crucial to both the Abraham and the Rachel and Leah narratives. The value of parenthood – whether the texts are concerned primarily with children or parents – has come under criticism from feminist and queer scholars, and so an interrogation of the construction of maternity, paternity, motherhood and fatherhood in these texts will form a part of this discussion.[96] The texts of motherhood have often been taken as liberating

---

92. Chapman, *House*, 44.
93. Ibid., 204.
94. Ibid., 219.
95. Brenner, *Intercourse*, 81–2.
96. Cheryl Exum responds to her previous analysis that the midwives of Exod. 1.8–2.10 were positive role models for women: 'By focusing solely on the surface

as they celebrate women's procreative power, and so have not been labelled as misogynistic. However, Esther Fuchs notes:

> Patriarchy…has little to gain from a total negation of women. It has much more to gain from valorizing the contribution of mothers to the patriarchal system. The interests of patriarchy are better served by routing the resourcefulness of mothers in the 'proper' direction. The proper direction is the sustenance and perpetuation of patrilineal continuity. Therefore, it is not women's procreative powers that are celebrated in most nativity narratives, but rather their initiative in obviating obstacles to patrilineal continuity.[97]

That is, women in these narratives are celebrated as much for their ability to continue the patriarchal line *through any means* other than and in addition to the simple ability to produce children; rather than celebrating a romanticized idea of *motherhood*, it celebrates the production of children and the intervention in familial politics.[98] Julie Parker's recent work on children draws attention to the distinction between children as 'useful' and children as valued in the Hebrew Bible, suggesting a refocusing on children in biblical texts, noting that issues as broad as adoption, education, family ritual, warfare, slavery and incest 'are seen differently when focusing on the children'.[99] A 'childist' readings 'reframes questions of human responsibility towards all people, including those who are young', emphasizing 'children's active role in shaping culture, instead of seeing them as largely passive or victimized'. Parker argues: 'Adults often fail to notice how children strategize and act to accomplish goals, exert

---

structure of the text, on the ways literary devices and structures serve as guides to meaning, it limits us to describing, and thus to reinscribing, the text's gender ideology. I now see this method as confining, and as representative of the phallocentric drive to control and organize reading (and reality) into clearly defined categories.' Exum articulates something similar to doxa: 'patriarchy depends on women's complicity… [R]ewarding women for their complicity is one of patriarchy's most useful strategies, because it can often achieve a level of cooperation that force or threat cannot guarantee': Cheryl Exum, 'Second Thoughts about Secondary Characters', in Brenner, ed., *Feminist Companion to Exodus to Deuteronomy*, 79–80, in which Exum responds to her previous writing: Cheryl Exum, '"You Shall Let Every Daughter Live": A Study of Exodus 1.8–2.10', *Semeia* 28 (1983): 63–82.

97. Fuchs, *Sexual Politics*, 47.
98. Fewell and Gunn, *Gender*, 70. Fewell and Gunn note the irony of Hannah giving Samuel to Eli despite having 'done a fairly lousy job of raising his own sons'!
99. Julie F. Parker, *Valuable and Vulnerable: Children in the Hebrew Bible, Especially the Elisha Cycle*, BJS 355 (Providence, RI: Brown Judaic Studies, 2013), 10.

control, maintain relationships, and organize their lives'.[100] In Parker's work on children in the Hebrew Bible, she emphasizes that while children are integral to economic structures, they are valued in and of themselves. She cites examples of parents who 'simply seem to care for their children whom they love': Hagar and Ishmael (Gen. 21.16); Jacob and the children's journey (Gen. 33.13-14); Jochebed saving Moses (Exod. 2.3, 6-9); Ruth and the women celebrating the birth of a son (Ruth 4.16); David pleading for the life of his newborn child (2 Sam. 12.15, 18-22); the prostitute who pleads for the child's life before Solomon (1 Kgs 3.26-27); the wife of Jeroboam seeking the prophet's help and the people of Israel mourning (1 Kgs 14.12); the widow of Zarephath beseeching Elijah when her son is dead (1 Kgs 17.17-24); the widow of one of the sons of the prophet seeking Elisha's help to prevent them becoming slaves (2 Kgs 4.1-7); and the Shunammite woman seeking the reviving of her dead child (2 Kgs 4.17-35).[101]

As well as parental compassion, Stiebert notes the ways in which a child is expected to follow their parents: inheritance (Prov. 19.14); which prophets, career or gods to follow (1 Kgs 7.14; 2 Kgs 3.13; 1 Chron. 25.6); in honour and behaviour (Exod. 20.12; Deut. 21.8-21; 2 Sam. 7.14) although when this conflicts with obedience to God this is no longer approved (1 Kgs 22.52; 2 Kgs 21.21; Ezek. 20.18-21). Parker is undoubtedly right that greater attention should be paid to children in biblical texts, and highlights that not all texts talking about reproduction should be solely thought of as being about the economic benefit of children, or about extending the family unit through time. However, arguably some of these texts do not refer to the value of children in and of themselves, such as the child in Ruth 4.16, which will be argued is valued partially in terms of his ability to build up the deceased.

Tracy Lemos goes further and questions the conventional wisdom that children were economically valuable. She highlights that weak crop growth may make it more challenging to provide for a larger number of household residents, and that this may lead to more desperate measures:

> ...a household might consist of struggling tenant farmers, day laborers, a widow forced into prostitution to provide for her children, or debt slaves... [Some reconstructions] follow too closely the idealized portrait of the

---

100. Ibid., 17.
101. Ibid., 42. Stiebert also notes the extolling of a parent's love or compassion (Isa. 49.15; Pss. 103.13; 27.10); the horror of a parent's inability to save their children (Deut. 28.53; 2 Kgs 6.28-29; Lam. 4.10; Jer. 19.9; 47.3); the incentive to fight to protect ones family (Neh. 4.14; 5.2, 5): Stiebert, *Fathers and Daughters*, 34–5.

Israelite family found in some biblical texts and do not take into consideration the plethora of evidence that some Israelites did not hold property or have stable enough economic realities that they could afford to provide for very young children in the years before they [could contribute][102]

While Parker argued for the emotional importance of children, Lemos's work on violence and personhood takes a darker approach, surveying the acknowledged violence against children in the Hebrew Bible which 'is far more brutal than many scholars have wished to admit and in my view leads one in a particular direction—that is, toward the position that children, and young children, in particular, were not accorded the privileges and protections of personhood in ancient Israel'.[103] For example, arguing against the conventional wisdom that children are economically important, she states: 'this is important because the approach that stresses the economic value of children is left flat-footed in explaining the abundance of evidence for violence committed against children *by their own parents*'.[104]

Lemos notes that texts that *decry* violence against children emphasize familial relationship, not 'the tender age of victims'. Psalm 106.37-38, which discusses the sacrifice of children, refers 'their sons and their daughters' (בניהם ואת־בנותיהם) twice. The same phenomenon appears in Ezek. 16.20. The same phrase is used in discussions of child cannibalism (Lev. 26.27-28; Deut. 28; Jer. 19.9), as well as parents selling their children (Neh. 5). Lemos argues that the deliberate inclusion of בנותיהם, rather than simply the catch-all בניהם, suggests the horror depicted is meant to 'arouse compassion or obedience' in its explicit articulation of the parent-to-children relationship, 'rather than the particular age or innocence or vulnerability of children'.[105] The social value placed on children in the Hebrew Bible is ambiguous, and any denial of compassion for children is false. However, this does not detract from the thrust of the Abraham narrative, which emphasizes numerical descendants and continuation of name, and Rachel and Leah, which highlights their role in providing sons for Jacob, and winning his affection, not an innate maternal desire per se. Procreation is valorized not for the sake of children, but for the capital they accrue, and the narrative crafts behaviour and desire in terms of playing the game.

---

102. Lemos, *Violence*, 142.
103. Ibid., 168.
104. Ibid., 142 (emphasis original).
105. Ibid., 167–8.

3. *Regulating Sexuality*

If certain texts valorize exaggerated procreation, this is not a carte blanche for unrestrained sexual behaviour. Instead, sexuality is highly regulated, in a way that focuses on ensuring the paternity of the child. Legal material provides a framework for controlling sexuality, and the following two case studies will look at the regulation of sex within and without the family: Deuteronomy provides a framework for the boundaries of appropriate sexual behaviour within the broader community, while Leviticus has a detailed consideration of sexual appropriateness within the kinship group.

3.1. *Law and Narrative in Deuteronomy*

Deuteronomy construct women's sexuality as within the domain of the man, whether her husband or father.[106] The law has a focus on בנים, rather than the Priestly זרע, and promises a complete absence of infertility if the law is followed (7.3-4). The transmission of identity is primarily through the teaching of the law from parent to child (4.10).[107] The family unit is situated around the father, whose absence causes the unit to disintegrate into widows and orphans.[108] The legal material is highly gendered, and tends to speak of women 'as objects of action rather than as legal agents'.[109] Legal material focuses on establishing women's virginity (22.13-19),[110] and punishment for any lack of it (22.21-22), with virginity always understood in relation to the father or husband.[111] Legal texts offer clarifying criteria for determining if a woman is guilty of adultery (22.22), and the grounds for considering her to have been raped (22.23-29). Again, the offense is constructed as primarily an offence towards the father or husband, to the extent that if an unbetrothed virgin is raped, the attacker is to pay a fine to her father and he (the attacker) is to take her in marriage without the possibility of divorce.[112] Entrance into the congregation is

---

106. Extensive analysis of the legal material in relation to gender and sexuality can be found in Pressler, *View of Women*; Anderson, *Women*; Ellens, *Sex Texts*.

107. See also Deut. 4.25, 40; 5.14, 26; 6.2, 7, 20-21; 11.19, 21; 12.12, 18; 16.11, 14.

108. Fewell and Gunn, *Gender*, 71.

109. Lemos, *Violence*, 64.

110. Gordon J. Wenham, '*Betûlāh* "A Girl of Marriageable Age"', *VT* 22, no. 3 (1972): 326–48. To counter this, see Pressler, *View of Women*, 25–8.

111. Anderson, *Women*, 43. Jeffrey H. Tigay, *Deuteronomy*, JPSTC (Philadelphia: Jewish Publication Society, 1996), 204.

112. The woman's marital status defines 'the nature of the offense and the severity of the penalty'; intercourse with a married/betrothed woman 'violates her

limited to those with functioning male genitalia (32.2), emphasizing the importance of reproduction, and specific ethnic and national criteria are put in place (23.3-9). The prohibition of remarriage to a former wife who has married another man may be either protective of the wife or reflective of an attempt to control the boundaries between blurred family lines, along the line of the law of adultery, possibly minimizing questions about paternity.[113] A man is prohibited from going to war for the first year after marriage (24.5), in order to please his wife – possibly suggesting a period for procreation.[114] Furthermore, a woman who intervenes in a fight and seizes the genitals of her husband's enemy is to have her hand cut off. In this instance, Tikva Frymer-Kensky argues that the woman has threatened male authority, by threatening the male genitals, which are sacrosanct.[115] This context for the law of levirate marriage may suggest a thematic link with procreation.

Cheryl Anderson, in *Women, Ideology and Violence: Critical Theory and the Construction of Gender in the Book of the Covenant and the Deuteronomic Law*, argues that some legal material (Deut. 21.15-17, 18-21; 22.13-21; 23.1) construct generational difference, within a structure that privileges the male/father as primary head, from whom the mother can derive authority within specific contexts, and which delineates between the parental generation and the children.[116] The laws, however, legislate for social control: the body becomes the central location of social control, and we can discern bodies as socially constructed. Following theories of how contemporary law encodes the female body, Anderson distinguishes three forms of control in the Deuteronomic Law:[117]

---

husband's claim to exclusive possession of her sexuality'. The punishment of death is not contingent on whether the woman has consented, whereas when an unbetrothed woman is raped 'it is a financial injury to her father... [who is] to be compensated'. The injury to the woman is social, and 'not treated as assault': Pressler, 'Sexual Violence', 107.

113. Anderson, *Women*, 46. See also Jer. 3.1, which Pressler argues relates the law to sexual purity or pollution: Pressler, 'Sexual Violence', 60.

114. Anderson, *Women*, 66. See also the discussion of Wright in the Introduction.

115. Tikva Frymer-Kensky, 'Deuteronomy', in *Women's Bible Commentary: Expanded Edition*, ed. Carol Ann Newsom and Sharon H. Ringe (Louisville, KY: Westminster John Knox, 1998), 67. This relates to the symbolic status of the genitals in the oaths of Genesis.

116. Anderson, *Women*, 56–8.

117. Ibid., 69–72, following Mary Jo Frug, 'A Postmodern Feminist Legal Manifesto (An Unfinished Draft)', in *After Identity: A Reader in Law and Culture*, ed. Dan Danielsen and Karen Engle (New York: Routledge, 1995), 7–23.

1. The female body submits to male authority, moving primarily from the father's control to the husband's control. The woman is never free to have intercourse outside of this construct, augmented by the restrictions on her contact with the male genitalia (25.11-12) and the control of the husband over her sexuality after his death (25.5-10).
2. The female body is meant for sex with men. Male sexual activity is prohibited when women come under the domain of other men; however, it is acceptable in terms of prostitutes, female slaves and foreign women. Non-privileged women are particularly sexualized.
3. The female body is meant for maternity. The laws encourage a kind of perpetuation and reproduction of the male's household, and strictly control the sexual activity of women within this household.

Carolyn Pressler's schematization, while focusing more on family law than the construction of identity, has similar parallels, and she suggests three themes: order (within the family); integrity (at the boundaries of the family); and continuity (in the reproduction of the family).[118] She states:

> The Deuteronomic family laws examined have as their primary focus neither women, per se, nor men, per se, but the family. They support the family, however, by affirming parental and especially paternal authority, by asserting the husband's unilateral and exclusive claims over his wife's sexuality, and by addressing a man's need for a male heir. In these laws, the interests of the family are largely identified with the interests of the man.[119]

The law also constructs who and what a man is, through a series of intersecting elements, traits and practices.[120] Mark George lists who the Israelite male *can* have sex with, whether prohibited or not: 'married women, engaged women, former wives, father's wives, mothers-in-law, sisters, virgin women who are not engaged, temple prostitutes…sex through war'. Deuteronomy constructs a highly sexualized male, with the text fixated on all the different possibilities of male sexual activity.[121] All those who are excluded from the assembly are understood in terms of reproduction and kinship: those with their penis or testicles cut off,

---

118. Pressler, *View of Women*, 97–101.
119. Ibid., 101.
120. George, 'Masculinity', 68.
121. Ibid., 72–4.

the 'misbegotten', Ammonites and Moabites to the tenth generation, Edomites and Egyptians to the third.[122] George hints at perhaps the fundamental ideology of reproduction in Deuteronomy:

> The deity, however, has no female deity partner, either wife, consort, or virgin, with whom he may procreate, at least according to Deuteronomy. How does he perpetuate his name? Through his chosen people and their observance of his Torah. Should they fail to observe it, then Yhwh will blot out their names from upon the earth.[123]

YHWH's desire to be perpetuated, through his passing on of the law throughout generations, subsumes other masculinities within the text. This is tied up with social control in the laws itself: the term 'purge the evil' occurs within the sex laws three times (22.13-29) and elsewhere in the context of social and religious law (17.7, 12; 19.13, 19; 21.9, 21; 24.7); this is intended to 'ensure the integrity of the social fabric, which may be blemished and undermined by the presence of wrongdoing'. The formula's use in the sex laws implies 'that maintaining the proper relations between the sexes—particularly with regard to the uncompromising fidelity incumbent upon women to maintain toward their patron, be he father, present husband, or future spouse—is as critical to preserving the proper social order as maintaining exclusive fidelity to Yhwh'.[124] Here Cynthia Edenburg makes a crucial link: the sex laws are not a suggested moral compass but are deeply intertwined with Deuteronomy's notion of social stability, and this stability revolves around a form of family life that is highly controlled. Family is controlled, women's and men's bodies are controlled, and the fruit of these bodies is controlled.

This is crucial to our discussion as it demonstrates how the integrity of the family through the control of sexuality and gender is tied up deeply with social stability and continuation; male childlessness ruptures this stability, and laws such as Deut. 25.5-10 step in to correct this rupture. The inverse is seen in non-legal material and the threat of non-compliance with the law, not just infertility and adultery, or the migration of children, but the cannibalization of offspring (28.53-57): 'you will eat the fruit of your womb' (ואכלת פרי־בטנך). Here a reversal of the stable, generational and reproducing paradigm throughout Deuteronomy breaks down in horrific acts of the eating of children – parents will eat their *own* sons and daughters, the fruit of their *own* womb, and the desperate woman

---

122. Ibid., 77.
123. Ibid., 76.
124. Cynthia Edenburg, 'Ideology and Social Context of the Deuteronomic Women's Sex Laws (Deuteronomy 22:13-29)', *JBL* 128, no. 1 (2009): 59.

will not even share the afterbirth or her new-born with her own children. These curses are the terms of the covenant (28.69), and the covenant is made with all those in Israel, explicitly טפכם, your children, and נשיכם, your wives or women (29.11), and future generations (29.15).[125] These future generations are invoked repeatedly (29.22, 29; 30.2, 19; 32.46) and further promises of prosperity are made (30.5, 9). Those who were not yet alive are to be gathered together periodically to hear the teaching (31.12-13), and there is a reference to YHWH's future smiting of Israel, that he would destroy children and the elderly, slaying them by the sword and removing their memory from among men (32.27) if they turn from the covenant. The one who turns away will have their name erased from under the heavens (29.20).

The focus here is on small generic families within a broader social framework, on the steady and controlled reproduction of a particular social order (the law), rather than on promises of excessive descendants as in Genesis. However, the text creates a discourse in which fidelity to the law results in a secure reproduction of the present community, the perpetuation of the male and his name, in a carefully regulated structure.[126] Familial relations are exclusively patrilineal and patriarchal. Women are frequently referred to and sometimes addressed, but their only power is that which they derive from their husbands and is only expressed through their motherhood. The text creates a system of sexual laws where the man can be in complete control of his wife/daughter's body and anything coming from this body. Virginity is highly prized, and adultery – whether the woman is engaged or married – is punished by death, except for a woman who is seized in the field. In this way, the control of women's bodies allows the man to guarantee any descendants will be his, and thus, the child is guaranteed to continue the man's name, removing ambiguity or competition. Deuteronomy ends with a rhetorical vision of what a lack of the compliance to the law will result in – the symbolic inversion of this social stability and the collapse of proper parent–child relations, with the erasure of one's name from under heaven.

3.2. *Incest Prohibitions: Regulating the Family*

Lot's sexual relations with his daughters in Genesis 19 starkly confronts us with the subject of incest. This narrative is made particularly interesting by several aspects: the lack of any overt condemnation of the act in

---

125. Tigay, *Deuteronomy*, 278.
126. Interestingly, Biale, *Blood and Belief*, 34, translates Deut. 34.7 (ולא־נס לחה) as 'his wetness has not abandoned him' and argues it implies Moses's fertility in old age.

Genesis 19; the presence of a specific prohibition against father–daughter incest is conspicuously missing from Leviticus 18 and 20; the inclusion of the act of producing progeny in desperation creates offspring and nations; and that Ruth, who we will come to later, is the fruit of one of these nations, the Moabites. The (apparent) lack of prohibition against father–daughter incest is made more intriguing when we realize the laws of Leviticus 18 and 20 appear to contradict the text of Deut. 25.5-10 (and Gen. 38) which attempts to mandate a widow and her brother-in-law to create offspring. Because of the centrality of intra-family dynamics and the importance of narratives that appear to permit incest in this analysis, it will be necessary to briefly explore the topic here, as well as using it as a further case study of the construction of intra-familial relations. By exploring how these prohibitions operate, it might be possible to clarify whether Deut. 25.5-10 contradicts Leviticus 18 and 20, or is operating in a similar structure.

Leviticus 18 and 20 contain a list of prohibited relations and various punishments for relations, respectively. The bulk of these relations can be categorized as 'incest', though it is important to note that there is no cross-cultural category of incest; while anthropological research demonstrates that incest taboos are 'universal, or near-universal', it is culturally specific to each context, and what may be prohibited or taboo in one context may be permissible or encouraged in another being understood, for example as 'close-kin marriage'.[127] Leviticus makes no distinction between 'blood' and 'marriage' incest, and 'the social is blurred by the lack of clear-cut differentiation between the two categories'.[128] We will review Leviticus 18 and 20, discuss it in relation to narrative texts, and suggest how incest can be understood socially, and therefore why it can be transgressed to maintain family stability.

Leviticus 18 is structured as follows:

1-5: General introduction about not following the practices of other nations

6: General command against 'approaching anyone near of kin to uncover nakedness':[129]

איש איש אל־כל־שאר בשרו לא תקרבו לגלות ערוה

---

127. Stiebert, *Fathers and Daughters*, 102–3. For example, brother–sister marriages were encouraged in Graeco-Roman Egypt: Brent D. Shaw, 'Explaining Incest: Brother–Sister Marriage in Graeco-Roman Egypt', *Man* 27, no. 2 (1992): 267–99.

128. Brenner, *Intercourse*, 90.

129. Jackson suggests that 'uncovering the nakedness' carries marital connotations, as the language switches at Lev. 18.19 to speak of intercourse which cannot involve marriage: Bernard S. Jackson, 'The "Institutions" of Marriage and Divorce in

7-18: Specifically prohibited list:
Nakedness of the father, which is the nakedness of the mother
Nakedness of the father's wife, which is the nakedness of the father
Nakedness of the sister, the father's daughter, or mother's daughter
Nakedness of the son's daughter, or daughter's daughter
Nakedness of the father's sister
Nakedness of the mother's sister
Nakedness of the father's brother, that is, his wife
Nakedness of the daughter-in-law
Nakedness of the brother's wife
Nakedness of a woman and her daughter, or her son's daughter or daughter's daughter
Taking a woman as a rival to her sister and uncovering nakedness while her sister is alive

19-23: Further prohibited sexual acts

24-30: Conclusion to not follow the practices of the other nations

Leviticus 20 contains punishments for these and other acts.[130] In v. 21, if a man takes his brother's wife, they will die childless (עֲרִירִים). This is an irony when compared to the command to produce offspring for the deceased in Deut. 25.5-10. The ordering of laws 'reveals the lack of any apparent logical order in the arrangement of the rules', and penalties, if given, 'are bewilderingly varied';[131] so much so that Johanna Stiebert, in

the Hebrew Bible', *JSS* 56, no. 2 (2011): 233 n. 48. Stiebert suggests 'the prohibited activity, "uncovering of nakedness", seems to be another technical term and a standard expression of Leviticus for what is clearly considered some sort of, possibly unlawful, gross indecency, incestuous penetrative sex': Johanna Stiebert, *First-Degree Incest and the Hebrew Bible: Sex in the Family*, LHBOTS 596 (London: Bloomsbury T&T Clark, 2016), 53.

130. Stiebert notes that incest is easy to conceal, suppress and deny and that the threats are 'first particularly harsh and secondly insistent about reminding potential offenders of the omniscience of God': Stiebert, *Fathers and Daughters*, 118.

131. Calum Carmichael, *Law, Legend, and Incest in the Bible: Leviticus 18–20* (Ithaca, NY: Cornell University Press, 1997), 8, suggests rather than poor arrangement, the laws are a response to narrative material in Genesis: 'the priestly lawgiver disapproved of what he found in some of his nation's traditions because these traditions condoned incestuous relationships', instead proposing the laws are a response to narrative material in Genesis and elsewhere (pp. 5–9). While compelling in places, and making sense of some of the arrangement of the law, Carmichael's argument

First-Degree Incest and the Hebrew Bible: Sex in the Family, suggests Leviticus 18 and 20:

> ...constitute in some respects rather odd expressions of legal formulations. Laws tend to be carefully worded and ordered, precise and concise, striving for consistency and comprehensiveness – yet here we have two groups of prohibitions that are in close proximity but at variance with each other. I would say that the overall tone of these lists – with their emotive expressions such as 'uncovering the nakedness', and the vivid reference to the land 'spewing out' its defiled inhabitants (Lev. 18:28) – is rather more shrill than legal language tends to be.[132]

Jonathan Ziskind maps out the historically dominant explanations for the lack of a daughter–father incest prohibition,[133] namely that it dropped out accidentally. However, he suggests opportunities for editors to have corrected this means it is unlikely it would be let slip. While some have suggested the writer wished to fashion it into a Decalogue, and so limited the number, Ziskind points out the more distant prohibited relations could be removed. Baruch Levine suggests that by prohibiting more distant relatives, daughters were automatically excluded:[134] father–daughter incest was instinctively understood to be wrong, so it did not need prohibiting, while Lev. 18.6's 'None of you shall approach anyone near of kin to uncover nakedness' of all his flesh/kin, אל־כל־שאר,[135] functions as a kind of umbrella ruling for close relations. Alternatively, the 'vagueness' of the prohibition concerning father–daughter incest is a kind of loophole: ownership of a daughter's sexuality is so strong that it cannot preclude the possibility of father–daughter sexual relations if the father so desires. For example, the Code of Hammurabi 154, rather than proscribing death, forces the father who has sexual intercourse with his daughter to flee the town.[136]

---

often stretches material to fit his scheme beyond the point of being compelling (see Stiebert, *Fathers and Daughters*, 126–9), and arguments, such as the Levitical writers hesitation about the Tamar and Judah narrative being about anti-Canaanism, is fairly tenuous (Carmichael, *Incest*, 19).

132. Stiebert, *Incest*, 62.

133. Jonathan R. Ziskind, 'The Missing Daughter in Leviticus XVIII', *VT* 46, no. 1 (1996): 125–7.

134. Baruch Levine, *Leviticus*, JPSTC (Philadelphia: Jewish Publication Society, 1994), 120.

135. Stiebert notes שאר in Lev. 21.2-3 includes mother, father, son, daughter, brother and a virgin sister 'close to him': Stiebert, *Incest*, 53.

136. Ziskind, 'Missing Daughter', 126.

Ziskind, however, points to a compelling understanding which does not suggest a permissiveness of father–daughter incest, but accounts for its absence in Leviticus 18. All relations are given with the second-person masculine singular possessive adjective, addressing an adult Israelite male: 'your mother', 'your father's wife', 'your sister…your father's daughter or your mother's daughter' and so on. The prohibitions, as they go on, 'become more immediate and personal'.[137] Rather than reiterating a command about adultery or rape, the writer employs terms like 'uncover the nakedness' to these prohibitions 'to be absolute…and to be lifelong, i.e., from the time the relationship was established by either birth or marriage, and not to end with death or divorce effected by the male relative whose linkage to a man defined the prohibition'.[138] He suggests, in defining relations in terms of kin, the logical prohibition against sex with a daughter would read 'you shall not uncover the nakedness of your daughter; her nakedness is your nakedness'; however, 'the impact of this truism was vitiated by the first half of the statement, that is, the prohibition itself'.[139] This would, argues Ziskind, be seen as an undermining of a father's authority with the family.

Stiebert notes that the argument made by Deborah Rooke somewhat corresponds to Ziskind's argument. For Rooke, Leviticus 18 and 20 remain 'an exercise in male bonding, that is, in protecting the kinship bonds between men by making sure that they are not in competition with each other for the same women'.[140] Rooke states that the prohibitions are directed at men, and sex is conceptualized as 'male initiated'.[141] To uncover the nakedness denotes shame and usually refers to female or feminine objects, so 'only the one who covered the woman was entitled to uncover her sexually'.[142] Rooke continues that:

---

137. Ibid., 127.
138. Ibid., 128. Ziskind understands these prohibitions as beneficial to the woman who can now not be 'handed around' the household for sexual use, including the widow obligated to the levirate 'who may not want such a marriage', contrasted with Tamar (Gen. 38) and the widow in Deuteronomy, who present themselves as being wronged.
139. Ibid., 129.
140. Deborah W. Rooke, 'The Bare Facts: Gender and Nakedness in Leviticus 18', in *A Question of Sex? Gender and Difference in the Hebrew Bible and Beyond*, ed. Deborah W. Rooke, HBM 14 (Sheffield: Sheffield Phoenix, 2007), 33.
141. Ibid., 23 n. 11.
142. Ibid., 27–8. Rooke compares the use of 'uncover the nakedness' referring to shame in Isa. 47.3, Ezek. 16.36-37; Ezek. 23; Hos. 2.11-12.

> On the assumption that exposure of a woman's nakedness is a way of claiming or expressing control over her sexuality, the prohibition against uncovering nakedness is a way of invalidating a given male's claim to sexual control of a given woman, by presenting his uncovering of her as a violation... [That it is used only of incest and not adultery or male–male intercourse] would suggest that the incest laws are addressing a situation where kinship links might lead men to think that they were entitled to sexual rights over particular women, and so the function of the 'nakedness' language in the prohibitions is to acknowledge this mistaken perception.[143]

So, for Rooke, Gen. 18.6 becomes 'no man of you shall approach any flesh of his (own) flesh to uncover nakedness',[144] emphasizing the bodily nature of kinship relations. The use of שאר, kin, for Rooke becomes a 'third category of body, a third gender', and notes that the bodies constructed as most threatening are constructed as male bodies in their relationship to the man addressed.[145] Rooke concludes that when viewed in light of hierarchical kinship structures, the most dangerous bodies are those that relate to 'paternal male relatives'. This is done most forcefully through the use of the nakedness formulation: 'incest is constructed not just as an offence or insult against another male but as an actual physical violation of his person'.[146] It is more than a violation against a person, as in adultery, but 'threatens the basic family structures and disrupts the social hierarchy in a more fundamental way than adultery does'.[147] Stiebert discusses the drawbacks of both Rooke and Ziskind's arguments, dealing with an incredibly complex text; however, their theses allow us to understand the social nature of the prohibitions in more detail.[148] Without attempting to 'solve' the case of the missing daughter, we are able to see that central to the prohibitions is both a heightened sense of the 'closeness' of even non-blood kin and how this contributes to the prohibition against sexual intercourse with them as being of the same flesh, as well as how the incest laws are a reflection of patriarchal kinship structures which emphasize male kinship.

---

143. Ibid., 27.
144. Ibid., 29.
145. The body of the father's wife (18.7-8), the body of the father's brother's wife (18.14), the body of the brother's wife (18.16), and the body of the granddaughter (18.10). Ibid., 31–2.
146. Ibid., 33.
147. Ibid.
148. See Stiebert, *Fathers and Daughters*, 113–15.

It has been suggested that Leviticus 18 and 20 reflect a later stage in the development of the legal tradition of levirate marriage, in which the Priestly writer effectively prohibits the practice through the inclusion of certain relations in the list of prohibited practices. Jackson, however, correctly notes in response to attempts to harmonize the passages that any conflict between this and other laws is a 'post-canonization conflict'. Additionally, he proposes texts belong to different traditions, therefore suggesting Leviticus 18 belongs to a 'religious' as opposed to legal tradition.[149] Stiebert compares the law to Lot's daughters, Judah and Tamar, and Ruth and Boaz, in her examination of incest in narrative texts. Some of the relationships prohibited in Leviticus 18 are depicted in narrative texts without opprobrium.[150] Stiebert notes that, whereas Leviticus addresses the male as the subject of incest, and despite contemporary evidence that suggests men are the perpetrators of incest against daughters, the pattern in the narratives is curiously one where the daughters take the 'incest initiative'.[151] Moreover, in these and other texts, incest is not the dominant theme but rather 'survival by trickery';[152] this stands in contrast to male-initiated incest which acts as an 'index of their ascending power and the father's political demise, or for sexual gratification'.[153] Also, the narratives lack the specific 'nakedness' terminology of the legal texts.[154] Stiebert suggests that rather than understanding the sexual relationships between family members as 'incestuous/illegal' they are better viewed as 'destabilizing/undesirable'.[155] As Stiebert puts it:

> Thus, while the primary thrust of the prohibitions is to attempt to promote the authority and allay the anxieties of the older generation (in particular older males), who may see themselves threatened particularly by younger males, there is also acknowledgment reflected in the lists of a need to accommodate the rights of other members of the household. The likelihood is that laws assigning sexual rights over women to particular males are aimed at

---

149. Jackson, 'Institutions', 233. For example, he suggests it is religious as they appear in the apodictic form and carry religious sanctions such as כרת and the loss of promised land, and appear to conflict with social institutions such as Jacob's marriages and Amnon and Tamar. For his distinction between religious and legal marriage, see 244–51.

150. Stiebert, *Fathers and Daughters*, 105.

151. Ibid., 106, and n. 20; Brenner, *Intercourse*, 93, makes the same point in the context of a discussion of women as sexual objects in legal and narrative texts.

152. Stiebert, *Fathers and Daughters*, 130.

153. Brenner, *Intercourse*, 101.

154. Ibid., 118.

155. Stiebert, *Incest*, 45.

minimizing competition between men and, consequently, maximizing the odds of social stability. The probability of competition between women, too, is acknowledged – hence the laws proscribing sex with two sisters, or with a mother and her daughter, or grand-daughter.[156]

This goes some way to disentangling the seeming conflict between incest law and levirate marriage – they are part of the same structures of power: there is no conflict, if they are understood as sharing the same sense of doxa, of embodied appropriateness, sharing the same sense of naturalness. If the incest prohibitions act to ensure social stability, we can understand how the levirate could be used to complement understandings of incest; the brother can have intercourse with the widow as it is a strengthening of male bonding, with the brother of the deceased responding to *instability* and repairing broken familial relations.

4. Conclusion

For Foucault, 'power is tolerable only on the condition that it masks a substantial part of itself. Its success is proportional to its ability to hide its own mechanisms.'[157] For a particular social discourse to reproduce itself, is must repeatedly mask itself and prove itself as natural. By being redacted into the very beginning of the story and subsequently reinforced through narrative after narrative, the text creates a situation in which men have male progeny and women produce progeny for them. In Genesis's tapestry of discourses of reproduction, the ultimate valorized virtue for women is to prolong the family line; men, on the other hand, are presumed fertile and their right to progeny is privileged and unquestionable; moreover, their name and continuity become theologically mandated by YHWH.

The supremacy of male transmission of identity is seen most distinctly in the priestly discourse around circumcision, in which the father transmits identity through sons, and the covenant through the material inscription on the penis. In this inscription name, descendants, and land become subsumed within a male discourse and the building of capital both for individuals and dynasties. The perpetuation of the seed is explicitly associated with the name of Abraham, and its perpetuation is fetishized as a good in and of itself. However, a discourse which constructs men as the centre of the procreative narrative, to the extent women are

---

156. Ibid., 79.
157. Michel Foucault, *The History of Sexuality*. Vol. 1, *An Introduction*, trans. Robert Hurley (New York: Vintage, 1980), 86.

excluded from the genealogies, must also construct a place for women within the narrative to conscript them in. There are glimpses – such as for Sarah – of the building up of women's lineage. This tension between reproduction and honour is seen dramatically with Rachel and Leah. The narrative sketches a symbolic structure in which women's maternal value is not only emphasized, but in which some consideration to its value is offered in terms of loyalty to the man's line. The narrative does not deny the difficulty this creates for women, as demonstrated through the attention paid to Leah and Rachel's suffering; it does, however, suggest the suffering is worth the eventual outcome, and allows women to read themselves into the narrative. However, no relationship of power can be completely hegemonic, and we see hints of conflict, most notably in the desire of Sarah and Rachel to be 'built up'. While the text, from a feminist perspective, is problematic, it is arguably naïve to view it as pure ideology. It reflects a kind of doxa which is held between the reader and writer, between men and women. Here the interplay between symbolic capital and symbolic violence does not only take place in a field of external institutions; it takes place in the most intimate field of family life, of love, of attention. The field is so internalized in the characters of Rachel and Leah that rather than rational decision making, their habitus, their unconscious sense of how to play the game, is what spurs them to produce offspring for Jacob. Intimacy, love, rivalry all reflect aspects of the habitus, ways of attuning oneself to the masked models of power and capital, which seem natural in patriarchal society. Yet in it we also see the introduction of another competing and complementary field – the religious field – and sexual and reproductive presidency is taken from Jacob and put into the hands of the divine, while the divine appears to be a powerful agent in both Lean and Rachel's practice.

As well as narrative material, sexuality and reproduction are regulated legally. In Deuteronomy and Leviticus we saw, however, that the focus is not sexuality per se, but the integrity of the family. The importance of the integrity of the family is highlighted through the strict control of bodies, and within Deuteronomy very membership of the community is premised on the following and passing on of the law; this law ensures women's sexuality is only utilized in the service of the men under whose patronage she finds herself. Texts that limit male sexual autonomy enforce a broader social order: restricting a man's access to another's wife in Deuteronomy. Leviticus 18 and 20 further regulate sexuality within the household, delineating sexual appropriateness between kin. The restrictions, similarly to Deuteronomy, are not a personalized moral sense of appropriateness, but regulate male kinship and maintain social order. The incest laws appear to prohibit the kind of sexual intercourse mandated in levirate marriage. Once we understand the incest legislation as ensuring social stability, we can see how levirate marriage, rather than destabilizing the family unit, respond to insecurity and reinforce its.

These texts construct male bodies as sexualized and reproducing, and demonstrate the gendered importance of responding to the failure of men to reproduce: if the male fails to transmit name or seed, he not only ruptures the normal line of succession, but fails in his performative masculinity. The texts also construct women as reproductive, and normalize the submission of their bodies and sexuality to the productive prowess of men. The normality presented in these texts reveals the interplay between field and habitus, and suggests a paradigm for the woman's role in levirate marriage, both in the formal legislation of Deut. 25.5-10, and the ways different characters negotiate this law in the narratives of Tamar, Lot's daughters, and Ruth.

Chapter 6

THE HOUSE OF THE FATHER?

In establishing the significance of burial, name, reproduction, and kinship, the various themes have centred around the basic unit of the family. This chapter will outline how the בית אב, House of the Father, is integrated into the broader arrangement of society, how it is transmitted through the inheritance of property, how it is established through genealogy and safeguarded through relationships between parents and children, and how it can be erased.[1] This will make sense of the roles different actors play in the core texts (the father, the widow, the brother etc.), and will allow us to establish how responses to the death of the childless man are not centred around the deceased individual, but are rooted in the social order. The three basic social units in the Hebrew Bible in the first temple period are the מטה or שבט (rod, staff, or tribe), 'which brought together clans related by descent from a common ancestor';[2] the משפחה (clan), which is the intermediate between the larger tribe and the smaller family units;[3] and

---

1. Perdue suggests, for בית אב, the terms 'family household', 'extended family', or 'compound family': Leo G. Perdue, 'The Israelite and Early Jewish Family: Summary and Conclusions', in *Families in Ancient Israel*, ed. Joseph Blenkinsopp et al., The Family, Religion, and Culture (Louisville, KY: Westminster John Knox, 1997), 175. Meyers suggests 'family household', 'which more successfully reflects the integral relationship between kinship-linked persons and the material basis for their survival': Carol Meyers, 'The Family in Early Israel', in Blenkinsopp et al., eds., *Families in Ancient Israel*, 19. Both these suggestions, I would argue, obscure the significance of the male head of the house.

2. Naomi A. Steinberg, *The World of the Child in the Hebrew Bible*, HBM 51 (Sheffield: Sheffield Phoenix, 2013), 46.

3. Joseph Blenkinsopp, 'The Family in First Temple Israel', in Blenkinsopp et al., eds., *Families in Ancient Israel*, 50. Blenkinsopp does, however, note the fluid nature of these terms.

the בית אב, the house of the father, the more immediate 'nuclear' family, which will be explored more fully in the following discussion.⁴ We read in Josh. 7.14:

ונקרבתם בבקר לשבטיכם והיה השבט אשר־ילכדנו יהוה יקרב למשפחות
והמשפחה אשר־ילכדנה יהוה תקרב לבתים והבית אשר ילכדנו יהוה יקרב לגברים

Here we see the divisions set of שבט, משפחה, and בית, with an emphasis on counting the males, גברים.⁵ Paula McNutt suggests there are difficulties in understanding the precise kinship terms used throughout the text. According to McNutt, 'social categories refer to ideal and not necessarily empirical categories...members of Israelite society themselves (at whatever time) were probably not precise in their use of these terms'; the meaning changed over time, as organization became 'subsumed under the centralized state', with the possibility that society 'did not adhere to any single system'.⁶ However, it appears the 'house' was a consistent feature; therefore the 'house' needs to be explored more broadly.

1. *Defining the Family: House of the Father*

The work of Susan Gillespie on the house is highly productive for this study.⁷ Gillespie calls for a renewed focus on the house as the object of social analysis, especially in 'house societies', suggesting that focusing on the house is more productive than a classificatory approach as it focuses on 'practices and understandings by which relationships are constructed

---

4. Different definitions are possible, for example Meyers suggests 'village' alongside clan or region for משפחה: Meyers, 'Household Religion', 119. Levine argues the house and clan is more realistic than the more idealized tribe (שבט, מטה). He argues the בית אב was patrilocal and 'predicated on ownership of a shared clan residence', and argues for its durability over different forms of government: Baruch Levine, 'The Clan-Based Economy of Biblical Israel', in *Symbiosis, Symbolism, and the Power of the Past: Canaan, Ancient Israel, and Their Neighbors from the Late Bronze Age Through Roman Palaestina*, ed. William Dever and Seymour Gitin (Winona Lake, IN: Eisenbrauns, 2003), 445–54.

5. See also Num. 3.15.

6. Paula M. McNutt, *Reconstructing the Society of Ancient Israel*, Library of Ancient Israel (Louisville, KY: Westminster John Knox, 1999), 76. The analysis of the בית אב has often been in terms of household religion. See Meyers, 'Household Religion', 119, and literature referenced there.

7. I discovered Gillespie in Chapman's work on the House of the Mother, discussed below.

in everyday social life, rather than on abstract or idealized rules'.[8] Groups 'referred to by the term 'house' are corporate bodies, sometimes quite large, organized by their shared residence, subsistence, means of production, origin, ritual action, or metaphysical essence, all of which entail a commitment to a corpus of house property, which in turn can be said to materialize the social group'.[9] Houses 'define and socially reproduce themselves by the actions involved with the preservation of their joint property, as a form of material reproduction that objectifies their existence as a group and serves to configure their status vis-à-vis other houses within the larger society'. In house societies, taking the house as the focal point of study explores how the actions and structures of groups in their local context are 'intertwined with genealogy, that is, kinship through time'.[10] Houses are 'long-lived corporate entities', people 'belong' and 'construct their identities and configure their social interactions' in relation to the house. However, there is 'no single form of affiliation':

> Descent and inheritance may flow through either or both parents depending on circumstances; endogamy and exogamy may coexist; postmarital residence is contingent on a number of factors; and marriage patterns, exchange relations, co-residence, or shared labour may be the primary determinants of social relationships, rather than their outcomes.[11]

The forms of organizing society which anthropologists (and biblical scholars) often elevate to the governing principle of social organization – commonly matrilineal or patrilineal descent – are less determinative in a house society, which may account for the sub-nesting of women's houses.[12] According to Gillespie, a focus on the house can enable us to 'move beyond kinship as natural', instead focusing on the role of 'production, religion, gender, rank, wealth, and power' as 'principles and strategies of consanguinity and affinity'.[13]

---

8. Susan D. Gillespie, 'Beyond Kinship: An Introduction', in *Beyond Kinship: Social and Material Reproduction in House Societies*, ed. Rosemary A. Joyce and Susan D. Gillespie (Philadelphia: University of Pennsylvania Press, 2000), 1. Gillespie is building on the two decades of work on house societies, initiated by two publications of Lévi-Strauss: Claude Lévi-Strauss, *The Way of the Masks*, trans. Sylvia Modelski (Seattle: University of Washington Press, 1982); Claude Lévi-Strauss, *Anthropology and Myth: Lectures, 1951–1982*, trans. Roy G. Willis (Oxford: Blackwell, 1987).
9. Gillespie, 'Kinship', 1–2.
10. Ibid., 2.
11. Ibid., 7.
12. As will be discussed in relation to Chapman, below.
13. Gillespie, 'Kinship', 9.

6. *The House of the Father?*

A house needs to negotiate 'strategies for maintaining its estate and producing its members over multiple generations'; the 'maintenance of links between past and present...is a fundamental value even if, though publicly claimed, it may have little basis in fact'. Status is negotiated through 'illustrious founders, usually house ancestors' and authority is based on 'precedence extending back into a legendary or even primordial past';[14] it is built with stories of migration, settlement, ancestral shrines, accounts of contests to establish priority, all held together through material objects such as ancestral relics, features in the landscape, and the house itself. Material and immaterial property continue to link members to these narratives, and actualize the house through time. The immaterial becomes materialized: 'intangible property, such as names or titles, is continually embodied by living persons, often in a cycle of generations, as when grandchildren take the names, and hence the identities, of their grandparents'.[15] This all contributes to house perpetuity:

> There is an important distinction between people and the structures upon which house relationships are constituted. The physical house (or temple or shrine), heirlooms, ancestral relics, and immaterial property represent a concentration of value, which is the key component to the standing of the house as an institution and its prestige in relation to other houses. The house so objectified signifies stability over time, although it is often rebuilt or even moved.[16]

The embodiment of the house, and its perpetuity, 'offers people a kind of immortality'; 'it lengthens the temporal span of their individual identities because the house itself is a reference to the past, as social and historical memories are focused on houses or empty places where houses once stood'.[17]

Both textual and ethno-archaeological material suggest that despite the ambiguity in some of the classificatory terms, the בית אב was the 'basic building block for the tribal structure and continued as such throughout the entire period under consideration'.[18] Blenkinsopp suggests that dwelling complexes from the period account for 'a nuclear family unit of two parents and between two and four children... [T]he typical household would also have included some or all of the following: grandparents, the

---

14. Ibid., 9–11.
15. Ibid., 12.
16. Ibid., 13.
17. Ibid., 16.
18. Blenkinsopp, 'Family', 51–3.

families of grown children (since postmarital patrilocal residence must have been very common), an adopted child…a divorced adult daughter who had returned to the paternal homestead, male and female servants or slaves, and other dependents.'[19] The בית אב is generally presented as endogamous, patriarchal, polygynous, patrilocal, joined (multigenerational), and patrilineal.[20] It may consist additionally of marginal members: debt servants, slaves, concubines, resident aliens, sojourners, day labourers, orphans and Levites (Exod. 20.8-10; Deut. 5.12-15; 16.11, 14).[21] Most of population Iron Age I and II lived in small villages, made up of mostly clusters of houses.[22] Four-room houses were the dominant model (although there may have been courtyards as part of this, or additional floors). Ground floors were used for domestic activities, with sleeping perhaps taking place (during good weather, and in the summer months) on the roof; and when the בית אב needed to be expanded a new four-room house was built adjacent.[23]

The security of the household becomes the foundation of social stability: 'The *bēt 'āb* was the basic element of patriarchal and urban society. Deep concern for keeping it alive and intact is the shaping force behind the customs, law and world-view of ancient society.'[24] Carol Meyers suggests levirate marriage, redemption and jubilee provisions were intended to keep small land units intact,[25] and McNutt even suggests

---

19. Ibid. Blenkinsopp is basing his reconstruction on, among other things, Stager's now-classic survey of material remains: Lawrence E. Stager, 'The Archaeology of the Family in Ancient Israel', *BASOR* 260 (1985): 1–35. See also Perdue, 'Family', 174–7.

20. Philip J. King and Lawrence E. Stager, *Life in Biblical Israel*, LAI (Louisville, KY: Westminster John Knox, 2001), 39.

21. Perdue, 'Family', 174–7. See the construction of Micah's house in Josh. 17–18: King and Stager, *Life*, 9–19.

22. Obed provides a useful synthesis of the extensive literature: Oded Borowski, *Daily Life in Biblical Times*, ABS 5 (Atlanta, GA: Society of Biblical Literature, 2003), 14–15. See also the comprehensive summary in: Patricia Dutcher-Walls, 'The Clarity of Double Vision: Seeing the Family in Sociological and Archaeological Perspective', in *The Family in Life and in Death: The Family in Ancient Israel: Sociological and Archaeological Perspectives*, ed. Patricia Dutcher-Walls, LHBOTS 504 (New York: T&T Clark, 2009), 1–15.

23. Borowski, *Daily Life*, 16–21.

24. Zafrira Ben-Barak, *Inheritance by Daughters in Israel and the Ancient Near East: A Social, Legal and Ideological Revolution*, trans. Betty Sigler Rozen (Jaffa: Archaeological Center Publications, 2006), 1.

25. Meyers, 'Family', 13–21.

that levirate marriage demonstrates the centrality of the survival of the 'nuclear family'.[26] The household is the primary economic unit, and consists of persons, their material culture, and their activities; and the בית אב, rather than comprising solely a nuclear family, indicates the extended family through patrilineality, which transmitted the material aspects of the household.[27] However, its common translation has given 'the illusion that a Hebrew equivalent of the word "lineage" is woven throughout the biblical text when in reality biblical schools are theorizing the "house" through the imposed lens of a patriline'.[28] The basic kinship unit of the household is brought together around a man and woman, or sometimes multiple women, whether coequal wives or concubines, yet the בית אב could include multiple 'nuclear units', sharing resources.[29] While there are a few texts such, as Josh. 7.14, quoted above, which 'outline a complete hierarchy' of house-clan-tribe, Cynthia Chapman's idea of houses 'nesting' within larger kinship units is compelling. Chapman proposes that the house is nested within the village, 'and ultimately within a nation'.[30] For example, Rebekah refers to a house as a single dwelling (Gen. 27.15), whereas Joshua 'is likely referring to a collection of Ephraimite houses (Josh. 24.15) and Isaiah describes the entire nation as "O House of Jacob"'.[31] Even the small individual house could be anything from a small nuclear family to multi-generation extended families; however, whatever the arrangement, the house forms the foundational ideal. Yet the house is not static, and repeated emphasis is put on its perpetuation. Chapman argues that there is a 'constellation' of Hebrew terms that construct the patrilineal ideal:

---

26. McNutt, *Reconstructing*, 90.

27. Meyers, 'Household Religion', 120. For various constructions of the בית אב, and the near absence of the term in Priestly material, see McNutt, *Reconstructing*, 87–92.

28. Chapman, *House*, 21.

29. McNutt, *Reconstructing*, 91.

30. Chapman, *House*, 25. Chapman builds on work that has demonstrated within one house there may be multiple, smaller sub-houses: Stager, 'Archaeology', 22; Susan Ackerman, 'Household Religion, Family Religion, and Women's Religion in Ancient Israel', in *Household and Family Religion in Antiquity*, ed. John Bodel and Saul M. Olyan, The Ancient World: Comparative Histories (Malden, MA: Blackwell, 2008), 129–32.

31. See also Lawrence Stager's 'nested' Jerusalem – the house of the hierarchy, the house of the King, and the house of YHWH as the 'apex of authority in this three-tiered cosmion': Lawrence E. Stager, 'The Patrimonial Kingdom of Solomon', in Dever and Gitin, eds., *Symbiosis, Symbolism, and the Power of the Past*, 69–71.

'house of the father'…'paternal begettings'…'patrimonial inheritance'… 'designated heir'…'name'…'monument'…and 'seed'. These terms represent the 'stability and eternal nature of a foundational father's house as he passed his name, inheritance, and monument to his designated heir in an unbroken chain'.[32]

'Together', Chapman notes, 'these terms communicate what we might call ancient Israel's patrilineal "dogma"'.[33] Sexual relationships form the foundation for the perpetuation of the house, and the male–female sexual union seems to instigate the sub-nested house.[34] This often appears to take place through some form of union; however, to describe these unions as marriage is problematic. Joseph Fleishman suggests the verb, to take, is a *terminus technicus* for a legitimate marriage.[35] Bernard Jackson, on the other hand, while accepting the possibility that לקח may operate as a legal term, says that 'it remains to be decided whether it does so in any particular context'.[36] לאשה, often translated wife, constructed of ל, to/for, and אשה, woman, and which often follows לקח, is also ambiguous: Jackson notes that two of the four 'wives' of Jacob were 'handmaidens' provided by one or other of the primary co-wives and are described in Gen. 32.22 'as the *shifḥah* when given by Laban to Leah… and even

---

32. Chapman, *House*, 27.
33. Ibid., 28.
34. Bendor has argued that each son formed his own house, citing Deut. 20.5-9 that 'building a house, planting a vineyard and taking a wife are joined together, the nuclear cell becoming a unit existing in its own right', which 'symbolize life at a decisive state for a member of the *bêit 'āb* who has come to set up his own unit of existence in his *bêit 'āb*': Shunya Bendor, *The Social Structure of Ancient Israel: The Institution of the Family (*beit 'Ab*) from the Settlement to the End of the Monarchy*, JBS 7 (Jerusalem: Simor, 1996), 123–4. See also Deut. 28.30; Amos 5.11; Zeph. 1.12.
35. לקח has three meanings: 'a) to transfer to one's possession what someone else has given, that is, to receive (e.g. 1 Sam 8,3); b) to take hold of, to transfer to possession practically (e.g. Judg 11,13); c) to acquire, that is, to transfer something to one's ownership in return for money (during the Biblical period this appears only a few times, for example, in Prov. 31,16)… לקח, "take" in the case under discussion has a dual meaning: Shechem grabbed her, not to rape her but to transfer her to his possession by marrying her, and afterwards he engaged in intimate relations with her': Joseph Fleishman, 'Shechem and Dinah in the Light of Non-Biblical and Biblical Sources', *ZAW* 116, no. 1 (2004): 27.
36. He cites, for example, Gen. 34.2 where לקח denotes merely taking a woman: Jackson, 'Institutions', 226 n. 20. Lemos argues that לקח treats women as legal objects, but is not commercial language and they could not be sold: Lemos, *Violence*, 75–76.

when she is given to Jacob *le'ishah* by Leah'.³⁷ Jackson draws further on Gen. 16.3 and Gen. 30.4, stating that the terminology 'does not imply a full (or sometimes even any) marital status'.³⁸ In Exod. 21.4 the master gives the debt-slave the woman, יתן־לו אשה, even though the relationship is designed to last only six years. Thus, a problem exists in presuming that the noun always bears a sexual connotation and always carries the meaning 'wife', as opposed to, say, a temporary sexual union. He further suggests:

> the most striking illustration of the difficulty of assuming that *le'ishah* always denotes marriage occurs in the law of the foreign captive, Deut. 21.10-14, where לקח לאשה in Deut. 21.11 refers simply to the (here, non-consensual) sexual act…and once the relationship is regularized…the status of *ishah* is that of slave concubine rather than full wife, since were it not for the rape the master would have been entitled to sell her on as a slave.³⁹

Allen Guenther notes the ambiguity of marriage, stating that rather than asserting certain forms of marriage are early or late, 'we should be open to recognizing in them more rather than less complexity and variety in Israel's language of different marriage types'.⁴⁰ Brenner's definition of לקח, as meaning 'formalize a union' (with accompanying consummation),⁴¹ may be sufficiently ambiguous to avoid any contemporary connotations of white dresses and church weddings, and avoid romanticized ideas of levirate marriage. Jackson argues that the same institution may 'be both social and legal, understood differently and enforced differently by different social groups'.⁴² The complexities of the examples of marriage (or 'levirate marriage' specifically) as demonstrated in the texts extant to us should warn us against attempting to formulate too neat a definition of 'marriage' in ancient Israel.

Chapman's *House of the Mother* problematizes and clarifies conceptions of the בית אב, and the role of the male–female pairing. Chapman states that rather than being mere vessels who produce male heirs, 'foundational mothers became nations, kingdoms, military units, and household alliances'. She further argues that any examination of the house

---

37. Jackson, 'Institutions', 227.
38. Ibid., 227 n. 23.
39. Ibid., 227.
40. Allen Guenther, 'A Typology of Israelite Marriage: Kinship, Socio-Economic, and Religious Factors', *JSOT* 29, no. 4 (2005): 405.
41. Brenner, *Intercourse*, 93 n. 5.
42. Jackson, 'Institutions', 222.

of the father and kinship 'must account for the mothers who served as its building blocks, for the breasts and wombs that defined social and political alliances with the house of the father'.[43] Chapman here provides an important counter to the way gender and lineage is presented in some of the texts we have looked at. As Gillespie notes, houses are not constrained by single rules for kinship organization; instead, they are sites for negotiating and competing over kinship. Chapman's work is vital in highlighting both that women formed kinship units with their own networks of power and allegiance, and that the house is not a flat 'patriarchal' unit but, rather, multifaceted and continually evolving. The term House of the Mother appears four times in the Hebrew Bible (Gen. 24.28; Ruth 1.8; Song 3.4; 8.2). The בית אם, a unit nesting within the wider house, is a space in which marriage is negotiated, uterine children form kinship bonds not formed with the children of other wives of the father, and in which mothers build up their own house.[44] It is a physical dwelling, and a grouping of people.[45] For example, in the narrative of Sarah and Hagar in Genesis 25, Chapman views Sarah, Keturah and Hagar as having a nesting house within the house of Abraham; within each of these units the text presents the transfer of wealth: material wealth, including land, property and gifts, and immaterial wealth, including 'divine blessing, name, titles, mediated and unmediated pathways to Abraham as the foundational ancestor, and finally the origin story itself'.[46] Sarah, as Rachel did, can talk about being built up, which may relate to the verb בנה, but also sons, בנים:[47] 'aspirations of a wife in having a son were distinct from and yet supportive of the aspirations that a husband had in securing a male heir'; 'the verb "to be built up", however, communicates much more than maternal emotions; it signifies Sarai's…desire to inaugurate their own "house" within the house of their husbands through bearing a son'.[48] The House of the Mother has consequences for the status of wives or slaves: in Gen. 25.12 Hagar bore Isaac to Abraham, whereas in 25.19 Abraham begot Isaac; Isaac is defined solely as Abraham's son, whereas Ishmael is understood by reference to his mother.[49] In the distinction Ishmael becomes part of a 'satellite house of the mother rather than a paternally nested house of the mother'.[50] The

43. Chapman, *House*, 228.
44. Ibid., 56.
45. Ibid., 91.
46. Ibid., 39.
47. Ibid., 150.
48. Ibid., 151.
49. Ibid., 40.
50. Ibid., 41.

house forms a fundamental unit of social organization, one comprised of a patriarchal figure and attached to a dwelling of land. They appear to be formed through male–female sexual pairings; however, the nature of these pairings is ambiguous and should not be understood as a nuclear family of husband, wife, and 2.4 children. They are not flat institutions, and within them there can be any number of configurations; and within these configurations, rather than the hegemonic power of a man there may exist multiple and competing sub-houses, in which women build up their own houses. The house, following Gillespie, materializes identity, name and lineage in people who embody and perpetuate the house; this demonstrates to us the vital importance of levirate marriage in preventing the disembodiment of the house through childlessness. Gillespie's idea of 'long-lived corporate entities' also contributes to our understanding of how family, genealogy, and burial all create a narrative around the house, which must be transmitted, but also preserved.

2. *Transmitting Property and Family*

A primary mechanism for the preservation of the household can be seen in the regulation of land and property. Land carries economic significance, with the 'farm' as the basic productive unit, and texts such as Josh. 21.12 and Neh. 5.3 emphasize the communal nature of land in relation to farming. The moving of boundary stones, 'set up by former generations', is prohibited (Deut. 19.14; 27.17).[51] Land is not owned but is understood as a נחלת אבות, an inheritance from the fathers.[52] Even in an area which we may understand to be purely material or economic there are dynamics of kinship and lineage. The narrative of apportioning land by lot (Josh. 13–22) also has significance in terms of expressing Israel's eternal right to the land.[53] Land takes on connections with שם, the name. This is particularly prominent in Ruth, where the name is to be established on the property of the deceased. Pressler notes several more texts in which name

---

51. Ferdinand Deist, *The Material Culture of the Bible: An Introduction*, BibSem 70 (Sheffield: Sheffield Academic, 2000), 144.

52. Num. 36.3, 8; 1 Kgs 21.3, 3; Prov. 19.14. The relation between אחזה and נחלה has changed over time, though אחזה may relate to inalienable property from a sovereign, whereas נחלה is more broadly inheritance; see Stavrakopoulou, *Land*, 34 n. 21; Deist, *Material Culture*, 144. They may, however, in certain periods have become synonymous, or taken on the same meaning in different periods: Baruch Levine, *Numbers 21–36: A New Translation with Introduction and Commentary*, AB 4A (New York: Doubleday, 2000), 346.

53. Deist, *Material Culture*, 145. See Deut. 4.21, 15, 4; 19.10; Jer. 12.14.

and land are connected: to be called by the name of someone means to inherit through them (Gen. 48.6); Joseph's sons are called by the names of Ephraim and Manasseh in their inheritance; and 2 Sam. 14.4 and Num. 27.4 suggest the name is established through land.[54] The most common form of inheritance appears to be between father and son; the firstborn is to receive a double portion of the father's possession, and the father is unable to show preference by giving one son a double share (Deut. 21.15-17). We find a basic outline of inheritance law in Numbers 27, where the daughters of Zelophehad approach Moses in order to object that they cannot inherit: the daughters, as will be explored in detail in the next chapter, are concerned with the father's name disappearing from the משפחה. YHWH responds to their plea and we are told a line of succession is established: son, daughter, brother, uncle and nearest kinsman (Num. 27.8-11). The property is to stay within the בית אב primarily before passing to the wider משפחה. There is also evidence of alternative mechanisms for inheritance, ones which Milgrom relates to Zelophehad's daughters.[55] In the case of Sheshan, who has daughters not sons, the father gives his daughter to his Egyptian slave, Jarha, to bare him Attai (1 Chron. 2.34-35); through this marriage Sheshan facilitates inheritance and perpetuation of the family. Typical patterns of kinship are flexible and can be manipulated and played for the safe passage of the social order.

The concern of the elders in Numbers 36 is with the group's continuing right to land. Land is divided among the tribes (Josh. 14.1–19.51) and is to some extent inalienable – unless, for example, it is within a walled city (Lev. 25.29). '[T]he family estate, nominally that which was allotted at the time of the conquest, is not a material sale-commodity' and must 'be prevented from passing into the hands of strangers'.[56] In 1 Kgs 21.2-3 we read King Ahab of Samaria's request for Naboth's vineyard:

> And Ahab said to Naboth, 'Give me your vineyard, so that I may have it for a vegetable garden, because it is near my house; I will give you a better vineyard for it; or, if it seems good to you, I will give you its value in money'. But Naboth said to Ahab, 'The LORD forbid that I should give you my ancestral inheritance [נחלת אבתי]'.

---

54. Pressler, *View of Women*, 67.

55. Jacob Milgrom, *Numbers*, JPSTC (Philadelphia: Jewish Publication Society, 1992), 231. Milgrom also notes Neh. 7.63 and Ezra 2.61, which record priests who traced their lineage to Barzillai through the marriage of their father to one of the daughters of Barzillai and 'took his/their name'.

56. Westbrook, *Property*, 59.

Naboth is explicit that YHWH will not allow the sale of the inheritance of his fathers, even as an exchange. Ahab is distraught, and Jezebel devises a plan, which leads to Naboth's death, and Ahab takes possession of the vineyard. YHWH tells Elijah to go to King Ahab, and Elijah says to him that he will bring disaster on him and consume him: 'I will bring disaster on you; I will consume you, and will cut off from Ahab every male, bond or free, in Israel; and I will make your house like the house of Jeroboam son of Nebat, and like the house of Baasha son of Ahijah…' (1 Kgs 21.21-22). Further, he states that dogs will eat Jezebel, and anyone belonging to Ahab will be eaten either by dogs or birds (1 Kgs 21.20-24). Ahab humbles himself, and YHWH declares he will not bring disaster in his days, but '…in his son's days I will bring disaster on his house' (1 Kgs 21.29). There appears to be a kind of irony in the text, which suggests that because Ahab has willed the destruction of Naboth and the estate of his fathers, YHWH will destroy Ahab's house, and his progeny. Moreover, they will be prevented from an honourable burial. Tenancy of the land is not granted to individual Israelites but the 'family'; however, the family does not mean only one's kin, but 'a man's own heirs and successors in as direct a male line as is possible'.[57]

There is a mechanism of גאלה, 'redemption', which allows the return of land to its previous holder. Leviticus 25.25-28 is our only legal source on the redemption of land:

> If anyone of your kin [אחיך] falls into difficulty and sells [ומכר] a piece of property [מאחזתו], then the next-of-kin [גאלו הקרב] shall come and redeem what the relative has sold. If the person has no one to redeem it, but then prospers and finds sufficient means to do so, the years since its sale shall be computed and the difference shall be refunded to the person to whom it was sold, and the property shall be returned. But if there are not sufficient means to recover it, what was sold shall remain with the purchaser until the year of jubilee; in the jubilee it shall be released, and the property shall be returned.

If an אח, brother (though with more generic connotations of kin), sells his possession, the nearest redeemer is to come and redeem what the brother has sold. Westbrook suggests that the author assumes that 'no one would sell their family estate except out of economic necessity',[58] and understands it in the broader context of blood redemption (Num. 35.19) and buying back a relative from slavery (Lev. 25.47). According to Zevit,

---

57. Norman H. Snaith, 'The Daughters of Zelophehad', *VT* 16, no. 1 (1966): 125.
58. Westbrook, *Property*, 42.

The objective of these norms and their expression as laws was to maintain the cohesion of clan and tribal units and to maintain the integrity of ancestral land as an expression of wealth and status. A theological justification for insistence on what appears altruistic behaviour maintained that both Israel and the land were YHWH's. Although YHWH's right of lordship over the people and his land could be temporarily abridged under certain circumstances, it could not be annulled permanently (Lev 25,8–34.47–55).[59]

Land is intimately connected with the ancestors, as demonstrated by the presence of ancestral tombs or monuments as markers for land (Isa. 5.8; Hos. 5.10; Mic. 2.2; Job 24.2), which is not only 'an ancestral ideal' but also 'a matter of continued social integrity'.[60] Redemption, therefore, acts to prevent the alienation of land, and presumably therefore of ancestry. Zevit, however, discusses two texts, Isa. 5.8 and Mic. 2.2, in which the prophets are outraged by the practice of alienation of land, which indicates that the alienation is at least possible.[61] In Jer. 32.6-8, Jeremiah recounts his cousin approaching him: '…Buy my field that is at Anathoth in the land of Benjamin, for the right of possession and redemption is yours; buy it for yourself'. Jeremiah 32.9-14 tells of Jeremiah buying from his cousin Hanamel, an outright sale sealed with documentation, which Zevit suggests is a circumstance of alienable land.[62] According to Westbrook, there is a broader ambiguity in the law: it is unclear whether property is to be returned to the original owner, or rather simply the wider family.[63] While there is no fixed sequence for redemption of the land, Lev. 25.48-50 outlines the order of redemption for a slave: brother, uncle, cousin, nearest relative.

However, one group is conspicuously absent from the lines of transfer of property: the אלמנה, or widow. Eryl Davies notes that the presence of widow inheritance in other ancient West Asian law codes makes its absence in the biblical text more conspicuous.[64] There are continuous requirements not to oppress the widow, or to offer kindness such as allowing them to glean (e.g. Exod. 22.21-14; Deut. 14.28-29; 24.17-18;

59. Zevit, 'Dating Ruth', 584.
60. Stavrakopoulou, *Land*, 12. See also Lewis, 'Ancestral Estate', 608, who discusses texts which link ancestral tombs with land (Josh. 24.30, 32; Judg. 2.9; 1 Sam. 25.1; 1 Kgs 2.34, Gen. 23.8, 20).
61. Zevit, 'Dating Ruth', 584.
62. Ibid.
63. Westbrook, *Property*, 60–1.
64. Davies, 'Inheritance I', 138; Galpaz-Feller, 'Widow'; Ben-Barak, *Inheritance*, 243–6. Galpaz-Feller does note two ostraca from the Moussaieff collection; one, from the eighth century, appears to allow for a widow to inherit land temporarily: Galpaz-Feller, 'Widow', 240.

26.12; Ezek. 22.6-7; Prov. 14.31-32). Pnina Galpaz-Feller also outlines texts in which widows appear to have some level of economic stability (Judg. 17.1-6; 1 Sam. 25.42; 2 Kgs 8.1-3; Prov. 15.25; Job 24.3), although she regards the mainly negative description of the widow in biblical texts as a result of her alienation from the household she has joined at marriage, acknowledging the widows described as possessing wealth may have gained it from their bride-price.[65] Genesis 38.11 and Lev. 22.13 imply that a childless widow could return to her father's house. Hiers offers a slightly more optimistic picture of a widow's right to inherit, as we see from such texts as 2 Kgs 4.1-7, 2 Kings 8 and Prov. 15.25. The first two, however, involve a widow residing with a son, who may be simply supported by her offspring. Proverbs 15.25 is the most convincing, stating that YHWH will tear down the house of the proud, but maintain the widow's גבול, or boundaries, although no other context is given.[66] The transmission of land was highly regulated, with strict lines of transmission; while these lines normally involve men, transmission is allowed to daughters for the purpose of temporarily preventing the absorption of the בית אב into the wider clan. This measure ensures the integrity of the בית אב, and its intent can be seen most clearly in the corresponding lack of inheritance for widows – it is not a matter of economic provision for women, but right transmission of property between men. The transmission of property is articulated in highly *religious* terms, determined by YHWH, and so the relationship between property and household, family, tribe and nation is not one of simple economic exchange; rather, it is highly controlled as the transmission of property is highly symbolic. This suggests that any interpretation of levirate marriage as concerned with the inheritance of property or with the establishment of a 'title' needs to understand the texts more widely in their symbolic context, and understand how the property aspect interacts with other parts of discourse.

3. *Genealogies and Connection*

Genealogies offer a way of constituting familial lines through generations, and relate to Gillespie's 'long-lived corporate entities'. Meyers suggests

---

65. Galpaz-Feller, 'Widow', 234. Cf. Gen. 31.15 in which Laban's daughters complain 'he has been using up the money given for us'.

66. Richard H. Hiers, 'Transfer of Property by Inheritance and Bequest in Biblical Law and Tradition', *Journal of Law and Religion* 10, no. 1 (1993): 132–3. Hiers also notes Ruth 4.9, which is discussed below. However, it is not convincing that Naomi owned the land, in terms of requiring Ruth to glean, and needing Boaz to redeem it.

that the biblical household is linked conceptually through genealogies, which 'present an over-arching kinship dimension to Israelite society', and lend security and stability to social interactions.⁶⁷ This happens in part through rootedness in tradition: 'Genealogies provide a particular form for recalling the origins and "biography" of an individual, community, or culture. Their basic elements are names, data, and locations, connected by indications of mutual relationships.'⁶⁸

Genealogies are highly politicized tools, and a genealogy which is aiming to claim power positions and establish hierarchies will emphasize the depth of a family line. As a site where past, present and future interact, they contextualize the cultural, economic, socio-political and religious.⁶⁹ The most essential element is the name: 'A genealogy lives by its audience's ability to "read" the stories behind the names and to get arguments implicitly made by specific ways of linkage'.⁷⁰ The names connect individuals and groups within the society and family and define social rights and obligations.⁷¹ Far from being a rigid framework, a system of names is instrumental both in 'prolonging society through time and in granting meaning to all events'.⁷² The genealogical 'narrative' attached to claims on a piece of land is grounded in the same dynamic of legitimizing the present and future on stories of past names.⁷³ Of this legitimization, we can say that by 'offering a frame of reference to previous generations and of commemorating the dead, genealogies may be understood as a specific form of *memory*'.⁷⁴

This interplay between genealogies and memory manifests itself through an exclusive selection of persons that 'provides a basic trace of

---

67. Meyers, 'Household Religion', 119.

68. Ingeborg Lowisch, 'Genealogies, Gender and the Politics of Memory: 1 Chronicles 1–9 and the Documentary Film *Mein Leben Teil 2*', in *Performing Memory in Biblical Narrative and Beyond*, ed. Athalya Brenner and Frank H. Polak, BMW 25 (Sheffield: Sheffield Phoenix, 2010), 229.

69. Lowisch, 'Genealogies', 229.

70. Ibid.

71. Robert R. Wilson, 'The Old Testament Genealogies in Recent Research', *JBL* 94, no. 2 (1975): 181.

72. Iteanu, 'The Dead', 58.

73. Wilson found that in both comparative anthropological material, and oral ancient West Asian genealogies, there was an incredible amount of fluidity in the choice of names to reflect particular purposes. See Robert R. Wilson, *Genealogy and History in the Biblical World*, YNER 7 (New Haven, CT: Yale University Press, 1977), 48–136.

74. Lowisch, 'Genealogies', 230.

power dynamics within the community that establishes identity through its genealogies'.⁷⁵ Evidence from the Hammurapi Dynasty suggests a cultural milieu in which genealogies were not just a political record but one which provoked an active response from the present community. The dead listed were invited to partake of the food and drink offerings, suggesting the genealogy was used in the context of a *kipsu*-offering.⁷⁶ Genealogies are also able to navigate more complex relationships. In Genesis 4 the addition of Adah and Zillah 'interrupts the patrilineal flow':⁷⁷ 'Lamech's house is complex, containing two maternally headed sub-houses, each comprising two maternally identified siblings'.⁷⁸ This is not unique:

> What we see in this text is actually a biblical pattern: exclusively paternal genealogies give way to narratives that introduce households, and these households contain fathers, mothers, wives, concubines, slave wives, firstborn sons, second-born sons, daughters, foreigners and slaves. The introduction of women and maternally defined subgroups of kin disrupts the neatness of a patrilineal genealogy, marking divisions with a paternal line.⁷⁹

Chapman argues that, given the term תולדת ('the paternal begettings', used in genealogy and which 'approximates the idea of a patriline') occurs only 39 times, concentrated in the priestly source, the formula cannot be viewed as the main framework for understanding biblical kinship,⁸⁰ as each patriline yields 'to a more complex and often maternally subdivided household'.⁸¹ Chapman suggests that 'instead of referring to societies like ancient Israel as "Patriline", many anthropologists have begun to qualify the term, describing societies as favouring, preferring, or valuing male kinship links over female kinship links while nonetheless depending on both'.⁸² She states that in order to understand hierarchies in patrilineal societies, we have to take serious account of 'relationships formed through

---

75. Ibid., 231. Genealogies may also incorporate marginal figures into group identity: Wilson, *Genealogy*, 183.
76. Wilson, 'Genealogies', 174.
77. Chapman, *House*, 1.
78. Ibid., 2.
79. Ibid.
80. Ibid., 4. McNutt suggests the genealogies of the Priestly tradition 'are very likely stereotyped conceptions of the social structure of early 'Israel' that are meant to legitimate the writer's ideals about social relations at the time they were written down': McNutt, *Reconstructing*, 77.
81. Chapman, *House*, 5.
82. Ibid., 7.

maternal ties'.[83] Therefore while genealogies imply a male line of descent, Chapman's argument highlights the complexities inherent in narratives like Ruth, and how the genealogies which include examples of levirate marriage, rather than being precise and clean family trees, negotiate the narrative the text is telling.

4. *Regulating the Family: The Fifth Commandment*

To establish the depth of line, families need to enforce certain obligations. The discourse of land, longevity, and lineage can be seen in the following commandment:

> Honour your father and your mother [כבד את־אביך ואת־אמך], so that your days may be long [יארכון ימיך] in the land that the LORD your God is giving you. (Exod. 20.12)

> Honour your father and your mother, as the Lord your God commanded you, so that your days may be long and that it may go well with you in the land that the LORD your God is giving you. (Deut. 5.16)

The placement of the commandment, between those concerning God and those concerning society, may be significant; it suggests the importance of reverence and respect, and the connecting of divine order and social order. The fifth commandment, along with one related to the observation of the Sabbath, is the only one stated positively (do, rather than do not); along with the prohibition on creating idols, it is the only one with a promised reward.[84] William Propp places the reward in the context of land, kinship and ancestors:

> *Upon the soil*. Why is this necessary? Personal fulfilment is not just longevity; it is longevity on one's own ancestral soil, surrounded by numerous descendants, and culminating in interment in that very soil, among the bones of one's forebears.[85]

The keeping of the commandment is a predicate for social stability and order. It complements others texts which assert the importance of reverence for elders: rising before the elderly (Lev. 19.32); listening to

---

83. Ibid., 11.
84. Michael David Coogan, *The Ten Commandments: A Short History of an Ancient Text* (New Haven, CT: Yale University Press, 2014), 76.
85. William Henry Propp, *Exodus 19–40: A New Translation with Introduction and Commentary*, AB 2A (New York: Doubleday, 2006), 179.

the father and not despising the mother when they are old (Prov. 23.22); and taking care of parents when they are old (Sir. 3.12-13).[86] The inverse of the command is seen elsewhere in Exodus:

> Whoever strikes father or mother shall be put to death. (Exod. 21.15)

> Whoever curses father or mother shall be put to death. (Exod. 21.17)

According to Albertz, 'the cursing of parents is mentioned along with other crimes deserving the death penalty, because it violates the commandment to honour one's parents and disturbs both societal and divine order'.[87] Honour, כבד, may contain certain memorializing overtones, and if taken to include honour due to parents after death, may include some form of funerary or naming rites, and here the interplay between respect for YHWH, respect for ancestry, and the promise of descendants and permanence in the land comes out starkly. Brichto goes further, arguing that the commandment relates specifically to post-mortem care. Brichto suggests יארכון ימיך is better translated 'long endure' rather than 'your days may be long' which he argues suggests longevity for the individual; addressing the commandment collectively ('family, clan, tribe, people') 'makes tenancy and tenure of the sacred soil contingent upon proper behaviour toward one's progenitors'.[88] For Brichto, during their lifetime parents would have the economic ability to enforce respect; once dead, however, they 'require protection from disloyalty or impiety', including funerary or memorial rites, and the 'disposition of the patrimonial estate'.[89] Brichto sees the negative of the commandment present in several passages, particularly the death penalty for the rebellious son (Deut. 21.18-21), and two passages about disrespectful children (Prov. 20.20; 30): the disrespectful son cannot be relied upon to provide post-mortem care. Christopher Wright responds to Brichto's argument, particularly his focus on the land as integral to the commandment, while questioning whether the living or the dead are recipients of the commandment. Wright rejects Brichto's argument that the commandment relates to the veneration of ancestors 'without much clearer indication', especially considering the 'supporting laws and exhortations' which surround appropriate behaviour to the living.[90] Wright

---

86. Coogan, *The Ten Commandments*, 76.
87. Albertz and Schmitt, *Family and Household*, 411.
88. Brichto, 'Kin', 30.
89. Ibid., 31.
90. Christopher J. H. Wright, *God's People in God's Land: Family, Land, and Property in the Old Testament* (Grand Rapids, MI: Eerdmans, 1990), 154. Wright

maintains the emphasis on land in Brichto's explanation of the command, though he shifts the emphasis to the 'concern for the maintenance of the relationship between the *people* and God and the dependence of that relationship upon the stability and security of the household units'.[91] Rainer Albertz, responding to Brichto, suggests the commandment 'is as easily interpreted to refer to the living as to the dead', citing Mal. 1.16 where honouring a living father is in question.[92] Moshe Weinfeld cites Akkadian, Babylonian, Ugaritic, Second Temple and Rabbinic evidence that care for parents in old age, and appropriate death, morning and memorialization rites can be considered part of the same obligation: 'the fifth commandment is formulated in a positive and abstract manner so that it might encompass all the possible filial duties'.[93]

Edwin Zulu looks at the commandment in the context of African reverence for ancestors. Zulu's framework of Southern African approaches to reverence for parents and ancestors may offer a more nuanced approach than one that sees the command as a form of ancestor cult. He argues that in the southern African framework there is no separation between social and religious lives. As such, the necessity of participation in community, a strong belief in ancestors as 'spiritual functionaries', and the importance of ancestors as 'reminders and symbols of morals and sources of blessing in a particular society', heighten the importance of the fifth commandment.[94] The elderly are considered custodians of moral values, and this

---

does, however, fall into the trap of claiming any suggestion of ancestor veneration 'enjoyed no clear sanction from Yahwism'; though he suggests there may be a 'social background of folk-religious roots and associations'.

91. Ibid., 155.

92. Albertz and Schmitt, *Family and Household*, 411.

93. Moshe Weinfeld, *Deuteronomy 1–11: A New Translation with Introduction and Commentary*, AB 5 (New York: Doubleday, 1991), 310–11. Contextual evidence on the obligation to support living parents is well attested: Sumerian, Babylonian and Ugaritic texts, using the same *kbd* root, even stipulate how much food a child is to provide their parents: Marten Stol, 'Care of the Elderly in Mesopotamia in the Old Babylonian Period', in *The Care of the Elderly in the Ancient Near East*, ed. Sven Vleeming and Marteen Stol, SHCANE 14 (Leiden: Brill, 1998), 60–1. There is contextual ancient West Asian evidence to support the care of the deceased at death and after: Old Assyrian adoption contracts included the obligation to mourn, bury, perform funerary rites including *zakārum* ('to name, invoke') and *paqādum* ('to care for, sustain') Klass R. Veenhof, 'Old Assyrian and Ancient Anatolian Evidence for the Care of the Elderly', in *The Care of the Elderly in the Ancient Near East*, ed. Sven Vleeming and Marteen Stol, SHCANE 14 (Leiden: Brill, 1998), 125.

94. Edwin Zulu, 'Reverence for Ancestors in Africa: Interpretation of the 5th Commandment from an African Perspective', *Scriptura* 81 (2002): 478.

honour does not diminish after their death; through their moral authority they create lineages made up of the living and the dead, and those who are credible heads of communities continue to assert authority after death as ancestors.⁹⁵ Mothers and fathers are referred to as 'a second God', suggesting 'respect for parents is linked to one's relationship with God; that relationships are not cut off when people die'. Physical memorials such as pillars are bowed to, gifts are taken to graves, and reverence is shown through names given to children. Moreover, obedience to ancestors means a 'guarantee of their blessing'; the fact 'that one revere one's ancestors guarantees oneself a land ownership since it is through these ancestors that land is passed on to descendants', and connecting with ancestors keeps one within the 'family structure'.⁹⁶ Rather than imposing a strictly delineated boundary between the living and the dead, we can see that honour due to parents does not prevent the same honour being carried out after death as before – proper reverence, not striking or cursing parents, burial and appropriate memorialization, are all part of the same social context which ensures longevity in the land of the ancestors and perpetuation of the covenant through future generations.

5. *Erasing the Family: Cutting Off*

If the integrity of the family is so vital to social order, then its eradication is exceedingly threatening. There is a specific form of punishment that destroys the continuation of the family: cutting off. The Hebrew root כרת has three basic meanings (a) to cut; (b) to eradicate, set aside, exclude, cut off; and (c) to enter into, conclude a covenant, matter, agreement, or treaty.⁹⁷ It is used frequently in the niphal as an 'extermination formula', in conjunction with other terms, such as 'shall be cut off from his people'.⁹⁸ For example:

> But those who eat flesh from the LORD's sacrifice of well-being while in a state of uncleanness shall be cut off from their kin (ונכרתה הנפש ההוא מעמיה). (Lev. 7.20)

> Any uncircumcised male who is not circumcised in the flesh of his foreskin shall be cut off from his people (ונכרתה הנפש ההוא מעמיה); he has broken my covenant. (Gen. 17.14)

---

95. Ibid., 479.
96. Ibid., 480.
97. Eugene Carpenter, 'כרת', *NIDOTTE*.
98. Levine, *Leviticus*, 241. See also: Exod. 30.33, 38; 31.14; Lev. 7.20; Num. 9.13.

The normal pattern is niphal + subject + preposition + group(s).⁹⁹ Baruch Levine states that on the most elemental level it is a metaphor borrowed from the 'felling of trees and other forms of vegetation'.¹⁰⁰ גזר, a synonym to כרת, is at times attested to relate to the dead or near dead:¹⁰¹

> they flung me alive into a pit
> and hurled stones on me;
> water closed over my head;
> I said, 'I am lost (נגזרתי)'. (Lam. 3.53-54)

One can be cut off from the living (Isa. 53.8), YHWH's hand (Ps. 88.6), and the cult (2 Chron. 26.21). The dead of Ps. 88.6 are no longer remembered by God, and do not offer him praise. Olyan suggests Ezek. 37.11, a reference to the exiled community, uses גזר to suggest the exiled are like the dead, cut off from God and the cult, and forgotten by YHWH,¹⁰² particularly given the difficulty perceived by many in worshiping YHWH in foreign lands.¹⁰³ The existence of punishment is argued to ensure that the purity boundaries operating within a given system are maintained.¹⁰⁴ Donald Wold therefore establishes that the penalty of כרת operates within P's purity–impurity symbolic structure,¹⁰⁵ the priestly writer invoking 'the kareth curse for deliberate trespasses against the rules of personal conduct which define and preserve the distinction between the sacred and the impure'.¹⁰⁶ Levine concludes that כרת was used for religious offenses:¹⁰⁷ violation of the Sabbath and improper observance of festivals and holy days; violations of certain laws of purity; specific prohibited sexual unions, also regarded as a form of impurity; cultic offences, such as eating fat/blood and mishandling sacrificial substances; and failure to circumcise one's male child at eight days. The punishment appears to have been carried out by God, but sometimes with human help. Jacob

---

99. Carpenter, 'כרת'.

100. Levine, *Leviticus*, 241. Jer. 11.19; see also Isa. 56.3-5.

101. Saul M. Olyan, "We Are Utterly Cut Off': Some Possible Nuances of נגזרנו לנו in Ezek 37:11', *CBQ* 65, no. 1 (2003): 45.

102. Ibid., 48.

103. Cf. 1 Sam. 26.19; Ps. 137.4.

104. Mary Douglas, *Purity and Danger: An Analysis of Concepts of Pollution and Taboo* (London: Routledge & Kegan Paul, 1966), 132.

105. Donald J. Wold, 'The Kareth Penalty in P: Rationale and Cases', in *Society of Biblical Literature Seminar Papers*, SBLSP (Missoula, MT: Scholars Press, 1979), 1.

106. Wold, 'Kareth', 2.

107. Levine, *Leviticus*, 242.

Milgrom argues that the cardinal postulate of the priestly legislation is that sins against God are punishable by God and not man.[108] However, it is debatable whether consanguineous and incestuous marriages (Lev. 18.27-29) can be substantiated purely as 'sins against God'. Moreover, Jay Sklar notes that there are examples where 'sins against God' are punished by human agency. He notes, for example, Exod. 31.14:

> You shall keep the Sabbath, for holy it is to you; everyone who profanes it shall surely be put to death (מות יומת), for (כי) whoever does any work in it their spirit shall be cut off from among their people.[109]

According to Sklar, the hophal of מות 'indicated that the covenant community carries out the execution'. Moreover, contra Milgrom, who defines it as two punishments,[110] Sklar notes the use of כי an interpretation of one by the other – both act in compliment, however they are not the same. The 'high-handed sin' in Num. 15.27-31, where the individual who reviles the LORD is to be cut off, is then followed immediately by a case of a man found gathering sticks on the Sabbath (v. 32) who is then sentenced to death outside the camp (v. 35).[111]

The exact nature of what כרת means, and who is to exact the punishment, was a widely debated issue in the Second Temple and Rabbinic periods.[112] Many commentators still prefer a translation of כרת which implies 'driven out of the community', 'excommunicated' and 'outlawed'.[113] The term also carries with it a series of 'qualifiers', such as 'cut off from among their people' (Lev. 17.4, 10; 20.3, 6, 38), terms indicating separation from the wider social and cultic community; thus excommunication seems explicit.[114] However, this fails to take into account the broader relationship of כרת with death. The interpretation of premature death of the sinner is suggested by texts such as Exod. 31.14; however, an understanding of כרת as meaning premature death or execution does not demonstrate its fullest meaning. Leviticus 20.2-3 references execution by a man and

---

108. Milgrom, *Numbers*, 405–6.

109. Attempting a literal translation as possible.

110. Milgrom, *Numbers*, 407–8.

111. Jay Sklar, *Sin, Impurity, Sacrifice, and Atonement: The Priestly Conceptions*, HBM 2 (Sheffield: Sheffield Phoenix, 2005), 19.

112. William Horbury, 'Extirpation and Excommunication', *VT* 35, no. 1 (1985): 31–4.

113. See the literature listed in Philip J. Budd, *Leviticus: Based on the New Revised Standard Version*, NCBC (London: Marshall Pickering, 1996), 122.

114. Sklar, *Sin*, 16.

כרת simultaneously, implying the two are complementary as opposed to synonyms.[115] This is fleshed out outside of legal material; for example, 1 Sam. 24.21 reads:

> ...Swear to me therefore by the LORD that you will not cut off my descendants [זרע] after me, and that you will not wipe out my name from my father's house.

Here seed is cut off. In Ruth it is the name that becomes cut off:

> I have also acquired her to...raise up the name of the dead on his inheritance (להקים שם־המת על־נחלתו), in order that the name of the dead may not be cut off from his kin and from the gate of his place (ולא־יכרת שם־המת מעם אחיו ומשער מקומו).[116]

Psalm 109.13 states:

> Let his descendants be cut off (יהי־אחריתו להכרית בדור אחר) in the generation after and let their name be blotted out (ימח שמם).[117]

Here cutting off posterity allows for the blotting out of the name in the next generation, the three passages linking כרת and the extermination of progeny/the name.[118] Wold suggests that the threat to exterminate offspring would result in an *emotional* response from the potential culprit,[119] which would act as a deterrent, as outlined by Douglas. However, I would argue that Wold is underestimating the importance of descendants to the culprit – it is not only that the loss of descendants would affect the individual man emotionally, but that the individual would want to ensure the continuation of his line to maintain his name and memory. It is precisely within this discourse that the deterrent works. It affects the continuity of the individual and his line in perpetuity. It not only affects the individual's mortality but prevents the social legacy which would ensure the man is remembered – without his lineage, through the destruction of his seed, the individual is removed from existence. It is through descendants that the individual is incorporated into the living community after his death has caused his social exclusion; with the removal of descendants

---

115. Jacob Milgrom, *Leviticus 1–16: A New Translation with Introduction and Commentary*, AB 3 (New York: Doubleday, 1991), 460.
116. Ruth 4.10, author's translation.
117. Author's translation.
118. See also 1 Kgs 11.16; 14.10; 21.21; Ps. 37.28, 38.
119. Wold, 'Kareth', 5–6.

any mechanism for social reintegration and therefore continuation and memory are removed.

In Lev. 20.20-21, as noted above, one of the penalties for illicit sexual relationships is that the couple will die childless; although כרת is not mentioned, the parallel laws (Lev. 18.14-16) are subsumed under the כרת penalty (18.29).[120] According to Wold, the measure repeatedly recalls the *lex talionis*, the measure for measure principle. As the Passover commemorates the sparing of the Israelite firstborn, desecration of the Passover (Exod. 12.15) results in כרת – 'if God's sparing of Israel's children is not ceremonially remembered, God will bring a curse on the offender's children so as to leave him without descendants'.[121] כרת is prescribed for failure to circumcise, an act instituted (Gen. 17.12) with the promise of numerous progeny (17.5), God's presence in perpetuity (17.7) and the land of Canaan as an inheritance (17.8).[122] Here the punishment would act as the inverse of the thing the rite was intended to signify. Wold relates the punishment of כרת in Lev. 20.2-5 for Molech worship to the punishment exacted in Ezek. 23.47, that the rebels are killed along with their sons and daughters.[123] In this text we see these themes coming together conceptually:

> Say further to the people of Israel:
>
> Any of the people of Israel, or of the aliens who reside in Israel, who give any of their offspring to Molech shall be put to death; the people of the land shall stone them to death. I myself will set my face against them, and will cut them off from the people, because they have given of their offspring to Molech, defiling my sanctuary and profaning my holy name. And if the people of the land should ever close their eyes to them, when they give of their offspring to Molech, and do not put them to death, I myself will set my face against them and against their family, and will cut them off from among their people, them and all who follow them in prostituting themselves to Molech. (Lev. 20.2-5)

The cutting off is connected to ancestors, not just in the context of the one who gives any of their offspring to Molech, but even the one who closes their eyes to it. Moreover, punishing blasphemers with כרת (Num. 15.30-31) carries a level of retribution – 'if one deliberately desecrates God's name, God will remove his name from his people – he shall be

---

120. Sklar, *Sin*, 17 n. 24.
121. Wold, 'Kareth', 5.
122. Ibid., 15.
123. Ibid., 20–1.

made extinct'.[124] The term may also refer to the stopping of the individual joining ancestors after death in the context of references to being gathered to one's ancestors,[125] although Milgrom asserts that this punishment would not be exclusive and would function in line with the more evidenced punishments.[126] The punishment is also used in the context of public offices:[127] 1 Sam. 2.33 states Eli's descendants will be cut off from the priestly office, as part of the punishment. Jeremiah states David would not be cut off from the throne of Israel:

> For thus says YHWH, never shall be cut for David (יכרת לדוד) a man to sit on the throne of the house of Israel.[128]

Here, to be cut off is again linked with descendants and lineage. Budd suggests that the repeated phrase 'from your kin' in texts which describe כרת suggests disinheritance and is deprived of his family and property rights,[129] which presumably is incorporated in the punishment, due to the interaction between land and lineage. Cutting off is used as a *lex talionis* for crimes related to descendants and the transmission of the covenant; through its various associations it comes to stand for the complete annihilation of the person, whether through death, or the destruction of seed, name and offspring. It thus, inversely, relates to texts of continuity and perpetuation of the family line – and explores an individual's punishments in the context of the whole community, even into the future. It provides a highly productive base to understand levirate marriage; connecting the previous discussion of lineage and descendants with both the eradication of name and the destruction of post-mortem continuity.

6. *Conclusion*

Within the biblical text, 'family' forms the stable social unit of society. And, while existing in various forms throughout the biblical period, בית אב remains central. This central social and economic unit is transmitted down through time in various capacities, from genealogies to

---

124. Wold, 'Kareth', 24.
125. Milgrom, *Numbers*, 407; Gordon J. Wenham, *The Book of Leviticus*, The New International Commentary on the Old Testament (London: Hodder & Stoughton, 1979), 242.
126. Milgrom, *Numbers*, 407.
127. Levine, *Leviticus*, 241–2.
128. Jer. 33.17, my translation.
129. Budd, *Leviticus*, 122.

property, with identity, name and lineage materialized through it. It is possible to separate off these various aspects of the integrity of the family, for example by suggesting the prominence of economic concerns over social ones, but in the various texts we have looked at these varying concerns (the transmission of names through genealogy, the transmission of property through inheritance) seem to coalesce around the symbolic בית אב which forms the focus of social continuity. That is, it is methodologically simplistic to try and divorce the study of property and inheritance from the cultural symbolic system in which it exists. The בית אב is the locus of familial power: the structures of power it relates to ensure its reproduction, and individuals internalize this and act to its benefit. The transmission of property carries a theological significance as the land is presented as apportioned to each community individually, and various regulations ensure the correct movement of property throughout generations. These generations are marked through genealogies, in which a collection of names tell the story of the בית אב, as well as rooting it in the more distant tribal ancestors. These family units are comprised of social relationships; the fifth commandment demonstrates how these social relationships are prescribed and the duties and obligations they carry, even after death.

However, the family can also be erased. It can also be erased through specific punishments such as cutting off, and is threatened through the alienation of land. Through exploring the penalty of cutting off, the importance of family continuity through time is highlighted; the existence of the individual and lineage are intertwined, so much so that the verb כרת is at different times used for seed, name or in reference to individuals. Therefore, if the cutting off of name, seed and individual ruptures the regular social order and threatens the integrity of the family, mechanisms are used to prevent and correct this. Having established the symbolic significance of the family unit, these mechanisms – levirate marriage, the erection of monuments, the realigning of family property – will now be examined.

Chapter 7

Mechanisms of Continuity

Thomas Mann, in his novel *Joseph and his Brothers*, beautifully grasps Tamar's desire, in a way biblical scholars have often been blind to: that Tamar wanted and loved Judah, not for himself, but in the pursuit of an 'idea'.[1] But what is this idea? What does Tamar long for? The proceeding chapters have set the foundation for understanding what this idea is, and why – rather than being a mechanical working of a law – it excites such devotion in its service. In this chapter, we will examine eight texts that look at responses to male childlessness (or, rather, sonlessness) in the face of death. Rather than reducing these texts an individual concern – such as property – we will read each text closely and search how they dialogue with each other and reflect the same paradigm, and how this paradigm shapes the responses the text constructs.

1. *Lot's Daughters: Genesis 19.30-38*

> And Lot…was afraid to dwell in Zoar, and he dwelt in a cave, he and his two daughters. And said the firstborn to the younger: 'Our father is old, and there is no man on earth to come in to us as is the way of all the earth (כדרך כל־הארץ). Come, let us make our father drink wine, and we will lie with him, that we may preserve life out of our father's seed (ונחיה מאבינו זרע). And so they made their father drink wine that night; and the firstborn went in, and lay with her father; and he did not know when she lay down or when she arose.[2]

The next day, the younger sister repeats the act. The elder bore a son named מואב, Moab, 'from my father', and the younger bore a son named

---

1. Thomas Mann, *Joseph and his Brothers*, trans. John E. Woods (New York: Knopf, 2005).
2. As stated in the Introduction, translations of the key texts in this chapter are my own.

בֶּן־עַמִּי, Ben-ammi, 'son of my kin'. This passage takes place immediately after the narrative of the destruction of Sodom and Gomorrah, where Lot offers his daughter's bodies to the men of the town, asserting his total control over the women's bodies; this is particularly poignant as the daughters in effect reverse the power dynamic and take control of the father's body. Lot is perceived to be ignorant of the events, which pass without judgment, although some commentators presume the story invokes a natural disgust.[3] The text does imply the father would have a deep reservation, thus the need for the daughters to make him drink wine beforehand. The narrative plays on a drive for female agency, which Robert Polhemus suggest could be contrasted with a kind of stereotype of a male rational-mind embodied in the father, who fails to act.[4] Victor Hamilton, in his commentary, stigmatizes the women through references to 'their lifeless womb' and 'perpetual barrenness', neither of which the text asserts, and so re-inscribes sexist conceptions, highlighting the strength of discourses over women's reproductive bodies and their influence over readings of the text.[5] The daughters express their determination in the words of the older: ונחיה מאבינו זרע, through the root חיה, suggesting a 'making alive' of the seed of the father. I would argue that the primary concern here, contra Hamilton, is not *per se* with the desire to bear children, much less to have intercourse with their father, but with their desire to continue the line of their father, in the context of disaster and seeming destruction of all life around them.[6] However, there is an ambiguity: the daughters are concerned that there is no one for them to have intercourse with, while also being concerned about raising life from the father's seed; so their motivations may be a complex of concerns around female childless, the continuing of life, and the need to perpetuate

---

3. Von Rad, for example, recognizes that there is no judgment in the narrative. However, he perceives the narrative as potentially an original Moabite tradition, which glorified the 'wild determination of both ancestral mothers': von Rad, *Genesis*, 244. This is contrasted with the approach of Hamilton, who presumes the text evokes disgust: Hamilton, *Genesis: 18–50*, 51. For an overview of perspectives on the neutrality of the text, and those who ascribe either praise or blame to the daughters (and to Lot), see Stiebert, *Incest*, 157–66.

4. Robert M. Polhemus, *Lot's Daughters: Sex, Redemption, and Women's Quest for Authority* (Stanford, CA: Stanford University Press, 2005), 10–11.

5. Hamilton, *Genesis: 18–50*, 51.

6. Hamilton does suggest that the claim there is no man on earth (בארץ) is hyperbolic, arguing that Zoar was spared, and so the text may refer to a hesitation about *who* will carry on their father's line in the absence of sons (for Lot) or husbands (for the daughters): ibid.

the father's seed. Stiebert suggests the daughters are choosing the lesser of two evils, 'namely "emergency incest" over extinction'.[7] Stiebert suggests this may be understood partly by regarding the story as myth, 'characterized by moral indifference', providing 'a frame of reference for examining universal themes'.[8] The phrase כדרך כל־הארץ implies a givenness and universality to sexual relations: women's penetration is presented as natural. If we approach the text as an ambiguous exploration of the theme of reproduction and survival, it presents an (albeit awkward) situation with a provocative solution. It may be that to Lot's daughters the entire human race had been exterminated,[9] in which case the narrative may negotiate the various tensions of, on the one hand, the extinction of a line, and on the other hand a possible transgression of an incest taboo. Polhemus posits the purpose of the narrative may be to demonstrate that, for the sake of children, *all* is required or allowed.[10] The root חיה may indicate an animating or making alive the seed already dormant in the man, rather than preservation, comparable to the seed coming out from Abraham's inner parts. I would argue that the behaviour of the daughters is partially ambiguous because it reflects the paradigm running throughout these texts, in which reproduction is mandated despite the transgression of taboos. Creating progeny with their father, though done irregularly, is doxic; however, the text casts the daughter's behaviour as doxic, whereas the conscious engagement of the father is denied.

2. *Levirate Law: Context*

If Lot's daughters can be regarded as a myth-type narrative of perpetuating the father's line, other texts contain accounts more traditionally termed 'levirate marriage'. We read in Lewis's 1725 *Origines Hebrææ: The Antiquities of the Hebrew Republick* a brief explanation of the levirate:

---

7. Stiebert, *Fathers and Daughters*, 135. Stiebert draws on the term used by Susanne Scholz, *Sacred Witness: Rape in the Hebrew Bible* (Minneapolis, MN: Fortress, 2010), 170.

8. Stiebert, *Fathers and Daughters*, 135. Stiebert later contrasts this text with contemporary research on incest, which demonstrates father–daughter incest is almost universally initiated by the male and unwanted by the daughter, and intensely damaging: ibid., 140–2.

9. Speiser, *Genesis*, 145.

10. Polhemus, *Lot's Daughters*, 10.

7. *Mechanisms of Continuity*

> The Law next to be explained…is commonly called the Law of the *Levirate*: The Obligation of it was, that if a Man died without Issue, leaving a Widow behind him, the Brother of the Deceased was bound to marry the Widow of his Brother.[11]

This is the oldest known citation of the term levirate in the English language,[12] and points us immediately to the problem of terminology. The practice accounted for in Deut. 25.5-10 (and other texts) is generally referred to either by the English term levirate marriage or the Hebrew term יבום,[13] based on the root יבם, which appears in Deut. 25.5-10, Genesis 38 and Ruth. The word levirate is derived from the Latin *levir* meaning 'brother-in-law' and is combined with the word marriage (with all the cultural baggage it carries), suggesting, on face value, a practice in which a brother-in-law is to marry the widow of his brother. As early as 1725 the practice had, according to Lewis, become 'commonly' called the law of the levirate. Deuteronomy 25.5-10 appears to sit quite comfortably with this terminology; the one obligated to act is something akin to a brother-in-law, and the use of לחק לאשה suggests the union taking place is some form of marriage. This association between the term levirate marriage and Deut. 25.5-10 has continued in scholarship to the present. However, the other texts (Gen. 38 and Ruth) are considered somehow anomalous as they do not involve a brother-in-law, and are ambiguous as to whether there is a permanent union between the widow and family member. Here the terminological problem becomes apparent: the Hebrew root יבם is not the equivalent of the Latin *levir*, and even the Vulgate fails to utilize *levir* in its translations.[14] The root of יבם, even using other ancient West Asian

---

11. Lewis Thomas, *Origines Hebrææ: The Antiquities of the Hebrew Republick. In Four Books* (London: Printed for Sam Illidge under Serle's Gate, Lincoln's-Inn-New-Square; and John Hooke at the Flower-de-luce over-against St. Dunstan's Church in Fleet-street, 1725), 3:268.

12. According to the Oxford English Dictionary, and my own investigations.

13. According to Kutsch, the term is found widely in later layers of Hebrew, Aramaic and Syriac. Middle Hebrew also has *yibbum* (levirate marriage), *yebamut* (consummation of levirate marriage), *yebama* as subject 'be taken in levirate marriage': Ernst Kutsch, 'יבם', *TDOT*. These changes may reflect something like the understanding of the practice as a distinct 'institution' that the usage of the root in biblical texts seems to avoid.

14. David Robert Mace, *Hebrew Marriage: A Sociological Study* (London: Epworth, 1953), 95. Mace notes the difficulty of deriving the definition from the Latin *levir* and the term *marriage*: 'the term is also used in a wider sense to describe cases

languages, cannot be defined with any confidence, and Weisberg notes the limits of ancient West Asian material in illuminating our understanding of the biblical levirate.[15] Burrows argues for progenitor/progenitress as a root, however even he concedes the meaning may have changed by the 'biblical' period.[16] 'Brother-in-law' seems misguided, attempting to define יבם as brother-in-law by its occurrence in texts that deal with 'levirate marriage', despite that in two of the three it is not the brother-in-law who acts as levir. Kutsch suggests a suitably vague definition 'a special kind of relationship', though he does add 'by marriage';[17] however, לקח לאשה cannot be confidently translated marriage, even if the narratives supported this. Mace suggests a definition focused on the act, though maintains the 'husband's brother' within it: 'the word which is used is a special one which means 'to perform the duty of a husband's brother'.[18] Thompson and Thompson note the same confusion between the Hebrew and Latin, and translate יבום as 'progenitor marriage', based on the above understanding of the derivation; while the etymology is flawed, arguably their translation is more accurate to the institution than 'brother-in-law marriage'.[19] I will continue to use the flawed term 'levirate marriage' and 'levirate' here in the discussion, since alternating between an alternative in my text and the traditional when referencing the secondary literature would become confusing. On the other hand, in translation the root יבם, in its various forms, will simply be transliterated, both to give a sense of the recurrence of the technical term throughout the passage, and to see what a reading would look like without the term 'brother-in-law'.

Within Deut. 25.5-10, Genesis 38 and Ruth the institution appears to operate very differently, and occasionally in scholarship one of the two narratives is referred to as not being about real levirate marriage, partially for the reasons just explained, and Brichto suggests a considerable amount of energy has been wasted on trying to determine whether Genesis 38 and Ruth are 'levirate marriage'.[20] Conversely, various attempts have been

---

where a more distantly related kinsman becomes the woman's husband, and even where his function is merely to beget children without marriage to her at all'. Nouns derived from the root occur in masculine and feminine form (Deut. 25.7, 9; Ruth 1.15) and the piel form of the verb (Gen. 38.8; Deut. 25.5, 7). Ruth 1.15 does use the term יבמתך, for sister-in-law, but this is in the context of the levirate.

15. Weisberg, 'Discontent', 403 n. 1.
16. Burrows, 'Background', 6–7.
17. *TDOT*, 'יבם'.
18. Mace, *Hebrew Marriage*, 96.
19. Thompson and Thompson, 'Legal Problems', 84.
20. Brichto, 'Kin', 12 n. 16.

made to work out the discrepancies between the texts. Michael Matlock is among those who view the law of Deuteronomy 25 as codifying an old institution:

> A comparison of this Genesis example with the Deuteronomic law reveals that the custom had changed by Deuteronomic times. For example, the levir's duty was obligatory and enforced by the father, and noncompliance ensured in death in Genesis (see vv. 8-11). However, in Deuteronomy, a choice is given to the levir; if he decides not to marry his dead brother's wife, he will receive public shame but not death. A variant custom of the levirate marriage occurs in the book of Ruth in which the 'redeemer' (גאל) is not Ruth's dead husband's brother but rather his closest living relative. Also, the variant custom in Ruth attests that the closest relative may choose to marry the dead man's wife; but when he decides not to marry her, there is no penalty of death.[21]

While Matlock attempts a kind of chronological legal progression, Weisberg focuses on the 'common denominator' in the three texts, which she views as anxiety over the reluctance of men, such as Onan, to fulfil the institution, which leads to her own historical reconstruction of each text reflecting decreasing obligation.[22] Here Weisberg views the text as a reflection of real day-to-day concerns:

> Women view levirate unions as opportunities to ensure family continuity and provide widows with security. Men, in contrast, see levirate unions as a threat to their understanding of paternity and their desire to protect their own interests. Through this opposition of men and women, biblical authors alert us to tensions between family and communal responsibilities, on the one hand, and the desires and concerns of individuals, on the other.[23]

Others, such as Thompson and Thompson, have noted that genre plays a part:

> Because Ruth and Genesis XXXVIII are stories we should not expect them to be transparent applications of Deuteronomy which gives only the general and ordinary circumstances of the customs, since it is a *legal* text. A straightforward legal application of the levirate would not provide the suspense necessary in the making of a good story. As stories, the narratives of Ruth

---

21. Michael D. Matlock, 'Obeying the First Part of the Tenth Commandment: Applications from the Levirate Marriage Law', *JSOT* 31, no. 3 (2007): 304–5.
22. Weisberg, 'Discontent', 405.
23. Ibid., 405–6.

and Genesis XXXVIII maintain a tension and suspense in the mind of the hearer by using the levirate custom in situations where the outcome is not obvious, and is not discovered until the climax of the narrative.[24]

Thompson and Thompson are surprisingly rare in understanding the texts as differing in content due to genre, rather than legal practice. Burrows, on the other hand, in his historical construction, suggests we 'only have' Deuteronomy, Genesis and Ruth as evidence of practice, disregarding any other texts as pertinent. He goes on to exclude Genesis 38, as it 'is not a typical instance', stating 'we cannot use the story…to show what was the prevailing law or custom in ancient Israel', and Ruth, as it is defined as akin to levirate but 'not quite the same', plus its additional complexities make it a separate issue. Therefore, 'that leaves us only the law given in Deuteronomy as a source for the normal procedure in levirate marriage among the Hebrews'.[25] Burrows narrows down to the extent that not even 'levirate inspired' texts apply to a discussion of the levirate. Rather than determining which texts are applicable, or constructing their diachronic progression, we will, instead, consider the texts on their own terms and bring them into dialogue with each other in the conclusion.

2.1. *Deuteronomy 25.5-10*

If brothers dwell together (ישבו אחים יחדו), and one of them dies and has no son (ובן אין־לו), the wife of the dead (אשת־המת) is not to be married outside to a strange man (החוצה לאיש זר). Her *yibamah* shall go in to her (יבמה יבא עליה), taking her in union (ולקחה לו לאשה), and *yibmah* her (ויבמה), and the firstborn son (בכור) which she bears shall raise the name of the dead brother (יקום על־שם אחיו המת), that his name may not be blotted (ולא־ימחה שמו) from Israel. But if the man does not desire to take his *yibim* (יבמתו), then his *yibim* shall go up to the gate to the elders and say, my *yibam* (יבמי) refuses to raise up for his brother a name (להקים לאחיו שם) in Israel; he will not *yibimi* (לא אבה יבמי)'. Then the elders of his city shall call to him and speak to him. If he stands firm, and says, 'I do not want to take her', then his *yibim* shall approach him in the presence of the elders, and pull his sandal from his foot (נעלי מעל רגלו), and spit in his face (וירקה בפניו), and declare, 'So shall be done to the man who does not build up his brother's house (לא־יבנה את־בית אחיו)'. And his name shall be called in Israel 'The house of him whose sandal was pulled off (ונקרא שמו בישראל בית הלוץ הנעל)'.

---

24. Thompson and Thompson, 'Legal Problems', 88.
25. Burrows, 'Levirate Marriage', 23.

The context of the law is ambiguous:²⁶ preceding it is a law pertaining to two men in a dispute (25.1-3), and a law on muzzling an ox while it is threshing (25.4); and following it is a law dictating that if two men fight and the wife of one seizes the opponent's genitals by the hand, then her hand is to be cut off (25.11-12), as well as regulations on weights and measures (25.13-16) and finally the commandment to 'blot out the memory (זכר) of Amalek from under heaven' (25.17-19). The previous collection of laws in Deuteronomy 24 does not appear to have any strong connection; however, there are some 'familial similarities': three of the laws relate to two sets of men in some sense struggling against each other; and vv. 17-19 are concerned with the preserving (or rather, wiping out) of memory, and uses the same verb, מחה, as vv. 5-10. Suggestions have been made that 25.11-12, the woman who seizes another man's testicles, relate to vv. 5-10, through a concern with 'procreation', that is, that the wife is threatening the man's procreative power.²⁷ The basic structure of the law is as follows:²⁸

> Prostasis, stating conditions for the law to take place:
> (1) two brothers dwell together
> (2) one brother dies
> (3) the dead brother has no sons
>
> Apodosis, stating the consequence of the conditions:
> (1) Basic stipulation
>   a. Negatively stated
>   b. Positively stated
>   i. Re: the woman
>   1. יבם
>   2. לקחה
>   3. יבמה
>   ii. Re: the name
>   1. positive
>   2. negative
> (2) Contingency if levir refuses to perform
>   a. prostasis
>   b. apodosis

---

26. Matlock, 'Obeying'. Matlock understands the Deuteronomy as structured around the Decalogue, with levirate marriage connected to the tenth commandment.

27. Matlock connects them through reference to brothers, a wife, concern for procreative power, and a shared form כי + verb + subject + יהדו: ibid., 304. Pressler echoes this, also noting the similarity in terminology (אשת, יחד, אחים): Pressler, *View of Women*, 63.

28. Adapted from Ellens, *Sex Texts*, 252–3.

The text itself recounts a situation where two brothers dwell together, and one dies without a son, and the process whereby the brother of the deceased takes his brother's widow and fathers a firstborn who 'raises' the name of the deceased brother. In this way the deceased brother's name is not blotted out.

Deborah Ellens's chapter on Deut. 25.5-10 in *Women in the Sex Texts of Leviticus and Deuteronomy* is the fullest review of the discussion in recent scholarship, with a substantial discussion and comprehensive references to past scholarship on the issue. Ellens suggests explanations fall into four groups: (1) those to do with progeny; (2) inheritance of property (land or sexual); (3) welfare of widows; (4) perpetuation of the deceased name. Ellens notes that most scholars take a 'variety of stances within the four groups', sometimes emphasizing one single aspect (such as Neufeld, and the widow's welfare); combining several competing concerns, or excluding one or more of the concerns from the combination. Ellens notes that the perpetuation of the name is often included with a combination of the first three, and may be accompanied with other factors such as ancestor worship or 'vague notions' concerning 'continued existence' in this world after his death. The following discussion will look at each relevant part of the text in depth.

2.1.1. *'When brothers dwell together'*. The question of the numbers of brothers being present is not addressed.[29] אח itself as a term should be inferred by context;[30] however, there is no reason here to presume it is speaking about anything other than two men brought up together, of the same father. The term 'together' is also somewhat ambiguous, and may mean either living together on the same family estate because their father is still alive or because they have not yet divided the estate after his death;[31] or living near each other in the same vicinity,[32] such as in Gen. 36.7 where dwelling together 'means dwelling close enough to use the same pasture land'.[33] It has been suggested that this could have been a typical scenario, rather than restrictive: for example, 'say two brothers

---

29. This point, which had not occurred to me, was, of course, picked up by the rabbis, who suggest the brothers are all asked in order from oldest to youngest, and if they all decline, the oldest must oblige; Mish. Yev. 4.5. See: Tigay, *Deuteronomy*, 223 n. 27.

30. It can mean nephew (Gen. 14.16), peoples (Jer. 3.8; Mal. 1.2) or be a term of endearment (2 Sam. 1.26; Song 4.9-12). See Parker, *Valuable and Vulnerable*, 49.

31. See also Pressler, *View of Women*, 64. Pressler uses other ancient West Asian legal texts to determine this.

32. Cf. Gen. 13.6.

33. Tigay, *Deuteronomy*, 231.

dwell together'.³⁴ If it is restrictive, it could imply, at minimum, the union 'was obligatory only if the levir's home, where the widow and her future child would reside, was close to that property'.³⁵ Joseph Blenkinsopp suggests: 'Since Israelite law did not provide for the widow to inherit the property of her husband, the danger of alienating the ancestral holding, the *naḥălăh*, does not seem to have been an issue as far as this stipulation was concerned, quite apart from the fact that the brothers are residing together, in the same household'.³⁶ While the issue is not that of alienation of property, it is probably also true that the clause implies some issues of property or inheritance, and has been taken by some as the clause which 'necessarily ties the levirate practice of that law to issues concerning inheritance of landed property'.³⁷ Westbrook draws on this idea, suggesting that the father has died and the estate is yet to be divided, and constructs elaborate scenarios in which Genesis 38 reflects a father who is still alive with an undivided estate, Deut. 25.5-10 a situation in which the father is dead but the estate still undivided, and Ruth a situation in which the father is dead *and* the estate alienated.³⁸ However, as noted above, the clause cannot be understood simply as a fear of the alienation of property.

2.1.2. *'The man dies without a son'*. The term used in v. 5, בן, is ambiguous, and we cannot say for certain whether this is only contingent on a man dying without a son, or more generally without a child.³⁹ However, most agree that the use of masculine-only בכור, first-born, in v. 6 qualifies בן in v. 5, so that it 'must refer to male progeny'.⁴⁰

34. Thompson and Thompson, 'Legal Problems', 89. They suggest 'the Israelites were not so legalistic'; their perspectives, which suggests an ambiguity in practice, provides a stark contrast to some of the overly ambitious reconstructions of the minutiae of ancient practice and law.
35. Tigay, *Deuteronomy*, 231.
36. Blenkinsopp, 'Family', 64.
37. Ellens, *Sex Texts*, 254.
38. Westbrook, *Property*, 78.
39. For example, בן can mean a child of either gender (Gen. 3.16) and sometimes the emphatic בן זכר is used for a male (Jer. 20.15): Neufeld, *Ancient Hebrew Marriage Laws*, 82. The term has meanings ranging from grandson (Gen. 11.31; 1 Sam. 9.9-11; 2 Chron. 22.9) to a member of a professional organization (2 Kgs 4.1; Isa. 19.11; Ezra 2.61). For a full survey of the language around children and offspring, see Parker, *Valuable and Vulnerable*, 46–74.
40. Ellens, *Sex Texts*, 252 n. 13; Westbrook, *Property*, 82; Pressler, *View of Women*, 65. The LXX translates בן with σπέρμα, and בכור with παιδιον, 'little children', which implies a decisive change in gendered vocabulary: Ernst Kutsch, 'יבם', *TDOT*; Neufeld, *Ancient Hebrew Marriage Laws*, 82.

2.1.3. *'The wife of the dead is not to be married outside to a strange man'.* Jeffrey Tigay suggests, based on Deut. 22.23-24, that אשת המת can also imply fiancée. The Hebrew is slightly ambiguous in its use of לאיש זר, as it does not specify whether this is outside of the משפחה or the בית אב.[41] If the concern was not to marry outside of the משפחה, the purpose of the law could primarily be to keep the נחלה within the נחלה of the clan.[42] However, the text seems more concerned with the immediate בית אב, specifically the brother of the deceased. This also becomes important in terms of determining the purpose of the law:

> In spite of some possible advantages to the childless widow, the law does restrict her behavior, by stipulating that she cannot marry outside of the family, even when her relationship with a male, her husband, has technically ended. In other words, this law, and others like it, result in a female being under the control of her father, and then her husband where her husband's control (or that of his family) continues even after his death.[43]

If this is true, then it detracts from any notion that the underlining purpose of the legislation is for the widow's advantage. It also emphasizes that the social relationships in the family transcend the death of the man.

2.1.4. לקח, בוא *and* לקח, יבם may suggest, as discussed above, that he is to take her 'as his wife',[44] or into a formal union, and the use of לקח, בוא and יבם denote sexual intercourse.[45] However, the following clause states that the purpose is not to provide a marriage but to raise the name of the dead through this sexual union. It is here that the Levitical law against incest is apparently transgressed.[46] The widow's agency in the union is

---

41. Zevit, 'Dating Ruth', 577. Pressler, *View of Women*, 65 n. 6. compares it to 1 Kgs 3.18 and Job 19.15, where it implies outside of the household.

42. This would be comparable to the concern in Num. 36 that the daughters of Zelophehad would marry outside of the משפחה.

43. Anderson, *Women*, 47.

44. Tigay, *Deuteronomy*, 232. Cf. Deut. 21.14.

45. Neufeld argues 'he shall go into her…' suggests the union took place by consummation: Neufeld, *Ancient Hebrew Marriage Laws*, 84.

46. For example, Westbrook suggests either that the incest law only counts during the lifetime of the deceased, or the levirate law is a *lex specialis* and so is exempt from the Levitical prohibition. He notes the case of the Hittite HL 193-195, in which two laws operate side-by-side, one stating that a brother can take the widow without punishment after the husband's death, the other stating that if the husband is alive it is a capital crime: Westbrook, *Property*, 86. Compare this to Mace, who suggests that Lev. 18 is a Priestly attempt to prohibit the law of the levirate, suggesting that

absent; however, it is noted that the retention of the widow's sexuality by the family cannot be seen as a full form of ownership of her; for example, there is no provision in law for the husband/father-in-law to be able to 'sell' her.[47] Ellens suggests 'this willingness, even eagerness, on the part of the woman is a function of her desire to fulfil her duty/destiny... It is the purpose for which the levirate law secures her sexuality as property.'[48] Mace notes:

> The most puzzling feature of the Hebrew levirate, however, still requires explanation. It lies in the extraordinary fact that a people like the Hebrews, who were so scrupulously jealous in the matter of the paternity of their children, should be prepared to reckon the son of a living man as that of his deceased brother. It is true that if any offspring other than his own were likely to be reckoned as belonging to a man, it would be that begotten upon his wife by such a closer relative as his brother. But even when that has been said, the obstacle remains formidable.[49]

Pressler argues that the law regards the principle of leaving a son as more important than the principle of 'biological paternity'[50] or incest prohibitions, arguing this is even more striking as her study underlines the gravity of the offence of adultery in the Deuteronomic legislation.[51] There is a further noteworthy suggestion in Sefer Ha-Hinnukh, that the offspring of the union can be counted as of the deceased's flesh, since when the mother married the man she became 'bone of his bone and flesh of his flesh' (cf. Gen. 2.23) and the brother is also partly his brother's flesh.[52]

2.1.5. *'Shall raise the name of the dead'*. In terms of the actual wording of the passage, 'in vv. 6 and 7, the greatest concern is to perpetuate the deceased's name and clan'.[53] However, the precise meaning of יקום על-שם אחיו המת is 'somewhat elusive', and Pressler is probably correct that it is unlikely that the term 'refers to being given the name of the deceased man in any literal sense', such as being named after the father, or taking any form of last name, and to my knowledge no piece of scholarship

---

the penalty threatened in Lev. 20 of childlessness may be a direct response to the law under discussion here: Mace, *Hebrew Marriage*, 110 n. 4.
   47. Burrows, 'Background', 8.
   48. Ellens, *Sex Texts*, 258 n. 28.
   49. Mace, *Hebrew Marriage*, 115.
   50. A term which, arguably, carries certain anachronistic associations.
   51. Pressler, *View of Women*, 68.
   52. Sefer Ha-Hinnukh no. 553. Quoted in: Tigay, *Deuteronomy*, 232 n. 23.
   53. Matlock, 'Obeying', 305.

on the subject argues this; among the various interpretations of שם, the most significant disagreements are over it having some connotations of property.[54] Most commentaries combine the various purposes of the law, for example Cairns states: 'In the early period its aim was threefold: to perpetuate the deceased's name and clan, to preserve the balance in land inheritance, and to provide for the widow'.[55] Richard Nelson argues: 'it is important to note that the law makes no direct mention of inheritance, economic matters, or the protection for the widow… [W]hatever benefits the widow may receive are not mentioned.'[56] Burrows, writing in 1940, offers three reasons for need of the levirate custom:[57] 'provision of an heir for his property', 'continuation of his personal life in the life of his son, according to a deep-seated conception of the ancient world', and 'welfare in the hereafter as dependent upon the performance of ancestral rites'.[58] Notably, however, the welfare of the widow, typically included in later scholarship, is missing. Burrows, instead, understands the economic implications of the widow first in terms of the value of retaining her for the family, and briefly mentions that the enactment of the law would probably provide provision for her support.[59] Westbrook states the law of levirate marriage would be a 'remarkably roundabout way' to provide protection: 'the brother is obliged not only to marry the widow but also to beget a child and pay the expense of raising that child and supporting the widow until such time as the child will be able to support his mother'. Moreover, he suggests that it is not a case of the widow being 'inherited', stating: 'this would make the levirate a right, whereas in the biblical sources it is clearly presented as a duty, and an onerous one at that'.[60] Moreover, Chapman demonstrates that the house of the mother remains a place where if a marriage ended, a woman could return to find refuse

---

54. Pressler, *View of Women*, 66.

55. Ian Cairns, *Word and Presence: A Commentary on the Book of Deuteronomy*, ITC (Grand Rapids, MI: Eerdmans, 1992), 216.

56. Richard D. Nelson, *Deuteronomy: A Commentary*, OTL (Louisville, KY: Westminster John Knox, 2002), 297–8.

57. Burrows, 'Background', 2.

58. For Example, he quotes an unspecified Babylonian text 'May he [i.e. the god Ninurta] deprive him of his son, the water-pourer…the son, the water-pourer, may he take away from him… May he tear out his boundary-stone, destroy his name, his seed, his offspring, his descendants from the mouth of men, and may he not let him have a son and a pourer of water', quoted from H. Schaweffer, 'The Social Legislation of the Primitive Semites', 49.

59. Burrows, 'Background', 7.

60. Westbrook, *Property*, 72.

and economic support.⁶¹ If we can eliminate protection of the widow as a purpose behind the law, and the law does not refer to the son being given his father's name as some sort of last name, this leaves us then with the tension remaining in the term שם: between Westbrook's 'title' and Pedersen's 'soul', which would also suggest the name would continue to have genealogical functions.

2.1.6. *'If the man does not desire'*. Speculating on the text's silence as to why the brother would refuse, Tigay suggests five scenarios:⁶² (1) he might not 'care' for his brother's wife; (2) he might feel that she had brought his brother bad luck;⁶³ (3) if his brother is dead and heirless, he may be able to inherit a larger share of his father's estate; (4) he may already be married and not desire an additional wife; (5) he may be concerned with the cost of supporting the widow and a child, and that this cost may well diminish his own estate. Further, there is the possibility that the firstborn, as well as inheriting from the deceased, may inherit part of the brother-in-law's own personal property.⁶⁴

2.1.7. *'His* yibim *shall go up to the gate to the elders'*. Weisberg correctly argues that 'the language of the ritual suggests that the widow represents her deceased husband', and that her words underscore the primary concern of the text around the deceased's need for progeny,⁶⁵ while Westbrook suggests there may be undisclosed reasons for the widow's protest, such as wishing to be freed from the union (acknowledging the Deuteronomist does not contemplate this) or to free herself of 'the stigma from barrenness'.⁶⁶ Particularly of interest is Weisberg's suggestion that the combination of being represented so strongly through the widow, and the shame imposed on the unwilling brother, can operate as a kind of 'comfort' to the childless man.⁶⁷ The punishment, through the removal of a shoe, has been connected to the removal of the shoe in Ruth 4. Notably, however, there is a gap in Ruth 4, in both context and practice. Moreover, shoes take on various symbolic meanings in biblical texts and

---

61. Chapman, *House*, 74, as we will see in Ruth 1 where the women may return to Moab.
62. Tigay, *Deuteronomy*, 332–3.
63. See, for example, Genesis 38.
64. Matlock, 'Obeying', 307.
65. Weisberg, 'Discontent', 409–10.
66. Westbrook, *Property*, 84.
67. Weisberg, 'Discontent', 413.

the presence of the shoe should not indicate sameness.[68] While it is widely acknowledged the spitting is intended to bring about shame,[69] Carmichael argues that rather than the sandal removal being a legal transaction, it too is shaming,[70] especially considering the name given to the brother (v. 10).[71] Carmichael views Deut. 25.5-10 as a legal construction responding to the ambiguities of Genesis 38, suggesting the 'lawgiver is only interested in the circumscribed case of the two brothers because he confines his interest to the circumstances described in Genesis 38'.[72] He says:

> The punishment he decides is to have the brother's widow symbolically imitate what Onan did to Tamar and hence remind the offending brother and the public bystanders that what he is in fact doing to her by refusing to have intercourse invites comparison with Onan's odious act. Thus the drawing off of the sandal (as in the Arab divorce ceremony the sandal symbolizes a woman or woman's genitals) from the man's foot (in Hebrew the foot can allude to the male sexual organ) signifies, by a process of transference, the man's withholding conception. Moreover, when after removing his sandal she spits in his face this action is a symbolic reminder of Onan's spilling of the semen on the ground.[73]

While Carmichael's argument is overconfident, it does point to the range of symbolic possibilities. Tigay suggests that there is an equity present

---

68. Pressler notes three different symbolic meanings of shoes: casting a shoe over something is a symbol of power in Ps. 60.10; going barefoot as a sign of mourning (Ezek. 24.17, 23); and a sign of humiliation/capture (Isa. 20.2): Pressler, *View of Women*, 70–1.

69. Ibid., 65 n. 9. Cf. Isa. 50.6; Job 30.10; Num. 12.14. Carmichael also notes that most biblical references to spitting refer to contemptuous spitting: Num. 12.14; Isa. 50.6; Job 30.10. רק (spittle) occurs euphemistically for semen in b. Nid. 16b, but Carmichael offers no biblical evidence. Calum Carmichael, 'A Ceremonial Crux: Removing a Man's Sandal as a Female Gesture of Contempt', *JBL* 96, no. 3 (1977): 331.

70. The sandal appears to have carried associations with property. See Ps. 60.9, where the treading of boundaries (cf. Gen. 13.17; Deut. 1.36; 11.24; Josh. 1.3) is associated with the promise of descendants to Abraham (Cairns, *Word and Presence*, 217).

71. Carmichael, 'Ceremonial Crux', 321 n. 1. Carmichael notes other examples of removal of the sandal being shaming in Isa. 20.2-4

72. Ibid., 328 n. 22.

73. Ibid., 329. Carmichael explores the euphemistic associations of רגליים: Gen. 49.8-12; Exod. 4.25; Deut. 28.57; 2 Sam. 11.8, 11; 2 Kgs 18.27 and Isa. 6.2; 7.20; 36.12; Jer. 2.25; Ezek. 16.25. The verb for removal in Deut. 25.9 has association of 'a man's loins/virility'; cf. Gen. 35.11; 1 Kgs 8.19; 2 Chron. 6.9; Hos. 5.6.

in the form of punishment, as he refused to build up his brother's house: 'the nickname degrades his own house; since he refused to protect his brother's name from obliteration, he acquires a pejorative nickname'.[74] The combination of the public refusal and the widow forcing the matter by public embarrassment suggest the concern is not for the widow's welfare but for the 'extended family, comprehended in terms of male relationships, into which she had married'.[75]

The purpose of the law is clear, though its meaning is ambiguous. The law casts the widow and the brother as ideally operating in the service of the deceased, and while the brother's non-compliance is mirrored in a form of public shame, the widow's non-compliance is not even considered. There are allusions to matters of property throughout the law: the brothers' dwelling together, the שם, the presence of the sandal; however, none of these are conclusive in terms of substantiating that the law is about property. Furthermore, the law is not concerned with the same issue as the law of redemption, that is, maintaining property within the משפחה; the focus is on the בית אב and the relations are in terms of the immediate confines of the household, albeit mediated through punishment by the wider community. The law suggests obligations between the widow, brother and the deceased, which override concerns about paternity, or any possible incest taboo that may have been in operation. We will now look at the practice in operation in two narrative texts.

2.2. *Judah and Tamar*

Genesis 38 is a multivalent text, and issues in interpretation stem in part from what Esther Menn calls its 'productive intertextuality', engaging Pentateuchal issues such as intermarriage with Canaanites, levirate marriage, incest, prostitution, and with an immediate context of the Joseph narrative and a wider context of the Davidic kingship.[76] It also appears as a surprising 'variation on the theme of infertility, which is so prevalent in Genesis',[77] and of the struggles between brothers. Due to its richness, 'all parts of the story of Judah and Tamar are significant'.[78] Weisberg

---

74. Tigay, *Deuteronomy*, 234. Rofé understands this as a 'symbolic talio': Alexander Rofé, 'Family and Sex Laws in Deuteronomy and the Book of the Covenant', *Henoch* 9, no. 2 (1987): 151–2.

75. Zevit, 'Dating Ruth', 578.

76. Esther Marie Menn, *Judah and Tamar (Genesis 38) in Ancient Jewish Exegesis: Studies in Literary Form and Hermeneutics*, JSJSup 51 (Leiden: Brill, 1997), 13.

77. Van Dijk-Hemmes, 'Limits', 80.

78. Martin Greenberg, 'Judah and Tamar', *Dor Le Dor* 16, no. 2 (1987): 124.

suggests it is unclear 'whether Tamar acts to preserve her husband's name and lineage or whether she acts to preserve her connection to Judah's family',[79] and this question will guide our discussion. There is a fair amount of debate as to the dating of Genesis 38, from Davidic (or earlier) to Persian,[80] coming in part from an its disconnect from the surrounding Joseph narratives;[81] that said, there have been attempts, notably by Robert Alter, to demonstrate how there are strong connections between this passage and its context.[82] In addition to territorial associations,[83] there are connections to the Davidic monarchy and Ruth, with the birth of twins perhaps emphasizing the genealogical line.[84] The short narrative has a developed thematic structure, initiated 'by indicating in the first five verses that the pericope of Genesis 38 dwells on procreation of Judah's progeny'. The verses establish a 'basic sequence of male and female actions'[85] (saw, took, went into, and then conceived, gave birth, named), which stand in stark contrast to the stories of childlessness and waiting

---

79. Sharon Pace Jeansonne, *The Women of Genesis: From Sarah to Potiphar's Wife*. (Minneapolis, MN: Fortress, 1990), 98.

80. For example, for a very early dating, see John A. Emerton, 'Judah and Tamar', *VT* 29, no. 4 (1979): 414. For a very late one, see Mark G. Brett, *Genesis: Procreation and the Politics of Identity*, OTR (London: Routledge, 2000).

81. Wildavsky discusses the tendency among scholars to suggest the narrative is wholly divorced from the surrounding context: Aaron Wildavsky, 'Survival Must Not Be Gained Through Sin: The Moral of the Joseph Stories Prefigured Through Judah and Tamar', *JSOT* 19 (1994): 37. For example, he cites von Rad, who states 'every attentive reader...can see that the story of Judah and Tamar has no connection at all with the strictly organized Joseph stories' (von Rad, *Genesis*, 356).

82. Robert Alter, *The Art of Biblical Narrative* (New York: Basic Books, 1981), 5–13. See also Brett, for example, who notes a link it to Gen. 37 and 38, 'insofar as Judah's character is called into question both by his empty discourse concerning 'brotherhood' and by his failure to live up to the *kinship* obligations laid on him by his daughter-in-law Tamar': Brett, *Genesis*, 113.

83. Sarna argues that the association of all the places mentioned – Adullam, Chezib, Timnah and Enal – being contained within the later territory of the tribe of Judah cannot be an accident, with the text possibly reflecting the movement of the tribe into the region and concerned with the history of the clan of Judah: Nahum M. Sarna, *Genesis*, JPSTC (Philadelphia: Jewish Publication Society, 1989), 264.

84. Abasili highlights particularly 'the future kings of Israel will come from the tribe of Judah' (cf. Gen. 49.8-12) (Abasili, 'Genesis 38', 286). Adullam is also connected with David's life, Bathshua and Tamar are linked with the biography of the king, and at the close of the narrative, Perez gains pre-eminence and becomes ancestor of David (see Sarna, *Genesis*, 264).

85. Menn, *Judah and Tamar*, 16.

throughout Genesis. This is, according to Johanna van Wijk-Bos, 'offset' in the second part by terms for death (vv. 7, 10) and waste (v. 9).[86] Male kinship terms abound (son, vv. 3, 4, 5; firstborn, vv. 5, 7; brother, vv. 8, 9) and Tamar is twice identified in relation to men (brother's wife, vv. 8, 9).

Judah settles near 'a certain Adullamite' named Hirah and takes a Canaanite woman:

> And she conceived and bore a son; and called his name Er. And she conceived again and bore a son and she called his name Onan. And yet again she bore a son, and she called his name Shelah. (Gen. 38.3-5)

The woman, though not named, names the sons. Judah takes a wife for Er named Tamar, and the text implies she is Canaanite also;[87] however, 'Er, the firstborn of Judah, was wicked in the eyes of YHWH, and YHWH put him to death',[88] with the epithet בכור used repeatedly (Gen. 38.7-8).[89] We then read:

> Then Judah said to Onan, 'Go in to the wife of your brother (בא אל־אשת אחיך) and *yabem* (ויבם אתה); and raise up seed for your brother (והקם זרע לאחיך)'. But Onan knew that the seed (זרע) would not be his, and when he went into the wife of his brother, he spoiled it on the ground (ושחת ארצה), so that he would not give seed (זרע) to his brother. (Gen. 38.8-9)

YHWH puts Onan to death, and Judah tells Tamar: 'remain a widow in the house of your father until Shelah, my son, is grown', from Judah's undisclosed fear Shelah would die too.[90] There is no suggestion of anything like a marriage union, with Onan only commanded to בא אל, without the verb לחק.[91] Nahum Sarna suggests Onan spills his seed as there is no

---

86. Johanna W. H. van Wijk-Bos, 'Out of the Shadows: Genesis 38; Judges 4:17-22; Ruth 3', *Semeia* 42 (1988): 42.

87. Maurice E. Andrew, 'Moving from Death to Life: Verbs of Motion in the Story of Judah and Tamar in Gen 38', *ZAW* 105, no. 2 (1993): 268.

88. *Genesis Rabba* appears to suggest the rabbis recognized that the denial of procreation is related to Er's wrongdoing, suggesting 'he would plough on the roof' (a euphemism for anal sexual intercourse), hinting towards an overall theme of failure to procreate; see: Jacob Neusner, *Genesis Rabbah: The Judaic Commentary to the Book of Genesis: A New American Translation*, BJS 104 (Atlanta, GA: Scholars Press, 1985), 3:209.

89. Abasili, 'Genesis 38', 281.

90. Some texts presume a widow can return to her father's house (Lev. 22.13; Ruth 1.8) presumably with a right to marry (Ruth 1.9).

91. Belkin, 'Levirate and Agnate', 279.

possibility of 'voluntary renunciation by the brother-in-law';[92] however, alternative explanations are viable, such as Onan choosing to deceive in order to avoid shame, or to prevent a rival inheriting the double-share of the firstborn. Either way, YHWH's annihilation of Onan displays both 'his approval of Judah's instruction to Onan', and 'his support for the levirate law and the gravity of refusing to fulfil such a duty'.[93] Leonard Mars, from a specifically anthropological approach, argues that there is clear social disapproval confirmed by divine action in capital punishment, suggesting that to raise up seed for a brother 'involves an act of altruism, of self-sacrifice in which self-interest is set aside for the sake of a brother and for one's family',[94] and so the text affirms the value of this self-sacrifice in a narrative context with a strong taboo attached to failure. He even goes as far as to say that Onan's crime 'was not coitus interruptus but was in fact murder, an hypothesis which would explain the severity of his punishment'.[95] By not fulfilling his obligation, Onan destroys his brother's post-mortem life. Drawing on the meaning of זרע as both semen and descendants, Mark Brett states 'Tamar's initiatives can be read as preserving the seed of the family, as opposed to Onan who wastes it for purely selfish reasons';[96] and this filial failure may move the sexual relationship back into the category of incest, a capital offence, moving Onan from an approved social-sexual role to a prohibited one.[97]

Judah's wife dies, and after the time of mourning he goes to Timnah to shear his sheep. Tamar, still in mourning, replaces her widow's garments with a veil, and sits at the entrance to Enaim on the road to Timnah.[98] We are told:

> She saw that Shelah was grown up, and she had not been given to him as a wife/woman (לא־נתנה לו לאשה). (Gen. 38.14)

92. Sarna, *Genesis*, 256.
93. Abasili, 'Genesis 38', 281.
94. Mars, 'Onan's Crime', 432.
95. Ibid., 435.
96. Brett, *Genesis*, 114.
97. Sarna, *Genesis*, 267.
98. While the veiling has often been taken by commentators as an explicit symbol of prostitution, it has been argued that the intention is simply to hide her face, in light of the LXX, Vulgate, and later rabbinic interpretation which appear to separate the aspect of veiling and prostitution, as well as ancient West Asian material which prohibits prostitutes from veiling: John R. Huddlestun, 'Unveiling the Versions: The Tactics of Tamar in Genesis 38:15', *JHS* 3 (2001).

Judah does not know who she is, and, thinking her to be prostitute (ויחשבה לזונה), asks, 'let me come in to you'.⁹⁹ Tamar here seemingly presumes Judah's sexual appetite.¹⁰⁰ Tamar makes him give her his signet, cord and staff as deposit, and she conceives by him, and puts back on the garments of her widowhood. The objects constitute a kind of signature, and מטה, while understood as Tamar asking for his staff, could be a sexual euphemism,¹⁰¹ or function as a homonym of the 'tribe' of Judah.¹⁰² The theme of intercourse is woven in with kinship and patterns of lineage and continuity. Judah's friend the Adullamite is unable to find the 'prostitute' to swap the gifts, and he and Judah decide to put the incident behind them. The narrative skips about three months, and Judah is told that Tamar has 'played the whore' (זנתה) and is pregnant. Hearing this, Judah orders Tamar is to be brought out and burned (הוציאוה ותשרף). The punishment at once both highlights Judah's double standards and deals with the 'problem' of Tamar's existence, with Judah ironically taking action where he would not before.¹⁰³ Tamar is brought out and declares it was the owner of the signet cord and staff who made her pregnant: 'Then Judah acknowledged them and said, "She is more righteous than I, since I did not give her to my son Shelah". And no more did he lie with her' (Gen. 38.26). J. A. Soggin suggests the extravagant form of penalty can be attributed to the story's 'fairy tale' like quality, in which penalties are threatened but never executed, particularly since, according to Soggin, as a widow Tamar is not guilty of adultery.¹⁰⁴ Aside from the oddness of viewing this text as being like a 'fairy tale', Soggin's suggestion that Tamar is not guilty of adultery fails to understand the full extent of the dynamics of widowhood in the context of the levirate, where the childless widow's sexuality is still maintained by the household of the husband, even after death.

---

99. Adelman notes the use of the irony of the passage; the root ידע points to the woman who is 'in the know' about identity while the men 'know' 'only through the flesh', and the entrance of Enaim, בפתח עינים, suggests the opening of eyes while also veiling Tamar from Judah (Adelman, 'Seduction and Recognition', 90, 93).

100. Abasili, 'Genesis 38', 282.

101. Wildavsky, 'Survival', 41.

102. Danna N. Fewell and David M. Gunn, *Narrative in the Hebrew Bible* (New York: Oxford University Press, 1993), 40.

103. Ibid., 42.

104. J. A. Soggin, 'Judah and Tamar (Genesis 38)', in *Of Prophets' Visions and the Wisdom of Sages: Essays in Honour of R. Norman Whybray on His Seventieth Birthday*, ed. David J. A. Clines and Heather A. McKay, JSOTSup 162 (Sheffield: JSOT, 1993), 283.

The narrative skips to the birth of twins. One begins to come out and has a crimson thread tied to his wrist; he then withdraws, and his sibling is firstborn and named Perez, and the other Zerah.[105] Perez and Zerah compensate for the loss of Er and Onan, and 'history, which has been stopped by Judah and his sons, sets back in motion'.[106] Perez 'became proverbial for fruitfulness',[107] and the text leaves us little information on the fate of Tamar; however, it lays some clues. We are told that Judah did not have intercourse (ידע) with Tamar again, and any possibility of a union with Shelah is not mentioned. Fuchs suggests:

> Even after Judah recognizes that he was wrong in withholding Shelah from his daughter-in-law, he is not shown to make up for his unjust treatment of Tamar. Why does the narrative avoid the issue of Tamar's marriage to Shelah? The reason seems obvious: despite the repeated references to Tamar's marriage, the issue at the heart of our narrative is the disruption of the patrilineal chain. Once mended through the birth of Zerah and Perez, there seems to be a little justification for dealing with Tamar and Shelah. Having reached its telos – the birth of male heirs – the narrative comes to an end. A closer examination of Tamar's plan and actions reveals that her goal – in perfect congruence with patriarchal interests – is to give birth to male heirs, not to be married to Shelah.[108]

Tamar will 'not become part of the patrilineal genealogy', it is not her 'right' or her 'privileges' that concern the narrator.[109] Instead, the offspring of Judah and Tamar's intercourse re-establish the line of Judah, and even when she is mentioned, such as in Ruth 4.12, it is concerning Judah.

There is a difficulty in drawing out a central theme to Genesis 38.[110] Several commentators take the widow as the central concern, but we are already faced with the patriarchal leanings of the text in the initial verses,

---

105. Here we see one of the great themes of Genesis, competition between siblings, reaching back even to the womb: Mars, 'Onan's Crime', 438.
106. Van Dijk-Hemmes, 'Limits', 82.
107. See Ruth 4.12; cf. Andrew, 'Moving from Death to Life', 268.
108. Fuchs, *Sexual Politics*, 72–3.
109. Ibid., 73.
110. Abasili, 'Genesis 38', 227. For example, Niditch argues for an interpretation based around the stability and health of Israelite social structure (Niditch, 'The Wronged Woman Righted', 144); Coats argues it is about the women's right to conceive (Coats, 'Widow's Rights', 465); Menn concludes it is about transition from one generation of males to the next (Menn, *Judah and Tamar*, 15); Wijk-Bos argues it is about righteousness (Johanna W. H. van Wijk-Bos, 'An Eye Opener at the Gate:

as the deaths are 'described as those of sons, not of husbands', indicating the primacy of the father, and issues of generational continuity, over the widow.[111] Menn suggests that the description of Judah's isolation from his siblings in v. 1 and the account of the birth and naming of the twins in the final vv. 27-30 implies 'the central issue driving the narrative consists of the transition from one generation of males to the next'.[112] Menn couples this with motifs of birth and naming in vv. 3-5, which she proposes mean 'Genesis 38 may be viewed as a double tale of procreation, in which initial biological and social discontinuity is twice overcome',[113] first, in vv. 1-5, with Judah's explicit concern with his eldest son in his instructions to Onan, confirming 'that the central movements of the plot involve generational transitions', and next in vv. 6-30, with its resolution. This transition 'from father to sons is a fundamental and recurrent structure in biblical literature, undergirding both the extended birth narratives and the skeletal genealogies'.[114] Judah's exclamation of Tamar's righteousness is not in Tamar's individual decisions (prostitution, deception, incest, etc.), but instead 'is communal, specifically directed towards relationship with other people',[115] a 'devotion to the law',[116] despite differences with Deuteronomy 25. Regardless of the apparent silence about Tamar and her perspective, some have understood the plot to be about her economic protection or desire for offspring:

> Powerless members of society who are wronged cannot always confront the perpetrators of injustice. The society in which they live may ignore the poor... After Tamar's husband Er dies, Onan is required by law to have intercourse with her and to marry her in order that she may have a child and that she might continue to be supported.[117]

George Coats and Genesis 38', *Lexington Theological Quarterly* 27, no. 4 [1992]: 120–1); Brueggemann claims it does not make clear its intents (Walter Brueggemann, *Genesis*, IBC [Louisville, KY: John Knox, 1982], 308).

111. Ellen van Wolde, 'Texts in Dialogue with Texts: Intertextuality in the Ruth and Tamar Narratives', *BibInt* 5, no. 1 (1997): 10.
112. Menn, *Judah and Tamar*, 15.
113. Ibid.
114. Ibid.
115. Andrew, 'Moving from Death to Life', 267.
116. Yairah Amit, 'Narrative Analysis: Meaning, Context and Origin of Genesis 38', in *Method Matters: Essays on the Interpretation of the Hebrew Bible in Honor of David L. Petersen*, ed. Joel M. LeMon and Kent Harold Richards, SBLRBS 56 (Atlanta, GA: Society of Biblical Literature, 2009), 279.
117. Jeansonne, *Women of Genesis*, 98.

Sharon Jeansonne here suggests an emotional and economic drive from Tamar for her own benefit; Westbrook, however, against almost all commentators, notes 'Tamar in Genesis 38 appears to be in no material distress'.[118] Jeansonne forces Judah's irresponsibility further, stating that although Judah is aware of the custom 'concerning widows and the levirate marriage', he fails to 'specify the totality of these obligations to his son Onan':

> Eschewing the obligation of marriage, and thus any responsibility for Tamar, he tells his son to have sexual intercourse and father a child, but does not specify that Onan should marry Tamar. Indeed, he expresses no concern for his daughter-in-law, who now has no means of support.[119]

Jeansonne at the end claims that 'although Tamar will no longer be a childless widow, she remains a widow denied the right of levirate marriage',[120] defining the levirate around the act of 'marriage'. George Coats suggests that, 'according to the levirate custom, a widow should not be left childless', and 'Tamar can expect only conception of a child'.[121] While removing the obligation for marriage, Coats subtly works in a desire for a child as the primary want of Tamar. Through this, Coats has an optimistic interpretation of the entire plot:

> If one assumes that the levirate custom, at least at this stage in history, concerns only the widow's right to conceive a child, the ending fits. Tamar is satisfied. Judah is satisfied. The reader knows that justice, particularly when widows are concerned, finally wins out.[122]

Aaron Wildavsky states that Onan's spilling of his seed is so wrong because it gives Tamar no opportunity 'to complain openly that she has been wronged' and seek redress in order to 'maintain her reputation'.[123] Deborah Sawyer suggests that her status as a 'non-person' between the two houses illustrates 'the dire situation women could face without the protection of the levirate marriage law'.[124] Arguably, however, it is

---

118. Westbrook, *Property*, 72.
119. Jeansonne, *Women of Genesis*, 101.
120. Ibid., 105–6.
121. Coats, 'Widow's Rights', 463–4.
122. Ibid., 465–6.
123. Wildavsky, 'Survival', 39.
124. Sawyer, *God, Gender and the Bible*, 62.

precisely because of the law (or cultural practice) that she is in such a dire situation, neither 'released' in order to remarry nor protected by the father-in-law's family, but instead her sexuality objectified as a kind of property for the cause of patrilineal procreation, under her father-in-law's authority.

Fuchs draws our attention to Tamar's concern, not for herself, but for 'Judah's patrilineal continuity',[125] despite 'questionable' sexual conduct.[126] In the disruption and chaos caused by premature death, previously taboo things – incest,[127] prostitution, trickery, female sexual autonomy – suddenly become valorized. I would suggest the valorization here is precisely related to the taboo; if the taboo exists to ensure paternity and sexual control over women for the purpose of progeny and perpetuation, here these taboo acts suddenly perform the function for which they exist: patriarchal sexual control in the service of the community's continuity. There are, however, some tensions in the text. We end up with a genealogy in Ruth that excises Er out in favour of Judah, the twins effectively becoming Judah's offspring – demonstrating perhaps the emphasis is not on the individual man who died but the right continuation of a line.[128] Judah's reaction to Tamar's sexual behaviour, sentencing her to death, contrasts with his own sexual freedom. The imbalance, according

---

125. Compare this to Wildavsky, who states that 'by using the sexual act in a moral, community-enhancing manner, so that the community emerges united in fulfilling God's command...its strength [grows]'. Both see it as serving a community purpose, however Wildavsky attempts an 'ethical' reading: Wildavsky, 'Survival', 42.

126. Fuchs, *Sexual Politics*, 69.

127. Abasili, 'Genesis 38', 286. Abasili presumes had Judah known, he would have been charged with incest. However, there is no reason to assume that Judah could not have acted as the levir (otherwise, why was Tamar not convicted of incest?).

128. Sarna, *Genesis*, 266. Cf. Gen. 46.12; Num. 26.20-22; 1 Chron. 2.4. Leggett argues against those who presume that because genealogical records list Perez as Judah's, it is valid reason to read the widows welfare as the thrust of the text (such as Coats, 'Widow's Rights', 462) or suggest the point of the practice has been ignored (Mace, *Hebrew Marriage*, 109): 'It is not valid to give precedence to later genealogical references over the clear statements of the narrative. Because of the difficulty of interpreting the genealogies of the Bible, the inclusion of Perez and Zerah as sons of Judah in Gen. 46.12 and Num. 26.19-20 should not, in the absence of additional evidence, be regarded as a final evolutionary stage of the levirate. As a possible example within a genealogy the use of both the real father as well as the father by means of the levirate, note should be taken of Zerubbabel who is called the son of Pedaiah (1 Chron. 3.19) and the son of Shealtiel (Ezra 3.2, 8; 5.2; Neh. 12.1; Hag. 1.12, 14)': Leggett, *Levirate and Goel*, 36–7.

to Fewell and Gunn, is 'symptomatic of the relation between men and women in the social world of the story'.[129] Tamar's 'tricksterism' is exercised primarily from a place of powerlessness,[130] and through this she 'brings about a number of fundamental reversals...[forcing] Judah to change his behavior'.[131] Despite not overturning patriarchal assumptions, Tamar's story does 'call into question' Judah's dominance and power.[132]

2.3. *Ruth*

Whereas Genesis 38 can perhaps be understood as a narrative working of Deut. 25.5-10, Ruth appears to combine the institutions of the levirate with that of redemption (Lev. 25.25-34). This combination has left biblical scholars at times a little flummoxed:

> The legal problems of the book of Ruth should be treated as Bertrand Russell treated the question of life after death: with a noble and unyielding despair.[133]

Levine laments: 'For all its charm, the book of Ruth produces a certain *malaise*'.[134] Hermann Gunkel suggested Ruth was devoid of historical work;[135] however, by the time of the publication of Rowley's article in 1947 all the significant debates about dates, purpose, legal difficulties and historical value were established.[136] The fundamental difficulty stems from the apparent combination of something that looks like Deut. 25.5-10 (levirate marriage) and looks like Lev. 25.25-34 (redemption), but which does not quite match either and appears to confuse two apparently separate institutions into one.[137] The conflict between Ruth and Leviticus/

---

129. Fewell and Gunn, *Narrative*, 38.
130. Brett, *Genesis*, 114–15.
131. Van Dijk-Hemmes, 'Limits', 82.
132. Van Wijk-Bos, 'Eye Opener', 121.
133. Michael D. Goulder, 'Ruth: A Homily on Deuteronomy 22–25?', in McKay and Clines, eds., *Of Prophets' Visions and the Wisdom of Sages*, 307.
134. Levine, 'In Praise of the Israelite *Mišpāḥâ*', 95.
135. 'Die Erzählung enthält nichts Geschichtliches', quoted in Rowley, 'Marriage', 79 n. 12.
136. Ibid., 77–9.
137. Here I am following the consensus that we can be confident that Ruth is a relatively 'late' text that would know some form of Deuteronomy and Leviticus. Berlin suggests a number of reasons for a postexilic context: (1) שוב occurs twelve times in the first chapter, and even Ruth is called 'the one who returned' (1.22; 2.6) despite never having been to Judah; (2) the family and relocation recall Joseph and the story of Abraham (Gen. 12.10); (3) though Moab is generally depicted negatively

Deuteronomy has provoked a range of solutions, prominently: attempts to synthesize the two texts; seeing them as diachronic differences in legal practices; or to seeing Ruth as a commentary or midrash on Deuteronomy.

These reconstructions of legal practices, however, are fragile. Derek Beattie claims:

> since legal procedure forms, in a sense, the framework of civilization and law is, by its nature, both definite and widely known, a story-teller, if he is to maintain the credibility of his fiction, will not create a legal situation which his audience will know to be impossible.[138]

However, he continues, in line with his argument that Ruth is an older text than the scholarly consensus would assume, that 'It must also be admitted that this general viewpoint is valid only in cases where an author may expect his audience to be familiar with the milieu in which the story is located', and that 'the author clearly intended the legal situation to be credible to his audience may be presupposed from the care which he took to explain the obsolete custom of removing a show as a symbol of abdication of interest.[139]

throughout the Hebrew Bible it is the location 'from which the people of Israel entered the land' after the exodus; as with the exodus God takes notice, פקד (cf. Gen. 50.24-25; Exod. 3.16; 4.13); (4) the period of the Judges in which the story is set mirrors the postexilic situation, with the Davidic monarchy 'anticipated in the future both in Judges an after the exile', along with references to Bethlehem, Judean lineage through Judah and Tamar, and the genealogy at the end, pointing to 'the restoration of the Davidic monarchy' (Berlin, 'Legal Fiction', 12–13). Goulder adds additional arguments: the presence of Aramaisms in the text; that the text is a *family novelle* like Tobit or Susanna or Joseph and Aseneth; that it is about a woman like Esther, Judith and Susanna; that it is edifying 'in which faithfulness to God in time of trial comes to happy ending', like Esther and Job; and that it was classed with the Ketuvim despite 'belonging by subject with the former prophets'. He also relies on deliberate anachronisms such as 'in the days when the judges judged' or Orpah 'going back unto her gods' (cf. Judg. 11.24) or 'the custom in the former time', and understands Ruth as drawing on texts which are no longer understood, or as a polemic against Ezra–Nehemiah (Goulder, 'Ruth: A Homily', 312–18). Zevit critiques some of these arguments (a welcoming attitude towards non-Israelites, Aramaisms, the inclusion in the Ketuvim), suggesting that additional arguments about 'late Hebrew' vocabulary, the dating of its orthography, and seeing Ruth as the 'development' of the institutions of levirate marriage, land redemption, and a widow's right to inherit still ultimately point to a late dating (Zevit, 'Dating Ruth', 574–6).

138. Beattie, 'Book of Ruth', 252.
139. Ibid., 252-3.

Levine, in direct response, suggests that the presence of a legal detail 'does not prove the applicability of the actual legal instruments referred to in the story', and suggests 'the author of Ruth was capable of legal leaps, of glossing over the prerequisites for invoking certain Israelite laws, while at the same time exploiting the very dynamics of those laws to enhance the intricacy of his plot'. Instead, the author was 'an artful manipulator of legalities! He [sic] transposed *laws* into *legal themes.*' The author 'utilized the formulas and technicalities of the legal *dicta* in a meta-legal way; and in so doing, successfully confounded generations of scholars!'[140] Thompson and Thompson suggest that the legal differences between Deuteronomy 25, Genesis 38 and Ruth are 'not contradictions at all, but only differences in the forms of the texts',[141] legal and narrative; however, they go on to suggest that narratives should be given more weight as they are 'concrete examples of the custom as it was actually practiced'.[142] Here, as in most scholarly work, Ruth is read as a kind of newspaper article, recounting a lived historical experience. This suggests a kind of legal stability in biblical texts across not only centuries, but the entire colonization and rebuilding of a nation, which would be deemed farcical if we were dealing with almost all other literature.

Ruth is a thematically rich text, dealing with death, kinship, gender, levirate marriage, redemption, inheritance and property, fertility, ethnicity, the Davidic kingship, all the time making textual allusions to our core themes with the use of שם, בית and כרת.[143] Due to the length and

---

140. Levine, 'In Praise of the Israelite *Mišpāḥâ*', 96.
141. Thompson and Thompson, 'Legal Problems', 79.
142. Ibid., 84. They offer no explanation for why this would be, and the suggestion seems unlikely, confusing narrative and case study.
143. Sutskover suggests matters of fertility and land are weaved into 'the massive net of cultural memories that accompany them'. In the first few verses: בית לחם, implying bread; שדי מואב, relating to field; Ephrat, derived from אפר or פרה, implying either soil or multiplication. This is contrasted with names like Mahlon, possibly from the root חלה, 'to be sick', or the Arabic *mahala*, 'barrenness or craftiness', or מחה, annihilate, and Chilion derived from כלה, to perish. Terms like native land, ארץ מולדת, include the lexeme land but also a fertility lexeme derived from ילד. There is a concentration of language relating to land, crop abundance, terms like seed (Ruth 4.12), which is polysemic, implying both progeny and crop, terms relating to harvesting, winnowing, threshing floors, terms relating to food and eating. These are complemented by sexual terms such as בוא, שכב, גלה, מרגלתיו. This continues to the birth of Obed, his name stemming from the verb עבד, to till, also being representative of fertility. 'The execution of the two transactions [levirate and redemption] in one is unique to the book of Ruth, and is in keeping with its two dominant lexical fields' (Sutskover, 'The Themes of Land and Fertility in the Book of Ruth', 283–94).

complexity, we also see competing voices arising, ones dealing with lack of offspring for the dead (4.5, 10) and the need to provide support for two widows (3.1), with the former 'voiced by a man, while the latter concern is attributed to a woman'.[144] Elimelech and Naomi resided in Moab; later, their sons Mahlon and Chilion took wives, Ruth and Orpah. All the men died, however, and the women all set out back to Judah. Seeing this, Naomi asks them to turn back to their mother's house, a place Chapman associates with marriage negotiations:[145]

> ...why will you go with me? Are there still for me sons inside me, that they may be to you husbands?... [E]ven if I should have tonight a husband and also bear sons, would you wait until they were grown? Would you then refrain from having husbands? (Ruth 1.11-13)

Her speech contains hints that Naomi could, in different circumstances, raise a son for Ruth or Orpah, implying a kind of levirate union, and possibly a preferable partner to the one Ruth eventually takes.[146] Ruth goes with Naomi, and eventually Naomi hatches a plan, and sends her to the threshing-floor of Boaz where she is to surprise him. In Ruth 3.9, at the threshing floor, Ruth reveals to Boaz that he is a גאל, or redeemer. Boaz appears to understand the implications of this, as after praising her he states:

> And now, although it is true that I am a kinsman-redeemer (גאל), yet there is a kinsman-redeemer nearer than I (גאל קרוב ממני). Stay this night, and in the morning, if he will 'perform the duty of kinsman-redeemer for you', good; let him redeem (אם־יגאלך טוב יגאל). If he does not want to act as kinsman-redeemer for you, then I will be kinsman-redeemer for you (וגאלתיך אנכי), as lives YHWH. Lie down until morning. (Ruth 3.12-13)

Boaz calls the redeemer to the gate:

> And he said to the kinsman-redeemer, 'The portion of land, which belonged to our brother Elimelech, is Naomi selling, who has returned from the country of Moab. And I thought to tell you of it, to say: Buy it in the presence of those sitting, and the elders of my people. If you will redeem it, redeem it; but if you will not redeem it, tell me, so that I know; for there

---

144. Weisberg, 'Discontent', 418.
145. Chapman, *House*, 61.
146. Tigay, *Deuteronomy*, 483 n. 13. Mace suggests that this passage implies that levirate marriage did not apply to women past a certain age, but this seems to read legal precedent into Naomi's heartfelt plea (Mace, *Hebrew Marriage*, 109).

is no one except you to redeem, and I come after you.' So he said, 'I will redeem it'. Then Boaz said, 'On the day you acquire the field from the hand of Naomi, then also Ruth the Moabite, the widow of the dead man, you will acquire (קניתה *kere*, קניתי *ketiv*), to raise the dead man's name on his inheritance'. And the kinsman-redeemer said, 'I cannot redeem it for to me lest I ruin my own inheritance. Redeem for yourself my right of redemption, for I cannot redeem it.'

The text hints at levirate marriage using the term 'the wife of the dead' (אשת המת), which only occurs in Ruth 4.5 and Deut. 25.5.[147] It is, however, problematic for several reasons.[148] In v. 5 the obligation to take Ruth appears to be conjoined to the law of redemption; the redeemer then declines lest it damages his inheritance. There is a textual conflict over whether the text should follow the *ketiv*, קָנִיתִי, or *qere*, קָנִיתָה, which may read: 'The day you acquire the field from the hand of Naomi, I am acquiring Ruth the Moabite'.[149] Whichever reading is preferred, on realizing that that Ruth will raise a child, he refused, on the ground of damage to his inheritance.[150] We then read:

> Now this [was the custom] in former times in Israel concerning redeeming and concerning exchanging (על־הגאולה ועל־התמורה): to confirm all things, one took off (שלף) the man's his sandal, and gave it to the other; this was a testimony in Israel. (Ruth 4.7)

---

147. Agnethe Siquans, 'Foreignness and Poverty in the Book of Ruth: A Legal Way for a Poor Foreign Woman to Be Integrated into Israel', *JBL* 128, no. 3 (2009): 450. Siquans article raises another legal conflict between Ruth and Deuteronomy: marriage with a Moabite (cf. Deut. 23.3).

148. The text appears to suggest Naomi is in possession of the land; however, it is not necessary, for our discussion, to go into this matter in detail, apart from to say there are convincing alternative interpretations. For example, Zevit suggests that מכר does not necessarily entail outright sale, that the involvement of a גאל in Ruth suggests sale has not occurred, and that, based on Ruth 2.2, we can be reasonably confident that no field is under Naomi's control (Zevit, 'Dating Ruth', 585).

149. For a detailed discussion of the arguments for both the *qere* and *ketiv*, see Zevit, 'Dating Ruth', 595–9. Zevit expresses a preference for the *ketiv* as the *qere* 'links the role of *gō'ēl* to that of levir and implies that the later was obligatory, facts about which Mr. Almoni [the nearest redeemer] was totally unaware'. See also Beattie, 'Book of Ruth', 264.

150. Discerning the reason for refusal involves elaborate reconstructions. Such a route is taken by Hiers, who creates a number of preconditions such as the redeemer being childless and being in fear the child Ruth produces will take the double share of his inheritance: Hiers, 'Transfer', 136.

It is suggested that the removal of the sandal here is related to the removal of the sandal in Deuteronomy 25.[151] Yet, while there may be an allusion, Carmichael is right in stating that 'the difference is significant: in Deuteronomy, the sandal is a publicly disgracing act; whereas in Ruth it is transactional; the verbs used to remove the sandal are different in both texts; and, in one the shoe is removed by the woman and the other the shoe is removed by the man'. Carmichael suggests that in Ruth the handing over of the sandal symbolizes the transference of property and, potentially, the right to 'acquire the woman'; and from this connection scholars have mistakenly understood the two ceremonies as the same.[152] We are informed in Ruth 4.10 that the sandal was taken off, and Boaz states to the people he has acquired all that belonged to Elimelech, Chilion and Mahlon, and:

> ...Ruth the Moabite, the wife/woman/widow (אשת) of Mahlon, I have also acquired[153] to be my wife/woman (לאשה), to raise up the name of the dead on his inheritance (להקים שם־המת על־נחלתו), in order that the name of the dead may not be cut off from his kin and from the gate of his place (ולא־יכרת שם־המת מעם אחיו ומשער מקומו); you are witnesses today.

Here is the most explicit reference to levirate marriage: the use of the term 'to raise the name of the dead' and 'that the name of the dead may not be cut off'.[154] Then, in Ruth 4.11-12, the people respond:

> May YHWH make the woman coming into your house like Rachel and Leah, who the two of them built up the house of Israel (בנו שתיהם את־בית ישראל); and may you do well in Ephrathah and create a name in Bethlehem (ועשה חיל באפרתה וקרא־שם בבית לחם); and may your house be like the house of Perez, who Tamar bore to Judah, from the seed which the YHWH will give you from this young woman.

---

151. Scholars have proposed that the ceremony is 'exactly the same' (Zevit, 'Dating Ruth', 580); or, a 'nicer' version, where the spitting is removed (Goulder, 'Ruth: A Homily', 310).

152. Carmichael, 'Ceremonial Crux', 324. Westbrook suggests that the author's explanation reflects their awareness of the 'different intent' of the shoe ceremonies here and in Deuteronomy (Westbrook, *Property*, 83 n. 4).

153. Lemos notes that this is the only occurrence of 'proprietary language' used in relation to marriage, whereas Deut. 25.5-10 and Genesis 30 do not: Lemos, *Violence*, 76.

154. Goulder also notes Deut. 25.5 and Ruth 4.13, 'go into her and take her as a wife'; and Deut. 25.7 and Ruth 4.1-2 going up to the 'gate of the elders': Goulder, 'Ruth: A Homily', 308.

The text invokes Rachel and Leah, and Tamar and Judah. Carmichael also suggests connections to Lot and his daughters, due to her status as a Moabite and her lying with a kinsman, and that a story 'that acknowledges the past lives of Rachel, Leah and Tamar is likely also to have taken stock of the tradition about Lot's Daughters'.[155] Chapman explores the recollections of Rachel and Leah in the book of Ruth, in its Judahite, exilic context. Ruth 4.11-12 references Ruth producing children in Ephrathah and bestowing a name in Bethlehem; it recalls Gen. 35.16-21 and 'evokes a territory infused with the memory of infertility overcome at great cost to the mother, and the birth of a son whose line produced a king'.[156] However, it also alludes to David, whose father was 'an Ephrathite of Bethlehem' (1 Sam. 17.12). The invoking of Perez, Tamar and Judah, however, references the house of Leah. The passage therefore plays with both the maternal houses of Rachel and Leah, but in the service of the unity: 'if the book of Ruth is the birth story of the Davidic kingdom, this blessing imagines the house of David as the united house of all Israel'.[157]

Boaz appears to act as *levir* to Ruth; Boaz, having acted as father figure, now goes on to act as husband.[158] As with Tamar, Ruth has 'achieved the purpose of the levirate with one who was not her *levir*'.[159] A child, Obed, is born 'to Naomi' (not Elimelech or Mahlon, or Ruth),[160] and in Ruth 4.21 is included as the son of Boaz in the genealogy of David. Various rather systematic attempts have been made to reconcile the seeming conflict in the genealogical naming, however the logical gymnastics involved (such as in Harold Rowley suggestion) ironically point to the ambiguity inherent in the conflict over who is named.[161]

155. Carmichael, 'Ceremonial Crux', 331. Adelman notes that whereas Gen. 19 and 38 are characterized by disguise and drunkenness, incest and deceit, 'Ruth reads like a pastoral romance replete with images of reapers in late spring, acts of loving-kindness [etc.]': Adelman, 'Seduction and Recognition', 90.

156. Chapman, *House*, 221.

157. Ibid.

158. Stiebert, *Fathers and Daughters*, 151.

159. Levine, 'In Praise of the Israelite *Mišpāḥâ*', 105.

160. Doniger suggests this is as Boaz is of Naomi's generation, is Naomi's brother-in-law (4.3), and that she is substituting her older self for the desirable younger Ruth (in reversal of Rachel/Leah and Shelah/Judah). She suggests 'Obed is "Naomi's baby" because he should have been born (physically) to Naomi or (officially) to Naomi's dead son': Wendy Doniger, *The Bedtrick: Tales of Sex and Masquerade* (Chicago: University of Chicago Press, 2000), 260.

161. Rowley's neat reconstruction is based on a range of variables: whether Boaz already has a child, the distinction between legal paternity and actual paternity, whether Ruth is taken also as a wife, whether Boaz's patrimony could be divided, whether genealogically Mahlon and Boaz's lines 'unite' in the son: Rowley, 'Marriage', 98.

In her compelling 'Levirate Fiction: Levirate *cum* Land Redemption in Ruth', Adele Berlin examines three conventional approaches to understanding the legal implications and the relationship between levirate and the law of redemption:

1. *True-to-life approach*: Berlin discusses approaches such as those of Zevit who attempt to construct a change in the legal institution over time, or Westbrook who attempts to understand the underlying legal principle.[162] Berlin notes the presumption, in Beattie quoted above, that the narrator must maintain legal credibility; however, even Beattie acknowledges that this only applies when the text is contemporary to the law. Berlin suggests that due to the consensus of a much later dating of Ruth, this becomes problematized.
2. *Midrashic Approach*: The midrashic approach suggests Ruth is the re-working of Torah texts, but sees 'the re-interpretation of Torah laws as the main goal of the book'.[163] Berlin highlights the benefits of this yet suggests it is anachronistic, and are not midrashic as 'the interpretation of Torah law *per se* is not the primary goal of the book', suggesting the use of Torah in Ruth 'is better seen as part of the larger phenomenon of scripturalization or inner biblical interpretation'. Therefore, 'in invoking biblical texts, legal and non-legal, Ruth is no different from any number of late biblical and postbiblical works',[164] with Ruth alluding to (possibly) Lot's daughters, Judah and Tamar in Genesis 38, the stories of Leah and Rachel, famine and relocation, the book of Judges, David and legal material.

---

162. See also Thompson and Thompson, who think Deuteronomy as a typical example and not normative, for instance, who can perform the levirate: Thompson and Thompson, 'Legal Problems', 71–4.

163. Berlin, 'Legal Fiction', 5. Berlin draws on Fischer's feminist interpretation of Ruth as Midrash, André LaCocque's 'Christian' midrash and Joshua Berman's rabbinic influenced reading, and draws out the inherent problems in each. For example, Berman suggests Ruth is a 'legal homily', unfolding in the order of the materials found in Deut. 24.16–25.10, drawing on what he sees as the interconnectedness of 'ideas, words or motif' in Joshua Berman, 'Ancient Hermeneutics and the Legal Structure of the Book of Ruth', *ZAW* 119, no. 1 (2007): 23. See also André LaCocque, *Ruth: A Continental Commentary*, trans. K. C. Hanson, CC (Philadelphia: Fortress, 2004); Irmtraud Fischer, 'The Book of Ruth: A "Feminist" Commentary to the Torah?', in *Ruth and Esther: A Feminist Companion to the Bible*, ed. Athalya Brenner, FCB 2nd Series 3 (Sheffield: Sheffield Academic, 1999).

164. Berlin, 'Legal Fiction', 9.

3. *Fictional Approach*: In this approach the levirate never actually functioned as in Ruth, where the *levir* and the *go'el* are the same; for example, Berlin suggests that the Deuteronomic text requires the estate has not been divided, and so there is no estate of the deceased to redeem. Berlin argues that the author created a 'legal fiction', drawn from the practice of levirate and redemption, in 'a fictional work that employs fictional or imaginary legal practices, which, in this case, bear an obvious resemblance to Torah laws but depart from it'.[165] This is highlighted in the transfer of the shoe, which transfers 'the right or obligation to be the *go'el* and the *levir*'.[166] This also takes place in the combination of להקים שם and על נחלתו, 'explicitly connecting the levirate with the estate of the deceased which is being redeemed'. Berlin suggests that the ceremony of the shoe is fictional since the audience needed to have it explained to them, 'even though they are presumed to know about the levirate and the land-redemption'.[167]

Berlin suggests a compelling explanation for the combination of the two institutions in the book of Ruth which avoids unanswerable questions about the text reflecting historical development of the laws or an over optimistic understanding of the text as early midrash:

> The combination of the levirate and the land redemption is most apt for a story of Judean return. They are two sides of the same coin: the preservation of the family and its estate. The *go'el* keeps land within the family, and the levir ensures that there is a family to possess the land. These are the Torah's legal institutions designed to ensure the continuity of the family and of its inherited landholdings when they are in jeopardy. The levirate takes effect when a family line is about to disappear, and the redemption of land takes effect when the land is in danger of being alienated from its proper owner. As a metaphor, this is exactly the situation faced by the postexilic Judeans, whose continuity as a national entity was in danger, and whose inherited land had passed to outsiders (Lam. 5.2).[168]

---

165. Ibid., 10.

166. Berlin suggests the '*halitzah-ge'ullah*' (*halitzah* being the removal of the shoe to decline the levirate) are hybridized by the author to solidify the notions of levirate and land redemption (ibid., 10–11).

167. Berlin suggests that there is little difference between 'creating fictitious historical events and creating fictitious legal events' (ibid., 11).

168. Ibid., 13.

Beyond the legal institutions, the 'broader conceptual framework' reflects an interest in progeny and land as 'the two components of the divine promise to the patriarchs that became a key ideological concept in postexilic writings of return'.[169] Matthew Suriano suggests a further conceptual linking between the *go'el* and levirate marriage, through his discussion of Job 19.23-27, in which he suggests the *go'el* carries obligations which relate to the care of the dead and post-mortem protection. If we follow Suriano's argument, it can help to open ways of understanding how aspects of redemption and levirate marriage can be symbolically linked.[170] Where some have taken the emphasis on property in Ruth as the key through which to read Deut. 25.5-10 and Genesis 38, this approach allows us to understand not how property is key to levirate marriage but how the two things work in tandem, brought together creatively in the narrative of Ruth. The book of Ruth seeks to tell the tale of family stability and perpetuation, and does so by connecting land, name and progeny, centring it around the movement between generations.

3. *Widow of Tekoa*

In the next text, we see the fear of the destruction of offspring expressed. The following passage takes places in the context of David's anger at his son Absalom for having his first son Amnon killed. We read in 2 Sam. 13.30 that David had been led to believe that all the king's sons had been killed.[171] Joab sends a wise woman from Tekoa to David to act in the role of a mourner. The woman comes to David and falls on her face:

> 'Save me, O king!' And the king said to her, 'What troubles you?' And she answered, 'Alas, I am a widow; my husband is dead. Your servant had two sons, and they fought with each other in the field; there was no one to separate them, and one struck the other, and killed him. And now has risen up the whole clan against your servant. They said, "Deliver him who struck

---

169. Ibid., 14.

170. Suriano, 'Death, Disinheritance, and Job's Kinsman-Redeemer'. Suriano makes conceptual links between the *go'el*, memorial monuments, care of the dead and יבם in Ruth. He states: 'The role assumed by Boaz, however, related as much to the dead (Mahlon) as it did to the living (Ruth), which is made clear in his petition before the elders of Bethlehem, stating that he will marry Ruth "to raise up [להקים] the name of the dead upon his inheritance that the name of the dead not be cut off from among his brothers" (Ruth 4.10; cf. v. 5). This passage in Ruth employs the same verbal root [√קום] that is used in Job 19.25 to describe the action of Job's kinsman-redeemer.'

171. Although this is later remedied in 2 Sam. 13.35.

his brother, that we may kill him for the life (נפש) of his brother who he killed, even if we will destroy the heir also". And so, they would extinguish my ember that remains, and leave to my husband neither name nor remnant (שם ושארית) on the face of the earth.' (2 Sam. 14.1-7)

Larry Lyke notes the commonality between the text and narratives of brothers struggling, particularly Deut. 25.11, the 'woman with a cause' trope (Gen. 38; Deut. 25.5-10; Ruth), and also women 'seeking the king's adjudication' (1 Sam. 25; 1 Kgs 3; 2 Kgs 6; Esther), arguing a commonality of 'themes, vocabulary, and imagery' between 2 Sam. 14.1-20, Deut. 25.5-10 and Deut. 25.11-12, and noting the 'Davidic' associations between Genesis 38, Ruth and 2 Sam. 14.1-20. In these texts women attempt to ensure the progeny of their dead husbands, and strive to preserve the husband's name and legacy. The text also relates in its context to the issues of taking another's wife and incestuous relations, such as Amnon–Tamar–Absalom, Absalom–concubines–David, Adonijah–Abishag–Solomon. He further notes that given this background, we see 'David would be acting in his own self-interest, given that the name he would preserve is his own'.[172]

Trying to invoke empathy, the woman's case rests on the family destroying her dead husband's heir,[173] presenting the widow's concern for loss of son or breadwinner as secondary, instead focusing on the husband's name and remnant.[174] Her family, her line, her lineage (although it is then placed in the context of her husband) is perceived as a fire, but one which is dying. The remaining son is an ember; he can go out like a dying fire or be used to light more kindling. If the family were to put out the ember, the consequences would be clear – the father would have neither name nor remnant. If the son is extinguished, so would be the father, his name would be snuffed out through the destruction of his line. Presumably, then, should the son live and produce an heir, the ember would ignite a fire; however, it is the original spark of the father that would be continued in the fire, his name would live on through the offspring.[175] This text draws on the themes of the texts of levirate marriage but discusses these themes

---

172. Larry L. Lyke, *King David with the Wise Woman of Tekoa: The Resonance of Tradition in Parabolic Narrative*, JSOTSup 225 (Sheffield: Sheffield Academic, 1997), 89–99.

173. Lewis notes that in v. 11 the avenger is referred to as the גאל הדם, blood redeemer, which he relates to the redeemer in Ruth: Lewis, 'Ancestral Estate', 607–8.

174. Mace, *Hebrew Marriage*, 102.

175. In v. 16, the woman uses the term נחלת אלהים. Lewis understands נחלת אלהים as a reference to the ancestral estate, understanding the text in relation to Deut. 25.6-7 and Num. 27.4, and also suggests that נחלת אלהים could be a parallel to נחלת אבות in 1 Kgs 21: Lewis, 'Ancestral Estate', 604.

in figurative language. Moreover, the text is ambiguous about the need to raise anything like Westbrook's 'title' over the land of the deceased, as the man in his lifetime has presumably established this; however, it is working within the same symbolic structure as our other texts. The concern for name here extends to one who has already had a son, and focuses the man's perpetuity in the figure of the son; it also highlights the emotional plea of preserving the husband's name, pointing us towards an interpretation which is not simply legal but suggests substantive post-mortem continuity, the eradication of which provokes fear.

4. *Monuments*

While being the focus of the preceding five texts, progeny is not the only way to respond to death. Two texts respond to fear of dying childless with the erection of monuments; however, both these texts do so with reference to progeny, and occupy the same symbolic field.

4.1. *Absalom's Monument*

> And Absalom had taken (לקח) and set up for himself (ויצב לו), in his lifetime, a monument (מצבת) which is in the King's Valley, for he said, 'I have no son (בן) to keep remembrance of my name (בעבור הזכיר שמי)'; he called the monument after his own name (ויקרא למצבת על־שמו), and it is called Absalom's Monument (יד אבשלם) to this day. (2 Sam. 18.18)

The text uses both מצבה and יד to describe the monuments. As discussed previously, such stela may be erected 'in any one of several loci', that is, not necessarily attached to a grave.[176] While some, such as Olyan, have understood this monument as a locality for offerings, this is problematized by the fact that the monument acts *in place* of offspring. Absalom is setting up a monument to his name as he is without a son, therefore it leaves questions open as to who would produce the offerings at the מצבה. This suggests use of the stone as a representative of the dead, rather than only as a site for mortuary rites. While texts such as the Ugaritic *Tale of Aqhat* wish that there may be a son in the house of the father to 'set up the stele of his ancestral god',[177] B. G. Ockinga compares Absalom's lament to an eighteenth-century Egyptian stele, which calls on the living on earth to look upon the stela and see the 'imitator' of the deceased, and refers to it as an heir and remembrance, as Absalom had 'no suggestion that he expected his son to provide him with a memorial stela'. Terms like

---

176. Olyan, 'Family Religion', 119.
177. Ockinga, 'Note', 32; see 2 Aqhat i.24ff.

imitator and heir can only be used in this context for a person. Ockinga suggests the situation is similar 'because Absalom did not have a son who would keep his name in remembrance, he is said to have erected himself a memorial stela to fulfil this function: the Egyptian examples provide us with a much closer parallel than does that from Ugarit, the one usually referred to by commentators'.[178] While not a direct comparison, there *is* precedent in ancient West Asia and North Africa for viewing the monument not simply as a place of offering but as an *imitator*. Absalom's words suggest this, by highlighting the *remembrance* of his name. This shifts the paradigm being looked at in these texts further: here the text deals with a response to childlessness with a similar frame of reference to levirate marriage, but one which understands שם in a context that cannot be reduced to a legal title but is more to do with remembrance. The monument here appears to stand for substantial, material continuity of the dead, perpetuated through memory. The biblical text records that Absalom's name is still invoked 'to this day'.

4.2. *Isaiah 56.3-5*

In Isa. 56.3-5 monuments are again sites which respond to childlessness:

> Nor let the eunuch (הסרים) say,
> 'Behold, I am a dry tree (עץ יבש)'.
> For thus says the LORD:
> To the eunuchs who keep my Sabbaths,
> who choose what pleases me
> and hold fast my covenant,
> I will give (ונתתי) to them, in my house and my walls (בביתי ובחומתי),
> a monument and a name (יד ושם)
> better than sons and daughters (טוב מבנים ומבנות);
> An everlasting name (שם עולם) I will give to them
> that shall not be cut off (אשר לא יכרת).

יד ושם is typically translated something like 'a memorial and a name', and this יד ושם is said to be better than sons and daughters, and the name that is everlasting[179] will not be 'cut off'.[180] Stavrakopoulou suggests

---

178. Ibid., 32–4.
179. Stavrakopoulou notes that שם עולם carries 'connotations of divinity and deification, as is suggested by its application to Yhwh' (cf. Gen. 21.33; Exod. 3.15; 1 Kgs 9.3; 2 Kgs 21.7; Isa. 63.17; Ps. 135.13) (Stavrakopoulou, *Land*, 124).
180. See the previous discussion of כרת for the full connotations. Stavrakopoulou notes similar uses of cut off: Isa. 14.18-22; 48.19; Jer. 9.21; Nah. 1.14; cf. Ruth 4.10. See also Deut. 25.5-6; Judg. 21.17; Job 18.16-19; Ps. 109.13; Jer. 11.19; 55.13 (ibid.).

that the יד can be understood in terms of mortuary cults, 'manifesting the ritualized remembering and cultic presence of the dead', while שם 'is the post-mortem memorialized "name" of the dead, invoked in the cult to perpetuate (by remembering) their ongoing existence';[181] thus they both form part of the same symbolic complex. Dwight van Winkle argues against proposals that יד ושם should express 'portion or share' as opposed to 'memorial stele'. Contra G. Robinson, who argues that the context is the fear that foreigners may not get a due portion in Israel, van Winkle demonstrates that vv. 6-7 are in response to the lament of the eunuch. Winkle also rejects Sara Japhet's proposal that the unusual verb נתן with יד suggests it must mean something else, arguing that her sample of the expression is too small to draw any strong conclusions, and noting examples of נתן and שם go together to refer to the spread of one's fame and reputation, which Japhet overlooks.[182] However, he goes on to suggest יד ושם is best rendered 'memorial stele', citing a few examples from the ancient Mediterranean that contain hands on steles, though acknowledging these are open to a wide interpretation. Once we consider the following clause, 'an everlasting name', we should not disregard the previous use of שם as simply qualifying the term יד but accept that it stands independently. Stavrakopoulou holds these two different ideas in tension:

> The territorial dynamics of the mortuary cult are also evident in this remarkable text, for as Sara Japhet observes, יד can also mean 'portion' or 'share', and is synonymous with חלק, which is often employed of an 'inheritance' or possession of a 'share' of land, and which in its own turn is also rendered within the same semantic field to the use of שם as a reference to a designated claim to or occupation of land, or an inheritable land holding.[183]

---

181. Ibid.
182. Dwight W. van Winkle, 'The Meaning of *Yād Wāšēm* in Isaiah LVI 5', *VT* 47, no. 3 (1997): 377–82. *Pace* the arguments to the contrary set forth by G. Robinson, 'The Meaning of יד in Isa 56,5', *ZAW* 88 (1976): 282–4, and Sara Japhet, '*Yd Wšm* [Isa. 56:5]—A Different Proposal', *MAARAV* 8 (1992): 69–80.
183. Stavrakopoulou, *Land*, 124. See also Num. 26.53-62; 27.3-4; Ruth 4.19. Zevit also suggests a funerary context, comparing the use of יד here to its combination in Isa. 57.8 with זכרון 'comprehending *yād* as referring to a funerary marker or cenotaph of sorts (cf. 2 Sam. 18.18 and Isa. 56:5) and associating it with *zikkārōn*, a memorial, filling the role of a living descendant who would invoke the memory of the dead (cf. 2 Sam. 18.18) may evoke a funerary context': Zevit, *Religions*, 529 n. 56.

By seeing the territorial dynamics, Stavrakopoulou plays on the language used as multifaceted, rather than reducing it to an idiom for property.[184]

Chan and Wright respond to the notion of Isaiah 56 as a form of 'prophetic Torah' which revises legal texts, specifically here the ban on the eunuchs' membership of the assembly in Lev. 21.16-23 and Deut. 23.2. They cite several considerations: the term סריס does not occur in the legal texts, and mutilated genitalia are not '*eo ipso* a sign of a person's status as a eunuch'. Isaiah 56.3-5 is not primarily concerned with entrance into the cultic community per se, which is the matter of concern in Deut. 23.2, but with memorialization, and in Isaiah 56 the eunuch is never actually depicted entering the sanctuary. The concern expressed by the eunuch is that of impotence or infertility; the eunuch draws in v. 3 upon the arboreal metaphor 'to express their inability to sire children and produce a namesake'.[185] Chan and Wright argue that rather than a matter of inclusion in the temple, YHWH's promise to the eunuch falls within *Totenpflege*/care for the dead, drawing on similarities between this text and 2 Sam. 18.18. By erecting a monument and a name in the temple,[186] amidst the deity's presence, the eunuch will have a part 'in the future age, when "my salvation will come and my deliverance will be revealed" (56:1b)'. They argue the memorial and name afforded by YHWH is best understood not as a surrogate son, but as that of a king–servant relationship, 'superior to a child insofar as the deity himself guarantees its permanence',[187] ultimately

---

184. See further: 'חלק is also the legacy of the territorial dead of the valley (נחל־חלקי) in Isa. 57:6… Thus, while Japhet assumes that the expression יד ושם in 56:5 is simply a metaphorical reference to the "enduring right" of the eunuch to a spiritual "share" within the temple community (cf. Josh. 22.24-25), the vivid mortuary cult imagery of this verse, set within its broader context of dynastic regeneration, suggests that the poet is exploiting the ambivalence of language here (anticipating the attack on mortuary cults in the oracle following shortly after, in 57:3-13), so that the memorial and territorial connotations of יד ושם are intentionally aligned, invoking close inter-relation of ancestor cult and claims to place' (Stavrakopoulou, *Land*, 125).

185. Michael J. Chan and Jacob L. Wright, 'King and Eunuch: Isaiah 56:1-8 in Light of Honorific Royal Burial Practices', *JBL* 131, no. 1 (2012): 101 n. 9. They compare Ps. 1.3; Jer. 11.19; 17.7-8, and associate this with terms used such as פרה (Gen. 1.22, 28; 26.22; Exod. 23.30; Jer. 3.16) פרי (Gen. 30.2; Deut. 7.13; 28.4; 30.9; Ps. 21.11; Lam. 2.20) and זרע (Gen. 3.15; Num. 5.28; 1 Sam. 1.1; 2.20; Nah. 1.14).

186. Chan and Wright draw on the strong tradition throughout the region in the ancient world where temples acted as deposits for 'material representations that served as a memorial of an individual or of a group' (Wright and Chan, 'King and Eunuch', 102).

187. They undertake a considerable survey of the role of eunuchs in various ancient societies: ibid., 103–16.

suggesting 'trito-Isaiah elevates their status, demonstrating not only to the eunuchs but also to his fellow Jews that YHWH has a deep concern for the eunuchs and their plight', in response to considerable negative attitudes displayed towards eunuchs in ancient texts,[188] and may resonate with the wider community's 'anxiety about its own future'.[189]

Stavrakopoulou suggests that 'Yhwh himself is thus imaged in 56.3-5 as an active participant in his own version of a mortuary ritual, simultaneously playing the role of descendant and ancestor',[190] which is particularly significant in terms of general perceptions of YHWH's aversion to the dead. This text may also be subverting the 'kinship contexts of ancestral cults':

> First, in asserting that the Yhwh temple can offer the community the regenerative and memorializing functions of the ancestral cult, the dead are rendered redundant, and the mortuary rituals associated with the household are appropriated and subsumed within the cultic control of the 'central' sanctuary. Second, the foreigner and the eunuch to whom the divine promise of יד ושם is made represent those without a traditional claim to the area, neither past nor pending: the foreigner is without local ancestors to mark his place, and the eunuch is without descendants to maintain his place.[191]

Here the symbolic associations of name, land, monument and descendants are used but are crafted into a new ideological alliance, materialized through the monument. It also draws on discourse around gender and sexuality, and there is a further dynamic which may emphasize the reproductive nature of the text. While מצבה is the most common term for monuments of this kind, the writer uses יד; and יד, from the Hebrew 'hand', can mean a memorial monument, such as in 2 Sam. 18.18 where it appears to act synonymously. However, the term is also euphemistic of a phallus. Zevit suggests this as a possibility, but that it remains opaque in terms of the Hebrew.[192] However, the context of a סריס,

---

188. They suggest Est. 2.21-23 is indicative of this.
189. Chan and Wright, 'King and Eunuch', 117.
190. Stavrakopoulou, *Land*, 125. For Stavrakopoulou, this carries a highly political dimension: 'Isa. 56:1-8 and its imaging of the entombed temple, the setting of Yhwh's שם in the temple is rendered a bold assertion of the deity's perpetual occupation of the city, memorialized as an enduring post-mortem name, and marking the metaphorical emergence of the community's deity from the "death" of cultic destruction and displacement': ibid., 130.
191. Ibid., 125.
192. 'Treating it as a term indicating "monument" or as a euphemism indicating "phallus", both of which could be viewed metaphorically as arm-shaped, might work

whose lament is framed in terms of his inability to produce offspring, is responded to by a יד, suggesting at least a euphemistic gloss to this alternative reading of יד.

The text responds to the same concerns as the texts of levirate marriage, namely, the concern of the non-producing male who fears eradication of the name. In its response to childless men, the text asserts the eunuch's place in the reproductive culture, playing on procreative language but rectifying his failure to slot into that culture. It also, as in 2 Sam. 14.1-7, presents the paradigm in the highly emotional language of the eunuch's plight, and explicitly promises perpetual memorialization as the benefit of the monument, keeping the name alive eternally.

5. *Zelophehad's Daughters*

One unusual feature of Isa. 56.3-5 is that the everlasting name is to be better than sons *and* daughters. The implications of this are not drawn out in Isa. 56.3-5, but it raises important questions about the place of daughters who have been seemingly absent in other texts. Numbers 27 and 36 deal explicitly with Zelophehad dying without sons but *with* daughters.[193] In Numbers 27 we are presented with the case of the daughters:

> Came forward the daughters of Zelophehad, son of Hepher, son of Gilead, son of Machir, son of Manasseh, of the families of Manasseh son of Joseph. And these were the names of his daughters: Mahlah, Noah, and Hoglah, and Milcah, and Tirzah.[194] They stood before Moses and before Eleazar

in translation, but each demands some fancy-footed eisegesis in a subsequent discussion'. Zevit also discusses the combination of יד and זכרון in Isa. 57.8, which may also play with the idea of memory and masculinity: 'Rendering *yād*, "penis", which is possible and reading *zikkārōn* thought *zākār*, "male", which is forced, connects these words clearly to beds and closed doors and can somehow be interpreted to phallic symbols. But the Hebrew still remains opaque after this type of experimentation' (Zevit, *Religions*, 529 nn. 53–56).

193. The daughters also appear Num. 26.33; Josh. 17.3-6; and 1 Chron. 7.

194. Shemesh suggests 'naming the daughters, who will inherit his portion, is a response to their fear that Zelophehad's name will be forgotten' (Yael Shemesh, 'A Gender Perspective on the Daughters of Zelophehad: Bible, Talmudic Midrash, and Modern Feminist Midrash', *BibInt* 15, no. 1 [2007]: 84). While this is certainly possible, there are other plausible reasons such as lineages being traced back through the daughters (cf. 1 Chron. 7.15, which although not listing the daughter's names, references them in terms of Zelophehad). Sterring goes further and suggests המלכת, in 1 Chron. 7.18, is Zelophehad's daughter מלכה, stating that 'at least one of the women of Zelophehad's family has succeeded in letting her name survive

7. Mechanisms of Continuity

the priest and before the leaders, and all the congregation...to say: 'Our father died in the wilderness; but he was not in the company of those who gathered together against YHWH in the company of Korah, but for his own sin he died; and he had no sons (בנים). Why should the name of our father be diminished (יגרע שם־אבינו) from among his clan (מתוך משפחתו) because he had no son? Give to us a possession among the brothers of our father (אחזה בתוך אחי אבינו)'.

...And YHWH spoke to Moses to say: 'Right are the daughters of Zelophehad in what they say; indeed, you shall give them a possession of inheritance among the brothers of their father (אחזת נחלה בתוך אחי אביהם) and pass the inheritance of their father to them. And to the sons of Israel you shall speak, to say "If a man dies, and has no son, then you shall pass (והעברת) his inheritance (נחלת) on to his daughter. If he has no daughter, then you shall give his inheritance to his brothers. If he has no brothers, you shall give his inheritance to the brothers of his father. And if he has no brothers of his father, then you shall give his inheritance to the closest kin of his clan, and he shall possess it."'

While a victory for the daughters, the language used is that of male continuity. The daughter's actions are particularly bold (speaking before the congregation; noting their father's lack of involvement in the rebellion of Korah; winning divine approval; making legal precedent; obtaining an inheritance); however, we are aware already that 'the nature of their request emphasizes their father's posterity, not personal advantage'.[195] Without a son the name will be lost (גרע) and the estate would presumably transfer elsewhere in the clan. Levine suggests that:

> The concern expressed by Zelophehad's daughters reflects an individualistic mentality, aimed at preserving the 'name' of the paterfamilias, and not a clannish or tribal mentality that would be more concerned with retaining land within the larger, socioeconomic unit.[196]

---

independently': Ankie Sterring, 'The Will of the Daughters', in Brenner, ed., *Feminist Companion to Exodus to Deuteronomy*, 96.

195. Stiebert, *Fathers and Daughters*, 65.

196. Levine, *Numbers 21–36*, 345. Levine suggests the verb גרע carries 'mathematical' connotations, to subtract or withdraw (see also Deut. 4.2; 13.1), which may suggest the wider משפחה also maintains some form of perpetuation of the name, communally. Ben-Barak, comparing it to other examples (Exod. 5.11; Lev. 27.18; Isa. 15.2; Jer. 48.37) understands 'why should our father's name be diminished in his father's house', as carrying the meaning of 'lowered in status'. This would accord, at least in part, with an understanding of the name as related to reputation or renown: Ben-Barak, *Inheritance*, 17 n. 11.

While the use of 'individualistic' is problematic (after all, we are already in this text alone dealing with multiple generations), it does seem the concern over the inheritance and name is about the father and בית אב, rather than the wider משפחה.[197] It is through keeping the inheritance within the smaller family unit that the daughters can ensure a material continuity which will prevent the father's name disappearing. As we will see, this is later modified to keep the land within the larger tribe structure; however, even with the guarantee the land will stay in the family (evident in the daughters' plea in v. 4) there is a narrower concern for a single household's continuity.

Although the daughters come forward, they are initially referred to as 'the daughters of Zelophehad', and the 'story proceeds at once to enumerate their paternal genealogy, listing Zelophehad's forebears', so much so that the word בן appears five times in the opening verse.[198] The words of their petition twice mention their father, and twice the absence of sons, while 'give *us* a possession' only comes at the end; their case is not framed as justice for women but as justice for their father and his name and memory.[199] Further, while the daughters inherit the land, the text makes a distinction: in vv. 9-11, the land is to be given, נתן, to the relatives; in v. 8, however, we read it is to be העברתם, moved or transferred to them.[200] Jacob Milgrom suggests we can make two assumptions based on this passage: that a name exists as long as it is attached to land; and that Zelophehad's name would be perpetuated through his grandsons. It seems to be conceptually within a similar frame of reference as levirate marriage, and there are a variety of views as to how the legislation relates diachronically to Deut. 25.5-10.[201]

---

197. Ben-Barak, *Inheritance*, 5.

198. Shemesh, 'Gender Perspective', 83.

199. Ibid., 26. Sakenfeld notes that: 'although this was doubtless a more existential concern for the male Israelite, it is not unreasonable to suppose that the daughters themselves participated in and assumed this cultural perspective. Certainly the narrator would have assumed that the daughters assumed it' (Katharine Doob Sakenfeld, 'Feminist Biblical Interpretation', *Theology Today* 46, no. 2 [1989]: 157).

200. Sterring, 'Will of the Daughters', 91. Milgrom suggests the use of the verb implies something of transferring to the unqualified instead of qualified: Milgrom, *Numbers*, 231.

201. According to Milgrom, the text is presuming the levirate could not be carried out, and that the daughters are unmarried (Milgrom, *Numbers*, 231). Compare this to Budd, who suggests that Num. 27 is filling in the 'legal gaps' of Deut. 25.5-10 (Philip J. Budd, *Numbers*, WBC 5 [Waco, TX: Word, 1984], 301). For Levine,

The law is later moderated as the heads of the ancestral houses of the clans of Gilead (of Machir, of Manasseh) come to speak to Moses. They complain that Moses was commanded to give the inheritance of 'our brother Zelophehad to his daughters', however:

> If they are [married] to one from the sons of the [other] tribes (והיו לאחד מבני שבטי) of the sons of Israel as wives/women (נשים), then will be taken their inheritance from the inheritance of our fathers and added to the inheritance of the tribe into which they will be; so from the allotted portion of our inheritance it will be taken. And when comes the jubilee of the sons of Israel, then will be added their inheritance to the inheritance of the tribe into which they will be; and so from the inheritance of the tribe (מטה) of our fathers will be taken their inheritance. (Num. 36.3-4)

Moses declares that they are right, and that the YHWH has commanded that the daughters can join with who they think best, but:

> Only to the clan of the tribe of their father (למשפחת מטה אביהם) may they become women/wives (לנשים), so that no inheritance of the sons of Israel shall go around from tribe to tribe; for every one of the sons of Israel shall keep the inheritance of the tribe of his fathers. (Num. 36.6)

The elders of the משפחות request that Moses prohibit the daughters of Zelophehad from marrying outside of the tribe, lest the land be lost from the נחלה, ancestral inheritance. According to Jacob Weingreen: 'It is to be noted that economic implications flowed directly from the establishment of the legal rights of daughters to inheritance, where there were no sons, and a secondary rule became necessary to safeguard the economic interests of the tribe'.[202] YHWH rules that the daughters may marry whom they choose, but only למשפחת מטה אביהם (Num. 36.6). Here we see the preservation of the inheritance in the מטה; however, the text also focuses attention on the בית אב by default. If the concern were preventing the alienation of the נחלה from the משפחה, it would be sufficient to allow the property to simply be inherited within the משפחה itself; however, by the presence of the daughters inheriting, and the wording of בתוך אחי אבינו, the matter of maintaining the integrity of the בית אב itself comes

---

'cousin-marriage replaced levirate marriage, merely moving the process forward by one generation... [T]he provisions of Numbers 36 bind the daughters of the deceased to the sons of their father's brothers' (Levine, *Numbers 21–36*, 358).

202. Jacob Weingreen, 'The Case of the Daughters of Zelophehad', *VT* 16, no. 4 (1966): 519.

into view. Zafrira Ben-Barak suggests the inheritance laws both preserve the father's name and memory, and the patrimony that was its economic, social and legal basis from generation to generation, 'the two components' of the integrity of the בית אב.²⁰³ Deuteronomy 21.16-17 reinforces the right of the firstborn to receive a double share of property from his father, and prohibits the father from using his discretion and handing it to another son. Stiebert notes that there are examples of the continuation of kinship bonds between fathers and daughters: a priest may defile himself by attending his daughter's funeral (Lev. 21.2), and a widowed/divorced daughter without children can return to her father's house (Lev. 22.12-13); we also have indications of daughters being *granted* some sort of property by their father (Gen. 21.14-16; 1 Sam. 1.4; Job 42.15).²⁰⁴ However, as we see in the daughter's claim to inheritance, their request emphasizes their father's posterity: it 'cannot be assumed that women's inheritance is empowering: if it merely indicates that the inheriting daughter is a conduit for property from her father to her father's male kin, it confers some economic advantage but not necessarily any further independence or autonomy'.²⁰⁵ Ben-Barak suggests the daughters serve as 'hereditary placeholders' waiting for the next man to resume the chain of inheritance.²⁰⁶

The tension here is drawn out between the social units discussed in the text: the בית אב, the משפחה, and the מטה. The initial ruling does not present itself as primarily concerned with the inheritance of daughters *for the sake of* the daughters inheriting. The focus is that a אחזת נחלה can be established for the father so that his name is not wiped out from his משפחה. The inheritance and this name are therefore closely linked, as shown in their movement between the בית אב and the משפחה: the name is not to be lost from among the משפחה, which is established by the daughters inheriting, and presumably creating a family line which will continue the בית אב, and it is reasonable to surmise from the later objection that even if they married outside the מטה, they would still ensure the fathers name did not disappear. The broader concerns of the מטה, however, are considered in the second ruling, which is purely about land and not name. The daughters' concern is like that of levirate marriage – the continuation of the father's name so it is not lost from among his near kin group – however the continuation relates

---

203. Ben-Barak, *Inheritance*, 3.
204. Stiebert, *Fathers and Daughters*, 65, 67.
205. Ibid., 66.
206. Ben-Barak, *Inheritance*, 163.

to the physical inheritance which they would otherwise lose. The text is ambiguous as to how any sexual union the daughters take on would relate to Zelophehad (would the children be counted in the patriline of the daughters or of the man?). However, it suggests that the material integrity of the נחלה is here vital to allow, if Ben-Barak is correct, the daughters to act as placeholders.

6. Conclusion

This chapter has surveyed a variety of texts (legal, narrative, prophetic), from different traditions within the wider biblical corpus, and any attempt to reduce them into one single idea – through, for example, tracing the development of the levirate institution – fails to understand how they reflect different contexts and genres, and that even within a snapshot of any society there are always competing ways of negotiating norms and law. However, they all reveal traces of a similar field, of discourse that involves the perpetuation of the male and the household, in response to the failure of the male to have achieved this in his lifetime. Moreover, they almost all require the use of women's agency in the service of this. The terminology used is distinct: שם, זרע, חיים, נחלה. However, despite these distinct words, a similar paradigm is at work. Even when one term is used, such as שם, it appears to operate in a way that is at once nothing to do with property in one text (Isa. 56.3-5), and everything to do with property in another (Num. 27). Rather than attempting to collapse these different nuances together, I would argue they each reflects a broad paradigm that centres on the perpetuation of the small family unit through the male line, the successful transmission of which appears to accrue symbolic and material capital. They do this, however, with a focus on individual males, and in texts such as Isa. 56.3-5 we see how the communal need for reproduction coalesces around the perpetuation, the memorialization, of the individual; both the individual and community rely on each other. Whereas these texts are typically read separately, it is possible to see how the narrative of Lot's daughters reflects a similar discourse to Tamar and Judah, or how the plea of Zelophehad's daughters reflects the same concern as the eunuch in Isaiah 56.

All these texts reflect the concern of males, or the family of males, of dying without sons, without a specific mechanism to perpetuate the name, seed or estate, which builds up the individual, household and family. Read alongside each other, they also demonstrate the wide concern of the paradigm, questioning some of the dominant readings of levirate marriage, such as that it is about welfare of the widow or tied up with inheritance. Moreover, while they correspond to the perpetuation of the family unit, there is also individual concern with being remembered even if sons cannot be provided.

In the Conclusion it will be demonstrated how the various concerns – name, property, gender, afterlife – all construct a kind of 'reproductive futurism' which articulates the relationship between the individual concern for remembrance and the stability and perpetuation of the family unit.

CONCLUSION

1. *Overview*

The biblical levirate has undergone much interpretation, even since ancient times. We see this in Josephus, who crafts a series on contrasting rationales onto the law:

> When a woman is left childless on her husband's death, the husband's brother shall marry her, and call the child that shall be born by the name of the deceased and rear him as heir to the estate; for this will at once be profitable to the public welfare, houses not dying out and property remaining with the relatives, and it will moreover bring the women an alleviation of their misfortune to live with the nearest kinsman of their former husbands. (Josephus, *Ant.* 4.8.23)[1]

Indeed, the institution appears to have undergone creative interpretation and change within the biblical texts themselves. This has led to the practice being debated and disputed, with scholarship at times being suffocated from an overly historical or legal approach. This monograph took as its starting point the premise that any institution, any rule, any idea, operates within particular social structures of power. That is, following Bourdieu, the texts we read were produced under certain forms of power which produced a way of understanding the world, a doxa, which we have traces of now in the text. Within these structures of power, people internalize the structures to operate in certain ways, often playing the field for the best possible outcome. Moreover, these relations of power construct identities like male and female as distinct, and the relations of power in these identities, though under constant negotiation, are never equal. We, therefore, read our core texts as the remains of a particular

---

1. Flavius Josephus, *Jewish Antiquities I–IV*, trans. Henry St. John Thackeray and Ralph Marcus, Loeb Classical Library 210 (Cambridge, MA: Heinemann; Harvard University Press, 1930).

discourse and sought to understand how they operate within this. With ethnographic material from contemporary societies, we have attempted to probe aspects of the boundaries and outlines of an ancient culture which relate to the subject of this paradigm, which examines responses in texts to the death of a male who has no living children. Looking at death, names, reproduction, the family, it was demonstrated how each operates with a keen concern on the *social*, and how this idea of social kinship congeals around the בית אב.

As demonstrated, death is not 'the end'; social ties between the living and the dead remain. This is seen keenly, for example, in the communal aspects of burial that connects with textual references to being gathered to one's ancestors. Conversely, to deny communal burial, or to mutilate a body, disturbs one's post-mortem existence. While some scholarship suggests an active deified dead, a more nuanced understanding points not to a relation between living and dead focused around worship of a deified dead, but one which understands commemoration and veneration of the dead as part of the typical social context. This context roots the dead in the world of the living, seen in the use of the dead in claims to land, physically represented through tomb or monument. The material commemoration of the dead was of crucial importance, and is made manifest through the preservation of the dead in their tombs, the communal nature of proper burial, and the establishing of monuments. These maintain the connections between the living and the dead and prevent 'dreaded death after death',[2] while also shaping claims to land and identity. Thus, death is not a rupture of the deceased from the living, but can be the inclusion of the dead in the wider social dynamics of the community. However, even the dead can lose social and symbolic capital, and the poor treatment of the dead can be an act of actual or symbolic violence.

The importance of social connection and memory is carried through to the discussion of names, which cross the boundaries of the living and the dead. The name is more than a descriptive label, but has a substantive connection to the one named. The detachability of the name allows it to cross social boundaries, whether between the human and the divine or the living and the dead. It crosses these boundaries most persistently in its connection to progeny, with name and progeny symbolically linked in various texts. The destruction of offspring relates to the destruction of name, and offspring and name work in tandem, either preserved or destroyed, to ensure the perpetuation, or destruction, of the individual and the wider social unit. Names take on a substantive presence and

---

2. Schmitt, 'Memory as Immortality', 87.

are seen to dwell under heaven or be inscribed in books, or physically represent the tribes of Israel before YHWH. In this way, they take on a performative function, and without this performance they lose their vibrancy. The promise of a name is tied up with the promise of progeny, and through this progeny, the names of ancestors are made great (Gen. 48.16), and are remembered in genealogies. However, to destroy one's name is equivalent to destroying the person, and often takes form through the destruction of progeny and therefore memory (Jer. 11.19). Names, like burial, accrue capital, and the erasure of a name diminishes it. Names are therefore powerful tools in various social fields, intimately connected with the embodied agent.

The name and house are built up through children, primarily sons, with men cast as reproductive. Understandings of kinship have transformed through the last few decades, and a Western, medicalized understanding of procreation is limited in its applicability to other cultures. Through, for example, circumcision, identity is transmitted as something both male, embodied, and connected to procreation, and through circumcision male power is constantly rearticulated. Procreation language is tied up with seed, explored through agricultural symbolism, and materialized through the fruitful cut of circumcision. In various texts, the importance of male procreation is emphasized. However, these come with a counterpart: the use of female sexuality. Women are constructed as using their sexuality in aid of male reproduction; the story of Rachael and Leah demonstrates not only how their sexuality is valued, but their worth is understood *through* their ability to produce sons for their husband; the text not only *suggests* the importance of 'motherhood' (though primarily understood in terms of production of children, not maternal affection) but *understands* women through these terms, producing knowledge about their roles and bodies. Whereas a contemporary feminist perspective finds the narrative of Leah and Rachel disturbing, if we follow Bourdieu this does not automatically imply it is an ancient piece of 'propaganda'; instead, it reflects a doxic, shared understanding of female sexuality and bodies. This takes the form of male use of the whole female sexuality of their household; when infertility occurs (perceived primarily as the fault of the woman) the male is 'offered' female slaves in service of his right to create heir and progeny. However, at times women such as Sarah (Gen. 16.2) and Rachel (Gen. 30.3) are *built up* from the production of offspring, and we are told Hagar's זרע will be multiplied (Gen. 16.10); women in the texts use strategies, and their habitus can compete in the field and built up capital. The strength of kinship structures can, however, come under threat internally from unregulated sexuality. Deuteronomy highly regulates women's sexuality, and prohibits men's sexuality from infringing on the women of other men, particularly protecting the man's ability to ensure paternity, done in service of an orderly and cohesive transmission from generation to generation, which in Deuteronomy is understood primarily in the service of the transmission of YHWH's Torah. Failure to comply results in punishment by YHWH, which takes on the form of the erasure of descendants and land. Incest taboos help to strengthen male bonding and control sexuality within the household, to ensure the correct relation of men to other men.

The ability to procreate takes on practical importance in the transmission of the family. Without a stable family unit, which regulates women's sexuality and proscribes proper intra-familial relations, the ability to perpetuate the male line is threatened. The social structure forms around the מטה/שבט, the משפחה and the בית אב, which are constructed primarily in terms of the males (Num. 3.15; Josh. 7.4). The בית אב forms the foci of the social world, and the importance of its integrity shapes social laws and norms. This is seen no more clearly than in the transmission of land, which is understood to belong not primarily to individuals but to social groups. The communal structure is transmitted through the transference of land from one generation to another. The land is not merely an economic possession, but is tied up with ancestors and takes on theological importance in its gifting from YHWH. Through the proper transference of land, the cohesion of the בית אב and wider משפחה is ensured, and this transmission is primarily centred around the male line (though occasionally being held by daughters as place holders), and excludes widows. The materiality of property relates to the materiality of the body in the grave, to the extent they are enmeshed. The transmission of property and family, and the transmission of the materiality of the male reproductive process, is manifest in genealogies which connect generations and strengthen kinship. Generational relations in the family home are closely guarded, such as in the command to honour father and mother – a text which mandates forms of behaviour which continue even after death. However, the transmission from generation to generation is threatened through a form of punishment, כרת, which destroys progeny and disrupts patrilineal continuity. כרת demonstrates that the destruction of land, progeny and name, rather than something abstract, evokes real fear. Instead of these fields – death and burial, names, sexual reproduction, social organization – being separate ones, they in fact share what Bourdieu called 'structural homologies' – that is, they map onto each other, forming a whole structure of society, and therefore influencing how individuals internalize these structures in their habitus.

With this context of name–land–progeny, we came to look at eight texts that respond to men dying without sons. Each is concerned with the perpetuation of the male in various forms and through various mechanisms. Through an examination of each text we have discussed the use of women primarily as agents of male perpetuation; and while some such as Eryl Davies may have read the concerns of the widow as of primary importance, this appears to be alien to the internal concerns of the texts themselves. Exploration of the symbolic associations of each passage drew us back to the tension between Pedersen, who understands the transmission of the name as a form of afterlife, and Westbrook who understands it in terms of a legal concept. The same discourse is in operation even when שם is not the primary concern, such as Genesis 38. Moreover, even when שם appears as the focus, it can appear in texts which are predominantly concerned with property and texts which do not focus on it at all. However, all the texts described the perpetuation of the man in embodied, materialized terms. Therefore, a more nuanced understanding is necessary, and one which relates to Brichto's analysis in 'Kin, Cult, Land and Afterlife – A Biblical Complex', which tries to understand how these different dynamics work in relation to each other, albeit with more measured understandings of the different symbolic interactions at work.

2. *Property and Progeny*

Pressler takes on some of Westbrook's conclusions on Deut. 25.5-10.[3] She suggests that Westbrook's definition of 'title' for שם 'seems overly precise'. Through drawing on only limited occurrences of the term שם 'to define its univocal legal meanings', Westbrook has, as discussed above, severely restricted his understanding of the passage. Pressler critiques Westbrook's insistence that the law only has one goal as restrictive, arguing that social institutions 'arise out of complex factors and tend to serve multiple purposes', suggesting the perpetuation of the man's name has more to do with the continuing possession of ancestral land than establishing a legal claim to land. I would broadly agree with Pressler on these points. Westbrook, by attempting to discern a univocal legal meaning, failed to understand that it works in a cultural system in which שם cannot be reduced to a term such as 'title' but can only be fully understood in its symbolic context. As demonstrated, it has other connotations, and operates in multiple fields at the same time. Ellens responds to Pressler's critique of Westbrook:

3. Pressler, *View of Women*, 67 n. 17.

Pressler cites 2 Sam 18.18 and Isa 56:4-5 as two examples of 'establishment of the name' by means other than inheritance of the land. These examples also support Westbrook's understanding. In these examples the name is fixed to a memorial object. Just as attachment of the name to an object establishes the name, so also does attachment of the name to the land.[4]

Ellens reiterates that if Westbrook's term is right, then 'establishment of a *proper connection* between the dead man and the landed inheritance is the core of the levirate law', and 'that if a man has established the proper connection to the land, then his name can continue in either a descendant who inherits or in a collateral who inherits'.[5] Ellens relies on Westbrook's idea of a 'fourth scenario', where brothers have divided the land, and the man inherits before he dies, and so title has been established and the levirate does not need to occur. Thus, for Ellens, the narrative of Zelophehad's daughters is not about the transmission of property as much as it is about Zelophehad's failure to 'effect a proper connection to the land'. If he had established 'title', then a 'collateral' could inherit. For Ellens, the problem is that the brother of the dead inheriting and establishing the name of the dead is an unbelievable 'legal fiction', so a more believable fiction must take place. This more believable fiction is the levirate, and through this a 'true division' takes place.[6] However, this falls into the same trap as Westbrook. Ellens suggests that a monument acts in the same way as land in establishing the name in a form like a title, but this does not mean that the name *has* to be reduced to monument or land. I would argue, conversely, that it is land and monument which allow a form of materiality to be attached to the name. We have seen in Genesis 38 the levirate in operation in a form that is concerned with זרע, not שם. Here a precise understanding of the levirate as concerned with the name as a legal title becomes more ambiguous. It is not that name and property are separate, but that there is more to the relationship between name and property than a specific legal term. Pressler terms this connection the 'property-progeny-name', carried down from father to son.[7] This 'property-progeny-name' is inextricably tied up with a 'patrilineal, patriarchal family structure'.[8] This 'property-progeny-name' is, crucially, one of the dominant modes of symbolic capital in the Hebrew Bible, and thus the 'patrilineal, patriarchal, family structure' must be reproduced. There

4. Ellens, *Sex Texts*, 255.
5. Ibid.
6. Ibid., 256.
7. Pressler, *View of Women*, 73.
8. Ibid.

are various attempts to articulate this synthesis. Thompson and Thompson suggest:

> In Israel a man's 'name' comes to mean his property to such an extent that his name achieves thereby an existence separate from his own person. On the other hand, his person is continued through his progeny. The effort, therefore, to maintain one's name becomes precisely the effort to keep progeny and property (name and person) together; i.e., to keep one's property within his immediate family.[9]

Burrows, also, understands a continuation of the personal life in the life of the son, tied up with ancestral rites, but understands this taking place in the context of 'the provision of an heir for his property, so that it might be kept in the family and in the normal line of inheritance'.[10] This 'progeny-property-name' was expressed in a different form by Brichto, with an emphasis on ancestral cult. The fact is, as acknowledged by Westbrook, the importance of the name, of establishing connection to property, can only be understood by its theological, ideological, or symbolic significance. Meir Malul offers a way to begin to articulate this:

> When we realize that even the male members of society do not actually own a piece of landed property, and at most only possess it in the sense of enjoying its usufruct, the female members' assumed claim to such a 'land of the fathers (*'ābôt*)' seems indeed ludicrous... The very idea of ownership in ancient times has to be construed in a completely different sense than is expected by an average modern person. Following the Hohfeldian philosophy of law, ownership is defined in sociological terms, and property is characterized as a social entity. A person could not have any legal relationship with a piece of property, for legal relationships can exist only between persons. That is: a person's relations vis-à-vis a piece of property are predicated upon his position within the social matrix and his relationships with the other members of the social group. In these terms, it is only as a full and legitimate member that one can have access to the group's property, to an extent which depends upon his hierarchical location with the social matrix. The conclusion of the foregoing is that no person can own immovable property, and the 'ownership' of the latter is vested with the social group as a whole... '[T]he land shall not be sold for ever: for all the land is mine; for ye are strangers and sojourners with me' (Lev. 25.23; cf. Ex. 19:5).[11]

9. Thompson and Thompson, 'Legal Problems', 87.
10. Burrows, 'Background', 3.
11. Meir Malul, *Knowledge, Control and Sex: Studies in Biblical Thought, Culture, and Worldview* (Tel Aviv-Jaffa: Archaeological Center, 2002), 256–7. I was drawn to look at Malul's work through a reference by Ellens, *Sex Texts*, 253 n. 15.

Malul draws on Ahab and Naboth (1 Kings 21) to demonstrate how 'for the familial household to continue its existence, its landed property should remain intact'.[12] Land is not merely a legal entity, a possession, which can be owned or transferred. Land is imbued with social meaning, it is a field where social meaning is played out, and this social meaning is apparent in the use of ancestors to establish claims to land, to the importance of its transmission into the future. At its most basic level, that of the בית אב, land is tied up with social continuity throughout the generations, it materializes it just as progeny materialize the זרע; it operates not under the auspices of a 'name' but along a symbolic complex of name, descendants and land, all of which congeal around the patrilineal בית אב and transmit its social-symbolic essence and structure through generations. Land operates not as the perpetuation of the name but in *service* of the perpetuation of the name:[13]

> A man's 'name' exists only in connection with his patrimony, the two principles inseparably intertwined in foundation of the *bēt 'āb*. He who inherits the patrimony becomes the legitimate heir, and through the inheritance preserves the father's name, keeps the patrimony within the family, and continues the dynasty of the *bēt 'āb*.[14]

It forms the essential social reproduction of ancient Israel, as understood in the context of its beliefs about death and the afterlife. It functions on 'this side' of the grave, but subsumes the grave into it, through social interaction with the dead and their geographical presence on its landscape. But it continuously projects itself into the future, securing itself through the control of sexuality (as in the sex laws of Deuteronomy), correcting itself in the place of failure (levirate marriage), and by tying itself up with the individual concerns and desires of individuals for continuity (Isa. 56 and the eunuch). In this way, it also gives life and continuity to the deceased. It is not a given social condition, but is utilized and manipulated in various services, for example to project YHWH as a superior to a Persian king.[15] Levirate marriage produced a son for the deceased who has died childless. If we follow contemporary anthropological understandings of kinship, the child raised in levirate marriage does not need to be a kind of legal fiction, a fictive child for the dead. Indeed, if we follow the incest prohibitions in Leviticus 19, the child is constituted of the same בשר,

---

12. Malul, *Knowledge*, 250.
13. Wright, 'Name', 147.
14. Ben-Barak, *Inheritance*, 18.
15. As in Chan and Wright, 'King and Eunuch'.

the same kin and flesh as the deceased as all the characters at play are under the same kinship-household.[16] If we stop understanding the fruit of the levirate union to be in some way a fiction, we can see how a child is produced for the deceased, in which he can be materialized even after death, and perpetuated in the same way as his name being remembered, to prevent his social eradication and the social eradication of his household. Social loyalty, reinforced by legal shaming, co-opts the brother (or kin) of the deceased to carry out the obligation to the dead brother, even if this may threaten his own economic prosperity. A child is produced to keep remembrance of the name of the dead, to protect his burial, his property, and perpetuate him through his own offspring.

This mechanism of perpetuation is not merely technical or disinterested; we have seen in Isa. 56.3-5 and 2 Sam. 14.1-7 that the thought of eradication of name and seed causes emotional distress. Let us turn again to Saul's cry:

> …Swear to me therefore by the LORD that you will not cut (תכרית) off my descendants after me (את־זרעי אחרי), and that you will not wipe out (ואם־תשמיד) my name from my father's house (שמי מבית אבי). (1 Sam. 24.21)

Saul's begging to preserve seed and name, to not be cut off, can be understood in terms of habitus, his desire and action attempting to play the game of survival. This is brought out more clearly in the threat of כרת which Saul invokes, the punishment of being cut off. כרת connects lineage and descendants with the eradication of name and abuse of corpses. As discussed, כרת is a *lex talionis* punishment for the failure to circumcise, failure to keep Passover, for incest, and giving offspring to Molech; it responds to a failure to keep normal patterns of lineage and procreation, and is a punishment that seems to not only cause destruction of life but also of post-mortem continuity. This all suggests that while there is a strong social dynamic at play, there is also an individual, personal urge, an internalization of the broader social paradigm, to protect and ensure one's existence after death, through burial, progeny, and monuments, and that these materialized, embodied forms of seed, corpse, name and land provide a substantive form of preventing the dreaded 'death after death'. That is, to exist after death requires something material one's existence can cling on to.

---

16. Janet Carsten, *After Kinship* (Cambridge: Cambridge University Press, 2004), 139, discusses how in non-medicalized understandings, flesh can come to be understood as shared through food and through living in the same household.

However, this paradigm of continuity is not general to all people in all social locations:

> One's status, that is, the conglomerate of rights and duties granted to him by the power of his location in the social matrix, which in turn is dependent upon his sex, age, role, and a myriad of other qualifications, is the criterion by which he gets rights of use in a certain object.[17]

That is, land 'as "property" is totally social: only when there is a social agreement (even a tacit one) can a certain object be defined as a property which "belongs" to a member of the society'.[18] This paradigm of perpetuation and continuity established through land, progeny and perpetuation of the name, is, as seen in genealogies, the privy of certain members of society; and society, following Bourdieu, is structured to keep these operations of power in the hands of certain members. It is fundamentally male, androcentric and patriarchal. It utilizes women's sexuality; in fact, it informs their habitus in such a way that procreation at any means is natural. It is inaccessible to slaves, to the foreigners without land, to those without economic resource. The inclusion of the eunuch in the paradigm (Isa. 56) can only take place because he is, initially, *excluded*. The inclusion of the eunuch, as an attempt at YHWH asserting his social control and usurping other social hierarchies, covers a failure of the patriarchal order to perpetuate itself. In this specific discourse, this form of *reproductive futurism*, invoking the symbolic aspects of name, land, progeny and lineage and formed around the בית אב, we can understand the responses to male death and the mechanisms in place to correct its failure.

3. Gender Reassessed

In asking if ancient Israel was patriarchal, Meyers states:

> Patrilineality is not the same as patriarchy. And male control of female sexuality does not mean male control of adult women in every aspect of household or community life… In agrarian societies in which a household's livelihood depends on its property (*naḥălâ*, 'inheritance'), the acute need for men to be sure their offspring were their own is manifest in regulations giving men control of female sexuality. Biblical legal stipulations concerning virginity, adultery, prostitution, levirate marriage, and childbirth

---

17. Meir Malul, ''*āqēb* "Heel" and *'āqab* "To Supplant" and the Concept of Succession in the Jacob–Esau Narratives', *VT* 46, no. 2 (1996): 194.

18. Ibid.

seek to assure that property remains within the male lineage; even Gen 3:16 ('he shall rule over you') likely concerns sexual control and not absolute male dominance.[19]

Meyers here refocuses our attention away from a generic understanding of ancient Israel as wholly oppressive towards women, and towards a more nuanced view of the way structures impact on the construction of gender.[20] Lemos, responding to Meyer's argument, welcomes her attention to the shortcomings of patriarchy 'as a model', though she finds it 'rather optimistic'.[21] Lemos looks at the place of women in Israelite society in terms of personhood, and finds it is inaccurate to speak of women as property,[22] and indeed that referring to women as property 'whether in general terms or in relation to their sexuality, is not only inaccurate, but also in some ways obscures our understanding of hierarchies and relations of dominance in these cultures'.[23] However, when we look at the lack of agency women have in legal texts, or the use of violence against women, their agency always exists in social hierarchies and their personhood is constructed as being unstable.[24] We have seen how this construction of gender operates in our texts. Women's habitus, their agency, often women's sexuality, is cast in the service of male reproductive futurism. In Genesis 19, Genesis 38, Deut. 25.5-10, Ruth, Numbers 27 and 2 Samuel 13 women frame their action as being done on behalf of men. The text constructs the use of their sexuality and agency not as an option but as a necessity, as a desire; women are constructed as necessary and valuable, but necessary and valuable especially in their ability to reproduce the social order and their loyalty to their men.

---

19. Carol Meyers, 'Was Ancient Israel a Patriarchal Society?', *JBL* 133, no. 1 (2014): 27.

20. Lemos, *Violence*, 77 n. 42.

21. Ibid. Lemos continues: 'while it is in no doubt that some women may have had some or even a great deal of agency in certain contexts, it is difficult to contest that women in other contexts – and in general – were subordinate to their husbands and fathers considering the repeated examples in biblical law and narratives where men are explicitly stated to be dominant over women, afforded life-and-death control over women, or where women are subject to capital punishment in cases where men are not (see, e.g., Gen 3.16; 19.8; 38.24; Lev 21.9; Deuteronomy 22; and Ezekiel 16, 23 [but *cf.* Hos 4.14]).'

22. Ibid., 72–8.

23. Ibid., 92.

24. Ibid., 94–5.

Moreover, we see time and time again how the dispositions of women's habitus lead them to play the game, both to build themselves up, but also because sexuality in the service of men is masked as natural and doxic. This ties into broader sexual discourse, such as Genesis 29–30, which articulates Rachel and Leah's value in terms of their sexual expediency in the service of their husbands. Contrary to some interpretations of Deut. 25.5-10 which understand the law as in service of the widow, the text does not consider the ability of the widow to deny her role, whereas the brother can decline his social obligation; her sexuality is the 'vehicle' in which the dead's progeny and property come to be.[25] Pressler states:

> Women did not carry on the family name; they did not regularly inherit family property (Deut 21:15-17). In a patrilineally structured society, women participate in the lineage of their husbands; they do not have lineages of their own. Deut 25:5-10 thus raises some questions about the continued existence of the lives of women, or the ongoing meaning of their lives. Presumably such meaning was understood to be derived from women's contribution to the continuation of their husbands' lineage when they mothered sons.[26]

Any social protection afforded her only takes place in the context of a patriarchal society and is derived from the men with whom she is in relation.[27] Moreover, any agent is competing in different fields at different times, and it is unsustainable to understand practice as solely isolated to one motivation. To attempt to separate the desire of the woman to produce a child, the desire to produce a child for her husband, and the desire to secure her status, does not recognize the way that various fields of play are internalized in a context – particularly when a model of symbolic capital is brought into play. Even texts which involve the cooperation of female characters together involve inevitable discrepancies in power and authority, as W. Gafney highlights in Naomi's sexual control of Ruth, her command to visit Boaz, with Ruth remaining throughout the text as 'Ruth, the Moabite woman'.[28] This is the context in which male reproduction is valorized and institutionalized.

The transmission of the covenant with Abraham draws on the discourse of land, name and progeny, while assimilating it into a wider Priestly theological construct. This takes its form, notably, in the rite of circumcision

25. Ellens, *Sex Texts*, 249.
26. Pressler, *View of Women*, 73.
27. Ibid., 74.
28. Gafney, 'Mother Knows Best', 31–2.

which places symbolic focus on the fruitful penis as the inscribed site of reproduction, a site which is only and exclusively in the male domain. Male desire for this does come out, however, in texts such as 2 Sam. 18.18 and Isaiah 56, where the desire cannot be projected onto women and instead is placed in the mouths of the unproductive men, who turn to non-reproductive means (monuments) to ensure their social continuity by tying their identity and name to fixed established monuments which represent them in their community; in Isaiah, this monument undermines the typical paradigm by becoming *better* than progeny. Here, masculinity, and its failure, is both undermined – eradicating the need for progeny – and corrected, creating a new construct of masculinity based on fidelity to YHWH, attainable by the eunuch who cannot reproduce sexually.

Power, however, can never fully mask its genesis. The discourses presented to us in the text are only images of the relations of power and knowledge in ancient Judah and Israel. The diversity of understandings in texts which respond to male death are evidence to the changing nature of the terms used, where aspects such as seed are emphasized over others. Moreover, within other texts we see competing emphases which point to the complexity and ambiguity of the discourse. Both Sarah and Rachel are said to build (בנה) themselves up, and the individual memory of Rachel and Leah's efforts are brought out in Ruth 4.11 when they are accounted as building the house of Israel. Rachel stands out again as a sign of the complexity of relations of gender in her role as ancestor (Gen. 35.19-20; 1 Sam. 10.2; Jer. 31.15). Further, narratives draw out the contradictions and double standards at play: as noted in Genesis 38, the narrative serves to highlight the permissiveness of Judah's behaviour, which is undermined by Tamar's loyalty.

4. *Conclusion: No Future?*

The texts examined in the present work – Genesis 19, Genesis 38, Numbers 27, Deut. 25.5-10, Ruth, 1 Sam. 18.18, 2 Samuel 13, Isaiah 56 – all deal with responses to the death of men without children. They all function within a symbolic structure we can term a kind of *reproductive futurism*, which serve to perpetuate and reproduce a social order, through material things – whether seed, land or monument – centred around the male but stretching both forward and backward through generations, and across the household and its wider role in the clan, tribe and nation. However, despite sharing in this same structure of power, they are all expressions of it rooted in their own historical, cultural and legal traditions. Attempts at establishing a chronology of some of these texts have been at times more and less successful; however, we have demonstrated that despite historical differences they exist within the same discourse, which is both in some ways familiar to us and in some ways foreign. Genesis 19, 38, Deuteronomy 25, and 2 Sam. 14.1-7 deal primarily with progeny and their survival or production; Ruth appears to conjoin this with an explicit focus on property, which is seen more clearly in Numbers 27; 1 Sam. 18.18 and Isaiah 56 deal with a scenario where the transmission of property or creation of progeny is not possible so they focus on the establishment of a monument in place of progeny for the perpetuation of the name. Though the different texts focus on the perpetuation of the male line through a series of different mechanisms (progeny, name, monument), these mechanisms are not to be considered alien to each other but part of the same symbolic complex that coalesces around the house and lineage of the father, even where, as in Isa. 56.3-5, the symbolic complex is circumvented. In these mechanisms, they respond to death, which though inevitable can be ameliorated through ensuring right social relations, whether through proper burial of the body in the tomb or the creation of progeny to continue the line. Through this, they prevent the 'dreaded death after death', which we can now suggest, forms something like a social annihilation; social continuation, on the other hand, is highly embodied and materialized. By social, this incorporates the security of the line through generations, incorporating the dead and the living, ideally reproduced by descendants in the future, secure in their landed holdings and able to transmit the social order into the future, all the time recalling the dead and remembering their burial sites. However, this social order is both personalized in individual desire to avoid annihilation, and at all times inequitable; it functions around the individual male and their relation to other male kin, and uses women's agency and sexuality in the service of this social order, side-lining their place in the order. This agency acts, in part, to repair the failure of men to reproduce the social order in the right way, through lack of children and more explicitly lack of sons. The reinforcement of masculinity is seen clearly in Isaiah 56, where the eunuch's masculinity is repaired by YHWH, who becomes the one who does the memorializing. However, occasionally we see gaps in this discourse, and women assert their place in the order and gain commemoration and dynasties in future generations.

In discussion of society we often hear a phrase, sometimes portrayed as an African proverb:[29] 'it takes a whole village to raise a child'. Our

---

29. Its source is, however, a matter of debate. See: https://www.npr.org/sections/goatsandsoda/2016/07/30/487925796/it-takes-a-village-to-determine-the-origins-of-an-african-proverb?t=1566571420307 (last accessed 23 August 2019).

fondness for this proverb may, it turns out, be founded on our own fascination with the figure of the Child as the primary concern of social order, to invoke Edelman's *No Future*. The biblical case may be somewhat different: it takes a child to raise a village. Without the child, without the monument, without the inheritance, there is nothing on which להקים שם המת, to raise the name of the dead, there is no material substance for the name or seed or memory to attach itself. Without this, the fears of the individual and the community conjoin, becoming the fear of social annihilation. Without the perpetuation of the present into the future, the dead lose their place in the social world and the living eventually become forgotten. It is once again apt to quote Rappaport:

> If no one any longer recited the *Shema*, 'The Lord our God the Lord is One' would cease to be a social fact, whatever the supernatural case might be. As far as present day society is concerned, Jupiter, Woden, En-Lil, and Marduk are no longer anything more than figments of ancient imaginings, for no one continues to establish or re-establish their being by calling their names.[30]

Without progeny, without land, without name, the ancestor, the father, the בית אב is lost; their conceptual relatedness, we have shown, appears to have been in operation throughout the many years spanning the Hebrew Bible's emergence/composition. With time, new understandings of perpetuation, of afterlife, of social order will have come into being; with new empires and the eventual shift to diaspora and exile new understandings of identity and personhood would have come into being. We may see this most prominently in Dan. 12.1-3:

> There shall be a time of anguish, such as has never occurred since nations first came into existence. But at that time your people shall be delivered, everyone who is found written in the book. Many of those who sleep in the dust of the earth shall awake, some to everlasting life, and some to shame and everlasting contempt. Those who are wise shall shine like the brightness of the sky, and those who lead many to righteousness, like the stars for ever and ever.

The names of the dead are written in the book, isolated from their kin and line. We see a new discourse is emerging, one which would shape Second Temple Judaism. Having established the prominent discourse operating in the redacted texts we have in the Hebrew Bible, it would now be possible to try, following a kind of Foucauldian archaeology, to fit these into a genealogy, and understand where the breaks between

---

30. Rappaport, *Ritual and Religion*, 297.

epistemes, structures of thinking, doxic periods, occurred. We can now focus in more narrowly to see how this is explored in specific texts, for example on how Isaiah may use the perpetuation of the family as a symbol to deal with the exile, as seen in Isaiah 56 and its competition with Persian kingship ideology. We can reread texts such as the Aqedah (Gen. 22) and understand the severity of Abraham sacrificing not just a son but also his social continuation. We can also outline the discourses of other ancient West Asian texts along with those of Second Temple Judaism, to try and establish a 'history of continuity and discontinuity', understanding continuity and social reproduction not as a given, but a construct of power, constantly at work to mask and reproduce itself. We see this change in Daniel, where a different form of post-mortem being is suggested more explicitly than in any other Hebrew Bible text,[31] one which would cause a rupture with the past, and which we see being contested in other Second Temple texts:[32] not this time raising a שם עולם, everlasting name, but instead being raised לחיי עולם, to everlasting life (Dan. 12.2).

---

31. See also: Isa. 36.19 and Ezek. 37.5.
32. For example, Mk 12.18-26. See m. Sanh. 10.1; Sir. 17.27-28; Wis. 3.1; and 4 Macc. 7.3 for evidence of the range of beliefs circulating in the period.

Bibliography

Abasili, Alexander Izuchukwu. 'Genesis 38: The Search for Progeny and Heir'. *Scandinavian Journal of the Old Testament* 25, no. 2 (2011): 276–88.
Ackerman, Susan. 'Household Religion, Family Religion, and Women's Religion in Ancient Israel'. Pages 60–88 in *Household and Family Religion in Antiquity*. Edited by John Bodel and Saul M. Olyan. The Ancient World: Comparative Histories. Malden, MA: Blackwell, 2008.
Ackerman, Susan, and Benjamin D. Cox. 'Rachel's Tomb'. *JBL* 128 (2009): 135–48.
Adelman, Rachel. 'Seduction and Recognition in the Story of Judah and Tamar and the Book of Ruth'. *Nashim: A Journal of Jewish Women's Studies & Gender Issues* 23 (2012): 87–109.
Adkins, Lisa. 'Introduction: Feminism, Bourdieu, and After'. Pages 3–18 in *Feminism after Bourdieu*. Edited by Lisa Adkins and Beverley Skeggs. Oxford: Blackwell, 2004.
Albertz, Rainer. *Israel in Exile: The History and Literature of the Sixth Century B.C.E.* Translated by David Green. SBLStBL 3. Atlanta, GA: Society of Biblical Literature, 2003.
Albertz, Rainer, and Rüdiger Schmitt. *Family and Household Religion in Ancient Israel and the Levant*. Winona Lake, IN: Eisenbrauns, 2012.
Albright, William. 'The High Places in Ancient Palestine'. Pages 428–58 in *Volume Du Congrès, Strasbourg 1956*. Edited by G. W. Anderson. VTSup 4. Leiden: Brill, 1957.
Allen, Michael. 'Male Cults Revisited: The Politics of Blood Versus Semen'. *Oceania* 68, no. 3 (1998): 189–99.
Alter, Robert. *The Art of Biblical Narrative*. New York: Basic Books, 1981.
Amit, Yairah. 'Narrative Analysis: Meaning, Context and Origin of Genesis 38'. Pages 271–91 *Method Matters: Essays on the Interpretation of the Hebrew Bible in Honor of David L. Petersen*. Edited by Joel M. LeMon and Kent Harold Richards. SBLRBS 56. Atlanta, GA: Society of Biblical Literature, 2009.
Anderson, Cheryl. *Women, Ideology and Violence: Critical Theory and the Construction of Gender in the Book of the Covenant and the Deuteronomic Law*. JSOTSup 394. London: T&T Clark, 2004.
Anderson, Janice C., and Stephen D. Moore, eds. *New Testament Masculinities*. SemeiaSt 45. Atlanta, GA: Society of Biblical Literature, 2004.
Andrew, Maurice E. 'Moving from Death to Life: Verbs of Motion in the Story of Judah and Tamar in Gen 38'. *ZAW* 105, no. 2 *Moving from death to life* (1993): 262–9.
Archer, Leonie. 'Bound by Blood: Circumcision and Menstrual Taboo in Post-Exilic Judaism'. Pages 38–61 in *After Eve: Women, Theology and the Christian Tradition*. Edited by Janet Martin Soskice. London: Collins Marshall Pickering, 1990.
Atkinson, Will. *Beyond Bourdieu: From Genetic Structuralism to Relational Phenomenology*. Cambridge: Polity, 2016.

Avrahami, Yael. 'Name Giving to the Newborn in the Hebrew Bible'. Pages 15–53 in *These Are the Names: Studies in Jewish Onomastics* (Hebrew). Edited by Aaron Demsky. Studies in Jewish Onomastics 5. Ramat-Gan: Bar-Ilan University Press, 2011.

Baden, Joel S., and Candida R. Moss, *Reconceiving Infertility Biblical Perspectives on Procreation and Childlessness*. Princeton: Princeton University Press, 2015.

Baloyi, M. E. 'The Christian View of Levirate Marriage in a Changing South Africa'. *Journal of Sociology and Social Anthropology* 6, no. 4 (2015): 483–91.

Barr, James. 'The Symbolism of Names in the Old Testament'. *BJRL* 52, no. 1 (1969): 11–29.

Beattie, Derek R. G. 'The Book of Ruth as Evidence for Israelite Legal Practice'. *VT* 24, no. 3 (1974): 251–67.

Beckman, Gary M., and Theodore J. Lewis, ed. *Text, Artifact, and Image: Revealing Ancient Israelite Religion*. Brown Judaic Studies, 2010.

Belkin, Samuel. 'Levirate and Agnate Marriage in Rabbinic and Cognate Literature'. *JQR* 60, no. 4 (1970): 275–329.

Bell, Catherine M. *Ritual Theory, Ritual Practice*. New York: Oxford University Press, 1992.

Ben-Barak, Zafrira. *Inheritance by Daughters in Israel and the Ancient Near East: A Social, Legal and Ideological Revolution*. Translated by Betty Sigler Rozen. Jaffa: Archaeological Center Publications, 2006.

Bendor, Shunya. *The Social Structure of Ancient Israel: The Institution of the Family (beit 'Ab) from the Settlement to the End of the Monarchy*. JBS 7. Jerusalem: Simor, 1996.

Benson, Susan. 'Injurious Names: Naming, Disavowal, and Recuperation in Contexts of Slavery and Emancipation'. Pages 177–99 in *An Anthropology of Names and Naming*. Edited by Barbara Bodenhorn and Gabriele vom Bruck. Cambridge: Cambridge University Press, 2006.

Berlin, Adele. 'Legal Fiction: Levirate Cum Land Redemption in Ruth'. *JAJ* 1, no. 1 (2010): 3–18.

Berlinerblau, Jacques. 'Ideology, Pierre Bourdieu's Doxa, and the Hebrew Bible'. *Semeia* 87 (1999): 193–214.

Berman, Joshua. 'Ancient Hermeneutics and the Legal Structure of the Book of Ruth'. *ZAW* 119, no. 1 (2007): 22–38.

Bernat, David A. *Sign of the Covenant: Circumcision in the Priestly Tradition*. AIL 3. Atlanta, GA: Society of Biblical Literature, 2009.

Berquist, Jon L. *Controlling Corporeality: The Body and the Household in Ancient Israel*. New Brunswick, NJ: Rutgers University Press, 2002.

Biale, David. *Blood and Belief: The Circulation of a Symbol between Jews and Christians*. Berkeley: University of California Press, 2007.

Blenkinsopp, Joseph. 'Deuteronomy and the Politics of Post-Mortem Existence'. *VT* 45, no. 1 (1995): 1–16.

———. 'The Family in First Temple Israel'. Pages 48–103 in *Families in Ancient Israel*. Edited by Joseph Blenkinsopp, John J. Collins, Carol Meyers, and Leo G. Perdue. Louisville KY: Westminster John Knox, 1997.

Bloch, Maurice. 'Teknonymy and the Evocation of the "Social" Among the Zafimaniry of Madagascar'. Pages 97–114 in *An Anthropology of Names and Naming*. Edited by Barbara Bodenhorn and Gabriele vom Bruck. Cambridge: Cambridge University Press, 2006.

Bloch-Smith, Elizabeth. 'The Cult of the Dead in Judah: Interpreting the Material Remains'. *JBL* 111, no. 2 (1992): 213–24.

———. 'Death in the Life of Israel'. Pages 139–43 in *Sacred Time, Sacred Place: Archaeology and the Religion of Israel*. Edited by Barry M. Gittlen. Winona Lake, IN: Eisenbrauns, 2002.

———. *Judahite Burial Practices and Beliefs about the Dead*. JSOTSup 123. Sheffield: JSOT, 1992.

———. 'Will the Real Massebot Please Stand Up: Cases of Real and Mistakenly Identified Standing Stones in Ancient Israel'. Pages 64–79 in *Text, Artifact, and Image: Revealing Ancient Israelite Religion*. Edited by Gary M. Beckman and Theodore J. Lewis. BJS 346. Providence, RI: Brown Judaic Studies, 2006.

Bodenhorn, Barbara. 'Calling into Being: Naming and Speaking Names on Alaska's North Slope'. Pages 139–56 in *An Anthropology of Names and Naming*. Edited by Barbara Bodenhorn and Gabriele vom Bruck. Cambridge: Cambridge University Press, 2006.

Bodenhorn, Barbara, and Gabriele vom Bruck. 'Entangled in Histories: An Introduction to the Anthropology of Names and Naming'. Pages 1–30 in *An Anthropology of Names and Naming*. Edited by Barbara Bodenhorn and Gabriele vom Bruck. Cambridge: Cambridge University Press, 2006.

Boer, Roland. *The Earthy Nature of the Bible: Fleshly Readings of Sex, Masculinity, and Carnality*. Basingstoke: Palgrave Macmillan, 2012.

———. 'Of Fine Wine, Incense and Spices: The Unstable Masculine Hegemony of the Book of Chronicles'. Pages 20–33 in *Men and Masculinity in the Hebrew Bible and Beyond*. Edited by Ovidiu Creangă. BMW 33. Sheffield: Sheffield Phoenix, 2010.

Borowski, Oded. *Daily Life in Biblical Times*. ABS 5. Atlanta, GA: Society of Biblical Literature, 2003.

Bourdieu, Pierre. *Distinction: A Social Critique of the Judgement of Taste*. Translated by Richard Nice. Cambridge, MA: Harvard University Press, 1984.

———. *In Other Words: Essays Towards a Reflexive Sociology*. Translated by Matthew Adamson. Stanford, CA: Stanford University Press, 1990.

———. *Language and Symbolic Power*. Edited by John Thompson Translated by Gino Raymond and Matthew Adamson. Cambridge: Polity, 1991.

———. *The Logic of Practice*. Translated by Richard Nice. Cambridge: Polity, 1990.

———. *Masculine Domination*. Translated by Richard Nice. Cambridge: Polity, 2001.

———. *Outline of a Theory of Practice*. Translated by Richard Nice. Cambridge Studies in Social Anthropology 16. Cambridge: Cambridge University Press, 1977.

———. *The Rules of Art: Genesis and Structure of the Literary Field*. Translated by Susan Emanuel. Cambridge: Polity Press, 1996.

Bourdieu, Pierre, and Loïc Wacquant. *An Invitation to Reflexive Sociology*. Chicago: University of Chicago Press, 1992.

Boyarin, Daniel. 'Are There Any Jews in "The History of Sexuality"?' *Journal of the History of Sexuality* 5, no. 3 (1995): 333–55.

Bray, Jason S. 'Genesis 23—a Priestly Paradigm for Burial'. *JSOT* 60 (1993): 69–73.

Brenner, Athalya. 'Female Social Behaviour: Two Descriptive Patterns within the "Birth of the Hero" Paradigm'. Pages 204–21 in *Feminist Companion to Genesis*. Edited by Athalya Brenner. FCB 2. Sheffield: Sheffield Academic, 1993.

———. *The Intercourse of Knowledge: On Gendering Desire and 'Sexuality' in the Hebrew Bible*. BibInt 26. Leiden: Brill, 1997.

Brenner, Athalya, and B. O. Long. 'Introduction'. Pages 1–10 in *Performing Memory in Biblical Narrative and Beyond*. Edited by Athalya Brenner and Frank H. Polak. BMW 25. Sheffield: Sheffield Phoenix, 2010.

Brett, Mark G. *Genesis: Procreation and the Politics of Identity*. OTR. London: Routledge, 2000.

Brichto, Herbert Chanan. 'Kin, Cult, Land and Afterlife – A Biblical Complex'. *HUCA* 44 (1973): 1–54.

Britt, Brian M. 'Erasing Amalek: Remembering to Forget with Derrida and the Biblical Tradition'. Pages 61–78 in *Derrida's Bible: Reading a Page of Scripture with a Little Help from Derrida*. Edited by Yvonne Sherwood. Religion/culture/critique. New York: Palgrave Macmillan, 2004.

Brueggemann, Walter. *Genesis*. IBC. Louisville, KY: John Knox, 1982.

Budd, Philip J. *Leviticus: Based on the New Revised Standard Version*. NCBC. London: Marshall Pickering, 1996.

———. *Numbers*. WBC 5. Waco, TX: Word Books, 1984.

Bunimovitz, Shlomo, and Avraham Faust. 'The Judahite Rock-Cut Tomb: Family Response at a Time of Change'. *IEJ* 58, no. 2 (2008): 150–70.

Burrows, Millar. 'The Ancient Oriental Background of Hebrew Levirate Marriage'. *BASOR* 77 (1940): 2–15.

———. 'Levirate Marriage in Israel'. *JBL* 59, no. 1 (1940): 23–33.

Burton, John W. 'Ghost Marriage and the Cattle Trade among the Atuot of the Southern Sudan'. *Africa: Journal of the International African Institute* 48, no. 4 (1978): 398–405.

Butler, Judith. *Excitable Speech: A Politics of the Performative*. New York: Routledge, 1997.

———. *Gender Trouble: Feminism and the Subversion of Identity*. New York: Routledge, 1990.

———. 'Imitation and Gender Insubordination'. Pages 307–20 in *Inside/out: Lesbian Theories, Gay Theories*. Edited by Diana Fuss. New York: Routledge, 1991.

Cairns, Ian. *Word and Presence: A Commentary on the Book of Deuteronomy*. ITC. Grand Rapids, MI: Eerdmans, 1992.

Carmichael, Calum. 'A Ceremonial Crux: Removing a Man's Sandal as a Female Gesture of Contempt'. *JBL* 96, no. 3 (1977): 321–36.

———. *Law, Legend, and Incest in the Bible: Leviticus 18–20*. Ithaca, NY: Cornell University Press, 1997.

Carroll, Robert P. 'Poststructuralist Approaches: New Historicism and Postmodernism'. Pages 50–66 in *The Cambridge Companion to Biblical Interpretation*. Edited by John Barton. Cambridge Companions to Religion. Cambridge: Cambridge University Press, 1998.

Carsten, Janet. *After Kinship*. Cambridge: Cambridge University Press, 2004.

Caserio, Robert L., Tim Dean, Lee Edelman, Judith Halberstam, and José Esteban Muñoz. 'The Antisocial Thesis in Queer Theory'. *PMLA* 121, no. 3 (2006): 816–28.

Chan, Michael J., and Jacob L. Wright. 'King and Eunuch: Isaiah 56:1–8 in Light of Honorific Royal Burial Practices'. *JBL* 131, no. 1 (2012): 99–119.

Chapman, Cynthia R. 'The Biblical "House of the Mother" and the Brokering of Marriage: Economic Reciprocity Among Natal Siblings'. Pages 143–70 in *In the Wake of Tikva Frymer-Kensky*. Edited by Steven Holloway, JoAnn Scurlock, and Richard Beal. Gorgias Précis Portfolios 4. Piscataway, NJ: Gorgias Press, 2009.

———. *The House of the Mother: The Social Roles of Maternal Kin in Biblical Hebrew Narrative and Poetry*. AYBRL. New Haven: Yale University Press, 2016.

Clines, David J. A. *Interested Parties: The Ideology of Writers and Readers of the Hebrew Bible*. JSOTSup 205. Sheffield: Sheffield Academic, 1995.
Coats, George W. 'Widow's Rights: A Crux in the Structure of Genesis 38'. *Catholic Biblical Quarterly* 34, no. 4 (1972): 461–6.
Collins, Peter. 'Virgins in Spirit: The Celibacy of the Shakers'. Pages 104–21 in *Celibacy, Culture, And Society: Anthropology of Sexual Abstinence*. Edited by Elisa J. Sobo and Sandra Bell. Madison, WI: University of Wisconsin Press, 2001.
Connell, Catherine, and Ashley Mears. 'Bourdieu and the Body'. Pages 561–76 in *The Oxford Handbook of Pierre Bourdieu*. Edited by Thomas Medvetz and Jeffrey J. Sallaz. New York: Oxford University Press, 2018.
Connerton, Paul. *How Societies Remember*. Themes in the Social Sciences. Cambridge: Cambridge University Press, 1989.
Coogan, Michael David. *The Ten Commandments: A Short History of an Ancient Text*. New Haven, CT: Yale University Press, 2014.
Cooper, Alan, and Bernard Goldstein. 'The Cult of the Dead and the Theme of Entry Into the Land'. *BibInt* 1, no. 3 (1993): 285–303.
Creangă, Ovidiu, ed. *Men and Masculinity in the Hebrew Bible and Beyond*. BMW 33. Sheffield: Sheffield Phoenix, 2010.
Crossley, Nick. 'The Phenomenological Habitus and Its Construction'. *Theory and Society* 30, no. 1 (2001): 81–120.
Csordas, Thomas J. *Body, Meaning, Healing*. Basingstoke: Palgrave Macmillan, 2002.
Dahood, Mitchell J. *Psalms I: 1–50. Introduction, Translation, and Notes*. AB 16. New York: Doubleday, 1966.
Davies, Eryl W. 'Inheritance Rights and the Hebrew Levirate Marriage: Part 1'. *VT* 31, no. 2 (1981): 138–44.
———. 'Inheritance Rights and the Hebrew Levirate Marriage: Part 2'. *Vetus Testamentum* 31, no. 3 (1981): 257–68.
Day, John. 'The Development of Belief in Life after Death in Ancient Israel'. Pages 231–57 in *After the Exile: Essays in Honour of Rex Mason*. Edited by John Barton and David James Reimer. Macon, GA: Mercer University Press, 1996.
Deist, Ferdinand. *The Material Culture of the Bible: An Introduction*. BibSem 70. Sheffield: Sheffield Academic, 2000.
Delaney, Carol. 'Cutting the Ties That Bind: Sacrifice of Abraham and Patriarchal Kinship'. Pages 445–67 in *Relative Values: Reconfiguring Kinship Studies*. Edited by Sarah Franklin and Susan McKinnon. Durham, NC: Duke University Press, 2001.
———. 'The Meaning of Paternity and the Virgin Birth Debate'. *Man* 21, no. 3 (1986): 494–513.
van Dijk-Hemmes, Fokkelien. 'Tamar and the Limits of Patriarchy: Between Rape and Seduction (2 Samuel 13 and Genesis 38)'. Pages 68–88 in *The Double Voice of Her Desire: Texts*. Edited by Jonneke Bekkenkamp and Freda Dröes, Translated by David E. Orton. Tools for Biblical Study 6. Leiden: Deo Publishing, 2004.
Dinshaw, Carolyn, Lee Edelman, Roderick A. Ferguson, Carla Freccero, Elizabeth Freeman, Judith Halberstam, Annamarie Jagose, Christopher S. Nealon, and Tan Hoang Nguyen. 'Theorizing Queer Temporalities: A Roundtable Discussion'. *GLQ: A Journal of Lesbian and Gay Studies* 13, no. 2 (2007): 177–95.
Doniger, Wendy. *The Bedtrick: Tales of Sex and Masquerade*. Chicago: University of Chicago Press, 2000.

Douglas, Mary. *Jacob's Tears: The Priestly Work of Reconciliation*. Oxford: Oxford University Press, 2004.

———. *Purity and Danger: An Analysis of Concepts of Pollution and Taboo*. London: Routledge & Kegan Paul, 1966.

Dutcher-Walls, Patricia. 'The Clarity of Double Vision: Seeing the Family in Sociological and Archaeological Perspective'. Pages 1–15 in *The Family in Life and in Death: The Family in Ancient Israel: Sociological and Archaeological Perspectives*. Edited by Patricia Dutcher-Walls. LHBOTS 504. New York: T&T Clark, 2009.

Edelman, Lee. 'The Future Is Kid Stuff: Queer Theory, Disidentification, and the Death Drive'. *Narrative* 6, no. 1 (1998): 18–30.

———. *No Future: Queer Theory and the Death Drive*. Durham, NC: Duke University Press, 2004.

Edenburg, Cynthia. 'Ideology and Social Context of the Deuteronomic Women's Sex Laws (Deuteronomy 22:13-29)'. *JBL* 128, no. 1 (2009): 43–60.

Eichrodt, Walther. *Theology of the Old Testament*. Translated by J. A. Baker. OTL 1. London: SCM, 1961.

Eilberg-Schwartz, Howard. *God's Phallus and Other Problems for Men and Monotheism*. Boston: Beacon Press, 1994.

———. *The Savage in Judaism: An Anthropology of Israelite Religion and Ancient Judaism*. Bloomington, IN: Indiana University Press, 1990.

Ellens, Deborah L. *Women in the Sex Texts of Leviticus and Deuteronomy: A Comparative Conceptual Analysis*. LHBOTS 458. New York: T&T Clark, 2008.

Emerton, John A. 'Judah and Tamar'. *VT* 29, no. 4 (1979): 403–15.

Exum, Cheryl. 'Second Thoughts about Secondary Characters'. Pages 75–87 in *Feminist Companion to Exodus to Deuteronomy*. Edited by Athalya Brenner. FCB 6. Sheffield: Sheffield Academic, 1994.

———. '"You Shall Let Every Daughter Live": A Study of Exodus 1.8–2.10'. *Semeia* 28 (1983): 63–82.

Fantalkin, Alexander. 'The Appearance of Rock-Cut Bench Tombs in Iron Age Judah as a Reflection of State Formation'. Pages 17–44 in *Bene Israel: Studies in the Archaeology of Israel and the Levant during the Bronze and Iron Ages in Honour of Israel Finkelstein*. Edited by Alexander Fantalkin and Assaf Yasur-Landau. CHANE 31. Leiden, Boston: Brill, 2008.

Fewell, Danna N., and David M. Gunn. *Gender, Power, and Promise: The Subject of the Bible's First Story*. Nashville: Abingdon Press, 1993.

———. *Narrative in the Hebrew Bible*. New York: Oxford University Press, 1993.

Finley, Moses I. 'The Ancient City: From Fustel de Coulanges to Max Weber and Beyond'. *Comparative Studies in Society and History* 19, no. 3 (1977): 305–27.

Fischer, Irmtraud. 'The Book of Ruth: A "Feminist" Commentary to the Torah?' Pages 24–49 *Ruth and Esther: A Feminist Companion to the Bible*. Edited by Athalya Brenner. FCB Second Series 3. Sheffield: Sheffield Academic, 1999.

Fleishman, Joseph. 'Shechem and Dinah in the Light of Non-Biblical and Biblical Sources'. *ZAW* 116, no. 1 (2004): 12–32.

Fortes, Meyer. 'Some Reflections on Ancestor Worship in West Africa'. Pages 122–42 *African Systems of Thought: Studies Presented and Discussed at the Third International African Seminar in Salisbury, December 1960*. Edited by Meyer Fortes and Germaine Dieterlen. London: Oxford University Press, 1965.

Foucault, Michel. *The History of Sexuality, Vol. 1: An Introduction*. Translated by Robert Hurley. New York: Vintage, 1980.

Franklin, Sarah, and Susan McKinnon. 'Introduction'. Pages 1–25 in *Relative Values: Reconfiguring Kinship Studies*. Edited by Sarah Franklin and Susan McKinnon. Durham, NC: Duke University Press, 2001.

———. *Relative Values: Reconfiguring Kinship Studies*. Durham, NC: Duke University Press, 2001.

Freeman, Elizabeth. *Time Binds: Queer Temporalities, Queer Histories*. Durham, NC: Duke University Press, 2010.

Frug, Mary Jo. 'A Postmodern Feminist Legal Manifesto (An Unfinished Draft)'. Pages 7–23 in *After Identity: A Reader in Law and Culture*. Edited by Dan Danielsen and Karen Engle. New York: Routledge, 1995.

Frymer-Kensky, Tikva. 'Deuteronomy'. *Women's Bible Commentary: Expanded Edition*. Edited by Carol Ann Newsom and Sharon H. Ringe. Louisville KT: Westminster John Knox, 1998.

———. *Studies in Bible and Feminist Criticism*. Philadelphia: Jewish Publication Society, 2006.

Fuchs, Esther. *Sexual Politics in the Biblical Narrative: Reading the Hebrew Bible as a Woman*. JSOTSup 310. Sheffield: Sheffield Academic, 2000.

Gafney, Wil. 'Mother Knows Best: Messianic Surrogacy and Sexploitation in Ruth'. Pages 23–36 in *Mother Goose, Mother Jones, Mommie Dearest: Biblical Mothers and Their Children*. Edited by Cheryl A. Kirk-Duggan and Tina Pippin. SemeiaSt 61. Atlanta, GA: Society of Biblical Literature, 2009.

Galpaz-Feller, Pnina. 'The Widow in the Bible and in Ancient Egypt'. *ZAW* 120, no. 2 (2008): 231–53.

Geertz, Clifford. *The Interpretation of Cultures: Selected Essays*. London: Hutchinson, 1975.

George, A. R, ed. *The Babylonian Gilgamesh Epic: Introduction, Critical Edition*. Oxford: Oxford University Press, 2003.

George, Mark. 'Masculinity and Its Regimentation in Deuteronomy'. Pages 64–82 in *Men and Masculinity in the Hebrew Bible and Beyond*. Edited by Ovidiu Creangă. BMW 33. Sheffield: Sheffield Phoenix, 2010.

Gevirtz, Stanley. 'West-Semitic Curses and the Problem of the Origins of Hebrew Law'. *VT* 11, no. 2 (1961): 137–58.

Giladi, Avner. *Infants, Parents and Wet Nurses: Medieval Islamic Views on Breastfeeding and Their Social Implications*. Leiden: Brill, 1999.

Gillespie, Susan D. 'Beyond Kinship: An Introduction'. Pages 1–21 in *Beyond Kinship: Social and Material Reproduction in House Societies*. Edited by Rosemary A. Joyce and Susan D. Gillespie. Philadelphia: University of Pennsylvania Press, 2000.

Gluckman, Max. 'Mortuary Customs and the Belief in Survival after Death among the South-Eastern Bantu'. *Bantu Studies* 11, no. 1 (1937): 117–36.

———. 'The Role of the Sexes in Wiko Circumcision Ceremonies'. Pages 145–67 in *Social Structure*. Edited by Meyers Fortes. Oxford: Clarendon Press, 1949.

Golden, Charles. 'Where Does Memory Reside, and Why Isn't It History?' *American Anthropologist* 107, no. 2 (2005): 270–4.

Goulder, Michael D. 'Ruth: A Homily on Deuteronomy 22–25?' Pages 307–19 in *Of Prophets' Visions and the Wisdom of Sages: Essays in Honour of R. Norman Whybray on His Seventieth Birthday*. Edited by Heather A. McKay and David J. A. Clines. JSOTSup 162. Sheffield: JSOT, 1993.

Greenberg, Martin. 'Judah and Tamar'. *Dor Le Dor* 16, no. 2 (1987): 123–5.

Guenther, Allen. 'A Typology of Israelite Marriage: Kinship, Socio-Economic, and Religious Factors'. *JSOT* 29, no. 4 (2005): 387–407.
Guyer, Jane I. 'Widow Inheritance and Marriage Law: A Social History'. Pages 193–219 in *Widows in African Societies: Choices and Constraints*. Edited by Betty Potash. Stanford: Stanford University Press, 1986.
Gwako, Edwins Laban Moogi. 'Widow Inheritance among the Maragoli of Western Kenya'. *Journal of Anthropological Research* 54, no. 2 (1998): 173–98.
Haddox, Susan. 'Favoured Sons and Subordinate Masculinities'. Pages 2–19 in *Men and Masculinity in the Hebrew Bible and Beyond*. Edited by Ovidiu Creangă. BMW 33. Sheffield: Sheffield Phoenix, 2010.
Hakim, Catherine. *Erotic Capital: The Power of Attraction in the Boardroom and the Bedroom*. New York: Basic Books, 2011.
Halberstam, Judith. *The Queer Art of Failure*. Durham, NC: Duke University Press, 2011.
Hamilton, Victor P. *The Book of Genesis: 18–50*. NICOT. Grand Rapids, MI: Eerdmans, 1995.
Hammer, Dean. 'Bourdieu, Ideology, and the Ancient World'. *The American Journal of Semiotics* 22, no. 1 (2006): 87–108.
Harker, Richard, Cheleen Mahar, and Chris Wilkes. 'The Basic Theoretical Position'. Pages 1–25 in *An Introduction to the Work of Pierre Bourdieu: The Practice of Theory*. Edited by Richard Harker, Cheleen Mahar, and Chris Wilkes. London: Macmillan, 1990.
Harris, R. Laird. 'Why Hebrew Shĕ'ōl Was Translated "Grave"'. Pages 75–92 in *The Making of a Contemporary Translation: New International Version*. Edited by Kenneth Barker. London: Hodder and Stoughton, 1987.
Hays, Christopher B. 'Re-Excavating Shebna's Tomb: A New Reading of Isa 22,15–19 in Its Ancient Near Eastern Context'. *ZAW* 122, no. 4 (2010): 558–75.
Heady, Patrick and Peter Loizos, eds. *Conceiving Persons: Ethnographies of Procreation, Fertility and Growth*. London: Continuum, 2003.
———. 'Introduction'. Pages 1–17 in *Conceiving Persons: Ethnographies of Procreation, Fertility and Growth*. Edited by Patrick Heady and Peter Loizos. London: Continuum, 2003.
Hendel, Ronald. 'Mary Douglas and Anthropological Modernism'. *JHS* 8 (2008).
Hess, Richard. 'Aspects of Israelite Personal Names and Pre-Exilic Israelite Religion'. Pages 301–13 in *New Seals and Inscriptions, Hebrew, Idumean, and Cuneiform*. Edited by Meir Lubetski. HBM 8. Sheffield: Sheffield Phoenix, 2007.
Hiers, Richard H. 'Transfer of Property by Inheritance and Bequest in Biblical Law and Tradition'. *Journal of Law and Religion* 10, no. 1 (1993): 121–55.
Hillers, Delbert. 'Some Performative Utterances in the Bible'. Pages 757–66 in *Pomegranates and Golden Bells: Studies in Biblical, Jewish, and Near Eastern Ritual, Law, and Literature in Honor of Jacob Milgrom*. Edited by David P. Wright, David N. Freedman, and Avi Hurvitz. Winona Lake, IN: Eisenbrauns, 1995.
Hoang, Kimberly Kay. *Dealing in Desire: Asian Ascendancy, Western Decline, and the Hidden Currencies of Global Sex Work*. Oakland, CA: University of California Press, 2015.
Hoffman, Lawrence A. *Covenant of Blood: Circumcision and Gender in Rabbinic Judaism*. CSHJ. Chicago: University of Chicago Press, 1996.

Horbury, William. 'Extirpation and Excommunication'. *VT* 35, no. 1 (1985): 13–38.
Howell, Signe. 'Self-Conscious Kinship: Some Contested Values in Norwegian Transnational Adoption'. Pages 203–23 in *Relative Values: Reconfiguring Kinship Studies*. Edited by Sarah Franklin and Susan McKinnon. Durham, NC: Duke University Press, 2001.
Hoy, David Couzens. 'Critical Resistance: Foucault and Bourdieu'. Pages 3–22 in *Perspectives on Embodiment: The Intersections of Nature and Culture*. Edited by Gail Weiss and Honi Fern Haber. New York: Routledge, 1999.
Huddlestun, John R. 'Unveiling the Versions: The Tactics of Tamar in Genesis 38:15'. *JHS* 3 (2001).
Humphrey, Caroline. 'On Being Named and Not Named: Authority, Persons, and Their Names in Mongolia'. Pages 157–76 in *An Anthropology of Names and Naming*. Edited by Barbara Bodenhorn and Gabriele vom Bruck. Cambridge: Cambridge University Press, 2006.
Hundley, Michael. 'To Be or Not to Be: A Reexamination of Name Language in Deuteronomy and the Deuteronomistic History'. *VT* 59, no. 4 (2009): 533–55.
Hurowitz, Victor A. 'Name Midrashim and the Word Plays on Names in Akkadian Historical Writings'. Pages 87–104 *A Woman of Valor: Jerusalem Ancient Near Eastern Studies in Honor of Joan Goodnick Westenholz*. Edited by Wayne Horowitz, Uri Gabbay, and Filip Vukosavovic. Biblioteca Del Próximo Oriente Antiguo 8. Madrid: Consejo Superior de Investigaciones Científicas, 2010.

———. 'Review of Sandra L. Richter, The Deuteronomistic History and the Name Theology: *Lešakkēn šemô šām* in the Bible and the Ancient Near East'. *JHS* 5, Review (2004).

Iteanu, André. 'Why the Dead Do Not Bear Names: The Orokaiva Name System'. Pages 51–72 in *An Anthropology of Names and Naming*. Edited by Barbara Bodenhorn and Gabriele vom Bruck. Cambridge: Cambridge University Press, 2006.
Jackson, Bernard S. 'The "Institutions" of Marriage and Divorce in the Hebrew Bible'. *JSS* 56, no. 2 (2011): 221–51.
Jacobs, Sandra. 'Divine Virility in Priestly Representation: Its Memory and Consummation in Rabbinic Midrash'. Pages 146–70 in *Men and Masculinity in the Hebrew Bible and Beyond*. Edited by Ovidiu Creangă. BMW 33. Sheffield: Sheffield Phoenix, 2010.
Jagose, Annamarie. *Queer Theory: An Introduction*. New York: New York University Press, 1996.
Japhet, Sara. '*Yd Wšm* [Isa. 56:5]—A Different Proposal'. *MAARAV* 8 (1992): 69–80.
Jay, Nancy. 'Sacrifice, Descent and the Patriarchs'. *VT* 38, no. 1 (1988): 52–70.

———. *Throughout Your Generations Forever: Sacrifice, Religion, and Paternity*. Chicago: University of Chicago Press, 1993.

Jeansonne, Sharon Pace. *The Women of Genesis: From Sarah to Potiphar's Wife*. Minneapolis, MN: Fortress Press, 1990.
Josephus, Flavius. *Jewish Antiquities I–IV*. Translated by Henry St. John Thackeray and Ralph Marcus. Leob Classical Library 210. Cambridge, MA: Heinemann; Harvard University Press, 1930.
Kaufmann, Yeḥezkel. *The Religion of Israel: From Its Beginnings to the Babylonian Exile*. Translated by Moshe Greenberg. London: Allen & Unwin, 1961.

Kelly, Raymond. *Constructing Inequality: The Fabrication of a Hierarchy of Virtue among the Etoro*. Ann Arbor, MI: University of Michigan Press, 1993.

———. 'Witchcraft and Sexual Relations: An Exploration in the Social and Semantic Implications of the Structure of Belief'. Pages 36–53 in *Man and Woman in the New Guinea Highlands*. Edited by Paula Brown, Georgeda Buchbinder, and David Maybury-Lewis. Washington, DC: American Anthropological Association, 1976.

Kertzer, David I. *Ritual, Politics, and Power*. New Haven, CT: Yale University Press, 1988.

King, Philip J., and Lawrence E. Stager. *Life in Biblical Israel*. LAI. Louisville, KY: Westminster John Knox, 2001.

Klawans, Jonathan. 'Pure Violence: Sacrifice and Defilement in Ancient Israel'. *HTR* 94, no. 2 (2001): 135–57.

LaCocque, André. *Ruth: A Continental Commentary*. Translated by K. C. Hanson. CC. Philadelphia: Fortress Press, 2004.

Laird, Donna. *Negotiating Power in Ezra-Nehemiah*. AIL 26. Atlanta, GA: SBL Press, 2016.

Lambek, Michael. 'What's in a Name? Name Bestowal and the Identity of Spirits in Mayotte and Northwest Madagascar'. Pages 115–38 in *An Anthropology of Names and Naming*. Edited by Barbara Bodenhorn and Gabriele vom Bruck. Cambridge: Cambridge University Press, 2006.

Lamont, Michèle. 'How Has Bourdieu Been Good to Think with? The Case of the United States'. *Sociological Forum* 27, no. 1 (2012): 228–37.

Lane, Jeremy. *Pierre Bourdieu: A Critical Introduction*. London: Pluto, 2000.

LaRocca-Pitts, Elizabeth C. *Of Wood and Stone: The Significance of Israelite Cultic Items in the Bible and Its Early Interpreters*. HSM 61. Winona Lake, IN: Eisenbrauns, 2001.

Lawler, Steph. 'Rules of Engagement: Habitus, Power and Resistance'. Pages 110–28 in *Feminism after Bourdieu*. Edited by Lisa Adkins and Beverley Skeggs. Oxford: Blackwell, 2004.

Layne, Linda. '"Your Child Deserves a Name": Possessive Individualism and the Politics of Memory in Pregnancy Loss'. Pages 31–50 in *An Anthropology of Names and Naming*. Edited by Barbara Bodenhorn and Gabriele vom Bruck. Cambridge: Cambridge University Press, 2006.

Leach, Edmund. *Social Anthropology*. New York: Oxford University Press, 1982.

———. 'Virgin Birth'. *Proceedings of the Royal Anthropological Institute of Great Britain and Ireland* (1966): 39–49.

Leggett, Donald A. *The Levirate and Goel Institutions in the Old Testament: With Special Attention to the Book of Ruth*. Cherry Hill, NJ: Mack, 1974.

Lemos, Tracy M. *Violence and Personhood in Ancient Israel and Comparative Contexts*. Oxford: Oxford University Press, 2017.

Levine, Baruch. 'The Clan-Based Economy of Biblical Israel'. Pages 445–54 in *Symbiosis, Symbolism, and the Power of the Past: Canaan, Ancient Israel, and Their Neighbors from the Late Bronze Age Through Roman Palaestina*. Edited by William Dever and Seymour Gitin. Winona Lake, IN: Eisenbrauns, 2003.

———. 'In Praise of the Israelite Mišpāḥâ: Legal Themes in the Book of Ruth"'. Pages 95–106 in *The Quest for the Kingdom of God: Studies in Honor of George E. Mendenhall*. Edited by Herbert Huffmon, Frank Spina, and Alberto R. Green. Winona Lake, IN: Eisenbrauns, 1983.

———. *Leviticus*. JPSTC. Philadelphia: Jewish Publication Society, 1994.

———. *Numbers 21–36: A New Translation with Introduction and Commentary*. AB 4A. New York: Doubleday, 2000.
Levine, Etan. 'On Intra-Familial Institutions of the Bible'. *Biblica* 57, no. 4 (1976): 554–9.
Lévi-Strauss, Claude. *Anthropology and Myth: Lectures, 1951–1982*. Translated by Roy G. Willis. Oxford: Basil Blackwell, 1987.
———. *The Way of the Masks*. Translated by Sylvia Modelski. Seattle: University of Washington Press, 1982.
Lewis, Theodore J. 'The Ancestral Estate (נחלת אלהים) in 2 Samuel 14:16'. *JBL* 110, no. 4 (1991): 597–612.
———. *Cults of the Dead in Ancient Israel and Ugarit*. HSM 39. Atlanta, GA: Scholars Press, 1989.
———. 'Family, Household, and Local Religion at Late Bronze Age Ugarit'. Pages 60–88 in *Household and Family Religion in Antiquity*. Edited by John Bodel and Saul M. Olyan. The Ancient World: Comparative Histories. Malden, MA: Blackwell, 2008.
———. 'How Far Can Texts Take Us? Evaluating Textual Sources for Reconstructing Ancient Israelite Beliefs about the Dead'. Pages 169–217 in *Sacred Time, Sacred Place: Archaeology and the Religion of Israel*. Edited by Barry M. Gittlen. Winona Lake, IN: Eisenbrauns, 2002.
Lipton, Diana. 'Remembering Amalek: A Positive Biblical Model for Dealing with Negative Scriptural Types'. Pages 139–53 in *Reading Texts, Seeking Wisdom: Scripture and Theology*. Edited by Graham Stanton and David F. Ford. London: SCM, 2003.
Lods, Adolphe. *Israel: From Its Beginnings to the Middle of the Eighth Century*. Translated by Samuel H. Hooke. The History of Civilization. London: Routledge & Kegan Paul, 1932.
Lovell, Terry. 'Thinking Feminism With and Against Bourdieu'. *Sociological Review* 1, no. 1 (2000): 11–32.
Lowisch, Ingeborg. 'Genealogies, Gender and the Politics of Memory: 1 Chronicles 1–9 and the Documentary Film Mein Leben Teil 2'. Pages 228–56 in *Performing Memory in Biblical Narrative and Beyond*. Edited by Athalya Brenner and Frank H. Polak. BMW 25. Sheffield: Sheffield Phoenix, 2010.
Lyke, Larry L. *King David with the Wise Woman of Tekoa: The Resonance of Tradition in Parabolic Narrative*. JSOTSup 225. Sheffield: Sheffield Academic, 1997.
Mace, David Robert. *Hebrew Marriage: A Sociological Study*. London: Epworth Press, 1953.
Mahmood, Saba. *Politics of Piety: The Islamic Revival and the Feminist Subject*. Princeton, NJ: Princeton University Press, 2005.
Malul, Meir. ' *'āqēb* "Heel" and *'āqab* "To Supplant" and the Concept of Succession in the Jacob–Esau Narratives'. *VT* 46, no. 2 (1996): 190–212.
———. *Knowledge, Control and Sex: Studies in Biblical Thought, Culture, and Worldview*. Tel Aviv-Jaffa: Archaeological Center, 2002.
Mann, Thomas. *Joseph and His Brothers*. Translated by John E. Woods. New York: Knopf, 2005.
Mars, Leonard. 'What Was Onan's Crime?' *CSSH* 26, no. 3 (1984): 429–39.
Martin, Diana. 'Chinese Ghost Marriage'. Pages 25–43 in *An Old State in New Settings: Studies in the Social Anthropology of China in Memory of Maurice Freedman*. Edited by Hugh D. R. Baker and Stephan Feuchtwang. Oxford: JASO, 1991.
Martin, Emily. 'The Egg and the Sperm: How Science Has Constructed a Romance Based on Stereotypical Male-Female Roles'. *Signs* 16, no. 3 (1991): 485–501.

Matlock, Michael D. 'Obeying the First Part of the Tenth Commandment: Applications from the Levirate Marriage Law'. *JSOT* 31, no. 3 (2007): 295–310.

Maynes, Mary Jo, Ann Waltner, Birgitte Soland, and Ulrike Strasser, eds. *Gender, Kinship, Power: A Comparative and Interdisciplinary History*. New York: Routledge, 1996.

McCarter Jr., Peter Kyle. *I Samuel: A New Translation with Introduction, Notes and Commentary*. AB 8. New York: Doubleday, 1980.

McNutt, Paula M. *Reconstructing the Society of Ancient Israel*. Library of Ancient Israel. Louisville, KY: Westminster John Knox, 1999.

Menn, Esther Marie. *Judah and Tamar (Genesis 38) in Ancient Jewish Exegesis: Studies in Literary Form and Hermeneutics*. JSJSup 51. Leiden: Brill, 1997.

Meyers, Carol. 'The Family in Early Israel'. Pages 1–47 in *Families in Ancient Israel*. Edited by Joseph Blenkinsopp, John J. Collins, Carol Meyers, and Leo G. Perdue. The Family, Religion, and Culture. Louisville, KY: Westminster John Knox, 1997.

———. 'Household Religion'. Pages 118–34 in *Religious Diversity in Ancient Israel and Judah*. Edited by Francesca Stavrakopoulou and John Barton. London: T&T Clark, 2010.

———. 'Was Ancient Israel a Patriarchal Society?' *JBL* 133, no. 1 (2014): 8–27.

Meyers, Eric M. 'Secondary Burials in Palestine'. *BA* 33, no. 1 (1970): 1–29.

Milgrom, Jacob. 'The Dynamics of Purity in the Priestly System'. Pages 29–32 in *Purity and Holiness: The Heritage of Leviticus*. Edited by Marcel Poorthuis and Joshua Schwartz. Jewish and Christian Perspectives 2. Leiden: Brill, 2000.

———. *Leviticus 1–16: A New Translation with Introduction and Commentary*. AB 3. New York: Doubleday, 1991.

———. *Numbers*. JPSTC. Philadelphia: Jewish Publication Society, 1992.

Morris, Ian. 'Attitudes toward Death in Archaic Greece'. *Classical Antiquity* 8, no. 2 (1989): 296–320.

Morrow, William. '"To Set the Name" in the Deuteronomic Centralization Formula: A Case of Cultural Hybridity'. *JSS* 55, no. 2 (2010): 365–83.

Muñoz, José Esteban. *Cruising Utopia: The Then and There of Queer Futurity*. New York: New York University Press, 2009.

Nelson, Richard D. *Deuteronomy: A Commentary*. OTL. Louisville, KY: Westminster John Knox, 2002.

Nestor, Dermot. *Cognitive Perspectives on Israelite Identity*. LHBOTS 519. New York: T&T Clark, 2010.

———. 'Merneptah's "Israel" and the Absence of Origins in Biblical Scholarship'. *Currents in Biblical Research* 13, no. 3 (2015): 293–329.

Neufeld, Ephraim. *Ancient Hebrew Marriage Laws: With Special References to General Semitic Laws and Customs*. London: Longmans, Green and Co, 1944.

Neusner, Jacob. *Genesis Rabbah: The Judaic Commentary to the Book of Genesis: A New American Translation*. Vol. 3 of *BJS* 104. Atlanta, GA: Scholars Press, 1985.

Niditch, Susan. 'The Wronged Woman Righted: An Analysis of Genesis 38'. *HTR* 72, nos. 1–2 (1979): 143–9.

Niehr, Herbert. 'The Changed Status of the Dead in Yehud'. Pages 136–55 in *Yahwism After the Exile: Perspectives on Israelite Religion in the Persian Era*. Edited by Rainer Albertz and Bob Becking. Studies in Theology and Religion 5. Assen: Royal Van Gorcum, 2003.

Noth, Martin. *Numbers: A Commentary*. Translated by James Martin. OTL. London: SCM, 1968.

Nyanzi, Stella. 'Widow Inheritance'. Pages 60–4 in *Men of the Global South: A Reader*. Edited by Adam Jones. London: Zed, 2006.

Oboler, Regina Smith. 'Nandi Widows'. Pages 66–83 in *Widows in African Societies: Choices and Constraints*. Edited by Betty Potash. Stanford: Stanford University Press, 1986.

Ockinga, B. G. 'A Note on 2 Samuel 18.18'. *BN* 31 (1986): 31–4.

O'Connor, David B. 'Thutmose III: An Enigmatic Pharaoh'. Pages 1–38 in *Thutmose III: A New Biography*. Edited by Eric H. Cline and David B. O'Connor. Ann Arbor, MI: University of Michigan Press, 2006.

Olyan, Saul M. 'Family Religion in Israel and the Wider Levant of the First Millennium BCE'. Pages 113–26 in *Household and Family Religion in Antiquity*. Edited by John Bodel and Saul M. Olyan. The Ancient World: Comparative Histories. Malden, MA: Blackwell, 2008.

———. 'Some Neglected Aspects of Israelite Interment Ideology'. *JBL* 124, no. 4 (2005): 601–16.

———. 'Unnoticed Resonances of Tomb Opening and Transportation of the Remains of the Dead in Ezekiel 37:12-14'. *JBL* 128, no. 3 (2009): 491–501.

———. '"We Are Utterly Cut Off": Some Possible Nuances of נגזרנו לנו in Ezek 37:11'. *CBQ* 65, no. 1 (2003): 43–51.

Owen, Margaret. *A World of Widows*. London: Zed Books, 1996.

Pardee, Dennis. *Ritual and Cult at Ugarit*. WAW 10. Atlanta, GA: Society of Biblical Literature, 2002.

Parker, Julie F. *Valuable and Vulnerable: Children in the Hebrew Bible, Especially the Elisha Cycle*. BJS 355. Providence, RI: Brown Judaic Studies, 2013.

Parkes, Peter. 'Fosterage, Kinship, and Legend: When Milk Was Thicker than Blood?' *CSSH* 46, no. 3 (2004): 587–615.

Pedersen, Johannes. *Israel: Its Life and Culture*. London: Oxford University Press, 1926.

Perdue, Leo G. 'The Israelite and Early Jewish Family: Summary and Conclusions'. Pages 163–222 in *Families in Ancient Israel*. Edited by Joseph Blenkinsopp, John J. Collins, Carol Meyers, and Leo G. Perdue. The Family, Religion, and Culture. Louisville, KY: Westminster John Knox, 1997.

Pitard, Wayne T. 'Tombs and Offerings: Archaeological Data and Comparative Methodology in the Study of Death in Israel'. Pages 145–68 in *Sacred Time, Sacred Place: Archaeology and the Religion of Israel*. Edited by Barry M. Gittlen. Winona Lake, IN: Eisenbrauns, 2002.

Polhemus, Robert M. *Lot's Daughters: Sex, Redemption, and Women's Quest for Authority*. Stanford, CA: Stanford University Press, 2005.

Potash, Betty. 'Wives of the Grave: Widows in a Rural Luo Community'. Pages 44–65 in *Widows in African Societies: Choices and Constraints*. Edited by Betty Potash. Stanford: Stanford University Press, 1986.

Pressler, Carolyn. 'Sexual Violence and Deuteronomic Law'. Pages 102–12 in *A Feminist Companion to Exodus to Deuteronomy*. Edited by Athalya Brenner. FCB 6. Sheffield: Sheffield Academic, 1994.

———. *The View of Women Found in the Deuteronomic Family Laws*. BZAW 216. Berlin: de Gruyter, 1993.

Preuss, Horst Dietrich. *Old Testament Theology*. Translated by Leo G. Perdue. Vol. II of *OTL*. Louisville, KY: Westminster John Knox, 1995.

Propp, William Henry. *Exodus 19–40: A New Translation with Introduction and Commentary*. AB 2A. New York: Doubleday, 2006.

von Rad, Gerhard. *Genesis: A Commentary*. Translated by John Marks. Revised. OTL. London: SCM, 1972.
———. *Studies in Deuteronomy*. Translated by David Stalker. SBT 9. London: SCM Press, 1953.
Ramsey, George W. 'Is Name-Giving an Act of Domination in Genesis 2:23 and Elsewhere?' *CBQ* 50, no. 1 (1988): 24–35.
Rappaport, Roy A. *Ritual and Religion in the Making of Humanity*. Cambridge: Cambridge University Press, 1999.
Rashkow, Ilona N. *Taboo Or Not Taboo: Sexuality and Family in the Hebrew Bible*. Minneapolis, MN: Fortress Press, 2000.
Reed-Danahay, Deborah. *Locating Bourdieu*. New Anthropologies of Europe. Bloomington, IN: Indiana University Press, 2005.
Rey, Terry. *Bourdieu on Religion: Imposing Faith and Legitimacy*. London: Equinox, 2007.
Ribar, John Whalen. *Death Cult Practices in Ancient Palestine*. PhD Diss., University of Michigan, 1973.
Richardson, Seth. 'Death and Dismemberment in Mesopotamia: Discorporation Between the Body and Body Politic'. Pages 189–208 in *Performing Death*. Edited by Nicola Laneri. OIS 3. Chicago: Oriental Institute of the University of Chicago, 2007.
Richter, Sandra L. *The Deuteronomistic History and the Name Theology: Lešakkēn šemô šām in the Bible*. BZAW 318. Berlin: de Gruyter, 2002.
Robinson, G. 'The Meaning of יד in Isa 56,5'. *ZAW* 88 (1976): 282–84.
Rofé, Alexander. 'Family and Sex Laws in Deuteronomy and the Book of the Covenant'. *Henoch* 9, no. 2 (1987): 131–60.
Rooke, Deborah W. 'The Bare Facts: Gender and Nakedness in Leviticus 18'. Pages 20–38 *A Question of Sex? Gender and Difference in the Hebrew Bible and Beyond*. Edited by Deborah W. Rooke. HBM 14. Sheffield: Sheffield Phoenix, 2007.
Rowley, Harold H. 'The Marriage of Ruth'. *HTR* 40, no. 2 (1947): 77–99.
Rubin, Gayle. 'The Traffic in Women: Notes on the "Political Economy" of Sex'. Pages 157–210 in *Toward an Anthropology of Women*. Edited by Rayna R. Reiter. Monthly Review Press: Routledge, 1975.
Rudman, Dominic. 'Mitteilungen: The Use of Water Imagery in Descriptions of Sheol'. *ZAW* 113, no. 2 (2001): 240–4.
Sahgal, Smita. *Niyoga: Alternative Mechanisms to Lineage Perpetuation in Early India: A Socio-Historical Enquiry*. Delhi: Indian Council of Historical Research, 2017.
Sakenfeld, Katharine Doob. 'Feminist Biblical Interpretation'. *Theology Today* 46, no. 2 (1989): 154–68.
Sanders, Seth L. 'Performative Utterances and Divine Language in Ugaritic'. *JNES* 63, no. 3 (2004): 161–81.
Sarna, Nahum M. *Genesis*. JPSTC. Philadelphia: Jewish Publication Society, 1989.
Sasson, Jack. 'Numbers 5 and the "Waters of Judgement"'. Pages 483–86 in *Women in the Hebrew Bible: A Reader*. Edited by Alice Bach. New York: Routledge, 1999.
Sawyer, Deborah. *God, Gender and the Bible*. Biblical Limits. London: Routledge, 2002.
Schattschneider, Ellen. '"Buy Me a Bride": Death and Exchange in Northern Japanese Bride-Doll Marriage'. *American Ethnologist* 28, no. 4 (2001): 854–80.
Schmidt, Brian B. *Israel's Beneficent Dead: Ancestor Cult and Necromancy in Ancient Israelite Religion and Tradition*. Winona Lake, IN: Eisenbrauns, 1994.

———. 'Memory as Immortality: Countering the Dreaded "Death after Death" in Ancient Israelite Society'. Pages 87–100 in *Judaism in Late Antiquity Part 4: Death, Life-After-Death, Resurrection and the World-To-Come in the Judaisms of Antiquity*. Edited by Jacob Neusner and Alan Jeffery Avery-Peck. HOS 49. Leiden: Brill, 2000.

Schmitt, Rüdiger. '"And Jacob Set up a Pillar at Her Grave...": Material Memorials and Landmarks in the Old Testament'. Pages 389–404 in *The Land of Israel in Bible, History, and Theology: Studies in Honour of Ed Noort*. Edited by Jacques Ruiten and J. Cornelis de Vos. VTSup 124. Leiden: Brill, 2009.

Schneider, David Murray. *A Critique of the Study of Kinship*. Ann Arbor, MI: University of Michigan Press, 1984.

Schniedewind, William M. 'The Evolution of Name Theology'. Pages 228–39 in *The Chronicler as Theologian: Essays in Honor of Ralph W. Klein*. Edited by Steven L. McKenzie, Matt Patrick Graham, and Gary N. Knoppers. JSOTSup 371. London: T&T Clark, 2003.

Scholz, Susanne. *Sacred Witness: Rape in the Hebrew Bible*. Minneapolis, MN: Fortress Press, 2010.

Schwartze, Lucas. 'Grave Vows: A Cross-Cultural Examination of the Varying Forms of Ghost Marriage among Five Societies'. *Nebraska Anthropologist* 25 (2010): 82–95.

Shaw, Brent D. 'Explaining Incest: Brother-Sister Marriage in Graeco-Roman Egypt'. *Man* 27, no. 2 (1992): 267–99.

Shemesh, Yael. 'A Gender Perspective on the Daughters of Zelophehad: Bible, Talmudic Midrash, and Modern Feminist Midrash'. *BibInt* 15, no. 1 (2007): 80–109.

Shilling, Chris. *The Body and Social Theory*. 3rd ed. London: SAGE, 2012.

Silva, Moisés. *Biblical Words and Their Meaning: An Introduction to Lexical Semantics*. Grand Rapids, MI: Zondervan, 1983.

Singer, Alice. 'Marriage Payments and the Exchange of People'. *Man* 8, no. 1 (1973): 80–92.

Siquans, Agnethe. 'Foreignness and Poverty in the Book of Ruth: A Legal Way for a Poor Foreign Woman to Be Integrated into Israel'. *JBL* 128, no. 3 (2009): 443–52.

Sklar, Jay. *Sin, Impurity, Sacrifice, and Atonement: The Priestly Conceptions*. HBM 2. Sheffield: Sheffield Phoenix, 2005.

Snaith, Norman H. 'The Daughters of Zelophehad'. *VT* 16, no. 1 (1966): 124–27.

Sobo, Elisa J., and Sandra Bell, eds. *Celibacy, Culture, And Society: Anthropology of Sexual Abstinence*. Madison, WI: University of Wisconsin Press, 2001.

Soggin, J. A. 'Judah and Tamar (Genesis 38)'. Pages 281–7 in *Of Prophets' Visions and the Wisdom of Sages: Essays in Honour of R. Norman Whybray on His Seventieth Birthday*. Edited by David J. A. Clines and Heather A. McKay. JSOTSup 162. Sheffield: JSOT, 1993.

Speiser, Ephraim A. *Genesis: Introduction, Translation and Notes*. AB 1. New York: Doubleday, 1964.

Spronk, Klaas. *Beatific Afterlife in Ancient Israel and in the Ancient Near East*. AOAT 219. Neukirchen-Vluyn: Butzon & Bercker Kevelaer, 1986.

Stager, Lawrence E. 'The Archaeology of the Family in Ancient Israel'. *BASOR* 260 (1985): 1–35.

———. 'The Patrimonial Kingdom of Solomon'. Pages 445–54 in *Symbiosis, Symbolism, and the Power of the Past: Canaan, Ancient Israel, and Their Neighbors from the Late Bronze Age Through Roman Palaestina*. Edited by William Dever and Seymour Gitin. Winona Lake, IN: Eisenbrauns, 2003.

Stamm, Johann Jakob. 'Names: In the Bible'. *Encyclopedia Judaica* 14:764–6.
Stavrakopoulou, Francesca. 'Gog's Grave and the Use and Abuse of Corpses in Ezekiel 39:11-20'. *JBL* 129, no. 1 (2010): 67–84.

———. *Land of Our Fathers: The Roles of Ancestor Veneration in Biblical Land Claims*. LHBOTS 473. New York: T&T Clark, 2010.

———. '"Popular" Religion and "Official" Religion: Practice, Perception, Portrayal'. Pages 37–58 in *Religious Diversity in Ancient Israel and Judah*. Edited by Francesca Stavrakopoulou and John Barton. New York: T&T Clark, 2010.

Steinberg, Naomi A. *The World of the Child in the Hebrew Bible*. HBM 51. Sheffield: Sheffield Phoenix, 2013.

Sterring, Ankie. 'The Will of the Daughters'. Pages 88–99 in *Feminist Companion to Exodus to Deuteronomy*. Edited by Athalya Brenner. FCB 6. Sheffield: Sheffield Academic, 1994.

Stiebert, Johanna. *Fathers and Daughters in the Hebrew Bible*. Oxford: Oxford University Press, 2013.

———. *First-Degree Incest and the Hebrew Bible: Sex in the Family*. LHBOTS 596. London: Bloomsbury T&T Clark, 2016.

Stol, Marten. 'Care of the Elderly in Mesopotamia in the Old Babylonian Period'. Pages 59–118 in *The Care of the Elderly in the Ancient Near East*. Edited by Sven Vleeming and Marteen Stol. SHCANE 14. Leiden: Brill, 1998.

Stone, Ken. *Sex, Honor, and Power in the Deuteronomistic History*. JSOTSup 234. Sheffield: Sheffield Academic, 1996.

Strathern, Marilyn. *Reproducing the Future: Essays on Anthropology, Kinship and the New Reproductive Technologies*. Manchester: Manchester University Press, 1992.

Sullivan, Nikki. *A Critical Introduction to Queer Theory*. New York: New York University Press, 2003.

Suriano, Matthew J. 'Death, Disinheritance, and Job's Kinsman-Redeemer'. *JBL* 129, no. 1 (2010): 49–66.

———. *A History of Death in the Hebrew Bible*. New York: Oxford University Press, 2018.

Sutskover, Talia. 'The Themes of Land and Fertility in the Book of Ruth'. *JSOT* 34, no. 3 (2010): 283–94.

Tappy, Ron. 'Did the Dead Ever Die in Biblical Judah?' *BASOR* 298 (1995): 59–68.

Thiselton, Anthony C. 'The Supposed Power of Words in the Biblical Writings'. *JTS* 25, no. 2 (1974): 283–99.

Thomas, Lewis. *Origines Hebrææ: The Antiquities of the Hebrew Republick. In Four Books.* Vol. 3. London: Printed for Sam Illidge under Serle's Gate, Lincoln's-Inn-New-Square; and John Hooke at the Flower-de-luce over-against St. Dunstan's Church in Fleet-street, 1725.

Thomas, Philip. 'No Substance, No Kinship? Procreation, Performativity and Temanambondro Parent–Child Relations'. *Conceiving Persons: Ethnographies of Procreation, Fertility and Growth*. Edited by Patrick Heady and Peter Loizos. London: Continuum, 2003.

Thompson, Charis. 'Strategic Naturalizing: Reproduction in an Infertility Clinic'. Pages 175–202 in *Relative Values: Reconfiguring Kinship Studies*. Edited by Sarah Franklin and Susan McKinnon. Durham, NC: Duke University Press, 2001.

Thompson, Dorothy, and Thomas Thompson. 'Some Legal Problems in the Book of Ruth'. *VT* 18, no. 1 (1968): 79–99.

Tigay, Jeffrey H. *Deuteronomy*. JPSTC. Philadelphia: Jewish Publication Society, 1996.

van der Toorn, Karel. 'Ancestors and Anthroponyms: Kinship Terms as Theophoric Elements in Hebrew Names'. *De-DE* 108, no. 1 (1996): 1–11.

———. *Family Religion in Babylonia, Syria and Israel: Continuity and Change in the Forms of Religious Life*. SHCANE 7. Leiden: Brill, 1996.

Tosh, John. 'Reviewed Work: Social Memory by James Fentress, Chris Wickham'. *Social History* 19, no. 1 (1994): 129–32.

Trible, Phyllis. *God and the Rhetoric of Sexuality*. OBT 2. Philadelphia: Fortress Press, 1978.

Ucko, Peter J. 'Ethnography and Archaeological Interpretation of Funerary Remains'. *World Archaeology* 1, no. 2 (1969): 262–80.

Vawter, Bruce. 'Intimations of Immortality and the Old Testament'. *JBL* 91, no. 2 (1972): 158–71.

Veenhof, Klass R. 'Old Assyrian and Ancient Anatolian Evidence for the Care of the Elderly'. Pages 119–61 in *The Care of the Elderly in the Ancient Near East*. Edited by Sven Vleeming and Marteen Stol. SHCANE 14. Leiden: Brill, 1998.

Wacquant, Loïc. 'A Concise Genealogy and Anatomy of Habitus'. Pages 528–36 in *The Oxford Handbook of Pierre Bourdieu*. Edited by Thomas Medvetz and Jeffrey J. Sallaz. New York: Oxford University Press, 2018.

Waltner, Ann. 'Kinship between the Lines: The Patriline, the Concubine, and the Adopted Son in Late Imperial China'. Pages 67–80 in *Gender, Kinship, Power: A Comparative and Interdisciplinary History*. Edited by Mary Jo Maynes, Ann Waltner, Birgitte Soland, and Ulrike Strasser. New York: Routledge, 1996.

Watson, Rubie S. 'The Named and the Nameless: Gender and Person in Chinese Society'. *American Ethnologist* 13, no. 4 (1986): 619–31.

Weinfeld, Moshe. *Deuteronomy 1–11: A New Translation with Introduction and Commentary*. AB. New York: Doubleday, 1991.

Weingreen, Jacob. 'The Case of the Daughters of Zelophehad'. *VT* 16, no. 4 (1966): 518–22.

Weisberg, Dvora E. 'The Widow of Our Discontent: Levirate Marriage in the Bible and Ancient Israel'. *JSOT* 28, no. 4 (2004): 403–29.

Weismantel, Mary. 'Making Kin: Kinship Theory and Zumbagua Adoptions'. *American Ethnologist* 22, no. 4 (1995): 685–704.

Wenham, Gordon J. '*Betûlāh* "A Girl of Marriageable Age"'. *VT* 22, no. 3 (1972): 326–48.

———. *The Book of Leviticus*. The New International Commentary on the Old Testament. London: Hodder & Stoughton, 1979.

Inhorn, Marcia C. and, Emily Wentzell. 'The Male Reproductive Body: Reproducing Masculinities through Sexual/Reproductive Medicine in the Middle East and Mexico'. Pages 307–19 in *A Companion to the Anthropology of Bodies and Embodiment*. Edited by Frances E. Mascia-Lees. New York: Wiley-Blackwell, 2011.

Westbrook, Raymond. 'The Law of the Biblical Levirate'. *RIDA* 24 (1977): 65–87.

———. *Property and the Family in Biblical Law*. JSOTSup 113. Sheffield: Sheffield Academic, 1991.

Westermann, Claus. *Genesis 12–36: A Commentary*. Translated by John J. Scullion. London: SPCK, 1985.

van Wijk-Bos, Johanna W. H. 'An Eye Opener at the Gate: George Coats and Genesis 38'. *Lexington Theological Quarterly* 27, no. 4 (1992): 119–23.

———. 'Out of the Shadows: Genesis 38; Judges 4:17-22; Ruth 3'. *Semeia* 42 (1988): 37–67.

Wildavsky, Aaron. 'Survival Must Not Be Gained Through Sin: The Moral of the Joseph Stories Prefigured Through Judah and Tamar'. *Journal for the Study of the Old Testament* 19.62 (1994): 37–48.

Wilson, Ian. *Out of the Midst of the Fire: Divine Presence in Deuteronomy*. SBLDS 151. Atlanta, GA: Scholars Press, 1995.

Wilson, Robert R. *Genealogy and History in the Biblical World*. YNER 7. New Haven, CT: Yale University Press, 1977.

———. 'The Old Testament Genealogies in Recent Research'. *JBL* 94, no. 2 (1975): 169–89.

van Winkle, Dwight W. 'The Meaning of *Yād Wāšēm* in Isaiah LVI 5'. *VT* 47, no. 3 (1997): 378–85.

Wold, Donald J. 'The Kareth Penalty in P: Rationale and Cases'. Pages 1–45 in *Society of Biblical Literature Seminar Papers*. SBLSP. Missoula, MT: Scholars Press, 1979.

van Wolde, Ellen. 'Texts in Dialogue with Texts: Intertextuality in the Ruth and Tamar Narratives'. *BibInt* 5, no. 1 (1997): 1–28.

Wright, Christopher J. H. *God's People in God's Land: Family, Land, and Property in the Old Testament*. Grand Rapids, MI: Eerdmans, 1990.

Wright, Jacob L. 'Making a Name for Oneself: Martial Valor, Heroic Death, and Procreation in the Hebrew Bible'. *JSOT* 36, no. 2 (2011): 131–62.

Wyatt, Nick. *Religious Texts from Ugarit: The Words of Ilimilku and His Colleagues*. 2nd ed. BibSem 53. London: Sheffield Academic, 2002.

Younger, K. L. 'The Phoenician Inscription of Azatiwada: An Integrated Reading'. *JSS* 43, no. 1 (1998): 11–47.

Zevit, Ziony. 'Dating Ruth: Legal, Linguistic and Historical Observations'. *ZAW* 117, no. 4 (2006): 574–600.

———. *The Religions of Ancient Israel: A Synthesis of Parallactic Approaches*. London: Continuum, 2001.

Ziskind, Jonathan R. 'The Missing Daughter in Leviticus XVIII'. *VT* 46, no. 1 (1996): 125–30.

Zulu, Edwin. 'Reverence for Ancestors in Africa: Interpretation of the 5th Commandment from an African Perspective'. *Scriptura* 81 (2002): 476–82.

Index of References

Hebrew Bible/Old Testament

Genesis

Ref	Page
1–11	134
1.12	132
1.20-22	132
1.22	136, 228
1.26-28	132
1.27	132
1.28	228
2.20	101
2.23	101, 138, 201
3.15	228
3.16	132, 199, 247
3.20	132
4	179
4.10	70
4.17–5.32	132
5.1-28	136
5.30-32	136
7.23	119
9.1	132, 136
9.7	132, 136
10.1-7	136
11.10-26	136
11.10-24	132
11.29-30	133
11.31	199
12.1-3	134
12.2	112
12.10	214
13	136
13.6	36, 198
13.15-16	134
13.17	204
14.16	198
15.2	134
15.4-5	135
15.15	64
15.16	64
16.2	46, 140, 239
16.3	171
16.10	134, 239
16.11	102
17	7, 135
17.1-8	136
17.5	102, 187
17.7	187
17.8	187
17.9-14	136
17.12	187
17.14	183
17.16	140
17.19	102
17.21	140
18.6	159
18.7-8	159
18.16	159
19	3, 7, 154, 247, 249, 250
19.8	247
19.30-38	190
21.8	131
21.14-16	234
21.16	148
21.33	226
22	252
22.17	2, 24
22.18	86
23.8	176
23.20	176
24	137
24.28	172
25	172
25.8	64, 67
25.11	83
25.12-18	136
25.12	172
25.19	172
26.22	228
27.15	169
28.3	136
28.10-22	89
28.18	86-88
28.22	88
29–30	248
29	141
29.14	138
29.23	141
29.27	141
29.28	39
29.30	141
29.31–30.24	141
29.32	141
29.33	141
29.34	141
29.35	142
30	219
30.1	142
30.2	228
30.3	239
30.4	39, 171
30.6	143
30.8	144
30.9	39
30.13	144
30.14	144
30.15	144
30.18-20	144
31.13	86, 88, 89

Index of References

Genesis (cont.)

31.15	177	38.7	207	5.11	231
31.44-54	88	38.8	3, 37, 44, 194, 207	6.2-3	106
31.45	86			6.12	137
31.53-55	84	38.9	207	6.30	137
32–33	50	38.10	207	12.15	187
32.22	170	38.11	177	17.8-16	118
32.28	102	38.14	208	17.14	118
32.29	144	38.24	247	19.5	243
33.13-14	148	38.25	73	20.4	86
34.2	170	38.26	209	20.5	65
34.8	39	38.27-30	211	20.8-10	168
34.12	39	38.29-30	38	20.12	148, 180
35.10-12	144	41.45	102	20.24	105
35.10	144	42.38	67	21.4	171
35.11	136, 204	44.29	67	21.15	181
35.14	86-88	44.31	67	21.17	181
35.16-21	220	46.6-27	136	22.21-14	176
35.17-20	145	46.12	213	23.24	88, 89
35.19-20	249	46.30	67	23.30	228
35.20	84, 86–8, 91	47.24	134	24.4-12	86
		47.29	137	24.4	86, 88
36.1-14	136	48.3	136	28.29	110
36.7	36, 198	48.6	174	30.33	183
37	206	48.16	112, 122, 239	30.38	183
37.2	146			31.14	183, 185
37.29	138	49.8-12	204, 206	32.32-33	118
37.35	67	49.25	135	34.13	88, 89
38	3, 4, 8, 27, 34–6, 39, 43, 44, 47, 52, 155, 158, 193, 194, 196, 199, 204–6, 210-12, 214, 216, 223, 224, 242, 247, 249, 250	49.29-32	75		
		49.29-31	75	*Leviticus*	
		50.5-6	75	7.20	183
		50.10	80	12.2	139
		50.13	75	12.3	139
		50.23	143	12.18	69
		50.24-25	215	15.2-3	138
				15.16-18	134
		Exodus		15.18	69
		1.7	136	17.4	185
		1.8–2.10	146	17.10	185
		1.15-21	46	17.13	138
		2.3	148	18	7, 155, 157, 158, 160, 162, 200
38.1-5	211	2.6-9	148		
38.3-5	207, 211	3.10	137	18.1-5	155
38.3	207	3.13-15	106	18.6	138, 155, 157
38.4	207	3.15	226		
38.5	207	3.16	215	18.7-18	156
38.6-30	211	4.13	215	18.14-16	187
38.7-8	207	4.25	204		

18.19-23	156	5.13	134	4.15	173
18.19	155	5.21-22	103	4.21	173
18.24-30	156	5.23-34	103	4.25	150
18.27-29	185	5.28	134, 228	4.40	150
18.28	157	9.13	183	5.4-5	104
18.29	187	12.14	204	5.9	65
19.20	134	14.18	65	5.12-15	168
19.23-25	137	15.27-31	185	5.14	150
19.28	64, 84	15.30-31	187	5.16	180
19.31	68, 84	15.32	185	5.23-27	104
19.32	180	15.35	185	5.26	150
20	7, 155–8, 160, 162, 201	16.3	73	6.2	150
		16.30	65, 67	6.7	150
		16.33	67	6.20-21	150
20.2-5	187	19.14	80	7.3-4	150
20.2-3	185	19.16-18	68	7.5	88, 89
20.3	185	20.5	134	7.13	228
20.6	185	26.19-20	213	7.24	31, 118
20.20-21	187	26.20-22	213	9.10	104
20.21	156	26.33	230	9.12	104
20.38	185	26.53-62	227	9.14	31, 118
21.2-4	138	27	4, 8, 35, 174, 230, 232, 235, 247, 249, 250	9.15-16	104
21.2-3	157			10.16	137
21.2	234			11.19	150
21.5	80, 84			11.21	150
21.9	247			11.24	204
21.16-23	228	27.1-11	38	12.1-18	84
22.4	134	27.3-4	227	12.3	31, 88, 89, 118
22.12-14	138	27.4	4, 174, 224, 232		
22.12-13	234			12.11	103
22.13	177, 207	27.8-11	39, 174	12.12	150
24.11-23	108	27.8	232	12.18	150
25.8-34	176	27.9-11	232	13.1	231
25.23	243	32.41-42	102	13.6	153
25.25-34	214	35.19	175	13.12	153
25.25-28	175	36	8, 174, 230	14.1	80
25.29	174	36.3-4	233	14.28-29	176
25.47-55	176	36.3	173	16.11	150, 168
25.47	175	36.6	233	16.14	150, 168
25.48-50	176	36.8	173	16.22	86, 88
26.1	86, 88			17.7	153
26.27-28	149	*Deuteronomy*		17.12	153
27.16	134	1.36	204	18.9-12	80
27.18	231	3.11	64	18.11	68, 84
		4.2	231	19.10	173
Numbers		4.4	173	19.13	153
3.15	165, 240	4.10	150	19.14	173

Index of References

Deuteronomy (cont.)

19.19	153		219, 223,	32.50	65
19.20	153		224, 232,	34.7	154
20.5-9	170	25.5-6	241, 247–9		
20.7	50	25.5	226	*Joshua*	
21.1-9	70		29, 37, 194,	1.3	204
21.8-21	148		199, 218,	7.4	240
21.9	153	25.6-7	219	7.9	31
21.10-14	171	25.6	224	7.14	165, 169
21.11	171		35, 199,	7.25-26	76
21.14	200	25.7	201	7.26	51
21.15-17	151, 174,		194, 201,	8.29	51, 76
	248	25.8-11	219	10.26-27	76
21.16-17	234	25.9	195	13–22	173
21.18-21	45, 151,	25.10	194, 204	14.1–19.51	174
	181	25.11-12	204	15.6	51
21.21	153		152, 197,	15.7	51
22	247	25.11	224	17.3-6	230
22.13-29	153	25.13-16	224	18.7	51
22.13-21	151	25.17-19	197	19.12	83
22.13-19	150	25.19	197	21.12	173
22.21-22	150	26.12	118	22.24-25	228
22.22	150	26.14	177	24.15	169
22.23-29	150	27.17	84	24.30	51, 176
22.23-24	200	28	173	24.32	176
23.1	151	28.4	149		
23.2	228	28.26	228	*Judges*	
23.3-9	151	28.30	76	2.9	51, 176
23.3	218	28.53-57	170	8.32	49
24.5	49, 151	28.53	153	9.53-54	49
24.7	153	28.57	148	11.13	170
24.16–25.10	221	28.58	204	11.24	215
24.17-18	176	28.69	105	13.17-18	108
25	34, 195,	29.11	154	16.31	75
	211, 216,	29.15	154	17.1-6	177
	219, 250	29.20	154	21.17	118, 119,
25.1-3	197	29.22	118, 154		226
25.4	197	29.29	154		
25.5-10	3, 4, 8, 24,	30.2	154	*Ruth*	
	26, 27, 29,	30.5	154	1.8	172
	34, 36, 37,	30.9	154	1.9	43, 207
	39, 47, 52,	30.19	154	1.11-13	217
	152, 153,	31.12-13	154	1.15	194
	155, 156,	32.2	151	1.22	214
	163, 193,	32.22	65-67	2.2	218
	194, 196–9,	32.27	154	2.6	214
	204, 214,	32.46	154	3.1	217
				3.9	39, 217

Index of References

3.12-13	217	25.25	109		225, 227–9,
4	50, 203	25.42	177		242, 249
4.1-2	219	26.19	184	21.5-9	70
4.3	220	28	42, 61	21.9-14	80
4.5	217, 218,	28.8	65	21.10	76
	223	28.13	64, 69	21.12-14	75
4.7	218	28.15	69	21.15-22	64
4.9	177	28.19	68, 84	22.6	65
4.10	3, 35, 52,			31.8-13	76
	186, 217,	*2 Samuel*			
	219, 223,	1	49	*1 Kings*	
	226	1.11-12	80	1.9	51
4.11-12	219, 220	1.20	49	2.6	67
4.11	145, 249	1.26	198	2.9	67
4.12	210, 216	2.32	75	2.10	64, 75
4.13	37, 219	3.31-37	80	2.34	176
4.16	148	3.31-32	75	3	224
4.17	38	3.31	80	3.18	200
4.21	220	4.12	69, 75	3.26-27	148
		5.6-9	102	6–7	4
1 Samuel		6	4	7.14	148
1	68	7	50	7.15-22	87
1.1	228	7.14	148	8	105
1.4	234	8.3	51	8.19	204
2.6	66, 67	8.13	30	8.27	105
2.20	228	8.18	30	9.3	226
2.33	188	11.8	204	11.15	49
7.12	51	11.11	204	11.16	186
8.3	170	12.15	148	13.21-22	75
9.9-11	199	12.18-22	148	13.30	76
10.2	51, 249	12.22-23	70	14.10	186
14.1-7	250	13–14	8	14.12	148
15.12	90	13	247, 249	14.23	86, 88
17.12	220	13.28	30	17.17-24	148
18.18	249, 250	13.30	223	21	224, 244
20.6	85	13.35	223	21.2-3	174
20.19	51	14	38	21.3	173
20.20-21	116	14.1-20	224	21.20-24	175
20.29	85	14.1-7	224, 230,	21.21-22	175
21.13	75		245	21.21	186
22.6	67	14.4	174	21.29	175
24.21	94, 114,	14.7	3	22.52	148
	118, 186,	14.16	224		
	245	18.9	105	*2 Kings*	
24.22	31	18.17	76	3.2	88
25	224	18.18	3, 4, 8, 37,	3.13	148
25.1	176		45, 86–91,	4.1-7	148, 177

2 Kings (cont.)		26.21	184	30.10	204
4.1	199	28.27	75	38.10	65
4.17-37	68	31.1	88	42.15	234
4.17-35	148				
6	224	Ezra		Psalms	
6.28-29	148	2.61-63	138	1.3	228
8	177	2.61	174, 199	6.5	66, 67
8.1-3	177	3.2	213	7.6	65
9.28	75	3.8	213	9.5	118
9.34-37	76	5.2	213	9.17	67
9.34	85			16.3	64
10.26-27	88	Nehemiah		16.4	85
10.26	88	4.5	119	18.5	67
10.27	88	4.14	148	20.1	105
13.21	68	5	149	20.2	30
14.27	31, 118	5.2	148	21.11	228
17.10	86, 88	5.3	173	27.10	148
18.4	88	5.5	148	30.3	67
18.27	204	7.63	174	30.9	66
21.6	84	7.64	138	31.17-18	66
21.7	226	12.1	213	31.18	67
21.21	148			33.21	30, 105
23.14	88	Esther		37.28	186
23.15-20	77	2.21-23	229	37.38	186
23.17	91			49.12	30
23.24	84	Job		49.14-15	67
23.30	75	3.12	70	49.15	65
		7.9	65, 67	55.15	67
1 Chronicles		11.8	67	60.9	204
2.4	213	14.12	70	60.10	204
2.34-35	174	14.13	67	69.28	118
3.19	213	14.21	68	72.20	113
7	230	17.13	65, 67	79.2	76
7.15	230	17.16	65, 67	83.11	76
7.18	230	18.16-19	226	86.13	65, 67
10.14	113	18.18	65	88.3	67
20.6-8	64	19.15	200	88.5-6	66
25.6	148	19.23-27	223	88.6-7	65
		19.25	223	88.6	184
2 Chronicles		21.13	67	89.48	67
6.9	204	21.21	68	103.13	148
12.20	75	21.26	65	106.28	80
14.2	88	24.2	176	106.37-38	149
14.3	88	24.3	177	109.13	118, 186, 226
22.9	199	24.19	67		
24.25	75	26.6	67	113.9	46

116.3	67	7.14	102	56.3-5	3, 8, 30,
135.13	226	7.20	204		45, 48, 88,
137.4	184	8.19-20	68, 84		89, 91,
139.8	67	8.19	64		184, 226,
141.7	67	14	114		228–30,
		14.9-22	115, 116		235, 245,
Proverbs		14.9-10	65		250
1.12	67	14.9	64, 67	56.3	228
5.5	67	14.11	67	56.4-5	242
7.27	67	14.15	67	56.5-10	86
9.18	67	14.18-22	226	56.5	32, 86, 87,
10.7	30	14.19-20	77		90, 227,
14.31-32	177	14.22	31		228
15.11	66, 67	15.2-3	80	56.6-7	227
15.24	67	15.2	84, 231	56.6	80, 87
15.25	177	19.3	64, 70, 84	57.3-13	228
19.14	148, 173	19.11	199	57.6	228
20.20	45, 181	19.19	51	57.8	227, 230
22.27-28	51	20.2-4	204	57.9	65, 67
23.14	67	20.2	204	60	131
23.22	181	22	75	63.17	226
27.20	67	22.12	84	65.4	65
30	45, 181	26.8	30	66.12-13	131
30.16	67	28.15	67	66.22	31
31.16	170	28.18	67		
		29.4	64, 84	*Jeremiah*	
Ecclesiastes		36.12	204	2.25	204
3.21	64	36.19	252	3.1	151
6.4	30	38.10	65, 67, 73	3.8	198
9.1-10	67	38.18	66, 67	3.16	228
9.5	61	40.26	99	6.10	137
9.10	66, 67	45.18-19	65	6.26	80
		47.3	158	8.1-3	80
Song of Songs		48.19	226	8.1-2	78
3.4	172	49	131	9.17-20	80
4.9-12	198	49.15	148	9.21	226
8.1-2	131	50.6	204	9.25	137
8.2	172	53.8	184	11.9	228
8.6	67	55.11	99	11.19	31, 114,
		56	14, 228,		184, 226,
Isaiah			244, 246,		239
5.8	176		249, 250,	11.22-23	114
5.14	65, 67		252	12.14	173
6.2	204	56.1-8	229	16.2	114
6.13	86, 87	56.1	228	16.4	76
7.11	65-67			16.5	85

Jeremiah (cont.)		26.41	137	*Habakkuk*	
16.6	84	31.14-18	65	2.5	65, 67
17.7-8	228	31.15-17	67		
19.9	148, 149	31.22	67	*Zephaniah*	
20.15	199	31.25	67	1.12	170
22.18-19	76	32.21	67		
23.6	102	32.27	67	*Haggai*	
25.33	76	37.5	252	1.12	213
26.23	76	37.11	184	1.14	213
31.15	24, 45, 249	37.17	67		
31.27	134	39.11	64	*Malachi*	
32.6-8	176	43.7-9	79, 86	1.2	198
32.8	45	44.7	137, 138	1.16	182
32.9-14	176	48	35		
33.17	188			New Testament	
41.5	84	*Daniel*		*Mark*	
41.9	76	12.1-3	251	12.18-26	252
43.13	86, 88	12.2	70, 252		
47.3	148			Pseudepigrapha	
47.5	84	*Hosea*		*4 Maccabees*	
48.37	84, 231	2.11-12	158	7.3	252
55.13	226	3.4	88		
		4.14	247	Apocrypha	
Lamentations		5.6	204	*Tobit*	
2.20	228	5.10	176	4.17	85
3.6	65	10.2	86		
3.53-54	184	13.14	65–7	*Wisdom of Solomon*	
4.10	148			3.1	252
5.2	222	*Amos*			
		5.11	170	*Ecclesiasticus*	
Ezekiel		6.10	80	3.12-13	181
6.8	39	8.10	37, 84	17.27-28	252
7.18	84	9.2	66, 67	30.18	85
16	247				
16.20	149	*Jonah*		*1 Maccabees*	
16.25	204	2.2	67	6.4	49
16.26	138	2.3-6	65		
16.36-37	158	2.7	65	Mishnah	
17.5	134			*Sanhedrin*	
20.18-21	148	*Micah*		10.1	252
22.6-7	177	1.16	80, 84		
23	158, 247	2.2	176	*Yevamot*	
23.30	138	5.13	88	4.5	198
23.47	187				
24.17	204	*Nahum*			
24.23	204	1.14	226, 228		

JOSEPHUS			*Hittite Laws*		*Phoenician Inscription*	
Jewish Antiquities			193-195	200	III.12–IV.3	119
4.8.23	38, 237					
			KAI		*RS*	
ANCIENT NEAR EASTERN			191	78	24.257	120
SOURCES			258	90	34.126	120
Code of Hammurabi						
154	157		*KTU*		QUR'AN	
			1.4 viii	65	Sura 2.223	123
Gilgamesh			1.6 vi.27-29	65		
XII:151	78		1.17.2.12-23	88		

Index of Authors

Abasili, A. I. 48, 206–10, 213
Ackerman, S. 76, 169
Adelman, R. 34, 47, 209, 220
Adkins, L. 17
Albertz, R. 66, 87, 90, 95, 103, 181
Albright, W. 85
Allen, M. 126
Alter, R. 206
Amit, Y. 211
Anderson, C. 40, 150, 151, 200
Anderson, J. C. 26
Andrew, M. E. 207, 210, 211
Archer, L. 138, 139
Atkinson, W. 13, 20
Atwook, M. 3
Avrahami, Y. 95, 99

Baden, J. S. 133
Baloyi, M. E. 52
Barr, J. 99, 101, 109
Beattie, D. R. G. 27, 215, 218
Belkin, S. 27, 28, 207
Bell, C. M. 21
Bell, S. 126
Ben-Barak, Z. 168, 176, 231, 232, 234, 244
Bendor, S. 170
Benson, S. 98
Berlin, A. 34, 47, 215, 221–3
Berlinerblau, J. 14
Berman, J. 221
Bernat, D. A. 140
Berquist, J. L. 133, 143
Biale, D. 135, 154
Blenkinsopp, J. 62, 83, 164, 167, 168, 199
Bloch, M. 95, 97, 102, 112
Bloch-Smith, E. 61–4, 68, 69, 71, 72, 79, 81, 83, 84, 87
Bodenhorn, B. 96–8, 101, 106, 107, 117

Boer, R. 26, 132, 137
Borowski, O. 168
Bourdieu, P. 14–21
Boyarin, D. 139
Bray, J. S. 62, 83
Brenner, A. 116, 133, 134, 140, 141, 145, 146, 155, 160, 171
Brett, M. G. 206, 208, 214
Brichto, H. C. 42–7, 181, 194
Britt, B. M. 118, 119
Bruck, G. von 96–8, 101, 107, 117
Brueggemann, W. 211
Budd, P. J. 185, 188, 232
Bunimovitz, X. 72
Burrows, M. 11, 27, 33, 194, 196, 201, 202, 243
Burton, J. W. 56
Butler, J. 24, 25, 101

Cairns, I. 202, 204
Carmichael, C. 156, 157, 204, 219, 220
Carpenter, E. 183, 184
Carroll, R. P. 11
Carsten, J. 245
Caserio, R. L. 24
Chan, M. J. 228, 229, 244
Chapman, C. R. 127, 130–2, 141, 146, 169, 170, 172, 179, 180, 203, 217, 220
Clines, D. J. A. 26
Coats, G. W. 40, 210, 212, 213
Collins, P. 128
Connell, C. 22
Connerton, P. 116, 117
Coogan, M. D. 180, 181
Cooper, A. 84, 88
Cox, B. D. 76
Creangă, O. 26
Crossley, N. 20
Csordas, T. J. 15

Dahood, M. J. 41, 64
Davies, E. W. 27, 37–40, 176
Day, J. 70
Deist, F. 173
Delaney, C. 125, 129, 130
Dinshaw, C. 23
Doniger, W. 220
Douglas, M. 11, 47, 184
Dutcher-Walls, P. 168

Edelman, L. 23, 24
Edenburg, C. 153
Eichrodt, W. 95
Eilberg-Schwartz, H. 10, 26, 136–9
Ellens, D. L. 34, 150, 197, 199, 201, 242, 243, 248
Emerton, J. A. 206
Exum, C. 147

Fabry, H. J. 95
Fantalkin, A. 72
Faust, A. 72
Fewell, D. N. 140, 143–5, 147, 150, 209, 214
Finley, M. I. 46, 63
Fischer, I. 221
Fleishman, J. 170
Fortes, M. 63
Foucault, M. 161
Franklin, S. 126, 127
Freeman, E. 24
Frug, M. J. 151
Frymer-Kensky, T. 143, 151
Fuchs, E. 140, 142, 147, 210, 213

Gafney, W. 47, 248
Galpaz-Feller, P. 34, 176, 177
Geertz, C. 11, 12
George, A. R. 78
George, M. 48, 152, 153
Gevirtz, S. 120
Giladi, A. 131
Gillespie, S. D. 166, 167
Gluckman, M. 63, 137, 138
Golden, C. 117
Goldstein, B. 84, 88
Goulder, M. D. 214, 215, 219
Greenberg, M. 205
Guenther, A. 171

Gunn, D. M. 140, 143–5, 147, 150, 209, 214
Guyer, J. I. 54
Gwako, E. L. M. 55

Haddox, S. 26
Hakim, C. 22
Halberstam, J. 24
Hamilton, V. P. 145, 191
Hammer, D. 13
Harker, R. 19
Harris, R. L. 67, 73
Hays, C. B. 75
Heady, P. 125–7
Healey, J. F. 65
Hendel, R. 11
Hess, R. 109
Hiers, R. H. 177, 218
Hillers, D. 99
Hoang, K. K. 22
Hoffman, L. A. 135, 138
Horbury, W. 185
Howell, S. 128
Hoy, D. C. 20
Huddlestun, J. R. 208
Humphrey, C. 106–8, 112, 113
Hundley, M. 95, 104–6
Hurowitz, V. A. 94, 95, 103

Inhorn, M. C. 124
Iteanu, A. 113, 114, 178

Jackson, B. S. 155, 156, 160, 170, 171
Jacobs, S. 140
Jagose, A. 25
Japhet, S. 227
Jay, N. 133, 137, 140
Jeansonne, S. P. 206, 211, 212

Kaufmann, Y. 68, 70
Kelly, R. 126
Kennedy, C. A. 85
Kertzer, D. I. 12
King, P. J. 168
Klawans, J. 84
Kutsch, E. 28, 193, 199

LaCocque, A. 221
LaRocca-Pitts, E. C. 86–8

Laird, D. 13
Lambek, M. 100–102, 108, 111, 112, 170
Lamont, M. 13
Lane, J. 999
Lane, M. 16
Lawler, S. 20
Layne, L. 100
Leach, E. 11, 125
Leggett, D. A. 28, 32, 38, 213
Lemos, T. M. 52, 96, 149, 150, 170, 219, 247
Levenson, J. D. 4
Lévi-Strauss, C. 166
Levine, B. 28, 157, 165, 173, 183, 184, 188, 214, 216, 220, 231, 233
Levine, E. 27, 41
Lewis, T. J. 41, 62, 65, 67, 69–71, 81–6, 88, 176, 224
Lipton, D. 118
Lods, A. 69
Loizos, P. 125–7
Long, B. O. 116
Lovell, T. 25
Lowisch, I. 178, 179
Lyke, L. L. 224

Mace, D. R. 193, 194, 201, 213, 217, 224
Mahar, C. 19
Mahmood, S. 20, 22
Malul, M. 243, 244, 246
Mann, T. 190
Mars, L. 32, 208, 210
Martin, D. 59
Martin, E. 129
Matlock, M. D. 195, 197, 201, 203
Maynes, M. J. 126
McCarter, P. K., Jr. 69
McKinnon, S. 126, 127
McNutt, P. M. 165, 169, 179
Mears, A. 22
Menn, E. M. 205, 206, 210, 211
Meyers, C. 80, 164, 165, 168, 169, 178, 247
Meyers, E. M. 76
Milgrom, J. 68, 69, 174, 185, 186, 188, 232
Moore, S. D. 26
Morris, I. 63
Morrow, W. 95, 104, 105

Moss, C. R. 133
Muñoz, J. E. 24

Nelson, R. D. 202
Nestor, D. 13
Neufeld, E. 37, 199, 200
Neusner, J. 207
Niditch, S. 40, 210
Niehr, H. 70
Noth, M. 38
Nyanzi, S. 55

O'Connor, D. B. 120
Oboler, R. S. 54
Ockinga, B. G. 89, 225, 226
Olyan, S. M. 62, 65, 74–6, 78, 85, 184, 225
Owen, M. 52

Pardee, D. 120
Parker, J. F. 147, 148, 198, 199
Parkes, P. 131
Pedersen, J. 29–32
Perdue, L. G. 164, 168
Pitard, W. T. 62, 63, 81, 82
Polhemus, R. M. 191, 192
Potash, B. 53
Pressler, C. 34, 40, 150–2, 174, 197–202, 204, 241, 242, 248
Preuss, H. D. 95
Propp, W. H. 180

Ramsey, G. W. 99
Rappaport, R. A. 121, 251
Rashkow, I. N. 139
Reed-Danahay, D. 16, 17
Reiterer, F. V. 95
Rey, T. 15, 16
Ribar, J. W. 81
Richardson, S. 78
Richter, S. L. 104
Ringgren, H. 95
Robinson, G. 227
Rofé, A. 205
Rooke, D. W. 158, 159
Rowley, H. H. 28, 214, 220
Rubin, G. 126
Rudman, D. 65–7

Sahgal, S. 53
Sakenfeld, K. D. 232
Sanders, S. L. 99
Sarna, N. M. 206, 208, 213
Sasson, J. 103
Sawyer, D. 25, 26, 212
Schattschneider, E. 57, 58
Schaweffer, H. 202
Schmidt, B. B. 2, 33, 34, 62, 80, 120, 121
Schmitt, R. 66, 87, 90–2, 181, 238
Schneider, D. M. 125
Schniedewind, W. M. 95, 103
Scholz, S. 192
Schwartze, L. 56, 59
Shaw, B. D. 155
Shelley, P. B. 1
Shemesh, Y. 230, 232
Shilling, C. 21
Silva, M. 104
Singer, A. 56
Siquans, A. 218
Sklar, J. 185, 187
Snaith, N. H. 175
Sobo, E. J. 126
Soggin, J. A. 209
Speiser, E. A. 143, 192
Spronk, K. 64
Stager, L. E. 168, 169
Stamm, J. J. 95
Stavrakopoulou, F. 41, 47, 51, 62, 63, 65, 74, 76–80, 85–8, 173, 176, 226–9
Steinberg, N. A. 164
Sterring, A. 231, 232
Stiebert, J. 10, 148, 155–7, 159–61, 191, 192, 220, 231, 234
Stol, M. 182
Stone, K. 10
Strathern, M. 126, 127
Sullivan, N. 24, 25
Suriano, M. J. 31, 62–5, 68, 70, 72–6, 78, 90, 223
Sutskover, T. 47

Tappy, R. 62, 70, 81, 84
Thiselton, A. C. 99
Thomas, L. 193
Thomas, P. 127
Thompson, C. 128
Thompson, D. 27, 32, 194, 196, 199, 216, 221, 243
Thompson, T. 27, 32, 194, 196, 199, 216, 221, 243
Tigay, J. H. 150, 154, 198–201, 203, 205, 217
Tosh, J. 116
Trible, P. 101, 135

Ucko, P. J. 82, 83

van Dijk-Hemmes, F. 47, 48, 205, 210, 214
van Wijk-Bos, J. W. H. 207, 210, 211, 214
van Winkle, D. W. 227
van Wolde, E. 211
van der Toorn, K. 68, 83, 84, 109, 110
Vawter, B. 42
Veenhof, K. R. 182
von Rad, G. 103, 134, 137, 142, 191, 206

Wacquant, L. 15, 17
Waltner, A. 127, 129
Watson, R. S. 110
Weinfeld, M. 182
Weingreen, J. 233
Weisberg, D. E. 4, 34, 128, 194, 195, 203, 217
Weismantel, M. 128
Wenham, G. J. 150, 188
Wentzell, E. 124
Westbrook, R. 28, 34–6, 41, 174–6, 199, 200, 202, 203, 212, 219
Westermann, C. 137, 142, 143, 145
Wildavsky, A. 206, 209, 212, 213
Wilkes, C. 19
Wilson, I. 104, 105
Wilson, R. R. 178, 179
Wold, D. J. 184, 186–8
Wright, C. J. H. 181, 182
Wright, J. L. 48–50, 228, 229, 244
Wyatt, N. 120

Younger, K. L. 119

Zevit, Z. 34, 86, 89, 176, 200, 205, 215, 218, 219, 227, 230
Ziskind, J. R. 157, 158
Zulu, E. 182, 183

www.ingramcontent.com/pod-product-compliance
Lightning Source LLC
Chambersburg PA
CBHW072126290426
44111CB00012B/1794